MW01029925

RECOMMENDATIONS FOR THE SERIES

"It is a pleasure to commend the Crossway Books series of homiletical commentaries authored by Dr. Kent Hughes. They will fill an enormous vacuum that exists between the practical needs of the pastor/teacher and the critical exegetical depth of most commentaries. With this series, evangelicalism may now claim its own William Barclay. While remaining true to the text and its original meaning, Dr. Hughes helps us face the personal, ethical, theological, and practical questions that the text wants us to answer in the presence of the living God and his illuminating Holy Spirit."

—Dr. Walter C. Kaiser, Jr.,
The Coleman M. Mockler
Distinguished Professor of Old Testament,
Gordon-Conwell Theological Seminary

"This series will minister to a pastor's soul as well as giving him an immense resource for his preaching. And it will minister to the parishioner wonderfully in personal Bible study. The reader will be filled with fresh thoughts about our Lord as well as joyful encouragement for himself. That is what happened to me in reading this."

—Dr. Kenneth N. Taylor,
Translator,
The Living Bible

"Now here's a refreshing look into God's Word through the eyes of an insightful and delightful teacher. Pastor Hughes sheds light on details that capture our imagination and deepen our understanding. This is no dry and ponderous commentary, but a unique window into the feelings, the textures, the teachings, the times, the very hearts of the New Testament writers."

—Frank E. Peretti,
Author,
This Present Darkness

"Conviction and clarity. Two words that characterize the powerful pulpit ministry of Kent Hughes. To hear him Sunday after Sunday—as I have for the last eight years—is to be confronted with the compelling message of God's Word and its uncompromising call upon the life of every believer. Pastor Hughes speaks straight to the heart."

—Harold B. Smith,
Former Vice President/Editorial,
Christianity Today

"Throughout the Christian centuries, from Chrysostom and Augustine through Luther, Calvin, and Matthew Henry, to Martyn Lloyd-Jones and Ray Stedman, working pastors have been proving themselves to be the best of all Bible expositors. Kent Hughes stands in this great tradition, and his exciting expositions uphold it worthily."

—Dr. J. I. Packer,
Author,
Knowing God

ACTS

Books in the PREACHING THE WORD Series:

JEREMIAH AND LAMENTATIONS:
From Sorrow to Hope
by Philip Graham Ryken

MARK, VOLUME ONE:
Jesus, Servant and Savior
by R. Kent Hughes

MARK, VOLUME TWO:
Jesus, Servant and Savior
by R. Kent Hughes

LUKE, VOLUME ONE:
That You May Know the Truth
by R. Kent Hughes

LUKE, VOLUME TWO:
That You May Know the Truth
by R. Kent Hughes

JOHN:
That You May Believe
by R. Kent Hughes

ACTS:
The Church Afire
by R. Kent Hughes

ROMANS:
Righteousness from Heaven
by R. Kent Hughes

EPHESIANS:
The Mystery of the Body of Christ
by R. Kent Hughes

COLOSSIANS:
The Supremacy of Christ
by R. Kent Hughes

1 & 2 TIMOTHY AND TITUS:
To Guard the Deposit
by R. Kent Hughes and Bryan Chapell

HEBREWS, VOLUME ONE:
An Anchor for the Soul
by R. Kent Hughes

HEBREWS, VOLUME TWO:
An Anchor for the Soul
by R. Kent Hughes

JAMES:
Faith That Works
by R. Kent Hughes

THE SERMON ON THE MOUNT:
The Message of the Kingdom
by R. Kent Hughes

PREACHING THE WORD

ACTS

The Church Afire

R. Kent Hughes

R. Kent Hughes, General Editor

CROSSWAY BOOKS

A DIVISION OF
GOOD NEWS PUBLISHERS
WHEATON, ILLINOIS

Acts

Copyright © 1996 by R. Kent Hughes.

Published by Crossway Books
a division of Good News Publishers
1300 Crescent Street
Wheaton, Illinois 60187

All rights reserved. No part of this publication may be reproduced, stored in a retrieval system or transmitted in any form by any means, electronic, mechanical, photocopy, recording or otherwise, without the prior permission of the publisher, except as provided by USA copyright law.

Cover banner by Marge Gieser

Photo of cover banner by Bill Koechling

Art Direction: Cindy Kiple

First printing, 1996

Printed in the United States of America

Unless otherwise noted, all Bible quotations are taken from *Holy Bible: New International Version*, copyright © 1978 by the New York International Bible Society. Used by permission of Zondervan Bible Publishers.

Library of Congress Cataloging-in-Publication Data

Hughes, R. Kent.
Acts / R. Kent Hughes
p. cm. — (Preaching the word)
Includes bibliographical references and indexes.
ISBN 0-89107-873-8
1. Bible. N.T. Acts—Homiletical use. I. Title. II. Series:
Hughes, R. Kent. Preaching the word.
BS2625.5.H84 1996
226.6'07—dc20 95-41952

15 14 13 12 11 10 09 08 07 06 05 04
15 14 13 12 11 10 9 8 7 6 5 4

To Marc and Lori Maillefer,
beloved colleagues and lovers of the church

Acknowledgments

Once again, deepest appreciation to my administrative assistant, Mrs. Sharon Fritz, for weekly typing and editing chapter manuscripts, and to Mr. Herbert Carlburg for further editing and for checking all references. Also, ongoing thanks to Mr. Ted Griffin for his expert editing of what is now over a dozen of my books.

But you will receive power
when the Holy Spirit comes on you;
and you will be my witnesses in Jerusalem,
and in Judea and Samaria, and to
the ends of the earth.

—Acts 1:8

Table of Contents

A Word to Those Who Preach the Word

There are times when I am preaching that I have especially sensed the pleasure of God. I usually become aware of it through the unnatural silence. The ever-present coughing ceases and the pews stop creaking, bringing an almost physical quiet to the sanctuary — through which my words sail like arrows. I experience a heightened eloquence, so that the cadence and volume of my voice intensify the truth I am preaching.

There is nothing quite like it — the Holy Spirit filling one's sails, the sense of his pleasure, and the awareness that something is happening among one's hearers. This experience is, of course, not unique, for thousands of preachers have similar experiences, even greater ones.

What has happened when this takes place? How do we account for this sense of his smile? The answer for me has come from the ancient rhetorical categories of *logos*, *ethos*, and *pathos*.

The first reason for his smile is the *logos* — in terms of preaching, God's Word. This means that as we stand before God's people to proclaim his Word, we have done our homework. We have exegeted the passage, mined the significance of its words in their context, and applied sound hermeneutical principles in interpreting the text so that we understand what its words meant to its hearers. And it means that we have labored long until we can express in a sentence what the theme of the text is — so that our outline springs from the text. Then our preparation will be such that as we preach, we will not be preaching our own thoughts about God's Word, but God's actual Word, his *logos*. This is fundamental to pleasing him in preaching.

The second element in knowing God's smile in preaching is *ethos* — what you are as a person. There is a danger endemic to preaching, which is having your hands and heart cauterized by holy things. Phillips Brooks illustrated it by the analogy of a train conductor who comes to believe that he has been to the places he announces because of his long and loud heralding of them. And that is why Brooks insisted that preaching must be "the bringing of truth through personality." Though we can never *perfectly* embody the truth we preach, we must be subject to it, long for it, and make it as much a part of our ethos as possible. As the Puritan William Ames said, "Next to the Scriptures, nothing makes a sermon more to pierce, than when it comes out of the inward affection of the heart without any affectation." When a preacher's ethos backs up his *logos*, there will be the pleasure of God.

Last, there is *pathos* — personal passion and conviction. David Hume, the Scottish philosopher and skeptic, was once challenged as he was seen going to hear George Whitefield preach: "I thought you do not believe in the gospel." Hume replied, "I do not, but *he does*." Just so! When a preacher believes what he preaches, there will be passion. And this belief and requisite passion will know the smile of God.

The pleasure of God is a matter of *logos* (the Word), *ethos* (what you are), and *pathos* (your passion). As you *preach the Word* may you experience his smile — the Holy Spirit in your sails!

R. Kent Hughes
Wheaton, Illinois

1

"You Shall Be My Witnesses"

ACTS 1:1-11

One reason I love to study the book of Acts is its uniqueness. It is *the* sourcebook for the spread of early Christianity. Without it we would know little about the apostolic church except what could be gleaned from Paul's epistles. It is the chronicle of the spreading flame of the Holy Spirit.

It is also a book with a splendid theme, tracing the work of the Holy Spirit through the birth, infancy, and adolescence of the Church. Its title could well be "The Acts of the Holy Spirit" or "The Acts of the Risen Christ Through the Holy Spirit Working Through the Church." Acts forms the perfect counterpart and contrast to the Gospels. In the Gospels the Son of Man offered his life; in Acts the Son of God offered his power. In the Gospels we see the original seeds of Christianity; in Acts we see the continual growth of the Church. The Gospels tell us of Christ crucified and risen; Acts speaks of Christ ascended and exalted. The Gospels model the Christian life as lived by the perfect Man; Acts models it as lived out by imperfect men.

The study of Acts is particularly important to us because it teaches us how to experience a stimulating, exciting life — how to make our lives count. One man said, "I have been a deacon in my church for years; built a church building, raised money, served on committees. But one thing my church never gave me was a relationship with Christ that would make my life exciting."[1] Rather than having an effervescent, relevant faith, this man found his life about as stimulating as a stale glass of ginger ale. He did not know the secret of Acts.

In our day one of the *nicer* things said about the institutional church is that it is "irrelevant." The book of Acts carries the remedy. Whether you are young and virile with Superman-like energy, or restless with what you have seen of a dull, ho-hum, business-as-usual Christianity, or at the age where you are receiving birthday cards that say things like "When it's time for a dental checkup, do you send out your teeth?" the message of Acts is for *you*!

The author of Acts was Luke the physician, and he begins with a reference to his already completed work on the life of Christ, which we know as the Gospel of Luke:

> *In my former book, Theophilus, I wrote about all that Jesus began to do and to teach until the day he was taken up to heaven, after giving instructions through the Holy Spirit to the apostles he had chosen. (vv. 1-2)*

Naturally Theophilus remembered, and his thoughts turned to Luke's great scroll and its remarkable account of Christ's life. He was thereby primed for what was to follow.

Then in verses 3-5 Luke continues with some new information as he tells Theophilus something more of the time after Christ's resurrection:

> *After his suffering, he showed himself to these men and gave many convincing proofs that he was alive. He appeared to them over a period of forty days and spoke about the kingdom of God. (v. 3)*

Luke is the only scriptural writer who tells us that Christ's post-resurrection ministry covered forty days. Evidently Jesus appeared at intervals, coming and going from Heaven at will, showing miraculous signs and instructing his disciples "about the kingdom of God."

Luke's record of the stunning encounter on the road to Emmaus is a typical example. Christ met the two followers in an altered physical form and "beginning with Moses and all the Prophets, he explained to them what was said in all the Scriptures concerning himself" (24:27), so that they later said (v. 32), "Were not our hearts burning within us while he talked with us on the road and opened the Scriptures to us?" The picture of those forty days is one of enraptured excitement, unfolding mystery, suspense, and anticipation.

Luke goes on in verses 4 and 5:

> *On one occasion, while he was eating with them, he gave them this command: "Do not leave Jerusalem, but wait for the gift my Father promised, which you have heard me speak about. For John baptized with water, but in a few days you will be baptized with the Holy Spirit."*

Christ's conversation with the apostles must have been awesome! It may have even led to all-night rap sessions. What was this baptism "with the Holy Spirit"? Would Jesus take them to the Jordan and rebaptize them? Would they hear a voice from Heaven like Jesus did? Rabbis had said the restoration of Israel's political fortunes would be marked by the revived activity of God's Spirit. So now some of the disciples burned with the hope of a political theocracy. Would they themselves be given supernatural powers? Peter probably wanted to go through walls just like the Master had done. What would be their duties? Certainly each one would have a special mission marked with incredible power and great success. They were forbidden to leave Jerusalem for now, but then . . . How long before this would happen? Jesus said, "In a few days." They could not wait!

In the midst of this ongoing, frenzied speculation, Jesus called the eleven together at the crest of the Mount of Olives. The apostolic band was aflame with expectancy.

> *So when they met together, they asked him, "Lord, are you at this time going to restore the kingdom to Israel?" He said to them: "It is not for you to know the times or dates the Father has set by his own authority. But you will receive power when the Holy Spirit comes on you; and you will be my witnesses in Jerusalem, and in all Judea and Samaria, and to the ends of the earth." (vv. 6-8)*

These were Jesus' final earthly words. It has been 2,000 years, and Jesus has not during that time planted his feet on *terra firma* and audibly addressed his followers. Perhaps that silence is intended to prevent anything from obscuring Jesus' last words, so they will continue to reverberate in the Church's ears.

Our Lord has laid down in the clearest terms the mission for those who are to follow him. This is the mission of the church that would dare to call itself New Testament — the mandate of apostolic Christianity.

Verse 8 is the key verse of the entire book of Acts. Chapters 1 — 7 tell of the witness "in Jerusalem," chapters 8 — 11 the witness "in all Judea and Samaria," and chapters 12 — 28 the witness "to the ends of the earth." This is the foundation on which to build an effervescent, exciting faith.

THE MISSION ITSELF

The core commission is seen in the heart of verse 8: ". . . and you will be my witnesses." We are to be "*witnesses*" for Christ! This is the recurring message of Acts. The word occurs no less than thirty-nine times. For example:

> *"God has raised this Jesus to life, and* we are all witnesses *of the fact." (2:32)*

> *"You killed the author of life, but God raised him from the dead.* We are witnesses of this.*" (3:15)*

> "We are witnesses of everything he did *in the country of the Jews and in Jerusalem." (10:39)*

> "'You will be his witness to all men *of what you have seen and heard.'" (22:15)*

This witness about Christ is often counterfeited but never duplicated. Perhaps you have had the experience of having some neatly dressed young men come to your door and, after some friendly conversation, invited them in, only to have them set up a flannelgraph while saying something like, "Wouldn't it be nice if we had prophets today?" They then present an incredible religious maze: the Aaronic priesthood, the priesthood of Melchizedek, a modern prophet from upstate New York (who was heralded by an angel with an Italian name), the Urim and Thummim (i.e., a pair of giant spectacles through which their prophet translated their sacred book), a "plan" that can promote you to the Terrestrial, Celestial, and finally Telestial Heavens, etc. An amazingly complex religious system given under the guise of being a witness for Christ's latter-day church, their gospel is in reality a complete reversal of the good news of Christ's grace.

The true witness to which Christ referred is not like that. To be a witness for Christ is to bring a message that is a marvel of simplicity: Jesus Christ is God come in the flesh; he died to pay for our sins; he was resurrected; now he is exalted in Heaven; he calls us to believe in him and so receive forgiveness of sins. This is good news. There is nothing to join, no system to climb — just a person to receive and, in him, eternal life.

Though this witness is simple, it requires costly commitment from its carriers. It radically touches our inner complexities — who we are deep inside. Not only must we have the message, the *logos*, the Word, but we must also attract the magnificent compliment that Sir Henry Stanley gave David Livingstone after discovering and spending time with him in Central Africa: "If I had been with him any longer, I would have been compelled to be a Christian, and he never spoke to me about it at all." [2] Livingstone's witness went far beyond mere words.

If we are to be effective witnesses for our Savior, we cannot be water boys in the game of life. We have to roll up our sleeves and pitch in. Our lives must display the inner reality of what we externally proclaim. That is why gospel flames raced across Asia. The apostles walked their talk. That is why Paul was able to reach the Praetorian guards while under arrest in Philippi (see Philippians 1:13). Are we witnesses like that?

This matter of *ethos* — who we are — demands absolute, soul-searching honesty because it is so easy to deceive ourselves. Those of us with a Bible-believing heritage who constantly hear and talk about spiritual things can by the sheer weight of discussion come to believe that we live up to what we talk about, even if we do not. Being an authentic witness demands an open, tender heart that is always growing in the experience it proclaims.

To be a witness we must have *logos* — the Word of Christ, *ethos* — the inner reality of what we proclaim, and *pathos* — passion. The apostles were passionate for Christ. Observe Peter at Pentecost, Stephen at his stoning, Paul before Felix. They fervently promoted their faith. They were a band of zealous believers who turned their world upside-down.

When George Whitefield was getting the people of Edinburgh out of their beds at 5 o'clock in the morning to hear his preaching, a man on his way to the church met David Hume, the Scottish philosopher and skeptic. Surprised at seeing him on his way to hear Whitefield, the man said, "I thought you did not believe in the gospel." Hume replied, "I do not, but *he does*."[3]

The message is simple, but the demand on the messengers is serious. For effective witness, there must the Word, the inner reality, the passion.

The command to be Christ's witnesses is for all true believers in him. There are no loopholes. No one can say, "This does not apply to me." Our honor exceeds that of any worldly ambassador, whether it to be Mainland China, France, or the private offices of the Prime Minister of England. Christ's last word to us is, "You will be my witnesses."

THE MISSION'S EXTENT

How far is this witness to spread? "In Jerusalem, and in all Judea and Samaria, and to the ends of the earth" (v. 8). We have heard these words so many times that it is difficult to feel their impact. But what a shock these geographical designations must have been to the disciples. Jerusalem? The Lord was crucified there. Judea? They had been rejected there. Samaria? Minster to those half-breeds? The ends of the earth? Gentiles too? The words were not only spiritually revolutionary, but socially and ethnically unheard of.

We all know the story. The Lord's outline was carried out to the letter. Jerusalem was filled with the preaching of the gospel, and 3,000 were saved in one day. Later Philip broke the taboos of Judea and crossed over into Samaria. Social revolution!

> Barbarian, Scythian, bond and free, male and female, Jew and Greek, learned and ignorant, clasped hands and sat down at one table, and

> felt themselves all one in Christ Jesus. They were ready to break all other bonds, and to yield to the uniting forces that streamed out from His Cross. There never had been anything like it. No wonder that the world began to babble about sorcery, and conspiracies, and complicity in unnameable vices.[4]

The good news of Jesus was even being whispered in Caesar's own kitchen (see, for example, Philippians 4:22).

How impressive is the scope of the missionary heart. Followers of Christ yearn for the gospel to go to the ends of the earth *and* into their own community. There can be no burden for distant unreached peoples without a burden for unreached neighbors. Christian believers see that it is their duty to cross over ethnic divisions. Christ demands a world heart! A heart that prays for those at home just as much as for those being touched by overseas missionaries. Jesus' final words to his Church demand expansive hearts.

Christ's words taken seriously are nothing less than the declaration of a benevolent war. They are a call for every believer — every forgiven sinner now following Christ — to spend and be spent. Nechayev, a nineteenth-century disciple of Karl Marx, was thrown into prison for his role in the assassination of Czar Alexander II. Prior to his death he wrote:

> The revolutionary man is a consecrated man. He has neither his own interests nor concerns nor feelings, no attachment nor property, not even a name. All for him is absorbed in the single exclusive interest in the one thought, in one passion — REVOLUTION.[5]

Although his motives and goals were wrong, Nechayev stated well the heartbeat of true commitment — the kind needed to accomplish the objectives of the Church, God's missile of salt and light hurled into the world to proclaim the triumphant message of sins forgiven and lives transformed. Too often we are overly concerned about personal comfort. If the Christian faith is worth believing at all, it is worth believing heroically!

Jesus' words are a call to zeal, and zeal — fervor, passion, urgent and loving service — is the medium by which the spiritual war is waged. Whether we are at home or bridging society's barriers or making our way to the ends of the earth, we are to be people of one thing — seeing one thing, caring for one thing, living for one thing — *to please God*. Whether we live, whether we have health, whether we have sickness, whether we are rich, whether we are poor, whether we get honor, whether we get slain, our deepest desire is to please him. And what does he want? "You will receive power when the Holy Spirit comes on you; and you will be my witnesses in

Jerusalem, and in all Judea and Samaria, and to the ends of the earth." The apostles did this, and we are to do likewise. What a call — to be personal witnesses of the Lord Jesus Christ! That is too much — it is too hard! And to demand that it be to the ends of the earth — impossible! That is why our Lord prefaced the statement with a promised provision of power.

THE MISSION'S POWER

"But you will receive power when the Holy Spirit comes on you." There was a brief interlude of about ten days, and then the Holy Spirit came upon the apostles, there were tongues of fire, they spoke in other languages, and spiritual *power* rolled through them. It was thus no surprise when Peter later walked by the Beautiful Gate, saw a lame man, and said, "Silver or gold I do not have, but what I have I give you. In the name of Jesus Christ of Nazareth, walk." And suddenly there was a high-jumping cripple in front of the temple. And again, John and Peter stood before the entire Sanhedrin and said, "Judge for yourselves whether it is right in God's sight to obey you rather than God. For we cannot help speaking about what we have seen and heard." Consider also the first gospel concert — in Philippi after Paul and Silas were beat up and tossed into the slammer. *Power!*

When the Holy Spirit comes upon followers of Christ, the most unlikely people become fountains of power. This spiritual power is always available, and he displays it according to his sovereign plans. God imparts his power when and how he wants to. Years ago when I was a youth pastor I noticed that a lot of young people would show up on Sunday morning, but when it came to Wednesday night Bible study I could hardly get a baker's dozen. I would have eight, then fifteen, then eight . . . I almost quit. I was so discouraged that I *had* to depend on the Lord. I remember finally just giving it all to the Lord, and one night when there were only eight a young man came to know Christ. He brought another young man to the group, and *he* came to know Christ. In two months my group went from fifteen to ninety, and then to 120! I only remember four Wednesday nights out of a year and a half that someone did not trust Christ!

This was a most unlikely occurrence, and it had nothing to do with me. The kids were praying and bringing their friends, and their friends were weeping, repenting, and trusting the Lord. There was life-changing power at work!

The power of the Holy Spirit is the supreme qualification and assurance of Christ's witnesses. The mission? To be "my witnesses." The mission's extent? "In Jerusalem, and in all Judea and Samaria, and to the ends of the earth." The mission's power? "When the Holy Spirit comes on you."

This is a dramatic text — Christ's final statement on earth and the key to the book of Acts. But then things became even more dramatic: "After he said this, he was taken up before their very eyes, and a cloud hid him from their sight" (v. 9). Some other versions suggest that the cloud came right down onto the mountain. That cloud may have been the *Shekinah* glory — a visible representation of the pleasure and presence of God. This was the same symbol that Moses had encountered on Sinai when God covered him with his hand so that Moses only saw the afterglow. It was the same cloud that traveled before Israel by day (a pillar of fire by night). It was the cloud that lay over the tabernacle and filled the temple. It was the cloud that Ezekiel saw depart over the east gate. It was the same presence that surrounded Jesus on the Mount of Transfiguration when his face shone forth like the sun (Matthew 17).

The apostles' hearts were pounding, and their eyes were wide as saucers as God powerfully underscored his Son's final words to his Church! The truth conveyed through these events should resound in the inner chambers of every believer's heart.

The ascended Christ was to be the confidence — the flame — of the apostolic movement. Having ascended, he now intercedes for the Church and has sent the Holy Spirit, "another Comforter" just like Himself. And so we can be his witnesses.

Verses 10 and 11 give us the stunning epilogue:

> *They were looking intently up into the sky as he was going, when suddenly two men dressed in white stood beside them. "Men of Galilee," they said, "why do you stand here looking into the sky? This same Jesus, who has been taken from you into heaven, will come back in the same way you have seen him go into heaven."*

The teaching here is clearly meant for a missionary church. "Jesus is returning again — so get going!" How does your life stack up? How does mine? Like a day-old glass of ginger ale? The life of a Christian can and should be exciting, effervescent. The key is genuine commitment to God's plan. Some of us are moved with such thoughts, but give us an hour watching our favorite sports team and it all vanishes — "the worries of this life." Or a young husband and wife who are struggling financially may feel unable to think about anything except their limited funds or an uncertain future, though in actuality that does not exempt them from being witnesses for Christ and following him. Regardless of the particular difficulties confronting us, we are called to be his witnesses.

Commitment is the key to a sparkling, meaningful life. *Logos*, ethos, pathos — what a life!

PRAYER

Our gracious Lord, the call is too high for any of us. But we thank you that the other Comforter who is just like Jesus is not only with *us but* in *us. God, help us to be giving, praying, sacrificing, honest, true, passionate believers, just like the apostles were. In Jesus' name, Amen.*

2

Expectant Prayer

ACTS 1:12-26

All of us find the chronicles of the Holy Spirit in Acts thrilling. That book abounds with rousing accounts of *apostolic power*—for example, Peter's confrontation of Ananias:

> *"Ananias, how is it that Satan has so filled your heart that you have lied to the Holy Spirit and have kept for yourself some of the money you received for the land? . . . You have not lied to men but to God." When Ananias heard this, he fell down and died. (5:3-5)*

Consider too Philip's amazing encounter with the Ethiopian eunuch, who after his baptism "did not see him again" because "the Spirit of the Lord suddenly took Philip away" (8:39). *Poof* and he was gone. Or Paul who, shipwrecked on Malta, built a fire for warmth, and a poisonous viper grabbed his hand, which he shook off into the fire and continued his conversation (28:3-5). Just another day in the life of an apostle. This is awesome apostolic power!

There was also *apostolic eloquence*. At Pentecost Peter preached with such conviction that the people "were cut to the heart and said to Peter and the other apostles, 'Brothers, what shall we do?'" (2:37). Paul reached such heights of persuasion before Agrippa that the king was forced to exclaim, "Almost thou persuadest me to be a Christian" (26:28, KJV). In such instances the Spirit of God uses the eloquence he has given to his servants to bring about great results in the kingdom.

There was also *apostolic joy*, for Luke tells us, "And the disciples were filled with joy and with the Holy Spirit" (13:52).

Ordinary people became fountains of divine power, eloquence, and joy.

There were outpourings of God's love and might in Jerusalem, in Samaria, in Caesarea . . . The power of the Holy Spirit erupted in Ephesus and Corinth and Rome, and such divine demonstrations have continued with intermittent flames throughout the course of history since then. Our hearts thrill at the stories of such wonderful times. Today the worldwide Church of Jesus Christ longs for the Spirit's power, eloquence, and joy!

Jesus promised that when he went away he would send another Helper to his people (John 16:7). God still sovereignly sends the mysterious winds of the Holy Spirit — his power, his comfort, his presence — to those who know and serve Jesus Christ. We do not know exactly why and how the Holy Spirit works, but we have been told what we must do to enjoy the fullness of the Spirit. Our situation is like that of the little boy who asked his grandfather, "Grandpa, what is the wind?" "I cannot explain the wind to you," the old fisherman replied, "but I can teach you to raise the sails!"[1]

The book of Acts shows us how to have the wind of the Holy Spirit in our sails. The attitude that makes way for the fullness of the Holy Spirit is the same attitude seen in Christ's followers just before the Holy Spirit was given on the Day of Pentecost.

EXPECTANT BELIEF (vv. 12-13)

In a word, the apostolic attitude that preceded the Holy Spirit's coming was *expectancy*. In the forty days between the Lord's resurrection and ascension he evidently traveled regularly between Heaven and earth. His encounter with the two disciples on the road to Emmaus was typical. The risen Christ would miraculously appear and perhaps perform a confirming sign or teach them from the Old Testament Scriptures. As a result, their hearts burned within them. The picture of those forty days was one of spiraling belief and flaming anticipation! There were heart-thumping gatherings in the Upper Room as one would give his account and then another. Sometimes the Master would come to them right through the walls!

As the days flew by and they obeyed his command to remain in Jerusalem, their optimistic belief and expectancy produced a wonderful but uncomfortable tension. They really *believed*, but the Ascension must have been the capper because as his last earthly instructions were ringing in their ears, they were surrounded by a luminous cloud (the *Shekinah* glory — the symbol of God's presence and favor). Then Jesus was gone!

Think of the walk back to Jerusalem after the angels told them to quit looking up and to get going, as described in 1:12: "Then they returned to Jerusalem from the hill called the Mount of Olives, a Sabbath day's walk from the city." It was only about two-thirds of a mile (1,100 meters) because this was all *The Mishnah* would allow.[2] Maybe they started out subdued, overwhelmed, stunned by the Ascension. Some probably were hardly aware that their feet were on the ground. Perhaps some pinched themselves. They returned to Jerusalem with great joy—mega-joy!

They went to the Upper Room, as verse 13 relates:

> *When they arrived, they went upstairs to the room where they were staying. Those present were Peter, John, James and Andrew; Philip and Thomas, Bartholomew and Matthew; James son of Alphaeus and Simon the Zealot, and Judas son of James.*

Though it is speculation, I personally believe this was the same Upper Room in which our Lord ate the last supper with the disciples. The Greek text says, "*the*" upper room" (not just any upper room). If this is correct, it is beautifully fitting that the Holy Spirit was given in the very same room in which Jesus promised him:

> *"And I will ask the Father, and he will give you another Counselor to be with you forever — the Spirit of truth. . . . I will not leave you as orphans; I will come to you." (John 14:16-18)*

It must have been a large room because 120 would soon squeeze in. In addition to the eleven apostles, there were Jesus' own mother Mary (this is the last mention of her in Scripture), Jesus' "brothers" (the very same brothers who had given him so much grief during his ministry, thinking he was out of his mind), and "the women" who had so faithfully ministered to Jesus during his life on earth (v. 14): dear Mary Magdalene, Mary of Clopas, Susanna, Joanna, Mary of Bethany, Martha (in the kitchen no doubt!), and many others. There were surely times when it was difficult for anyone to hear anything!

They stayed together because of one thing: they believed that the Holy Spirit was going to come upon them and they were going to receive promised power. They expected the infilling of the Holy Spirit. They had absolutely no doubt about it. No wavering. No discussion.

The sails must be hoisted to catch the winds of the Holy Spirit through *expectant belief.* Amazingly, the great R. A. Torrey was once a tongue-tied preacher. His early years in the ministry were torture for him. He preached three times each Sunday and committed his sermons to memory but nearly twisted the top button of his coat off as he forced the sermon out. When he finished, he felt a great sense of relief that his duty was over for another week. But then he would immediately think, "You have to begin tomorrow to get ready for next Sunday."

The glad day finally came when he realized that when he stood up to preach, though people would see him, there was Another whom they did not see but who stood by his side, and all the responsibility for results was upon his Lord. All Torrey had to do was to get as far back out of sight as possible and let Jesus do the preaching. Torrey came to truly believe what he already believed in principle: the Holy Spirit, sent by Jesus, was in him to do the work. Only then did the power come. From that day on, preaching became the joy of his life. He would rather preach than eat.

The primary problem with believers in this matter of the fullness of the Holy Spirit is their lack of believing expectancy. We believe it is possible for others but not for us. We believe that R. A. Torrey experienced it, and Jonathan Edwards, and Corrie ten Boom, and Joni Eareckson Tada, but it is out of our reach. Such thinking is misinformed. What needs to happen here? We do not have to broaden our belief or enlarge our understanding. We simply need to really believe — and so act upon — what we say we believe. Do we truly expect Christ to fill us with His Holy Spirit and thus empower our lives?

EXPECTANT PRAYER (v. 14)

Along with the apostles' confident anticipation came trusting prayer.

> *They all joined together constantly in prayer, along with the women and Mary the mother of Jesus, and with his brothers. (v. 14)*

Persistence. "They all joined together constantly in prayer." A. T. Robertson says this means, "they stuck to praying."[3] There was a commitment to prayer! The text reads literally, "were continually devoting themselves to *the* prayer," which suggests there may have been an appointed service of prayer. The last verse in Luke adds that they were "continually at the temple, praising God" (24:53). Sometimes they were in the temple and sometimes in the Upper Room, but they were *persistent.*

The one who wants his sail full of the breeze of the Spirit must have such perseverance in prayer. In Luke 11:13 Jesus says, ". . . how much more will your Father in heaven give the Holy Spirit to those who ask him!" We must ask, but persistence is the key. A hurried request soon forgotten and unrepeated will produce no fruit. Jesus prefaced his statement with the story of the man who went to his neighbor at night to borrow food for an unexpected guest and only received what he wanted by repeatedly banging on the door.

> *"I tell you, though he will not get up and give him the bread because he is his friend, yet because of the man's persistence he will get up*

> *and give him as much as he needs. So I say to you: Ask [literally, keep asking] and it will be given to you; seek [literally, keep seeking] and you will find; knock [literally, keep knocking] and the door will be opened." (vv. 8-9)*

The apostolic band believed so fully and fervently that they could not help but pray with persistence!

Unity. "They all *joined together* ["with one accord," KJV] constantly in prayer." This is amazing! Eleven disciples — strong-willed men, the kind who argued over who was going to get the best seat in the kingdom and who refused to wash one another's feet; Jesus' brothers who had been so perverse as to reject his messiahship; his mother and a whole houseful of women — rich, poor, chaste, unchaste — "*all*" of them were of one mind — literally, "of one heart and mind." How? They were all looking up to Christ at the same time for the same thing.

The Lord is pleased to pour his Spirit upon believers who are living in unity. At the end of Acts 4, the Church is described as being "one in heart and mind," with the result that "much grace" and "great power" came upon them (vv. 32-33). The breeze of the Holy Spirit refreshes the life of those who dwell in unity — those who through faith in Christ forgive, make restitution, and seek the healing and affirmation of others.

Dependence. Many years ago the great Bible teacher William R. Newell was concluding a conference in China for China Inland Mission, and as he left he said to the mission's leader, "Oh, do pray for me that I shall be nothing!" The director responded with a twinkle in his eye, "Newell, you are nothing! Take it by faith!"[4] The Upper-Room fellowship knew this implicitly. They knew that by themselves they could do *nothing*.

Some have criticized the apostles for resorting to the drawing of lots to discover Judas' replacement. Such critics forget two things: 1) Drawing lots was the time-honored way of determining God's will in Israel. Proverbs 16:33 says, "The lot is cast into the lap, but its every decision is from the LORD." 2) Even in the casting of lots the apostles cast themselves completely on God for the outcome in dependent prayer. The fullness of the Holy Spirit comes to those with poverty of spirit, to those who hunger and thirst for righteousness, to those who rely wholly on God.

A FINAL WORD

As believers we have received the full benefit of Christ's body and blood. Yet we can never have enough of Christ. Almost always when I am dining out, the waitress will say, "Can I warm your coffee?" I almost always respond, "Yes." No matter how hot the cup, given time and neglect, it becomes cold. Some of us need a spiritual warm-up. Some of us are almost empty. We need the refreshing filling or refilling of the Holy Spirit.

Would you like the wind of the Spirit in your sails? Believe that Christ will do just as he said. Join the expectancy of the Upper-Room fellowship. Believe that it is possible not only for others, but that it will happen to *you*. Ask expectantly. Ask him to fill your cup and make it overflow. Ask for the wonderful winds of God! ". . . how much more will your Father in heaven give the Holy Spirit to those who ask him!" (Luke 11:13).

PRAYER

O God, forgive us for being content with our own resources. Help us to recognize our poverty and to then call to you for the riches of the power of the Holy Spirit. And once we ask, help us to expect you to answer and provide. Help us to continue ever in sincere, heart-felt prayer, knowing that without you nothing good will transpire in our lives. May our sails be full with the wind of your Spirit as we carry out high adventures for your glory, in your strength. In Jesus' name, Amen.

3

Pentecost

ACTS 2:1-13

Among the most treasured memories of my years as a young father are my family's celebrations of the Fourth of July. A kaleidoscope of recollections comes to mind — our good friends and their children, backyard hotdogs and hamburgers, my wife Barbara's potato salad and apple pie, annual grudge-match touch football games, skinned elbows and bruised egos. Most of all I remember the children: shirts off, sunburned shoulders, tummies out, sticky, dirt-colored hands, and hair that at the end of the day looked and smelled like damp chicken feathers.

And of course the fireworks. I discovered early on that the best show is not the fireworks but the children's faces. Their expression of sheer joy and wide-eyed abandon is first white with the reflection of the phosphorus, then changes hues as the display continues, finally turning amber and then disappearing as the flame goes out, only to begin all over again.

While the departing luminous cloud at the ascension of Christ must have been an extraordinary sight, even more remarkable were the apostles' countenances. "They were looking intently up into the sky as he was going" (1:10). Imagine the rapture on their faces as they gazed upward until the cloud was only a spark in their eyes and the angels told them to get moving.

Those uplifted eyes set the tone for the ten days that followed as they looked for Christ's return via the indwelling of the Holy Spirit and an influx of spiritual power. They really did believe that Christ was going to send the Holy Spirit. There was no doubt. No wavering. Their confidence made them ready to have their cups filled and warmed with the Holy Spirit.

Also, during that ten-day wait between the Ascension and Pentecost they became increasingly aware of their *need* to be filled. During Christ's life they had known his exhilarating presence. Even during the forty days between the Resurrection and Ascension they had repeatedly been blessed by his visits. But during these ten days the disciples undoubtedly felt empty. They were more aware than ever of the importance of their Savior's presence — and now he was gone. The Master's words recorded in John 15:5, "Apart from me you can do nothing," were forever embedded in their consciousness. But their profound emptiness, as trying as it was, made them ready for Pentecost.

What happened to the apostolic band when the Holy Spirit came at Pentecost, what happens when the Holy Spirit personally fills us, and how can we prepare for it?

WHAT HAPPENED TO *THE APOSTLES AT PENTECOST (vv. 1-4)*

Verse 1 tells us that "the *day* of Pentecost" had arrived. This was fifty days after Passover, and that is what *Pentecost* means — "the fiftieth." (It came literally as a week of weeks after Passover and was also called "The Feast of Weeks.") Passover occurred in mid-April, so Pentecost was at the beginning of June. It was the best-attended of the great feasts because traveling conditions were at their best. There was never a more cosmopolitan gathering in Jerusalem than this one. It was the perfect time for the descent of the Holy Spirit of God.

A divinely arranged appropriateness in the feast of Pentecost provides the background for the giving of the Holy Spirit. Originally regarded as the "feast of the firstfruits," it was emphasized by a special offering of two baked loaves made from freshly gathered wheat, designated in Leviticus 23:17 as "firstfruits to the Lord." As the day of the firstfruits, Pentecost was eminently appropriate for the bestowal of the Holy Spirit and the conversion of 3,000 souls — firstfruits of an even greater harvest.

It was also fitting because by the time of Christ Pentecost was considered the anniversary of the giving of the Law on Mount Sinai, and thus it provided a perfect opportunity to contrast the giving of the Law with the giving of the Spirit. "The Spirit's coming is in continuity of God's purpose in giving the law and yet . . . the Spirit's coming signals the essential difference between the Jewish faith and commitment to Jesus . . . the former is Torah-centered and Torah-directed, the latter is Christ-centered and Spirit-directed."[1] Pentecost occurred by divine arrangement.

What happened on that special day?

When the day of Pentecost came, they were all together in one place. Suddenly a sound like the blowing of a violent wind came from

> *heaven and filled the whole house where they were sitting. They saw what seemed to be tongues of fire that separated and came to rest on each of them. All of them were filled with the Holy Spirit and began to speak in other tongues as the Spirit enabled them. (vv. 1-4)*

As the apostles' heads were bowed in prayer, a breeze began to move across them, and then it was *more* than a breeze. Literally, "an echoing sound as of a mighty wind borne violently"[2] roared through the house like the whirr of a tornado, so that their robes flapped wildly. The Spirit of God was coming upon them! A fiery presence was in their midst, and (as the Greek indicates) it suddenly divided into separate flame-like tongues that individually danced over the heads of those present. Fire had always meant the presence of God. Through John the Baptist, God had promised a baptism with fire (Matthew 3:11), and now it was here. They were "*filled* with the Holy Spirit" and in an electrifying instant began to speak in other languages — literally, "as the Spirit continued giving them to speak out in a clear, loud voice."[3] They spoke as clearly and powerfully as the Old Testament prophets.

This event may seem esoteric and mysterious, with its "wind," "fire," and supernatural utterance. It has a primal ring like the Greeks' earth, fire, wind, and water. But in the Jewish context the phenomenon was perfectly understandable. The Hebrew word for "wind," *ruah*, and the Greek word *pneuma* are both used for the Holy Spirit. Ezekiel used *ruah* to describe the Spirit of God moving over a valley of dry bones (representing a spiritually dead Jewish nation), so that suddenly there was thunder[4] and the clattering of bones as they came together "bone to bone." Then came the wonderfully macabre spectacle of growing sinews and flesh, and finally skin, and then Ezekiel's words at God's command:

> *Come from the four winds, O breath, and breathe into these slain, that they may live . . . they came to life and stood up on their feet — a vast army. (37:9-10)*

At Pentecost, the reviving winds of the Spirit came upon the apostles with incredible spiritual life and power. In a future day this will achieve final fulfillment in the Messianic Age. The apostles now had God's life-giving Spirit in a more intimate and powerful way than they had ever known — than *anyone* had ever known.

First "wind," then "fire." Fire is a symbol of God's presence throughout the Bible, beginning with Moses and the burning bush (Exodus 3:2-4) and continuing with the consuming fire on Mount Sinai (Exodus 24:17). The fire at Pentecost indicated God's presence, just as its resting on Israel demonstrated a corporate unity. However, a new significance came when the fire divided into flames dancing over the individual apostles. The Spirit now rests upon each believer individually. The emphasis from Pentecost onwards is on the personal relationship of God to the believer through the Holy Spirit. The inner pillar of fire burns away our dross, flames forth from our inner being, and brings to us a sense of God's presence and power. The fire of God!

First "wind," then "fire," then divinely empowered utterance. In the Old Testament, inspired speech was regularly associated with the Spirit's coming upon God's servants, as in the case of Eldad and Medad (Numbers 11:26-29) and of Saul (1 Samuel 10:6-12). Pentecost was the day par excellence of such speech. To the observant Jew, it was easy to see that the Holy Spirit had come. When he comes to God's people, he brings wind, fire, and utterance.

How did the apostles feel when the heavens began to roar so loudly that the sound attracted a vast multitude from all corners of Jerusalem? Surely there were some involuntary gasps or cries of surprise in the Upper Room. What was it like when the flames began flashing over their heads and they began speaking languages they did not know? Some began to speak in perfect Latin, others in an authentic Phrygian dialect. The burning expectancy of the last fifty days, the persistent emptiness, was suddenly fulfilled. What did they feel in relation to God and to one another? We get some idea from Ephesians 5:18-21, where Paul carefully explains the experience by first counseling the Ephesians to be filled and then explains what this means in four subordinate participles.

WHAT HAPPENED IN *THE APOSTLES AT PENTECOST (v. 4; Ephesians 5:18-21)*

> *Do not get drunk on wine, which leads to debauchery. Instead, be filled with the Spirit. Speak to one another with psalms, hymns and spiritual songs. Sing and make music in your heart to the Lord, always giving thanks to God the Father for everything, in the name of our Lord Jesus Christ. Submit to one another out of reverence for Christ.*

There was *communication*! They were to ". . . speak to one another with psalms, hymns and spiritual songs." On Pentecost and the following days, through the work of the Holy Spirit, believers were united in the core of their beings, they shared the same secret, and they discovered a depth and joy of communication they had not previously known. This spiritual exchange was best expressed by reading and teaching the Scriptures and by worshiping God with music.

My own experience has borne this out in my relationship with my wife. If we are both filled with the Holy Spirit and are open to God, there is wonderfully fulfilling communication. I have also found this dramatically true in my ministry experiences at camps and weekend retreats. Often when a retreat begins everyone is at arm's length. Some know Christ, some do not. Some are walking with the Lord, and others are not. But as the Spirit's ministry takes effect, some confess Christ and allow themselves to be filled with the Holy Spirit and to appropriate the fullness of God. Everyone revels in the joy of the Lord at such times. Where there is the fullness of the Holy Spirit, there is communication.

There was also *joy*! They were to "sing and make music in [their] heart to the Lord." The inner music of their souls went right up to God. One of the memorable figures of the great Welsh revival was Bill Bray, the Cornish coal miner. Billy was so alive that when he would descend the shaft in the morning he would pray, "Lord, if any of us must be killed today, let it be *me*; let not one of these men die, for they are not happy and I am."[5] He was preeminently a man of joy. Once, in a somber meeting when the people were commiserating over their difficulties,

> he arose smiling, and clapping his hands said: "Well, friends, I have been taking vinegar and honey but, praise the Lord, I have had the vinegar with a spoon and the honey with a ladle." His testimony was always one of joy and victory. Speaking concerning the Lord, he said: "He has made me glad and no one can make me sad; He makes me shout and no one can make me doubt; He it is that makes me dance and leap, and there is no one that can keep down my feet."[6]

He would have fit right in with those in the Upper Room. Acts 2:11 says they were "declaring the wonders of God."

There was also *thanksgiving*. They were "always giving thanks to God the Father for everything." Such action is supernatural. Certainly the apostles were not that way before the Spirit came upon them.

They were also in *subjection* to one another. As Paul says, "Submit to one another out of reverence for Christ." This had not previously been a part of the apostolic disposition. Their earlier concerns were more like who was going to get the chair next to Jesus in the Kingdom. Jesus washed their feet because they refused to serve one another. But with the coming of the Holy Spirit, they became able to submit to one another.

What a transformation! In all the emotion and ecstasy of Pentecost, this was going on deep down inside, and it then flowed out to others. Certainly there was only one Pentecost historically, but the benefits of the filling remain, and they are wonderful — a communicative spirit, a joyful spirit, a thankful spirit, and a yielding, serving spirit.

WHAT HAPPENED THROUGH *THE APOSTLES AT PENTECOST (vv. 5-13)*

> *Now there were staying in Jerusalem God-fearing Jews from every nation under heaven. When they heard this sound, a crowd came together in bewilderment, because each one heard them speaking in his own language. Utterly amazed, they asked: "Are not all these men who are speaking Galileans? Then how is it that each of us hears them in his own native language? Parthians, Medes and Elamites; residents of Mesopotamia, Judea and Cappadocia, Pontus and Asia, Phrygia and Pamphylia, Egypt and the parts of Libya near Cyrene; visitors from Rome (both Jews and converts to Judaism); Cretans and Arabs — we hear them declaring the wonders of God in our own tongues!" (vv. 5-11)*

The rushing wind brought together a great crowd, and the apostles stepped forth from the Upper Room and began to proclaim the gospel in the languages of the day. Their hearers were amazed because they saw these men were Galileans—ignorant, despised country bumpkins who had funny accents because they could not pronounce gutturals. But suddenly they had amazing linguistic powers. No matter what dialect he was using, each of the Twelve held forth on "the wonders of God."

The result? "Amazed and perplexed, they asked one another, 'What does this mean?' Some, however, made fun of them and said, 'They have had too much wine'" (vv. 12-13). Some committed the fatal error of attributing the supernatural to natural causes. They were "modern men." Spiritually indifferent, they flippantly made light of the most important things of life and went on their self-sufficient way. Others were "amazed" — literally, "distraught" — and utterly at a loss saying, "What does this mean?" These honest hearers sought answers, and wonderfully, as the chapter goes on to record, some 3,000 believed that day and were saved. What grace!

"What does this mean?" It means that the Holy Spirit brings new life to those who believe in Jesus Christ, and with that life comes a continuing power to those who are continually filled. It means fire in our lives, individually burning away the chaff and flaming out to those around us. It means the truth of God going forth from us in a way we would never have dreamed of — the divine utterance of God through us. It means communication, joy, thankfulness, submission.

What does this require of us? The same thing it required from the apostles and those 3,000 followers — *emptiness*, an acknowledgment that we need Christ. God helps us have faith and respond to the gospel, and that is how we become Christians and receive the saving baptism and fullness of the Holy Spirit. Then, once we are Christians, God's persistent work in our lives liberates us from the idea that we can live the Christian life on our own. Each time we acknowledge our inadequacy, he fills us with more of his Spirit so we can carry on his work. He will not fill our sails with the wind of the Holy Spirit unless we admit that the sails are empty. This requires humility and confession. The apostles were living in empty dependency until the filling came.

The key to the Spirit-filled Christian life is found in a paradox: cultivating an attitude of perpetual emptiness brings with it a perpetual fullness. Jesus said it like this: "Blessed are those who hunger and thirst for righteousness, for they will be filled."

PRAYER

Here's our cup, Lord. Warm it and fill it up, Lord! May all you intend to happen in our lives come to pass, through the power and presence of your Holy Spirit! Please continue to work in us and through us, producing a supernatural joy and praise in our hearts. May your fullness bring salvation to many around us, for your glory. In Jesus' name, Amen.

4

Peter's Greatest Sermon

ACTS 2:14-37

First sermons or new preaching situations are often memorable experiences. Spurgeon's Preacher's College had a tradition of giving students a text right on the spot and having them preach it to Mr. Spurgeon and the staff. On one particular day a student was given the subject of Zacchaeus. The student stood before them and said, "Zacchaeus was of little stature; so am I. Zacchaeus was up a tree; so am I. Zacchaeus came down; so will I."[1] And he sat down. Smart man! He probably had a great career.

Peter's first sermon was probably his best. It is perhaps, aside from our Lord's sermons, the greatest ever preached. Greatest because of the place it occupies in the history of redemption (it is the inaugural sermon of the age of grace), greatest by its pure results (there were 3,000 converts), and greatest by virtue of its being a model for apostolic preaching.

That it was even a good sermon is amazing because just fifty days earlier, Peter had committed the greatest denial of Christ in history. You will recall that he had a position of *primacy* among the apostolic band. He was always first in everything — first on the water, first with his mouth, first with the sword. This led to his fleshly *presumption*: "Lord, though all the rest of these men leave you, I never will. You are looking at a real man! A straight-ahead, honest-to-goodness go-getter. I will lay down my life for you." His primacy and presumption prepared the way for his infamous *plunge* when in a vile, craven manner, with words he had not used in years, he denied his Lord.

Just fifty days later he was the inaugural spokesman for the inception of the age of grace. Somehow Peter's experiences had prepared him for exceptional use. The situation in Jerusalem at that time was *not* an inviting situation for this first sermon. Fifty days earlier the Jews had murdered Peter's leader by slow torture and had gotten away with it. Now a huge, excited crowd that must have greatly exceeded 3,000 was in a side-show mood, having come to see the strange apostolic phenomena. Sure, some were honestly inquiring, "What does this mean?" (v. 12), but others said, "They have had too much wine" (v. 13). It was not an easy situation, and yet Peter did his greatest preaching on that occasion. A preliminary glance reveals several reasons why.

It was great because it was *simple*. First, the apostle answered their question; second, he told them about Christ; third, he enlisted commitment. There was none of the stuffy obscurity that comes so easily to preachers. A. J. Gossip tells how he once heard the great Principal Rainy of New College, Edinburgh enthusiastically discussing a certain preacher's scholarly sermons, when one of his friends asked: "Will the simple people to whom he preaches follow him at all?" "Well," replied Rainy, "they will have the comfortable feeling that something very fine is going on."[2] There was none of that with Peter's Pentecost sermon. It was absolutely clear and simple. The preacher must not assume intelligibility and simplicity — he must fight for it.

The sermon was great because it was *Scriptural*. Peter's message abounds with God's Word. Notice verse 16 where he says, "This is what was spoken by the prophet Joel" and in the following verses quotes Joel 2:28-32; or later, verse 25, where he says, "David said" and then quotes Psalms 16 and 110.

The sermon was great because it was *Christ-centered*. Look at verse 22, "Jesus of Nazareth," verse 23, "this man," verse 32, "This Jesus," and verse 36, "God has made this Jesus, whom you crucified, both Lord and Christ."

The sermon was great because it was *convicting*. "When the people heard this, they were cut to the heart and said to Peter and the other apostles, 'Brothers, what shall we do?'"(v. 37).

The sermon was great because it was *practical*. It began by answering the question "What does this mean?" (v. 12) and ended by answering the question "What shall we do?" (v. 37).

The sermon was great because it was *attention-getting and relevant*. You would be amazed to know what a preacher can see from his pulpit! I had a couple in my last church who would go to sleep on the front row with their heads propped against one another and their mouths open. A preacher can see his people look at their watches. That does not bother me too much, but I know I am in trouble when people start shaking their watches. Peter got their attention and spoke to the point, saying in effect, "We are not drunk. We have not had anything to drink yet because on this Pentecost holiday we have not made our sacrifices. That is an hour away, and our main meal is two hours after that. We do not drink wine before a meal. How can you be so ridiculous?"

What specifically made this sermon great?

HE SIMPLY EXPLAINED WHAT HAD HAPPENED (vv. 16-21)

Peter explained that what they were seeing was simply a fulfillment of the prophetic Scriptures (v. 16): "This is what was spoken by the prophet Joel." That is, "Joel told us all about this." Then (in verses 17-21) Peter quoted Joel 2:28-32, which describes the whole range of the age of grace (or of the Spirit), in which we live.

> *"'In the last days, God says, I will pour out my Spirit on all people. Your sons and daughters will prophesy, your young men will see visions, your old men will dream dreams. Even on my servants, both men and women, I will pour out my Spirit in those days, and they will prophesy.'" (vv. 17-18)*

All this was present that day in various ways among the apostolic band. Peter's life explicitly manifested these things, as the following chapters in Acts so marvelously record. He prophesied and was caught up in dreams and visions.

There had been no provision for, and no promise of, an abiding presence of the Holy Spirit in the life of any Old Testament saint. That is why King David prayed, "Do not . . . take your Holy Spirit from me" (Psalm 51:11). But the coming of the Holy Spirit at Pentecost changed all that. In the Upper Room Jesus made these promises:

> *"And I will ask the Father, and he will give you another Counselor to be with you forever — the Spirit of truth. The world cannot accept him, because it neither sees him or knows him. But you know him, for he lives with you and will be in you." (John 14:16-17)*

> *"But I tell you the truth: It is for your good that I am going away. Unless I go away, the Counselor will not come to you; but if I go, I will send him to you." (John 16:7)*

With the coming of the Spirit came the Spirit's indwelling, baptizing, sealing, and filling. This was something new — something wonderful and dynamic! Joel's prophecy told of the dawn of this wonderful age. The sunset of the age is described in verses 19-20:

> *"'I will show wonders in the heaven above and signs on the earth below, blood and fire and billows of smoke. The sun will be turned to darkness and the moon to blood before the coming of the great and glorious day of the Lord.'"*

This great age will end with the "day of the Lord" — a special manifestation of the Lord's power and glory and justice. These are marvelous thoughts, but an even greater fact is that during this age, as Joel so beautifully says (quoted in in verse 21), "'And everyone who calls on the name of the Lord will be saved.'" So Peter opened the great inaugural sermon of the new age of grace with the perfect quotation from the book of Joel. What a great way to begin!

It is in Peter's appropriation of Joel's prophecy that we see the ground of the greatness of this sermon: Peter was full of Scripture! Peter was not preaching with notes. He did not even know he was going to preach. There had been no conscious preparation. The point is, he knew Joel's messianic prophecy by heart.

Harry Ironside is a great example of a preacher full of God's Word. Under his mother's guidance Harry began to memorize Scripture when he was three. By age fourteen he had read through the Bible fourteen times, "once for each year." During the rest of his life he read the Bible through at least once a year. A pastor friend told me of a Bible conference at which he and Ironside were two of the speakers. During the conference the speakers discussed their approaches to personal devotions. Each man shared what he had read from the Word that morning. When it was Ironside's turn, he hesitated, then said, "I read the book of Isaiah." He was saturated with the Word of God.[3]

I can say with reservation that in the matter of scholarship and preaching, knowledge of the English Bible is of far greater importance than knowing Greek or Hebrew or mastering dogmatics. Karl Barth put it this way, imitating a Biblical warning: "If thou art a learned man, take care lest with all thy erudite reading (which is not reading God's Word) thou forgettest perchance to read God's Word."[4] If we are truly feeding on the Scriptures, the Spirit will be pleased to use us to communicate his truth.

Not only was Peter full of the Word, but he was full of the Spirit. The very Scripture that Peter quoted is a description of his state. The Upper-Room promise of the coming of *allos parakletos*, literally "another Helper" — one just like Jesus — had been dramatically fulfilled in Peter's life. Being full of the Spirit, it was just as if Christ were speaking in person. That is why the sermon was so great.

In applying this to our own lives, we must realize that there is an intimate connection being being filled with the Spirit and being filled with the Word. Ephesians 5:18-19 says,

> *Do not get drunk on wine, which leads to debauchery. Instead, be filled with the Spirit. Speak to one another in psalms, hymns and spiritual songs. Sing and make music in your heart to the Lord.*

Colossians 3:16 adds:

> *Let the word of Christ dwell in you richly as you teach and admonish one another with all wisdom, and as you sing psalms, hymns and spiritual songs with gratitude in your hearts to God.*

As we fill ourselves with God's Word and yield to it, we make ourselves available for the filling of the Spirit.

PETER EXPLAINED ABOUT JESUS (vv. 22-37)

Peter naturally moved from explaining what had happened to an explanation about Jesus. In verse 22 we have the *Incarnation*: "Jesus of Nazareth was a man . . ." In verse 23 we have the *Crucifixion*: "This man was handed over to you by God's set purpose and foreknowledge; and you, with the help of wicked men, put him to death by nailing him to the cross." Then in verse 24 we have the *Resurrection*: "But God raised him from the dead, freeing him from the agony of death, because it was impossible for death to keep its hold on him." Peter supported his argument for the Resurrection by quoting two mysterious Psalms that could only be fulfilled by Christ.

The first, Psalm 16:8-11, could not have been fulfilled by David because it speaks of someone whom the grave could not hold and who did not undergo decay. David's body remained in its grave and deteriorated. Peter explained this in verses 29-33:

> *"Brothers, I can tell you confidently that the patriarch David died and was buried, and his tomb is here to this day. But he was a prophet and knew that God had promised him on oath that he would place one of his descendants on his throne. Seeing what was ahead, he spoke of the resurrection of the Christ, that he was not abandoned to the grave, nor did his body see decay. God has raised this Jesus to life, and we are all witnesses of the fact. Exalted to the right hand of God, he has received from the Father the promised Holy Spirit and has poured out what you now see and hear."*

The second is Psalm 110:1, quoted in verses 34 and 35 of our text: "'The Lord said to my Lord: "Sit at my right hand until I make your enemies a footstool for your feet."'" Peter's argument was that this cannot be applied to David because he did not ascend to Heaven; therefore, it must apply to the resurrected Messiah.

Peter said, rightly, that these mysterious Psalms can be understood only if we believe in Christ's resurrection and ascension.

Peter's preaching was full of Christ — his incarnation, his crucifixion, his resurrection, and his ascension. That is why the sermon was so great! He concluded in verse 36: "Therefore let all Israel be assured of this: God has made this Jesus, whom you crucified, both Lord and Christ." Jesus could scarcely be lifted higher by human words. He is called "Lord," a title that would have particular appeal and meaning to Gentile ears. And he is called "Messiah," which meant so much to Jewish ears. "God has made this Jesus . . . both Lord and Christ."

Why was Peter's first sermon so great? Both Peter and his sermon were *full of Christ*, *full of Scripture*, and *full of the Holy Spirit*.

Just fifty days earlier, Peter had been full of presumption and pride, and on that fateful Passover night he fell in the most wretched spiritual plunge in history. The result was a profound emptiness, as profound as any man has ever known. That had necessitated a pre-Pentecost restoration of Peter on the shores of Galilee when the Lord asked Peter three times to declare his love. His emptiness made way for Pentecost and as profound a fullness as anyone has ever known! And Peter's overflowing fullness led him to tell Israel the truth about their spiritual bankruptcy. The crowd cried in desperation, "Brothers, what shall we do?" Their emptiness made way for their fullness as 3,000 believed in Christ and were saved. For them the sermon was truly great, because it led them to a supreme Savior.

It would be wonderful to hear a great sermon like Peter's, but it is even better to hear a sermon that is great *because of what it does to us*. It is entirely possible to hear good teaching or preaching for years and never personally hear it in the great way the 3,000 did. Charles Swindoll tells of a wedding where one of the wives of a leader of his church came to him and said, "My husband and I have been down at the beach for the past week, and my husband has walked the beach for hours and hours in the greatest agony. After several days he finally came in and threw himself down on the couch and wept for three hours. Then he asked Christ into his heart." That is a shocking story — one of the leaders in the church becoming converted to Christ!

In a sense, only the 3,000 that day heard Peter's great sermon. There are professing Christians who need Christ. They've heard, but they haven't heard. It is possible to be a respectable, well-taught, moral sinner. That is why the Lord said, in the Parable of the Tares, not to pull the tares out of the wheat field, because the roots are tangled together and we will pull out the wheat too. We cannot tell the difference.

It is possible to have everyone fooled and yet to know nothing of what the 3,000 heard. If you know no emptiness, you will not know the fullness of Christ in your life. If you have never come to the end of yourself and become "poor in spirit," you have never been truly open to the fullness of Christ and the true knowledge of him. Do we *hear* Peter's sermon? If not, the God of grace invites us to come honestly before him who sees all and to allow him to speak to us.

PRAYER

> *Our Father, we thank you for the work of the Holy Spirit. You have said that when the Holy Spirit comes, he will convict the world of sin. We pray, Lord, for those who may have it all together on the outside and yet not know you, that you would bring them to the place of the 3,000, those who had ears to hear. In Jesus' name, Amen.*

5

The Church Where the Spirit Reigned

ACTS 2:38-47

Peter's sermon on the Day of Pentecost was his first and his greatest. And when he closed with the words recorded in verse 36, "Therefore let all Israel be assured of this: God has made this Jesus, whom you crucified, both Lord and Christ," the multitude came under deep conviction. "When the people heard this, they were cut to the heart and said to Peter and the other apostles, 'Brothers, what shall we do?'" The people were convicted both of the Lordship of Christ and of their own sin. They did not try to deny what Peter said. They simply cried, "Brothers, what shall we do?" Not bad for a first sermon.

Peter responded by giving specific instructions to God's covenant people: "Repent and be baptized, every one of you, in the name of Jesus Christ for the forgiveness of your sins. And you will receive the gift of the Holy Spirit" (v. 38). Then he added significantly in verse 39, "The promise is for you and your children and for all who are far off — for all whom the Lord our God will call."

The promised gifts for all who truly believe extends even to the Gentiles, those who are "far off." So at Pentecost Peter saw the promise being extended to us today. Luke concludes the description of that victorious occasion by saying:

> *With many other words he warned them; and he pleaded with them, "Save yourselves from this corrupt generation." Those who accepted his message were baptized, and about three thousand were added to their number that day. (vv. 40-41)*

Three thousand spiritual newborns! Earlier that day in the Upper Room there had been 120. Now in a flash there were 3,000! Three thousand new children of God — 3,000 shepherding responsibilities for the apostles. One of the great days of my own ministry happened during the first year after we began a new church when, in response to an invitation, several families came forward to profess Christ. They represented a wide range of people — from our mailman and his wife to an aspiring stockbroker and his family. And the church was excited. After the service there was lots of laughter and abundant tears and embracing. As we were driving home, my wife and I discussed the future and what would become of those people, and I recall saying, "They mean a lot of joy — and a lot of trouble."

I was absolutely right about both things. Today there are continuing joys from those lives. But there were also long nights of counseling, conflicts over false doctrine, and great disappointments. New babies mean great responsibility and a lot of work. Those newly born-again believers were 3,000 bundles of joy *and* 3,000 accidents waiting to happen.

The crowd really believed and so were baptized, which for a Jew was a traumatic step. Just how traumatic is difficult for us to understand in our mildly Christianized culture, but in Jewish culture baptism was a rite for Gentile converts that symbolized a break with one's past and the washing away of all defilement.[1] Three thousand Jews took that revolutionary step that day. A. T. Robertson comments that the numerous pools in Jerusalem afforded ample opportunity for wholesale baptizing. What a day for Jerusalem!

First, there had been the 120 in the Upper Room, then the wind of the Spirit, then flames dancing above the Twelve, then supernatural utterances as they began to speak in other languages, then a huge crowd. Finally, there was Peter's greatest sermon, and now the pools of Jerusalem were clogged with converts waiting to be baptized.

The Holy Spirit was reigning, and with his rule vast responsibilities descended upon the apostles. They would have to look to the Spirit for guidance. Fortunately, thanks to the Lord, things fell naturally into place. The reign of the Spirit in the lives of the people and the apostles led to some practices that brought growth to all and made the apostles' task possible. Four things happened (or better, happen) in the church where the Spirit reigned. They were then, and still remain, keys to spiritual growth and maturity.

TEACHING (v. 42)

"They devoted themselves to the apostles' teaching . . ." Note carefully that this verse literally says, "They were *continually* devoting themselves to the apostles' teaching." It is very important that we note this term "continually devoting" because it governs the other characteristics of the church where the Spirit reigns. It denotes a steadfast and single-minded devotion to a certain course of action.

Many of us marvel at the free throw specialists in the National Basketball Association who when well into the game, breathing heavily, hurting from a foul, step to the free throw line and seldom miss (often maintaining an 80 percent success rate). How do they make it look so easy? By continual devotion to their task.

These 3,000 baby Christians were continually devoting themselves to God's Word as it came from the apostles. Think of those poor apostles — there were only twelve of them. There must have been nights when they fell into bed thinking they could never utter another word. What did they teach? The epistles? The epistles had not been written yet. The Gospels? There were no written biographies of Christ at that time. What, then, did they teach? The Old Testament, the sayings of Jesus as they recalled them, the Sermon on the Mount, the final conversations in the Upper Room . . .

These new Christians, under the reign of the Holy Spirit, were *hungry* for God's Word. They could not get enough of it. Being filled with the Spirit and being filled with God's Word go together. Ephesians 5:18-20 says:

> *Do not get drunk on wine, which leads to debauchery. Instead, be filled with the Spirit. Speak to one another with psalms, hymns and spiritual songs. Sing and make music in your heart to the Lord, always giving thanks to God the Father for everything, in the name of our Lord Jesus Christ.*

Colossians 3:16-17 says about the same thing except it begins with a charge to let the Word of God bear fruit within us:

> *Let the word of Christ dwell in you richly as you teach and admonish one another with all wisdom, and as you sing psalms, hymns and spiritual songs with gratitude in your hearts to God. And whatever you do, whether in word or deed, do it all in the name of the Lord Jesus, giving thanks to God the Father through him.*

Where the Spirit reigns, a love for God's Word reigns. Those early believers studied the Scriptures — God's communication to them. The early church knew nothing of the anti-intellectualism and the disdain for Biblical knowledge that characterizes some quarters of Christianity today.

The backbone of a healthy Christian life is teaching. Peter says, "Like newborn babies, *crave* pure spiritual milk, so that by it you may grow up in your salvation" (1 Peter 2:2). Teaching was the milk of the early church under the direction of the Holy Spirit. The example of an energetic nursing baby is a fitting example for us to pursue, even if we have already moved on to steak. Young believers must make sure they are feeding on the teaching of God's Word. There is much confusion today about the essential matters of our faith. In a non-reading, experience-oriented culture, solid Bible teaching is sometimes hard to find. Believers should beware of churches or Christian fellowships where the people do not carry their Bibles. Read your Bible. Mark it up. Each of us must make sure that sometime, somewhere in our week we are being taught.

When the Spirit reigns, God's people *continually* devote themselves to the study of his Word. That is the first characteristic, but more than study is needed. Once in introducing Richard Wurmbrand, I described my church as a Bible-believing church. He stopped me, paused, and said slowly, "Are you a Bible-*living* church?" Good question!

FELLOWSHIP (v. 42)

"They devoted themselves to . . . the fellowship." This kind of fellowship did not exist before the giving of the Holy Spirit at Pentecost. The Greek word used here (*koinonia*) is not even found in the Gospels. This is the first occurrence of the word in the New Testament. The root idea is "commonness" or "commonality." New Testament Greek is called *koine* Greek because it was the common Greek of the day — the street language of the people.

Every time this word is used in the New Testament, it denotes some kind of sharing — either sharing something with someone (for instance, in 2 Corinthians 8:4; 9:13 where it means an offering, collection, or contribution) or sharing in something someone else is experiencing. Here in Acts the emphasis of the word is on contributing or giving. The foundation of the early Christians' fellowship was giving. Verses 44 and 45 make this clear:

> *All the believers were together and had everything in common [Greek,* koina*]. Selling their possessions and goods, they gave to anyone as he had need.*

The early believers did not sell everything, as some have tried to say. Some still had houses, as verse 46 indicates: "They broke bread in their homes." Also, in Acts 5 Ananias and Sapphira owned property. The point is, the fellowship of the early church rested on a mutual generosity and sharing.

Fellowship cost something in the early church, in contrast to our use of the word *fellowship* today. Fellowship is not just a sentimental feeling of oneness. It is not punch and cookies. It does not take place simply because we are in the church hall. Fellowship comes through *giving*. True fellowship costs! So many people never know the joys of Christian fellowship because they have never learned to give themselves away. They visit a church or small study group with an eye only for their own needs (hardly aware of others) and go away saying, "There is no fellowship there." The truth is, we will have fellowship only when we make it a practice to reach out to others and give something of ourselves.

Fellowship is preeminently a work of the Holy Spirit.

> *May the grace of the Lord Jesus Christ, and the love of God, and the fellowship [*koinonia*] of the Holy Spirit be with you all. (2 Corinthians 13:14)*

Furthermore, fellowship happens as we draw close to the Godhead. First John 1:3 says:

> *We proclaim to you what we have seen and heard, so that you also may have fellowship [*koinonia*] with us. And our fellowship [*koinonia*] is with the Father and with his Son, Jesus Christ.*

As we experience *koinonia* with the Father and the Son, we draw closer to each other and enjoy fellowship (*koinonia*) with one another. I think the most beautiful illustration of this in the Bible is found in 2 Corinthians 8. In the fourth verse we see the Macedonian church begging for the privilege of participation (the word is *koinonia*) in an offering, a contribution. Those particular believers were extremely poor, and yet they determined to practice *koinonia* by giving to others. Why? I think the answer is given in verse 5:

> *And they did not do as we expected, but they gave themselves first to the Lord [fellowship with him] and then to us in keeping with God's will.*

That is *koinonia*. When we think about this Christian word we use and abuse all the time, we need to remember its link with giving. Do you want to have fellowship? You must be a giver.

When the Spirit reigns, God's people not only relate to the Word — they relate to one another in *koinonia* and sharing. "God setteth the solitary in families" (Psalm 68:6, KJV).

WORSHIP (v. 42)

Their worship consisted of two things: "the breaking of bread and . . . prayer." I believe "the breaking of bread" refers to the regular observance of the Lord's Supper, for two reasons. First, the reference comes between two religiously-loaded terms in verse 42 — "fellowship" and "prayers." And second, in verse 46 the phrases "broke bread" and "ate together" are purposely separated. After their principal meal they would take the remaining bread and wine and engage in the elevating remembrance of Christ's death. They "[continually] devoted themselves" to this. Christ and his atoning work were constantly before them, daily bringing their hearts upward in solemn and joyous contemplation.

Another way they worshiped was "prayer." The text should properly read, "the prayers," suggesting specific prayers, probably both Jewish and Christian. The early believers suddenly saw the old formal prayers through new eyes and also, in their new joy, created new prayers for praise — much as Mary did when she sang the Magnificat.

When the Spirit reigns, the hearts of God's people move up toward him and their relationship with him intensifies.

EVANGELISM (v. 47)

The final broad characteristic of the first church was evangelism: "And the Lord added to their number daily those who were being saved" (v. 47). As Robertson says, "It was a continuous revival day by day." When the Spirit reigns, God's people relate to the world as they should.

What happens in the church where the Spirit reigns? There is a radically wonderful reorientation of essential relationships.

Where the Spirit reigns, believers relate to the Word — teaching.
Where the Spirit reigns, believers relate to each other — *koinonia.*
Where the Spirit reigns, believers relate to God — worship.
Where the Spirit reigns, believers relate to the world — evangelism.

That is what God did for the 3,000 and what he wanted them to do for him. That is also want he wants to do for us and what he wants us to do for him.

This is such a beautiful package! Let me tie the bow on it with the concluding verses of the passage because they perfectly elaborate on verse 42.

As the Word went out, "Everyone was filled with awe" — not just because "many wonders and miraculous signs were done by the apostles," but because everything worked together to bring a profound sense of God.

This awe and soul-fear was not terror, but something like Isaiah experienced when he saw the holiness of God and cried, "Woe to me! I am ruined! For I am a man of unclean lips" (Isaiah 6:5). Such a response is the deep reaction of a frail, fallen being standing before the true God of love and righteousness. In the early church there was a sense of holiness much like that which the children of Israel had when Moses came down from Mt. Sinai — awe in the presence of Almighty God.

How we need this today! Nothing would promote revival more than a sense of awe before our holy God coupled with a sense of our own unworthiness. Verse 46 gives a beautiful picture of the worship in the early church:

> *Every day they continued to meet together in the temple courts. They broke bread in their homes and ate together with glad and sincere hearts.*

This was all marvelously balanced. It was both formal and informal, "in the temple" and "in their homes." Jesus had called the temple his Father's house, so they naturally went there to worship. Much of their time was spent on Solomon's porch with its marvelous view of the Mount of Olives (cf. 3:11 and 5:12). Also, since their communal meal could not be eaten on temple precincts, they broke bread from house to house.

The believers also had "glad and sincere hearts." "Glad" means "exulting gladness."[2] The *New English Bible* translates this "unaffected joy." When someone passed by one of the house fellowships, they not only heard solemn testimonies and hymns, they sometimes heard laughter! Sometimes we look like someone has put Clorox in our coffee, but in the early church they were human and full of joy.

The church under the rule of the Holy Spirit is devoted to teaching, fellowship, and worship, and evangelism flows forth as a result. Along with a sense of human sinfulness, the people's realization of God's holy presence enabled them to continually feel a sense of awe at his majesty. There was also genuine joy. What a beautiful picture — a church where the Spirit reigned.

PRAYER

Our Father, we yearn for the reign of the Spirit in our own lives. We long for your truth. We long for holiness and power in the Body of Christ. Our hearts long after you as the deer pants after the water brook. We long too for the salvation of the souls around us. In Jesus' name, Amen.

6

When Life Is Jumping

ACTS 3:1-26

It must have been tempting for some in the early church to try to preserve the apostolic fellowship, to linger in their Acts 2 experience, to cultivate an esoteric club-like atmosphere and, perhaps unknowingly, smother the Spirit's fire with exclusiveness. But they did not do this. What they experienced under the Spirit's reign was so explosive and expansive, they just had to get going! So in Acts 3 we see the church moving out into the world with healing power — Exhibit A of what a Spirit-filled church can do.

WHAT THE SPIRIT-FILLED CHURCH IMPARTS (vv. 1-11)

The example that Luke chose to share was Peter and John's encounter with a lame beggar. Verse 1 gives us the setting: "One day Peter and John were going up to the temple at the time of prayer — at three in the afternoon." The apostolic church had not yet broken with the temple, and so, as with all devout Jews, Peter and John continued their attendance at the designated times of prayer. Perhaps this time of day, even then, held special significance for them because it was the hour when Jesus cried from the cross, "It is finished" (John 19:30). Whatever the two apostles' reason, it was the busiest of the prayer times, and so they were part of a large throng moving into the temple.

Verse 2 completes the setting:

> *Now a man crippled from birth was being carried to the temple gate called Beautiful, where he was put every day to beg from those going into the temple courts.*

As Peter and John moved along with the flow of the crowd, they providentially encountered a beggar being borne on a litter to his usual post. He had been a congenital cripple for all of his life. Having never taken a step, he had to be carried everywhere he went. His begging post was one of the best spots in the entire city because it was at the Beautiful Gate, or Nicanor Gate, which Josephus tells us was fifty cubits high and forty cubits wide, was overlaid with Corinthian bronze, and was such a work of art that it "far exceeded in value those plated with silver set in gold."[1] What a compelling sight the impotent beggar made against the backdrop of such opulent surroundings! It was the perfect place to solicit funds. Further, Judaism considered almsgiving a meritorious art.[2] So the man's position at Israel's religious center would have profited him well.

Now came the divine encounter:

> *When he saw Peter and John about to enter, he asked them for money. Peter looked straight at him, as did John. Then Peter said, "Look at us!" So the man gave them his attention, expecting to get something from them. Then Peter said, "Silver or gold I do not have, but what I have I give you. In the name of Jesus Christ of Nazareth, walk. (vv. 3-6)*

Though they had not even come to the gate, the beggar caught sight of Peter and John, who probably looked like good prospects. So he began his mechanical beggar's wail, which he had undoubtedly repeated millions of times: "Gentlemen, just a few cents please . . ." Peter responded, "Look at us!" As the beggar turned expectantly Peter said, "Silver or gold I do not have." Perhaps the beggar began to frown. Perhaps he thought he was being mocked. But then came those immortal words: ". . . but what I have I give you. In the name of Jesus Christ of Nazareth, walk."

Dr. Luke is very careful to make sure we get the total impact of what happened next. Verses 7 and 8 tell us:

> *Taking him by the right hand, he helped him up, and instantly the man's feet and ankles became strong. He jumped to his feet and began to walk. Then he went with them into the temple courts, walking and jumping, and praising God.*

The poor man knew he could not walk, so he did not budge. But Peter, doing a typically Peter thing, grabbed him by the right hand and began to hoist him up. "Hey, old buddy, you're healed!" At that moment (the Greek says, "*instantly*") everything came together. One commentator says:

> Perhaps only medical men can fully appreciate the meaning of these words; they are the peculiar, technical words of a medical man. The word translated *feet* is only used by Luke, and occurs nowhere else. It indicates his discrimination between different parts of the human heel. The phrase *ankle-bones* is again a medical phrase to be found nowhere else. The word "leaping up" describes the coming suddenly into socket of something that was out of place, the articulation of a joint. This then is a very careful medical description of what happened in connection with this man.[3]

Sometimes we miss the drama and the significance of miracles like this one because we do not allow our imaginations to catch the fact that it happened *instantly*. In Matthew we read that one Sabbath Jesus told the man with the withered hand to reach out his hand, and as he did, his hand was healed. That hand was crippled, and before everyone's eyes it became whole. In Matthew 8 at the end of the Sermon on the Mount we learn of a leper who came through the crowd crying, "Unclean, unclean." The man was *full* of leprosy. He had grotesque features, and Jesus healed him in full view of the people. The man's eyebrows grew back, and his face took shape. His hair and his vocal cords were made whole. He was healed right before their eyes!

So it is with the text we are studying now. The man was healed in a flash. The text says, "He jumped to his feet and began to walk." Maybe a tentative step, then a less tentative step, followed by long, steady steps. He was saying to himself, "I cannot believe this! I'm walking! And I can jump too!" He began hopping around the temple terrace — leaping around and praising the Lord. With a volume not appropriate for most of our church services he was shouting, "Hallelujah! Praise the Lord! I've been healed!" It was a beautiful scene.

> *When all the people saw him walking and praising God, they recognized him as the same man who used to sit begging at the temple gate called Beautiful, and they were filled with wonder and amazement at what had happened to him. While the beggar held on to Peter and John, all the people were astonished and came running to them in the place called Solomon's Colonnade. (vv. 9-11)*

The word used here to describe how he was clinging to Peter and John is used several times in the New Testament for police arrest. He was holding on tight, perhaps partly from gratitude and partly from fear. "They recognized him as the same man who used to sit begging at the temple gate called Beautiful." Thanks to the miraculous power of God, the lame man was jumping, and everyone was flying high.

What does the Spirit-filled church impart? *It imparts what it has!* Notice verse 6:

> *"Silver or gold I do not have, but what I have I give you. In the name of Jesus Christ of Nazareth, walk."*

There is a spiritual axiom here: you can only give away what is truly yours. A friend of mine, Ian Barclay, is an art lover, and he longs to be able to paint. He can do all right with a pen or pencil. Some of his cartoons have been published in major newspapers. But on a recent trip to Italy he found himself longing to be able to paint like such masters as Michelangelo and da Vinci. But he cannot. He just does not have it in him. What it would take to paint like Michelangelo is the spirit of Michelangelo!

My friend will never have the spirit of Michelangelo, but he does have the spirit of Christ — the spirit of the most beautiful, complete man who ever lived! This is what Peter and John possessed, and this is what they gave. They had within them *the* Spirit, "another Counselor" (*allos parakletos*, John 14:15) — another Helper like Christ. "Christ lives in me," Paul said (Galatians 2:20), and Christ lived in Peter and John as well. They were members of the living Christ. They were "partakers of the divine nature" (2 Peter 1:4, KJV). They could impart the power of Christ because they were full of Christ.

The old commentator Cornelius a Lapide tells how Thomas Aquinas once called on Pope Innocent II while he was counting a large sum of money. "You see, Thomas," said the Pope, "the church can no longer say, 'Silver and gold have I none.'" "True, holy Father," said Thomas, "and neither can she now say, 'Arise and walk.'" What about us? What is our experience with Christ? The Spirit-filled church imparts what it has.

It imparts *healing*. The miracle was both literal and parabolic, because the Spirit-filled church dispenses more than care for the body — it brings healing to the soul. In place of spiritual lameness, there can be leaping!

The Spirit-filled church imparts *joy*. When the rejoicing cripple entered the temple, the echoing chambers resounded with his jubilation. Hallelujahs rang from the vast cedar ceiling of Solomon's Porch as everyone stopped (even the money changers) to watch the high-jumping cripple!

Erma Bombeck tells how she was sitting in church one Sunday when a small child turned around and began to smile at the people behind her. She was smiling, doing nothing else, not making a sound. When her mother noticed, she said in a stage whisper, "Stop that grinning — you're in church," gave her child a swat, and said, "That's better!" Erma concluded that some people come to church looking like their deceased rich aunt left everything to her pet hamster! In contrast, the Spirit-filled church overflows with joy!

It also imparts *wonder*. The temple regulars could not believe what they were seeing and hearing. As always happens when there is joy and power in the church, they became curious about what had happened and how.

The Spirit-filled church draws the world to itself and to its Savior.

HOW THE SPIRIT-FILLED CHURCH IMPARTS (vv. 12-20)

When the Spirit-filled church begins to exhibit power and healing, there is a danger to avoid — people may focus on Christ's servants rather than on Christ. John and Peter were quick to counter this, and in so doing they explained how the Spirit-filled church is able to impart what it has.

How did Peter and John heal the cripple? First and foremost, not by their own power.

> *When Peter saw this, he said to them: "Men of Israel, why does this surprise you? Why do you stare at us as if by our own power or godliness we had made this man walk?"*

They disavowed any power in themselves, unlike so many today who measure their ministry success by the number of times their name is in print. Peter and John rejected the people's adulation because they knew the power to heal was not theirs.

They went on to explain that the miracle happened through Christ's name (v. 16). Peter had already said this once, in verse 6 — "In the name of Jesus Christ of Nazareth, walk." Jesus was from Nazareth — he was a Nazarene, and this had been used to insult Christ during his life on earth. But now Peter waved it like a banner.

Not everyone had heard all this, so Peter explained it (in verse 16, leading up to it in verses 13-15).

> *"The God of Abraham, Isaac and Jacob, the God of our fathers, has glorified his servant Jesus. You handed him over to be killed, and you disowned him before Pilate, though he had decided to let him go."*

Peter thus reminded them that they had rejected Jesus when they said, "We have no king but Caesar!"

> *"You disowned the Holy and Righteous One and asked that a murderer be released to you."*

They had said, "Give us Barabbas."

"You killed the author of life, but God raised him from the dead. We are witnesses of this."

Now he was ready to make the definitive statement:

"By faith in the name of Jesus, this man whom you see and know was made strong."

The apostle was saying, "Listen, Israel! It is through the name of Jesus that this miracle has happened!" Many people decide who and what you are when they hear your name. The name Joni invokes a mental image. So does JFK or Pope John Paul II or Michael Jordan or Billy Graham. Names come to stand for one's character and power. Peter did this miracle on the basis of what Jesus is — his name.

More exactly, the healing happened through *faith in Christ's name*.

"By faith in the name of Jesus, this man whom you see and know was made strong. It is Jesus' name and the faith that comes through him that has given this complete healing to him, as you can all see." (v. 16)

The church had power because it had faith in Jesus' name — it fully trusted him!

This is so simple but so true. Faith in the name of Jesus Christ brings power to the church. Any man or woman who has ever done anything substantial for Christ has done so only by faith in his name. If we could assemble the great missionaries of the cross, we would have the most extraordinary collection of idiosyncrasies the world has ever seen. They would not understand each other. Some would not like each other. But there would be one common, exciting characteristic in them all — a flaming earnestness of belief in the power of the name of the Lord Jesus Christ.

We must remember that even our faith is a gift (Ephesians 2:8). It does not come through the resolution of human will but by asking God to grant it. Let us exalt and proclaim Jesus in all the fullness of his name, affirming our belief and living in faithfulness to him.

PRAYER

Lord, we believe. Help our unbelief. Increase our faith. Help us to be willing channels of your power — the power of the name of the Lord Jesus Christ. Please extend your healing forgiveness to others through us, your humble servants. In Jesus' name, Amen.

7

The Bliss of Persecution

Acts 4:1-22

The Acts 2 experience of the apostles' new life, rich teaching, satisfying *koinonia*, and joyful worship was expansive and expulsive — a rocket thrust that propelled them into a needy world. Acts 2 demanded Acts 3.

Likewise, the healing power of Acts 3 led the early church toward another inevitable step in its growth. Having been infused with the power of the Spirit, moving out into the world with regenerative healing power, the church now experienced opposition — its first persecution (Acts 4).

Persecution is an inevitable element of genuine Christian faith. In John 15:18-20 Jesus told his disciples:

> *"If the world hates you, keep in mind that it hated me first. If you belonged to the world, it would love you as its own. As it is, you do not belong to the world, but I have chosen you out of the world. That is why the world hates you. Remember the words I spoke to you: 'No servant is greater than his master.' If they persecuted me, they will persecute you also. If they obeyed my teaching, they will obey yours also."*

Jesus used *a fortiori* logic: what is true of the greater (namely, Christ) will also be true of the lesser (us). Jesus' Beatitudes conclude with predictions of persecution. As Christlike virtue is built upon Christlike virtue in his followers' lives, the reward is not fame or adulation but persecution! Paul, writing to Timothy to strengthen him in the ministry, said, "Everyone who wants to live a godly life in Christ Jesus will be persecuted" (2 Timothy 3:12).

The martyr Dietrich Bonhoeffer wrote from his Flossenberg cell in 1937:

> Suffering . . . is the badge of the true Christian. The disciple is not above his master. . . . Luther reckoned suffering among the marks of the true church, and one of the memoranda drawn up in preparation for the Augsburg Confession similarly defines the church as the community of those "who are persecuted and martyred for the gospel's sake." . . . Discipleship means allegiance to the suffering Christ, and it is therefore not at all surprising that Christians should be called upon to suffer.[1]

This is not all bad. As the late Bishop Sheen once said, "One advantage of being thrown on your back is that you face heaven." When the Spirit reigns in our lives, there will be persecution and a heavenly focus!

How did the early church respond to opposition?

When the healed beggar entered Solomon's Porch (NIV, "Solomon's Colonnade"), the white columns reaching up sixty feet to the cedar roof illustrated his joy as his voice reverberated throughout the great hall. Peter's sermon was equally dramatic as a large crowd gathered around them. And the presence of Exhibit A doing jumping jacks brought great credibility to what the apostle said.

> *The priests and the captain of the temple guard and the Sadducees came up to Peter and John while they were speaking to the people. They were greatly disturbed because the apostles were teaching the people and proclaiming in Jesus the resurrection of the dead. They seized Peter and John, and because it was evening, they put them in jail until the next day. But many who heard the message believed, and the number of men grew to about five thousand. (4:1-4)*

Certainly few in the temple could have missed the commotion. Soon "the priests" (Levites who were giving their annual service in the temple), "the captain of the temple guard" (the temple police chief), and "the Sadducees" came together and terminated the meeting. Those who believed now came to 5,000, but the leaders made the arrest anyway. There were undoubtedly some unhappy words between the crowd and the authorities.

Note the Sadducees' leading role in the incarceration. Little good can be said about this bunch. The Pharisees opposed Jesus for religious reasons (misguided conviction). The Sadducees' opposition, however, came largely from political motivations. This is why the Sadducees were not as involved in early persecutions against Christ. But as they saw the incipient threat to their political structure, they became implacable enemies. In the book of Acts persecution was largely Sadducean. They were the materialistic rationalists of their day — denying the supernatural, denying evil spirits, denying angels (see Acts 23:8). Above all, they denied the Resurrection (see Mark 12:18), which the apostles boldly preached. To the Sadducees, the Messiah was simply an ideal and the messianic age a process.

These men had gained special ascendancy during the intertestamental Maccabean period. During subsequent political regimes, they created a priestly nobility. They were the educated, wealthy elite. But they were also unprincipled collaborationists, political sycophants who would sell their mothers to stay in power. Though a minority, they controlled Jewish political and religious life. They were evil control freaks, and they did not want anyone rocking their boat.

As it was evidently too late in the day to hold a legal hearing, the Jewish leaders tossed Peter and John into jail. Possibly the healed beggar too, because he was with them in the following events (see 4:14). The story continues in verses 5-7:

> *The next day the rulers, elders and teachers of the law met in Jerusalem. Annas the high priest was there, and so were Caiaphas, John, Alexander and the other men of the high priest's family. They had Peter and John brought before them and began to question them: "By what power or what name did you do this?"*

The court assembled in concentric semicircles before Peter, John, and the ex-cripple, with the high priest seated in the middle. It would be difficult to imagine a more priggish, malevolent assembly of men than this group dominated by the Sadducees — highly sophisticated, twitty bluebloods who had come to take care of the Galilean hayseeds. Annas is called "high priest" here, but at this point in time this was more of an honorary title for him. Caiaphas, his son-in-law, was the actual high priest. Nevertheless, Annas was the ecclesiastical boss of Palestine.

Do you get the picture? Peter, John, and the healed beggar in their coveralls; the Sadducee-dominated Sanhedrin assembled for judgment. "By what power or what name did you do this?" The question was a subtle, deadly trap, because if the apostles' accusers could get them to attribute the healing to any power other than Jehovah, even though it was a bona fide miracle they could sentence them to death (see Deuteronomy 13:1-5).

This was the same mob that tried and condemned Christ. Most of us would be absolutely paralyzed. But what did Peter do? One thing is for sure — he did not run.

HOW THE EARLY CHURCH RESPONDED TO OPPOSITION (vv. 8-13, 19-20)

> *Then Peter, filled with the Holy Spirit, said to them: "Rulers and elders of the people! If we are being called to account today for an act of kindness shown to a cripple and are asked how he was healed, then know this, you and all the people of Israel: It is by the name of Jesus Christ of Nazareth, whom you crucified but whom God raised from the dead, that this man stands before you healed. He is 'the stone you builders rejected, which has become the capstone.' Salvation is found in no one else, for there is no other name under heaven given to men by which we must be saved." (vv. 8-12)*

Verse 13 says that the Sanhedrin noticed Peter and John's bravery — amazing in view of the circumstances. The apostles ministered beyond their natural abilities. The Sanhedrin observed that they were not educated or trained and yet gained ascendancy over the Palestinian elite in verbal combat. Christ's men responded to their persecutors with daring and aggressiveness.

Peter was unflinchingly personal:

> *"Then know this,* you *and all the people of Israel: It is by the name of Jesus Christ of Nazareth, whom* you *crucified. . . . He is 'the stone* you *builders rejected.'"*

Though most of the Sanhedrin were Sadducees and did not want to hear of the Resurrection, Peter hurled it at them like a flaming spear: "whom *you* crucified but whom God raised from the dead." Then came his stupendous claim in verse 12: "Salvation is found in no one else, for there is no other name under heaven given to men by which we must be saved." It is Christ or nothing! Christ or judgment! Christ or Hell! What marvelous, gracious aggression! And Peter had just begun!

What was the Sanhedrin's reaction? There was probably coughing and clearing of throats, uneasy shifting of position and straightening of robes, and certainly some exchanged glances and pounding hearts.

> *When they saw the courage of Peter and John and realized that they were unschooled, ordinary men, they were astonished and they took note that these men had been with Jesus. But since they could see the man who had been healed standing there with them, there was nothing they could say. (vv. 13-14)*

Incredible! They could think of nothing to say. Even the cynical, witty Caiaphas, who had so sardonically sealed Christ's death, stating, "It is better . . . that one man die for the people than that the whole nation perish" (John 11:50), now had nothing to say. Overwhelmed by the embarrassing silence, they dismissed the offending apostles of Christ.

> *So they ordered them to withdraw from the Sanhedrin and then conferred together. "What are we going to do with these men?" they asked. "Everybody living in Jerusalem knows they have done an outstanding miracle, and we cannot deny it. But to stop this thing from spreading any further among the people, we must warn these men to speak no longer to anyone in this name." Then they called them in again and commanded them not to speak or teach at all in the name of Jesus. (vv. 15-18)*

These incredibly hard-hearted men were so intent on protecting their own interests that a bona fide, undeniable miracle did not get through to them. They had no understanding of what was going on with this new resurrection sect.

Note Peter and John's supreme reply:

> *"Judge for yourselves whether it is right in God's sight to obey you rather than God. For we cannot help speaking about what we have seen and heard." (vv. 19-20)*

You probably could have heard a pin drop in that hall of hewn stone. Peter and John again responded with confidence and powerful freedom of speech, ministering beyond their human abilities. They responded daringly and aggressively and with integrity. No compromise.

Frederick the Great once called all his generals together. One of them, Hans Von Zieten, had duties to perform at his church that night and a Communion to participate in, so he refused to come. Later he was again invited to dine with all the generals and Frederick the Great. On that occasion they all made light of him and joked about his religious duties and about the Lord's Supper. Von Zieten stood and said to his intimidating ruler, "My lord, there is a greater king than you, a king to whom I have sworn allegiance, even unto death. I am a Christian man, and I cannot sit quietly as the Lord's name is dishonored, his character belittled, and his cause subjected to ridicule. With your permission I shall withdraw."

There was silence because the generals knew such a daring act could mean death. But Frederick the Great was so struck by Von Zieten's courage that he begged him to stay and promised him he would never again demean those sacred things. Long live the tribe of Hans Von Zieten!

Peter Cartwright was a great circuit-riding Methodist preacher in Illinois. An uncompromising man, he had come north from Tennessee because of his opposition to slavery. One Sunday morning when he was scheduled to preach, his deacons told him that President Andrew Jackson was in the congregation. Knowing Cartwright was used to saying whatever he felt God wanted him to say, regardless of how people might react, they warned him not to say anything that would offend the chief executive. He stood up to preach and said, "I understand President Andrew Jackson is here. I have been requested to be guarded in my remarks. Andrew Jackson will go to Hell if he does not repent." The audience was shocked. They wondered how the President would respond to this, but after the service he told Cartwright, "Sir, if I had a regiment of men like you, I could whip the world."

This is how the early church too responded to opposition — with beautiful integrity. The Sanhedrin could do nothing but release them, as verses 21-22 reveal:

> *After further threats they let them go. They could not decide how to punish them, because all the people were praising God for what had happened. For the man who was miraculously healed was over forty years old.*

WHY THE EARLY CHURCH RESPONDED AS IT DID (vv. 13, 8)

The answer is wonderfully clear in verse 13:

> *When they saw the courage of Peter and John and realized that they were unschooled, ordinary men, they were astonished and they took note that these men had been with Jesus.*

The fatal interrogation of Jesus on the eve of the crucifixion had made an unforgettable impression on the Sanhedrin. Though they would have liked to forget it, they simply could not. And now as the two apostles interacted with them, they could not help but be reminded of Jesus. The apostles were "unlearned " (KJV; that is, unlettered), and they were "ignorant" (KJV; the same root word for "idiots, unschooled"). But when they talked, they were so much like Jesus that the presence of Christ right then and there could not be denied. Peter's and John's companionship with Jesus had transformed them.

What the Sanhedrin did not perhaps understand was that the apostles were still companions of Jesus. They were indwelt with the Holy Spirit and with Christ (compare Romans 8:9-10). Their Lord was saturating their emotions, compelling their wills, energizing their bodies, so that the Sanhedrin was seeing not only them, but Christ. Not only that, but Peter and John, filled with the Holy Spirit, were in constant communication with their Lord. As Alexander Maclaren said, "A soul habitually in contact with Jesus will imbibe sweetness from him, just as garments laid away in a drawer with some . . . perfume absorb fragrance from that beside which they lie."[2] Seeing Peter and John, the Jewish leaders were seeing Jesus.

The apostles were able to respond to opposition as they did because they were walking with Christ. And as a result, "they [the members of the Sanhedrin] were astonished." This priggish, pompous, self-consciously superior, gospel-hardened group experienced wonder, awe. Perhaps some of them even came to Christ.

The lives of all who know the reign of the Spirit resound with a display of God's healing power that brings opposition and even persecution but also incredible joy. The Beatitudes describe this same process of persecution and spiritual bliss. "Blessed [happy, blissful] are those are persecuted because of righteousness, for theirs is the kingdom of heaven" (Matthew 5:10).

Later in Acts, when the apostles had been flogged at the orders of the same Sanhedrin, "The apostles left the Sanhedrin, rejoicing because they had been counted worthy of suffering disgrace for the Name" (Acts 5:41). When confronted by their enemies, they responded with amazing confidence, daring aggressiveness, and no compromise! Why? Because they had been with Jesus.

Practically, what does this mean for us? When we are filled with the Holy Spirit, Christ is the focus of our lives. The Holy Spirit does not promote himself. He promotes Christ.

Also, we cannot rest on the fact that we prayed for the Spirit's fullness five years ago or even last week. But as we engage in constant prayer for his fullness, the Spirit of Christ will consistently flow through us.

We must spend time in God's Word. The Bible is like a mirror set before us. The light of Christ reflects off the Word and into our faces, so that we shine forth Christ. We must remain in the Word — constantly learning, constantly being taught — not relying on what we have learned in the past, but interacting with it anew, so that Christ is projected throughout our entire lives.

We must spend time with God's people. We become like the people with whom we spend time, and the light of Christ flows out of his people and into those around them.

We must spend time in prayer, because as we fellowship with the Lord, the perfume of his life makes us the very "fragrance of [Christ]" (see 2 Corinthians 2:14).

PRAYER

O God, please fill us with your Spirit again and again. Help us to be disciplined in spending time in your Word, time with your people, time in prayer. May the world not be able to miss the fact that we have been with Jesus. Please help us to be humble and dependent upon the Holy Spirit, for your glory and honor. In Jesus' name, Amen.

8

When the Church Is Great

ACTS 4:32-37

The expansion of the early church was amazing. As Earle Cairns writes in his *Christianity Through the Centuries*:

> The number of active believers in Jerusalem after the Resurrection was estimated at approximately five hundred by Paul (I Cor. 15:6). . . . Pliny's letter proved that Christianity was strong in Asia Minor shortly after the beginning of the second century. During the first century it had been confined largely to the eastern section of the empire, with the Jews being given the first chance to accept Christianity as the gospel reached new cities. During the second century, expansion was rapid among the Greek-speaking Gentile population of the empire. The church in Alexandria became the chief church of Egypt. Christians could be found in all parts of the empire by 200.[1]

One of the reasons for the expansion was persecution. Christians who were forced to flee from Jerusalem won converts in Samaria. Others preached in Antioch, which was then the largest city in Syria and the nexus of Hellenistic culture. From there Christianity spread around the shores of the Mediterranean and around the world. Persecution, rather than thwarting Christianity, aided its expansion!

The main reason the Church spread as it did was that it is by nature expansive. Christ is the only way, and he set the supreme missionary example by giving his life for the world. This produced in his followers a mind-set of outreach, sacrificial service, and growth.

What was that first church like when it burst forth with news of God's love for a needy world? What is it that makes a church truly great?

All the believers were one in heart and mind. No one claimed that any of his possessions was his own, but they shared everything they had. With great power the apostles continued to testify to the resurrection of the Lord Jesus, and much grace was upon them all. There were no needy persons among them. For from time to time those who owned lands or houses sold them, brought the money from the sales and put it at the apostles' feet, and it was distributed to anyone as he had need. Joseph, a Levite from Cyprus, whom the apostles called Barnabas (which means Son of Encouragement), sold a field he owned and brought the money and put it at the apostles' feet. (vv. 32-37)

UNITY (v. 32)

Luke tells us that "All the believers were one in heart." They had a *unity of heart*. The Scriptures use the word *heart* to indicate the wellspring of our being, ". . . the central place to which God turns, where religious experience has its root, which determines conduct."[2] The heart is our inner spirit. The church in Acts was united in the deepest part of its being. They shared an inarticulate bond, a great secret. They could sense a fundamental unity with other believers.

Sometimes we meet someone, and before a word is spoken we sense a oneness with him or her. If we are true believers, we share a fundamental unity in the core of our beings.

This inner greatness also produced a *unity of soul*. "All the believers were one in . . . mind." They shared the same basic mental focus and thought about many of the same things. This came about as the fundamental, inarticulate unity of their hearts effervesced upward into their souls! They were truly soul brothers and sisters. This was the greatest, most profound, most satisfying unity the world has ever seen!

As a result, there was no division. This was astounding because, just a few days before, when 3,000 were converted, they came from everywhere! There were:

Parthians, Medes and Elamites; residents of Mesopotamia, Judea and Cappadocia, Pontus and Asia, Phrygia and Pamphylia, Egypt and the parts of Libya near Cyrene; visitors from Rome (both Jews and converts to Judaism); Cretans and Arabs. (2:9-11)

This does not mean these believers saw everything eye to eye. It is wrong to suppose, as sadly some do, that when believers dwell in unity they will carry the same Bible, read the same books, promote the same styles, educate their children the same way, have the same likes and dislikes — that they will become Christian clones. The fact is, the insistence that others be just like us is one of the most disunifying mind-sets a church can have because it instills a judgmental inflexibility that hurls people away from the church with lethal force. One of the wonders of Christ is that he honors our individuality while bringing us into unity.

There are different kinds of gifts, but the same Spirit. There are different kinds of service, but the same Lord. There are different kinds of working, but the same God works all of them in all men. (1 Corinthians 12:4-6)

Bishop Westcott said: "External visible unity is not required for the invisible unity of the church."[3] The early Christians certainly differed in their opinions on many things — food, clothing, language, customs. But they were united as to who Christ was, that he was Lord of all. All of them recognized the necessity of living for him. The Oxford Codex adds to this passage: "Neither was there any severance between them."[4] One heart, one soul, and *no severance*! They were founded and established on Christ.

No one has explained this better than A. W. Tozer:

Has it ever occurred to you that one hundred pianos all tuned to the same fork are automatically tuned to each other? They are of one accord by being tuned, not to each other, but to another standard to which each one must individually bow. So one hundred worshippers met together, each one looking away to Christ, are in heart nearer to each other than they could possibly be were they to become "unity" conscious and turn their eyes away from God to strive for closer fellowship.[5]

First John 1:7 puts it this way: "If we walk in the light, as he is in the light, we have fellowship with one another." King David painted a word picture of this in Psalm 133:1-3:

Behold, how good and how pleasant it is when brothers live together in unity! It is like precious oil poured on the head, running down on the beard, running down on Aaron's beard, down upon the collar of his robes. It is as if the dew of Hermon were falling on Mount Zion. For there the Lord bestows his blessing, even life forevermore.

In explaining how expansive unity is, David recalled a scene with obvious affection — the high priest being anointed with oil. When the oil was poured over his head, it ran down his beard and onto his robes. David used this picture to poetically portray how unity overflows to others, which David saw as wonderfully refreshing.

Jesus said in John 17:21, ". . . that all of them may be one, Father, just as you are in me and I am in you. May they also may be in us so that the world may believe that you have sent me." It was the believers' great unity that enabled the spread of the gospel. That bonded band of brothers and sisters conquered the world — Christ-followers who sailed the oceans and marched the continents to both throne and dungeon. When the church is great, there is great unity.

GRACE (vv. 32-33)

> *All the believers were one in heart and mind. No one claimed that any of his possessions was his own, but they shared everything they had. With great power the apostles continued to testify to the resurrection of the Lord Jesus, and much grace was upon them all. (vv. 32-33)*

"Much grace" here is literally "mega-grace." *Grace* — the gifts and favor God pours upon the undeserving. Christ came to an empty people and poured his grace upon them. We are saved by grace, healed by grace, nurtured by grace.

There is no appropriate response to grace except thanksgiving. The believers' hearts were like that of Jonathan's son, Mephibosheth, whom King David chose to graciously care for after Jonathan's death, promising that his land would be restored to him and that he would always have a place at the king's table. In response, "Mephibosheth bowed down and said, 'What is your servant, that you should notice a dead dog like me?'" The hearts of the Christians in the early church were full of God's grace, and it overflowed to those around them! When the church is great, there is abounding grace.

POWER

A great church also has "great power" — literally, "mega-power." The root for the Greek word translated "power" is the origin of our English word *dynamite*.

With explosive power they "continued to testify to the resurrection of the Lord Jesus" (v. 33). Despite all the counter-propaganda of the

Sadducees, the church received divine enablement to present the fact of the Resurrection. Paul later wrote in Romans 6:4:

> *We were therefore buried with him through baptism into death in order that, just as Christ was raised from the dead through the glory of the Father, we too may live a new life.*

They themselves had resurrection life, and as a result the people who heard believed. There was hard evidence (living eyewitnesses, etc.) to prove that Christ was alive. But for many it was enough to see him living in the lives of his followers. Their "great power" was resurrection power!

CARE

> *They shared everything they had. . . . There were no needy persons among them. For from time to time those who owned lands or houses sold them, brought the money from the sales and put it at the apostles' feet, and it was distributed to anyone as he had need. (vv. 32b, 34-35)*

If we focus on what seems to be the impracticality of this, or upon the seeming communism, we miss the point. Communism says practically, "What is yours is everyone's." Christianity says, "What is mine is yours." A generous, giving spirit permeated this great church. The overall atmosphere was one of care for one another.

This included *material care*. The *New International Version* well captures the sense of verse 34: "There were no needy persons among them. For from time to time those who owned lands or houses sold them, brought the money from the sales and put it at the apostles' feet." This spirit was especially evident in the Macedonian church, which begged Paul for the privilege of giving:

> *And now, brothers, we want you to know about the grace that God has given the Macedonian churches. Out of the most severe trial, their overflowing joy and their extreme poverty welled up in rich generosity. For I testify that they gave as much as they were able, and even beyond their ability. Entirely on their own, they urgently pleaded with us for the privilege of sharing in this service to the saints. And they did not do as we expected, but they gave themselves first to the Lord and then to us in keeping with God's will. . . . For you know the grace of our Lord Jesus Christ, that though he was rich, yet for your sakes*

he became poor, so that you through his poverty might become rich. (2 Corinthians 8:1-5, 9)

There was also *spiritual care*. Material sharing was just the tip of the iceberg. The believers were people-oriented. When Christians sincerely care for one another's material needs, they want to minister to spiritual needs as well — bearing one another's burdens, sympathizing with and praying for one another. In touch with others' hurts, they gladly sacrifice time and comfort for those who are in need.

A married couple I know had an ongoing interest in a single mother who could not pay her bills. They took her aside, told her they wanted to be her burden-bearers, and asked her for all of her bills. My friends are not wealthy, but they wrote out a check for each of that lady's bills! This is aggressive care in the name of Jesus!

Just how deep this care in the early church went is seen in the brief mention of Barnabas in verses 36-37:

Joseph, a Levite from Cyprus, whom the apostles called Barnabas (which means Son of Encouragement), sold a field he owned and brought the money and put it at the apostles' feet.

Barnabas was named after his spiritual gift — "Son of Encouragement," son of exhortation, son of consolation! Every mention of Barnabas in Acts pictures him as an encourager. For example, when Paul dropped poor John Mark, Barnabas came alongside and patched him up, so that he went on to live a productive Christian life.

Here in Acts 4 Barnabas' encouragement was highly effective. He did more than say, "Be warm and filled." He gave whatever he could. Such a life draws people to Jesus. In Jesus' own words:

"A new commandment I give you: Love one another. As I have loved you, so you must love one another. All men will know that you are my disciples if you love one another." (John 13:34-35)

Such love is something people can understand, and it is something they want desperately!

Luke's portrait of the great apostolic church still inspires believers today. I love what St. Ignatius said later of the church in Rome, which applies so beautifully here:

It was a church worthy of God, worthy of honor, worthy of congratulation, worthy of praise, worthy of success, worthy in purity, pre-

> eminent in love, walking in the law of Christ and bearing the Father's name.[6]

What about the church today? We build great buildings, but do we build great people? We may have well-oiled machinery and programs that are the envy of others, but how do we compare with the early church? When the church is great, there is a *greatness in unity*. As believers' hearts beat together in spiritual oneness, their fellowship of soul puts their common focus upon Christ. And when the world sees such great unity, it is impacted by the grace flowing from the church — *great grace*. There is also *great power*. People come to believe because they see resurrection life in the church. And when the church is like this, there is *great care* as its people expend their lives to help one another. How beautiful!

PRAYER

> *Our Father, we thank you that the Holy Spirit, through Luke the Apostle, has given this beautiful depiction of your great Church. Lord, we long to be people who have great unity, great grace, great power, great care, and a great outreach to those who are lost! Lord, please work in our lives to accomplish this. In Jesus' name, Amen.*

9

Keeping Things on the Up and Up

ACTS 5:1-16

Barnabas was a sparkling example of all the sterling qualities of the early church — unity, grace, power, caring — especially caring. His original name was "Joseph," but he was nicknamed "Barnabas" ("Son of Encouragement") because that is the way he was (4:36). In Acts 4 he sells his real estate on the island of Cyprus and lays the proceeds at the apostles' feet for distribution to the needy. Every time we meet Barnabas in Acts, he is helping someone.

Things were going great in the new church. Always the enemy of God's loving plan, Satan had already begun a counterattack of outward persecution through the civil and religious authorities (Acts 4). But that tactic was not terribly creative or effective, so now the devil tried a different strategy and attacked the church from within. His agents were a husband and wife. The wife's name was "Sapphira," Aramaic for "beautiful," and the husband's name was "Ananias," which in Hebrew means "God is gracious." Few people's lives have contradicted their names more dramatically. Acts 5 records nothing beautiful or gracious about this unhappy couple.

Verses 1 and 2 describe their actions:

> *Now a man named Ananias, together with his wife Sapphira, also sold a piece of property. With his wife's full knowledge he kept back part of the money for himself, but brought the rest and put it at the apostles' feet.*

Ananias and Sapphira had witnessed Barnabas' magnificent act and had seen the great respect that it drew from fellow believers. So they announced they too would sell their property and give it to the church.

However, they both agreed to claim to give the entire sale amount but hold some back, making everyone think they had given it all. If this happened today, Ananias would probably wait until the organ was playing "I Surrender All" and then haltingly come forward, laying his check at Peter's feet. Ananias and Sapphira's ruse was not a mere miscalculation in their checkbook but premeditated deception. This was pious pretense — religious sham — simulated holiness — Christian fraud.

What does God think of spiritual deception? This is an extremely serious issue for the Church. Ananias and Sapphira appeared to be Christians, and I believe they were, as did St. Augustine and Alexander Maclaren and such contemporaries as Richard Longenecker. We ourselves are terribly susceptible to their sin, a spiritual error to which believers still fall. Their punishment was a "sanctifying discipline" for the church (to use Jeremy Taylor's words).

This is an important but for some reason neglected text. Spurgeon in his sixty volumes of the Metropolitan Tabernacle Pulpit anthology *Twenty Centuries of Great Preaching* has no sermon on this text. Yet, it remains an immensely important passage of Scripture. Dr. Barnhouse, on the basis of this text, would never let his congregation sing the third stanza of "At Calvary:" "Now I have giv'n to Jesus everything; now I gladly own him as my King." "You see," he said, "if God acted in the same way today that he did in the fifth chapter of Acts, you'd have to have a morgue in the basement of every church and a mortician on the pastoral staff."[1] The truth is, we would not have a pastoral staff either!

Why did Ananias and Sapphira do what they did? Possibly the Christian life was new and mysterious to them, and they just wanted to be on the inside of things, to really belong. Or perhaps they craved special recognition by the leadership. Or maybe they were swept up by the bandwagon effect. Applause or acceptance or acclaim may have been overly important to them. At the worst, maybe they were making a crass attempt to rise within the power structure, though I doubt they began with such low intentions.

I think that when they saw Barnabas' great generosity, they genuinely wanted to follow suit. But their motivations were mixed and when the money was in hand, they could not live up to their avowed intention. They were undoubtedly new Christians, and the habits of the old life were only a breath away. They overestimated themselves, a common error of new believers.

SPIRITUAL DECEPTION PUNISHED (vv. 3-10)

Picture the scene. Ananias has just finished laying his gift at Peter's feet, and the organ has finished playing "I Surrender All." Ananias' heart begins to thump. He feels dizzy and confused. Why isn't Peter smiling?

Then Peter said, "Ananias, how is it that Satan has so filled your heart that you have lied to the Holy Spirit and have kept for yourself some of the money you received for the land? Didn't it belong to you before it was sold? And after it was sold, wasn't the money at your disposal? What made you think of doing such a thing? You have not lied to men but to God." (vv. 3-4)

Peter explained that Ananias did not have to give anything, but that in pretending to give everything he was now, instead of being filled with the Spirit, under Satan's control. In lying to the church, Ananias had lied to the Holy Spirit — that is, to God. And he was responsible for his actions because he had dreamed up this idea in his own heart. Poor, wretched Ananias!

When Ananias heard this, he fell down and died. And great fear seized all who heard what had happened. Then the young men came forward, wrapped up his body, and carried him out and buried him. (vv. 5-6)

The Greek word translated "gave up the ghost" (KJV; NIV, "died") is used in Acts to describe sudden, terrible, judicial death.[2] This was divine judgment.

"The young men" of the fellowship, suited by their strength for such a task, bore Ananias' corpse away and buried him. The first recorded burial in the Christian community was that of a hypocrite! Tragic!

We must be absolutely clear as to what Ananias' sin was. It was not casual deception. Rather, he feigned a deeper spiritual commitment than he had. We share Ananias' sin not when others think we are more spiritual than we are, but when we try to make others think we are more spiritual than we are. Examples of Ananias' sin today include: creating the impression we are people of prayer when we are not; making it look like we have it all together when we do not; promoting the idea that we are generous when we are so tight we squeak when we smile; misrepresenting our spiritual effectiveness (for example, saying, "When I was at the crusade in New York, I ran the whole follow-up program," when the truth is, you were a substitute counselor). When a preacher urges his people toward deeper devotion to God, implying that his life is an example when in actuality he knows it is not, he is repeating Ananias' sin! When an evangelist calls people to holy living but is secretly having an affair with his secretary, he is an Ananias! This gives us all a lot to think about, if we dare.

There was a much better way open to Ananias. "Peter and my friends, Sapphira and I were going to give everything, but we have decided to keep some for our needs. We would like to do the same as Barnabas did, but we do not feel we can at this time." If they had been honest, God would have used and multiplied what they did give.

Spiritual deception is heinous to God! When we lie to believers, we are not lying to them but to the Lord!

Ananias was already cold in his grave when Sapphira showed up.

> *About three hours later his wife came in, not knowing what had happened. Peter asked her, "Tell me, is this the price you and Ananias got for the land?" "Yes," she said, "that is the price." Peter said to her, "How could you agree to test the Spirit of the Lord? Look! The feet of the men who buried your husband are at the door, and they will carry you out also." At that moment she fell down at his feet and died. Then the young men came in and, finding her dead, carried her out and buried her beside her husband. (vv. 7-10)*

Imagine the effect this must have had on the church. Many knew the erring couple. No doubt, new friendships had developed with them. But now they were dead by God's hand. Luke says there was "great fear" in the church (v. 11), and along with it, I am sure, much soul searching and long bouts of prayer. We must not take the unyielding holiness and the judgment of God lightly. What if such a thing happened today? Can you imagine if a pastor or other church leader was speaking falsehood to the church and suddenly fell over dead? What would that do to us? We would surely begin to think about our own integrity or the lack of it.

Some have a hard time accepting this passage because Peter did not give Ananias and Sapphira time to repent. They say that Peter did not show Christ's compassion or restraint, that Christ's dealing with Judas, whose sin was a thousand times more heinous, did not descend to this level, and that the story of Ananias and Sapphira must therefore be fictitious.[3] They forget that Christ was trying to save Judas' soul. Here the future of the Church was at stake. Ananias and Sapphira were saved but dishonest and disobedient.

SPIRITUAL DECEPTION DISCUSSED

Why was God so severe? Because this was a pivotal time in church history. "The way Ananias and Sapphira attempted to reach their goals was so dramatically opposed to the whole thrust of the Gospel that to allow it to go unchallenged would have set the entire mission for the Church off course."[4] A similar thing happened in the case of Achan as the children of Israel prepared for a new era in the Promised Land. The destruction caused by spiritual pretense is clearly more far-reaching than we can imagine. We know it has poisoned the life of the Church throughout its history. "Hypocrite" is the secular cliché for the churchgoer, too often rightly so.

We know also that spiritual pretense diseases our relationships within the Church. Ephesians 4:25 says it perfectly: "Therefore each of you must put off falsehood and speak truthfully to his neighbor, for we are all members of one body."

Dante portrayed hypocrites in the Eighth Circle of Hell wearing gilded capes that were beautiful to the eye but were actually made of lead, producing the burdened cry, "O weary mantle of eternity."[5] Beautiful as hypocrites may be in appearance, they carry debilitating weight throughout life, suppressing the life of the church.

The consequences of deception are incalculable, and yet it comes to us so naturally. We are deceivers by nature. Satan, a liar from the beginning, brought about our fall by convincing us to believe his lies, making us children of deception. Our culture is riddled with untruth. Media advertising and hype provide us with a daily litany of hyperbolic deception: "easier to win than ever before," "toilet paper soft as a cloud." Unbiased samplings tell us most people prefer Coke — "The Real Thing." Strangely, equally unbiased samplings tell us most people prefer Pepsi. Smoke a Marlboro and you will become the epitome of big-country, bronco-busting masculinity. You will also smell like a camel and run the risk of dying from cancer!

We so naturally alter the facts. My three and a half pound smallmouth bass quickly becomes four pounds. Have you ever been talking freely and enthusiastically and suddenly realized that you were exaggerating? Deception is addictive. A short paragraph from William James's classic *Principles of Psychology* speaks powerfully to this point.

> Could the young but realize how soon they will become mere walking bundles of habits, they would give more heed to their conduct while in the plastic state. We are spinning our own fates, good or evil, and never to be undone. Every smallest stroke of virtue or of vice leaves its never so little scar. The drunken Rip Van Winkle, in Jefferson's play, excuses himself for every fresh dereliction by saying "I will not count this time!" Well! he may not count it, but it is being counted nonetheless. Down among his nerve cells and fibres the molecules are counting it, registering and storing it up to be used against him when the next temptation comes. Nothing we ever do is, in strict scientific literalness, wiped out. Of course, this has its good side as well as its bad one.[6]

That is basically true, though of course the grace of God can change us from the inside out. Nevertheless, habits of deceit are easily formed, hard to break. Realizing this, Dr. Samuel Johnson wrote long before William James:

> Accustom your children constantly to this [the telling of the truth]; if a thing happened at one window, and they, when relating it, say that it happened at another, do not let it pass, but instantly check them; you do not know where deviation from truth will end. . . . It is more from carelessness about truth than from intentional lying, that there is so much falsehood in the world.[7]

Because we are deceivers by nature and because we live amidst deception, spiritual deceit is all too common in the Church. God says in the most dramatic way that it should not be so. "Therefore each of you must put off falsehood and speak truthfully to his neighbor, for we are all members of one body." The body can only enjoy health and function correctly when each part passes the truth to the brain. If it calls hot cold and cold hot, it will dysfunction. The Body of Christ is sometimes ill because of falsehood.

Peter confronted Ananias and Sapphira about their heart deception. Their story is a call to confront ourselves. Do I practice spiritual deceit? Do I attempt to make others think I am more committed than I am? These are serious questions. In the larger picture, it is a matter of life and death — maybe not our own, but someone else's — perhaps our children, our grandchildren, our relatives, our neighbors. Possibly God is calling us to confront another believer, as Peter did. Nathan did the same to King David: "You are the man!" (2 Samuel 12:7). We must help each other remain honest and obedient to God.

Luke goes on to tell us in verse 11 that "Great fear seized the whole church and all who heard about these events." They began to honestly assess what God wanted of them and where they were in their spiritual lives. Verses 12-16 record a continuance of great power manifesting itself in remarkable wonders and the expansion of the Church. When the Church is great — with great unity, great grace, great power, and great care — it is perpetuated by great honesty. We must keep our spiritual life on the up and up!

This demands some practical steps. First, we should take an honest look at our lives regarding deceit. Are we truthful people? Do we engage in exaggeration and coloring? Are we promoting spiritual deception about our own commitments. Are we trying outwardly or subtly to make ourselves appear to be what we are not? Perhaps, to acquire objectivity, it would be helpful to seek the perspective of another person — your spouse, if you are married, or perhaps a trusted, honest friend.

Second, honestly lay the results before the Lord. Repent of all sin, relying on his grace. Ask him to remove habits of deception so that truth becomes a habit instead.

Third, covenant that with his help you will consciously refrain from lying in all its forms and will repent immediately from any failure in this area.

PRAYER

O God, show me any habits of deception in my life. I now renounce any lies I am using to make others think I am more spiritual than I really am. Cleanse me of all dishonesty, and help me to walk in the light as you are in the light. In Jesus' name, Amen.

10

The Liberty of God's Children

ACTS 5:17-42

When the early church moved out with its aggressive and expansive mind-set, a collision with the forces of darkness was inevitable. Peter and John and the ex-cripple experienced it first when they were arraigned before the imposing Sanhedrin and warned not to speak or teach in the name of Jesus. Their resistance and resilience were also predictable.

> *"Judge for yourselves whether it is right in God's sight to obey you rather than God. For we cannot help speaking about what we have seen and heard." (4:19-20)*

When Satan attacked the church from within with the deadly spiritual hypocrisy of Ananias and Sapphira, the church, responding to God's discipline, again rebounded with a resurgence of spiritual power, as recorded in Acts 5:12-16. We see the same phenomenon in Acts 5:17-42 as Luke records three consecutive waves of persecution — each succeeded by remarkable resiliency.

Being raised close to the Pacific Ocean in Southern California taught me a few things about waves. I have fond memories from my high school and college years of leaving home on hot August days when the thermometer was flirting with 100 degrees at 10 A.M., picking up some friends, and after thirty minutes on Beach Boulevard standing on the burning white sand by lifeguard station #3 at Huntington Beach and gazing at a large green surf crowned with white foam set against a horizon rimmed by the purple peaks of Santa Catalina Island. Air temperature 80 degrees; water temperature 69 degrees. Big surf. Perfect. On days like that, there is only one thing to do — hit the water. But you have to know a few essentials.

First, if you are wading out and suddenly observe a huge breaker poised menacingly above you, raised so high against the sky that tiny fish are swimming calmly about in its aquarium-like crest, you had better dive right into it. Otherwise, you will be right back where you began — minus some skin and pride. However, if you perform properly, you will easily pop up on the other side, buoyant and ready to move to deeper water. You do not have to be a great swimmer to get along in the surf. If you just take the time to learn a few simple techniques, you will soon be riding watery mountains, head and shoulders above, kicking in and out at will.

The ocean-surf metaphor applies beautifully to our study of the early church. The forces of evil tried to drown the new church with a flood of suppression, only to have it pop back up as alive and free as ever. Buoyant liberty in ministry rose above a hostile world. Acts 5 is helpful to all of us because though few of us will probably ever face such overt persecution as did the early church, none of us will ever entirely escape the world's repression either, which is more deadly than the Pacific surf. God has a message for today's church.

WAVE NUMBER ONE (vv. 17-25)

The first of three deadly waves of persecution is described in verses 17-18:

> *Then the high priest and all his associates, who were members of the party of the Sadducees, were filled with jealousy. They arrested the apostles and put them in the public jail.*

After the judgment of Ananias and Sapphira, the church continued to minister in unusual power — often in public, beneath the great colonnade of Solomon's Porch. In the midst of one of the sessions the temple police suddenly closed in, taking all twelve apostles captive and tossing them in jail. The Sadducees did this because they "were filled with jealousy." They were not trying to prevent heresy or protect the people or maintain God's honor. They were simply jealous.

Jealousy is always an ugly word. Proverbs 6:34 says, "Jealousy arouses a husband's fury." It is by nature destructive. These Sadducee leaders were envious of the popularity of the apostles and were self-protective of their own prestige. "The crowd should be gathering around *us*, not them." They were moved by the lowest and most contemptible motive. When their malevolence poured forth, the apostles found themselves in the city jail.

Though this would not be the last time the apostles would find themselves imprisoned, they were not at all like the prisoners the jailers had grown accustomed to. The apostles were cool, calm, and collected. If what we see later in Philippi is any indication, there were songs in the night, with Peter perhaps singing bass. The Jerusalem city jail had never seen anything like this, nor had the guards witnessed anything like what was about to happen.

> *But during the night an angel of the Lord opened the doors of the jail and brought them out. "Go, stand in the temple courts," he said, "and tell the people the full message of this new life." At daybreak they entered the temple courts, as they had been told, and began to teach the people. (vv. 19-21a)*

They were divinely delivered. Either God lulled the guards into sleep or the apostles were made temporarily invisible. Whatever happened, it must have been great fun to be out on the streets while the prison lay locked behind them. There is some divine humor here, too, because the Sadducees did not believe in angels. And yet here, right in their own city, were some close encounters of the spiritual kind.

Why the angelic intervention? God was teaching the Twelve that he can deliver his servants from the world's oppression anytime he sees fit. He delivered in a similar way two other times in Acts — once with Peter (12:6-11) and once with Paul and Silas (16:26ff.), though in the latter case God did not want his apostles to escape but to stay in the jail despite the doors being opened — perhaps an even greater witness.

In Acts 5 the angelic liberation was not only meant to free them, but to encourage them — and us! The apostles now knew that God could deliver them from the world's clutches anytime, anywhere!

If church traditions are correct, Matthew knew the reality of an angelic presence when he suffered martyrdom by the sword. So did Mark when he died in Alexandria after being dragged through the streets of the city. Luke experienced the same when he was hanged on a large olive tree in Greece. It was John's realization when he was scarred in a cauldron of boiling oil and lived his last days banished on an island. So it was with Peter as he was crucified upside-down in Rome, James as he was beheaded in Jerusalem, James the Less when he was thrown from a high pinnacle and beaten to death with a club, Philip when he was hanged, Bartholomew when he was scourged and beaten until he died, Andrew when he was bound to a cross and preached at the top of his voice to his persecutors until he perished, Thomas who was run through with a lance, Jude who was killed by executioners' arrows, Matthias who was stoned and then beheaded, Barnabas who suffered the same fate at Salonica, and Paul who was beheaded in Rome. On and on and on it goes.

All of these died knowing that God can deliver his people anytime he wants. Scripture says that when waves of persecution or trial come, God can deliver us *if he so wills*. No matter how dark or oppressive the wave, he can rescue us. Believe it!

Not only were the apostles divinely delivered — they were divinely commissioned. "Go, stand in the temple courts, and tell the people the full message of this new life" (v. 20). The language here suggests a command to exercise dogged steadfastness. They were to hold their ground, stand firm, and deliver the entire message of new life in Christ. Those following the path of the apostles are to proclaim the liberating message of life even in the midst of persecution.

Aida Skripnikova is on that path. Aida was born in 1941 in Leningrad when the Russian people were fighting to free themselves from their Axis invaders. As we know, the enemy was driven out, but that did not bring true freedom. In the fall of 1961 Aida came to know Christ as a nineteen-year-old, and with her new faith came the impulse to share it with others. Aida purchased some postcards with a beautiful picture by Claude Lorain representing a harbor at sunrise (chosen perhaps as a symbol of the spiritual sunrise she had discovered) and then wrote a poem on the reverse side. The poem expressed her perception of life and the need to find God. The poem was entitled: "Happy New Year! 1962."

Our years fly past
One after another, unnoticed.
Grief and sadness disappear,
They are carried away by life.
This world, the earth, is so transient
Everything in it comes to an end.
Life is important.
Don't be happy-go-lucky!
What answer will you give your creator?
What awaits you, my friend, beyond the grave?
Answer this question, while light remains.
Perhaps tomorrow, before God,
You will appear to give an answer for everything.
Think deeply about this,
For you are not on this earth forever.
Perhaps tomorrow, you will break
Forever your links with this world!
SEEK GOD WHILE HE IS TO BE FOUND.

Aida then took her postcards and stood on the Nevski Prospect (which is the Leningrad equivalent of Fifth Avenue in New York City) and handed out her cards to passersby. She was, of course, arrested. In April 1962 she was tried by a Communist court. She was exiled from Leningrad and lost her job as a lab assistant. She was arrested again in 1965 and was sent to a labor camp for a year. In 1968 she was arrested again and was sent to a labor camp for three more years.[1]

Perhaps Aida Scripnikova in her short Christian life had never read our text, but she obeyed the instinct of her heart and in the midst of unbelievable oppression shared the message of life! That day in 1961 when she came to know the Lord Jesus Christ, she was the freest soul in Leningrad!

"Go, stand in the temple courts, and tell the people the full message of this new life." In some Bible translations (including the RSV and NASB) "Life" is capitalized. The apostles were not only to speak about life, but *Life* — new life — "*this* new life" — a specific gift of grace from a loving God. Jesus brings us Life.

> *Then Jesus declared, "I am the bread of* life. *He who comes to me will never go hungry, and he who believes in me will never be thirsty." (John 6:35)*

> *Jesus answered, "I am the way and the truth and the* life. *No one comes to the Father except through me." (John 14:6)*

St. Irenaeus said, "The glory of God is a man fully alive," and that is true. When we become alive in Christ, God is wonderfully glorified!

> *In him was* life, *and that* life *was the light of men. (John 1:4)*

> *That which was from the beginning, which we have heard, which we have seen with our eyes, which we have looked at and our hands have touched — this we proclaim concerning the* Word of life. *The* life *appeared; we have seen it and testify to it, and we proclaim to you the eternal* life, *which was with the Father and has appeared to us. (1 John 1:1-2)*

Regardless of how hostile and oppressive our surroundings, no matter how philistine the workplace, how callous the students, how neurotic the neighbors, we are meant to share Christ by life and word.

The first big breaker had crashed upon the apostles, but they came through with buoyant liberation. With the first blush of daybreak they were back in the temple, on Solomon's Porch, giving out the goods. The Sanhedrin was just getting out of bed, but Christ's ambassadors were already hard at work.

> *At daybreak they entered the temple courts, as they had been told, and began to teach the people. When the high priest and his associates arrived, they called together the Sanhedrin — the full assembly of the elders of Israel — and sent to the jail for the apostles. But on arriving at the jail, the officers did not find them there. So they went back and reported, "We found the jail securely locked, with the guards standing at the doors; but when we opened them, we found no one inside." On hearing this report, the captain of the temple guard and the chief priests were puzzled, wondering what would come of this. Then someone came and said, "Look! The men you put in jail are standing in the temple courts teaching the people." (vv. 21-25)*

As Annas and his friends gathered in their chamber, Annas wore his most dignified and severe expression. Their gorgeous robes were arranged and the prisoners sent for. Then the report came, and their dignity hit the road. They were bewildered and perplexed, shaking in their sandals. What next?

WAVE NUMBER TWO (vv. 26-33)

The leaders collected themselves and prepared to pour another wave of suppression on the would-be preachers.

> *At that, the captain went with his officers and brought the apostles. They did not use force, because they feared that the people would stone them. Having brought the apostles, they made them appear before the Sanhedrin to be questioned by the high priest. "We gave you strict orders not to teach in this name," he said. "Yet you have filled Jerusalem with your teaching and are determined to make us guilty of this man's blood." (vv. 26-28)*

In this bitter reproach, we get a glimpse into the pathology of oppressors. Though they think themselves mighty rulers, they are guilt-ridden and are afraid that someone or something will displace them. Fear is both the method and the reward of tyranny. In this instance the religious rulers blurted out that the apostles were "determined to make us guilty of this man's blood." The truth is, *they* were the ones who said, "Crucify him!" (Matthew 27:22-23) and "Let his blood be on us and on our children!" (Matthew 27:25). Such fear and denial are trademarks of modern enemies of Christ as well. Those leaders' reproach was laced with the aroma of death because the apostles were showing contempt for the court's earlier ruling. The Sadducees now had all the evidence they needed.

How did the apostles respond to this second wave of spiteful opposition? With incredible buoyancy!

> *Peter and the other apostles replied: "We must obey God rather than men! The God of our fathers raised Jesus from the dead — whom you had killed by hanging him on a tree. God exalted him to his own right hand as Prince and Savior that he might give repentance and forgiveness of sins to Israel. We are witnesses of these things, and so is the Holy Spirit, whom God has given to those who obey him." (vv. 29-32)*

What magnificent liberation! They exalted Christ as "Prince and Savior." They made no attempt to palliate their opponents' guilt. They were fearless, walking in the footsteps of great saints such as Daniel and his friends. Do you remember the answer of Shadrach, Meshach, and Abednego when they stood before Nebuchadnezzar?

> *"O Nebuchadnezzar, we do not need to defend ourselves before you in this matter. If we are thrown into the blazing furnace, the God we serve is able to save us from it, and he will rescue us from your hand, O king. But even if he does not, we want you to know, O king, that we will not serve your gods or worship the image of gold you have set up." (Daniel 3:16-18)*

The very flames of oppression burned their bonds so that they walked freely in the fires of persecution. St. Athanasius found this to be true as well. "Athanasius *contra mundum* — Athanasius against the world!" Martin Luther experienced this too. "Here I stand. God help me. I cannot do otherwise." Aida Skripnikova had the same calm courage! "Seek God while he may be found."

How was this remarkable liberation and power gained? Obedience. Peter and the apostles began their answer by saying, "We must obey God rather than men!" (v. 29) and concluded by saying, "We are witnesses of these things, and so is the Holy Spirit, whom God has given to those who obey him" (v. 32). The witnessing power of the Holy Spirit is released through obedience to Christ, to the Word, to the inner voice of his guidance. Some good self-check questions are:

1. Am I living consistently in view of what I know about Christ?
2. Am I living a life that is in accord with what I am learning in the Scriptures?
3. Am I refusing to do what I know he wants?

4. Am I refusing to share my faith because of fear of rejection or appearing unintellectual or uncultured or any other reason?

We cannot have the power of the Holy Spirit if we are saying no to him.

WAVE NUMBER THREE (vv. 34-42)

The apostles were not only enduring the tides of persecution — they were surfing! Look at the effect of their courage: "But when they [the Sanhedrin] heard this, they were cut to the quick [literally, "sawn through"] and were intending to slay them" (v. 33, NASB). They were overcome by violent mental anguish and indignation.

Now came the final wave of suppression. Some think the Sanhedrin would have killed the apostles right on the spot if it were not for Gamaliel. I do not think so. They were too smart for that. But certainly the intervention of the venerable Gamaliel mitigated the extremity of the apostles' punishment.

Much can be said about this man, but suffice it to say that he was among the best of the Pharisees and a man of moderation. He was the grandson of the famous Rabbi Hillel and was so highly thought of that *The Mishnah* says of him, "Since Rabban Gamaliel the elder died there has been no more reverence for the law; and purity and abstinence died out at the same time."[2]

> *But a Pharisee named Gamaliel, a teacher of the law, who was honored by all the people, stood up in the Sanhedrin and ordered that the men be put outside for a little while. Then he addressed them: "Men of Israel, consider carefully what you intend to do to these men. Some time ago Theudas appeared, claiming to be somebody, and about four hundred men rallied to him. He was killed, all his followers were dispersed, and it all came to nothing. After him, Judas the Galilean appeared in the days of the census and led a band of people in revolt. He too was killed, and all his followers were scattered. Therefore, in the present case I advise you: Leave these men alone! Let them go! For if their purpose or activity is of human origin, it will fail. But if it is from God, you will not be able to stop these men; you will only find yourselves fighting against God." (vv. 34-39)*

Evidently, because of Gamaliel's rational entreaty a compromise was reached and the apostles were let off easy — easy, that is, if we think thirty-nine stripes is easy.

> *His speech persuaded them. They called the apostles in and had them flogged. Then they ordered them not to speak in the name of Jesus, and let them go. (v. 40)*

One by one they were whipped until the flesh parted. And one by one they experienced supernatural joy.

> *The apostles left the Sanhedrin, rejoicing because they had been counted worthy of suffering disgrace for the Name. Day after day, in the temple courts and from house to house, they never stopped teaching and proclaiming the good news that Jesus is the Christ. (vv. 41-42)*

Jesus said, "Blessed are those who are persecuted because of righteousness" (Matthew 5:10). I once heard Richard Wurmbrand describe this kind of joy. When he was in a Romanian prison, his tormentors ripped chunks of flesh out of him, and he had the scars to prove it. He was sentenced to solitary confinement, and for weeks or even months on end no one would speak to him in his tiny cell. Amazingly, during all of that there were times when he was overcome with joy. He would actually stand up in his weakened state and dance around his cell, confident that the angels were dancing with him.

He was released from prison unexpectedly, and as he left the prison dressed like a scarecrow, with his teeth rotted and in terrible shape, he met a peasant woman on the road carrying a basket of beautiful strawberries. When she offered him one, he started to take it but then said, "No thanks. I am going to fast." He went home to his wife, and they prayed and fasted as a memorial to the joy he had experienced in prison, asking God for the same kind of joy *outside* prison.

We are not expected to be perfect or faultlessly consistent in our faith and walk, but we are expected to be joyful. We are also expected to persevere. "Day after day, in the temple courts and from house to house, they never stopped teaching and proclaiming the good news that Jesus is the Christ" (v. 42). Similarly, the final verse in Acts describes the Apostle Paul's unswerving courage: "Boldly and without hindrance he preached the kingdom of God and taught about the Lord Jesus Christ" (28:31). The apostles were buoyant, resilient, liberated, victorious!

We flatter ourselves if we imagine we have known anything like the oppression they knew. But we also make a mistake if we imagine we are immune. We do face waves of opposition, though they are more subtle. Sometimes we do not even know they have overwhelmed us. But the enemy knows and celebrates because we no longer speak and teach "the full message of this new life" (v. 20). When we are in such a state, the world does not see the glory of men and women fully alive. Our disobedience has cut us off from the power of the Holy Spirit. There is no joy, no buoyance.

At such times we need to be set free and know again the liberty God has given to his children. When we take our stand for him, speaking the message of life, obeying him rather than men, we will feel the waves, but we will also feel his pleasure.

PRAYER

Our gracious Lord, the supreme example of these men as wave upon wave of oppression came upon them — as they surfaced so buoyantly — as they obeyed your command to speak — as they determined to "obey God rather than men" — as they rejoiced in their suffering — is all beyond us, for it is supernatural. God, we pray that you would teach us how to live out our faith amidst oppression, however it comes — to be buoyant and joyous and effervescent for Jesus. In Jesus' name, Amen.

11

Maintaining the Ministry

ACTS 6:1-7

When a certain Dallas church decided to split, each faction filed a lawsuit to claim the church property. A judge finally referred the matter to the higher authorities in the particular denomination. A church court assembled to hear both sides of the case and awarded the church property to one of the two factions. The losers withdrew and formed another church in the area.

During the hearing, the church courts learned that the conflict had all begun at a church dinner when a certain elder received a smaller slice of ham than a child seated next to him. Sadly, this was reported in the newspapers for everyone to read. Just imagine how the people of Dallas laughed about that situation! This brought great discredit not only to the church but to Jesus Christ![1]

The tiniest events sometimes cause great problems. Again and again a church has warded off a frontal attack only to be subverted from within.

Acts 6 shows us Satan trying to disrupt the inward peace of the early church. Wonderful things were happening as the new church grew by leaps and bounds. Three thousand received Christ at Pentecost. Another 2,000 were added shortly thereafter. Acts 5 tells us that many more were then added to the church. Satan, unhappy about God's successes, sowed a spirit of murmuring and gossip among God's people, hoping to set believer against believer.

Countless works for God have been destroyed in this way. God blesses a work, souls come to Christ, the church reaches its community, missionaries are sent out. Then someone complains that he or she is not appreciated or is being neglected. Perhaps this comes in the form of a critical glance, a name forgotten, a social gaffe, or some imagined offense. Bitter dissension ignites and spreads, and the whole work goes up in flames.

Acts 6 describes such a situation. The delicate unity of the early church became endangered, threatening the spiritual testimony of many thousands of believers.

THE APOSTOLIC MINISTRY ENDANGERED (v. 12)

We might think everybody would have been so occupied with each day's new blessings that there was no room for murmuring. Not so!

> *In those days when the number of disciples was increasing, the Grecian Jews among them complained against the Hebraic Jews because their widows were being overlooked in the daily distribution of food. (v. 1)*

Jerusalem had a large minority of Hellenistic (Greek-speaking) Jews — Jews who, though they spoke no Hebrew because they had lived abroad for centuries, returned to Jerusalem because it was their holy city. Many of these Jews had returned so they could spend their final days in Jerusalem — much like modern-day Zionists. As a result there was an abundance of Greek-speaking women who had outlived their husbands. Resentful, the native Aramaic-speaking Jews discriminated against the Hellenistic Jews, whom the Pharisees held in utter contempt, considering them second-class Israelites.

Then came Pentecost, and thousands of Aramaic-speaking Jews plus hundreds of Hellenistic Jews became one in Christ. However, conversion (wonderful as it was) did not erase all their prejudices. The Greek-speaking widows soon felt they were being shorted. When the other widows received two loaves of bread, they only got one. At least that is the way they saw it. So they "complained" about it. "Our Hebrew-speaking brothers are favoring their own people." The offense may have been more imagined than actual, but that made no difference to those who felt overlooked.

At any rate, word finally reached the apostles who, rightly perceiving that the situation was serious, called a congregational meeting. They saw that the corporate witness of the church was at stake. Jesus had said:

> *"A new commandment I give you: Love one another. As I have loved you, so you must love one another.* All men will know that you are my disciples if you love one another." *(John 13:34-35)*

Concerning this specific situation, Acts 6:2 tells us:

So the Twelve gathered all the disciples together and said, "It would not be right for us to neglect the ministry of the word of God in order to wait on tables."

The apostles' statement tells us that more than corporate witness was at stake. Evidently some had suggested that the way to dispel hard feelings between the foreign Jews and the hometown crowd was to have Peter, John, Philip, and the others divvy up the widows' goods. Though such counsel may have appeared sensible at first glance, it actually brought apostolic principles of discipleship and delegation under well-meaning but deadly attack. The power of the apostolic church would have been greatly diminished, and this glorious chapter of early-church history would have been sadly tamed.

Waiting on tables would have left the apostles little time for anything or anyone else. The apostles would have dried up spiritually under the pressure of serving meals plus all the counseling and preaching, with little time for preparation and prayer. Furthermore, if the apostles had agreed to personally run the food program, others might have hesitated to perform the slightest ministry without apostolic direction, and that would have fostered the overdependence we sometimes see today, with followers afraid to tie their shoes without getting permission from the pastor. Delegation is at the heart of developing followers.

The ill-advised suggestion must have been a substantial temptation for the apostles. No one wants others to think they see themselves as above common work. "You are not willing to wait on tables? Are you better than Jesus? He washed your feet, and you will not even set a plate before a hungry woman? Did not Jesus say, 'The greatest among you will be your servant' (Matthew 23:11)?"

This was also a temptation to think, "Things will not happen the way they should if I do not do them myself." By nature, we like to be the ubiquitous hand of God to others. Certainly no one can do the job the way *we* can. It is to the apostles' credit that they resisted this. In fact, in the years to come they would wash one another's feet again and again and would repeatedly refuse the temptation to set themselves up as little gods.

THE APOSTOLIC MINISTRY ENHANCED (vv. 2-4)

Beyond saying no to the suggestion, the apostles refused to assign blame and made the people part of the solution. Thus their ministry was increased through *spiritual delegation and discipleship*, and others grew spiritually. "Brothers, choose seven men from among you who are known to be full of the Spirit and wisdom. We will turn this responsibility over to them" (v. 3).

They allowed the congregation to choose men of impeccable character: "full of the Spirit . . . full of . . . wisdom." Morgan said concerning this:

> A man full of the Spirit is one who is living a normal Christian life. Fulness of the Spirit is not a state of spiritual aristocracy, to which few can attain. Anything less than the fulness of the Spirit for the Christian man is disease of the spiritual life, a low ebb of vitality. Fulness of the Spirit is not abnormal, but normal Christian life.[2]

These men — evidently the first deacons — lived in dependence upon God's Spirit and not their own strength. They knew how to take truth and apply it to a practical situation. They addressed the plight of the overlooked widows with sanctified common sense.

The apostles' act of delegation was supremely successful. Not only were the widows given good care, but two of the greatest New Testament saints came to full maturity and power under their new responsibilities. Stephen soon afterwards preached his epic sermon before the Sanhedrin and become the first martyr of the Church. Philip had a multifaceted ministry as God transferred him from place to place (consider, for example, his winning the Ethiopian eunuch to Christ immediately after successful mass evangelism in Samaria).

The apostles had served their Master wisely and skillfully, and their discipleship and delegation raised an army of Stephens and Philips to spread the gospel. The ministry of the apostles and of the church was multiplied marvelously!

This also came about because the apostles were able to maintain needed *spiritual discipline*. "[We] will give our attention to prayer and the ministry of the word" (v. 4) — prayer, preparation, and preaching.

"[We] will give our attention to *prayer* . . ." And pray they did! In this respect they were like Jesus who during his "life on earth . . . offered up prayers and petitions with loud cries and tears" (Hebrews 5:7). This contrasts sharply with today's average pastor who, according to a *Christianity Today* survey, spends only three minutes a day in prayer. Perhaps this is due to our feeling that we must be present at every meeting and have our hand on every ministry, producing an overcrowded schedule that leaves no time for personal fellowship with God. How much better it would be to emulate Andrew Bonar, who made these entries in his diary:

> I see that unless I keep up short prayer every day throughout the whole day, at intervals, I lose the spirit of prayer.
>
> Too much work without corresponding prayer.

> Today setting myself to pray. The Lord forthwith seems to send a dew upon my soul.
>
> Was enabled to spend part of Thursday in my church praying. Have had great help in study since then.
>
> Passed six hours today in prayer and Scripture reading, confessing sin, and seeking blessing for myself and the parish.[3]

The apostles' prayers were accompanied by "the ministry of the word" — *preparation.* The Greek word translated "ministry" here has the same root as the word translated "deacon" in the New Testament, and this root includes "dust," suggesting the idea of raising dust in a hurry — that is, being busy at work.[4] The apostles were laborers! Some wrote portions of Scripture under the inspiration of the Holy Spirit. They all prayerfully pored over the Old Testament, working hard at understanding and communicating the spiritual truths of God's Word. This is where shepherds often fall short today. Phillips Brooks said:

> I know of no department of human activity, from the governing of a great nation to the doctoring of a little body, where the disposition is not constantly appearing to invent some sudden method or to seek some magical and concise prescription which shall obviate the need of careful, comprehensive study and long-continued application. But this disposition is nowhere so strong, I think, as in the ministry.[5]

Dr. Donald Grey Barnhouse adds:

> No man is ever going to be able to fill the pulpit adequately unless he spends thousands of hours year after year in the study of God's word.[6]

Phillips Brooks called preaching "truth mediated through personality." The prophet prays over his message, personally absorbing every point. Then, with fear and trembling, God's spokesman steps before the people.

By divinely-directed delegation, the apostles not only freed others to grow in their service to God, but they freed themselves for prayer, preparation, and powerful preaching! Thus the spiritual ministry of the Church was enhanced.

Verses 5 and 6 describe the implementation of the apostolic plan:

> *This proposal pleased the whole group. They chose Stephen, a man full of faith and of the Holy Spirit; also Philip, Procorus, Nicanor,*

Timon, Parmenas, and Nicolas from Antioch, a convert to Judaism. They presented these men to the apostles, who prayed and laid their hands on them.

Everyone — the Greek-speaking Jews and the Aramaic-speaking Jews — came together and chose the favored seven. What a beautiful event — especially considering that all those chosen had Greek names. Though Hebraic Jews comprised the majority of the congregation, they chose Hellenistic Jews to administer the program! The Holy Spirit was reigning. The result?

So the word of God spread. The number of disciples in Jerusalem increased rapidly, and a large number of priests became obedient to the faith. (v. 7)

God's Word spread! The number of disciples increased! Priests believed!

When Satan does not succeed in stopping the church with a frontal assault, he attacks from within. This usually happens subtly — an invitation not sent, a job unnoticed, a critical comment overheard, jealousy over something that really does not matter (like the size of a ham slice). When the murmuring begins, the devil smiles.

Ken Taylor, in his *Romans for the Family Hour*, relates the following story:

One hot day a family traveling down the highway between Johnstown and Jamestown stopped at Farmer Jones's place to ask for a drink of water, which he gladly gave them.

"Where are you headed?" he asked them.

"We are moving from Johnstown to Jamestown to live," they told him. "Can you tell us what the people there are like?"

"Well, what kind of people did you find where you lived before?" Farmer Jones asked.

"Oh, they were the very worst kind!" the people said. "They were gossipy and unkind and indifferent. We are glad to move away."

"Well, I am afraid you will find the same in Jamestown," replied Farmer Jones.

The next day another car stopped, and the same conversation took place. These people were moving to Jamestown, too.

"What kind of neighbors will we find there?" they asked.

"Well," said Farmer Jones, "what kind of neighbors did you have where you lived before?"

"Oh, they were the very best! They were so kind and considerate that it almost broke our hearts to have to move away."

"Well, you will find exactly the same kind again," Farmer Jones replied.[7]

When believers are unhappy and begin to murmur, the first place to look for the problem is in their own hearts. Christians who were unhappy at their last church or town or job are probably unhappy where they are now. If they feel they have just cause for criticism, by all means they should express it to the right people in an appropriate way. But they must avoid murmuring or gossiping and must be willing to be part of the solution.

If the widows are being neglected, we should be willing to wait on tables. If the Sunday school needs help, we should be ready to assist however we can. If we see a need for a small group, perhaps we should host one. If we see the need for evangelism, we should be willing to share Christ.

We must not just complain but must be willing to lead, to delegate, and, above all, to serve.

PRAYER

Our Father, we thank you for this account of how the Holy Spirit repulsed the inward attacks of our enemy. We pray, God, that you would cause us to be a part of the answer, to examine our own hearts, to take our criticism to those who can do something about it, to lead in any way you desire — being willing to delegate to and equip others. Lord, help us to be willing to have you fill us and use us however you desire. In Jesus' name, Amen.

12

Standing Tall

Acts 6:8 — 7:60

On a cold night in 1961 I said good-bye to my soon-to-be-bride and pointed my Ford on the familiar path home. As might be suspected, I was in good spirits. A convulsing body in my headlights, sprawled across the gutter and curb, ended my reverie. Was it a seizure? A hit-and-run? A mugging — or maybe a would-be mugger feigning distress? What should I do? Adrenaline surging, I sped around the corner to a store, jumped out of my car, and ran in to call an ambulance. Suddenly, gazing through acrid smoke, I realized I was looking at the business end of a .38 revolver in the hands of a pale, wide-eyed teenaged employee of Holiday Liquor. Instinctively I sputtered something like, "Don't shoot . . . A man's lying in the street." To which the boy replied with a surreal calm, "Good — I got him."

As we stood there, an incredible picture loomed through the smoke. Behind the counter stood two middle-aged clerks, their white shirts growing increasingly red with blood. The tiny holes in the larger man's glasses revealed that they had been blasted with a sawed-off shotgun.

We all have memories of experiences when it seemed like time stood still, and that is how that day is for me. The gaping holes in the store's windows . . . wadding from expended shotgun shells . . . broken bottles pouring forth their contents . . . liquor mixing with blood on the tan asphalt tile . . . two bloodied clerks standing motionless in disbelief . . . the blond teenaged stock boy putting the cocked revolver up to my ashen face . . . my cautioning him not to shoot . . . the five evenly spaced holes that looked like cherry pits just above his kidneys. Most of all, I remember the bitter moaning of the dying young man in the street. On the verge of eternity, his lips poured forth the fullness of his heart — a litany of curses and hatred. At death he was miserably estranged from both men and God.

Death reveals who we really are. Consider the famous French philosopher Voltaire, who used to say concerning Christ, "Curse the wretch." He also boasted, "In twenty years Christianity will be no more. My single hand shall destroy the edifice it took twelve apostles to rear." Voltaire was proud, confident, cynical. But when he died, he cried in desperation, "I am abandoned by God and man! I give you half of what I am worth if you will give me six months' life. Then I shall go to hell; and you will go with me. O Christ! O Jesus Christ!"[1]

In contrast, the moment of death also sometimes reveals spiritual beauty. John Wesley died full of counsel, exhortations, and praise for God. His final words were, "The best of all is, God is with us. The best of all is, God is with us. The best of all is, God is with us. Farewell!"[2] Adoniram Judson, the great American missionary to Burma, suffering immensely at death, said to those around, "I go with the gladness of a boy bounding away from school, I feel so strong in Christ."[3] Jonathan Edwards, dying from smallpox, gave some final directions, bid his daughter good-bye, and expired saying, "Where is Jesus, my never-failing friend?"[4]

Acts 6:8 — 7:60 shows us the final day in the life of a man named Stephen — how he lived, what he said, how he died. Stephen's death revealed him to be a man whose heart beat with Christ's to the very last.

Stephen means "a crown" or "a garland." The Greek word was used for the reward given to a civic leader or to the crown of glory received by a victor in the Olympic Games. What a perfect name for the one who stood so tall on his final day and was crowned with the first Christian martyr's crown. Stephen's example shows us how to live and how to die. Never do we see the meaning and worth of life more clearly or more poignantly than in the final moments of a faithful Christian's life on earth.

LIVING AS CHRIST WOULD LIVE (6:8-15)

On that last day of his life Stephen lived as Christ lived. His story is introduced in 6:8 with the statement, "Now Stephen, a man full of God's grace and power, did great wonders and miraculous signs among the people." He, like Christ, was *full of grace*. In the New Testament "grace" refers to the unmerited, unlimited riches of God poured upon us through Christ. God's riches flowed through Stephen and onto those around him. But there is more. In pre-Christian times the word *grace* was used to describe the charm of a woman or of one's speech. The word's background suggests beauty, symmetry, rhythm, elegance, loveliness — and all of this was seen in Stephen.

"Full of . . . grace," Stephen possessed a charm of character that touched even those who did not know its source. Note the impression Stephen left on the Council (v. 15): "All who were sitting in the Sanhedrin looked intently at Stephen, and they saw that his face was like the face of an angel." Stephen possessed a winsomeness just like Jesus'.

God's grace can accomplish the same in us. Wesley humorously said, "One of the advantages of the grace of God is that it makes a man a gentleman without the aid of a dancing master."[5] Grace not only pays for our sins — it changes us. Oh, to be like Stephen — "full of God's grace"!

Verse 8 reveals that Stephen was also a man who shared *Christ's power*: "Now Stephen, a man full of God's grace and power, did great wonders and miraculous signs among the people." Acts 2:22 uses similar words about Christ: "Jesus of Nazareth was a man accredited by God to you by miracles, wonders and signs." Stephen would soon deliver a great sermon that gave the Sanhedrin a whipping they could not believe! This transpired through Jesus' power, not Stephen's. "You will receive power when the Holy Spirit comes on you; and you will be my witnesses . . ." (1:8).

Stephen also knew the power of perseverance! When the mob tore him limb from limb, he was just like Christ — no reviling, no recrimination, no self-defense. Even while on his knees (7:60), he stood tall. Christ's power enables us to *do* what we ought and to *be* what we ought.

Stephen was also a man who shared *Christ's wisdom*: "But they could not stand up against his wisdom or the Spirit by whom he spoke" (v. 10). The Scriptures use "wisdom" in different ways, but here it carries the idea of insight, just as in Ephesians 1:17 where Paul prays regarding "a spirit of wisdom and revelation, so that you may know him better." God had given Stephen a discerning mind and spiritual insight — an important quality we all need.

Stephen was also a man who shared *Christ's rejection*:

> *Then they secretly persuaded some men to say, "We have heard Stephen speak words of blasphemy against Moses and against God." So they stirred up the people and the elders and the teachers of the law. They seized Stephen and brought him before the Sanhedrin. They produced false witnesses, who testified, "This fellow never stops speaking against this holy place and against the law. For we have heard him say that this Jesus of Nazareth will destroy this place and change the customs Moses handed down to us." (vv. 11-14)*

The aroma of death permeates this entire passage. Young Stephen was already in the cemetery, if his enemies had their way.

Stephen was one of the seven Hellenistic (Greek-speaking, immigrant) Jews enlisted to serve the widows (6:1-6). The Hellenistic Jews were not very popular in Jerusalem, so Stephen's Hellenistic synagogue had a vested interest in his not making waves. In fact, when Stephen became too hot to handle, it was the Hellenistic Jews who delivered him to the Sanhedrin (v. 9). Moreover, they secretly brought trumped-up charges of blasphemy against him (v. 11). This "court" was the same group that had convicted Jesus. It even had the same high priest. Stephen was as good as dead. But on that final day Stephen was living as Christ would, and that was all that mattered.

SPEAKING AS CHRIST WOULD SPEAK (7:1-53)

Once the Sanhedrin heard all the charges, the high priest asked Stephen, "Are these charges true?" (7:1), though he was not really interested in anything Stephen had to say — a mockery of a trial. What followed was one of the most amazing and most potent sermons ever preached. Stephen knew his Bible and his Bible history. As he stood tall before the Council, he brought the theology of Christ down hard on the three great pillars of popular Judaism: the land, the law, and the temple — three false bases for confidence before God. He not only attacked those three sacred cows — he took them by the horns and turned them belly up.

The first sacred cow was *the land* (vv. 2-36). According to popular opinion, God gave special spiritual privileges to those living on the real estate of Palestine. The resulting veneration of the land and the status that went with it left little room for the saving work of Jesus the Messiah. Stephen argued that this was wrong. To prove his point, Stephen cited the case of Abraham in verses 2-8. Abraham spent considerable time in the land but did not live as if he had arrived at the height of God's purpose for him. Stephen began by saying in verse 2:

> *"Brothers and fathers, listen to me! The God of glory appeared to our father Abraham while he was still in Mesopotamia, before he lived in Haran."*

God revealed himself to Abraham even *before* he was living in the land. Stephen made a similar point in verses 4-5:

> *"So he left the land of the Chaldeans and settled in Haran. After the death of his father, God sent him to this land where you are now living. He gave him no inheritance here, not even a foot of ground."*

The point is, God blessed Abraham even though he did not yet occupy as much as a foot of the Holy Land. The land is not the blessing.

In verses 9-16 Stephen went on to show that the same was true of the twelve sons of Jacob. God blessed them through Joseph in Egypt even though the only part of the Holy Land they possessed was the family tomb.

Stephen's clinching example was Moses, described in verses 17-36. God met and took care of Moses and his people *outside* the Holy Land. Moses was raised in Egypt (vv. 17-22). He matured in Midian (v. 29). He was commissioned near Mt. Sinai, and God called the area "holy ground" (vv. 30-34). "Holy ground" is wherever God meets his people, and not just inside the borders of Palestine. The greatest miracles of Israel happened in Egypt, at the Red Sea, and in the desert — not in the Promised Land.

One cow down, two to go.

The next sacred cow was *the exaltation of the law and the veneration of Moses.* Stephen's basic argument (v. 37) built on Moses' words from Deuteronomy 18:15, when Moses predicted that God would raise up for the Jews "a prophet like me from your own people." The Jews' hope of redemption was not Moses' law, but Jesus himself.

Of course, the Jews in Moses' day rejected both Moses and the law anyway:

> *"But our fathers refused to obey him. Instead, they rejected him and in their hearts turned back to Egypt. They told Aaron, 'Make us gods who will go before us. As for this fellow Moses who led us out of Egypt — we don't know what has happened to him!'"* (vv. 39-40)

The law of Moses could not save the Israelites. Besides, Moses told them to look for another prophet.

The final sacred cow of Judaism was *the temple*. "God is surely with us — we have the temple." Stephen answered this foundation of false security in verses 48-50, quoting Isaiah 66:1-2:

> *"'Heaven is my throne, and the earth is my footstool. What kind of house will you build for me? says the Lord. Or where will my resting place be? Has not my hand made all these things?'"*

Three cows down! Twelve hooves pawing the air! "Gentlemen, Sanhedrin, rulers of Israel, Sadducees, Pharisees, listeners, you think you are *in* because you possess the land, the law, and the temple. But you are wrong — dead wrong!"

What does all this have to do with us today? *The land.* It is possible to imagine that since we live in a privileged nation where so much good has been done and so many godly people reared, we will surely inherit God's blessing. *The law.* Sometimes we, like the Jews of old, make a fetish out of

God's Word. We carry it with us, mark it appropriately, thumb it piously, but fail to let it take root in our hearts. *The temple*. It is easy to suppose that since we go to the place where God has chosen to meet his people, we will receive special blessings. Three times, not necessarily so! It is possible to have all these things and yet be pitifully and utterly damned, or saved but defeated and disobedient.

Stephen wanted to make sure no one missed his point, so he drove it home in verses 51-53:

> "You *stiff-necked people, with uncircumcised hearts and ears!* You *are just like* your *fathers:* You *always resist the Holy Spirit! Was there ever a prophet* your *fathers did not persecute? They even killed those who predicted the coming of the Righteous One. And now* you *have betrayed and murdered him* — you *who have received the law that was put into effect through angels but have not obeyed it."*

Stephen had become a bit strident, but rightfully so. Similarly, in a later era George Whitefield preached to a New England church three evenings in a row on "You must be born again." The message was so vigorous that the elders finally came to him and asked, "Mr. Whitefield, why do you keep preaching, 'You must be born again'?" Whitefield responded, "Because *you* must be born again!" Stephen wanted to get his message across: "*You* have sinned — *you* need a Savior!"

DYING AS CHRIST WOULD DIE (vv. 54-60)

Stephen's sermon was his death warrant, but he was standing tall. He had lived like Christ, he had spoken like Christ, and now he would die like Christ. In response to a godliness they wished to deny or silence, the Sanhedrin went berserk. "When they heard this, they were furious and gnashed their teeth at him" (v. 54). A preacher knows he is in trouble when the congregation begins to frown, but he is in worse trouble when they grind their teeth! Verses 57-59a tell the story:

> *At this they covered their ears and, yelling at the top of their voices, they all rushed at him, dragged him out of the city and began to stone him. Meanwhile, the witnesses laid their clothes at the feet of a young man named Saul. While they were stoning him, Stephen prayed, "Lord Jesus, receive my spirit."*

These respected, dignified aristocrats descended on young, innocent Stephen and executed him! Their action was illegal, brutal, immoral, but they did not care. They probably took him outside the city where the witnesses repeated their charges, threw him down an embankment (it was the witnesses' privilege to do so), and cast great stones on him, followed by more stones from the crowd. Frederick Buechner describes it this way:

> Stoning somebody to death, even somebody as young and healthy as Stephen, is not easy. You do not get the job done with the first few rocks and broken bottles, and even after you get the man down, it is a long, hot business. To prepare themselves for the work-out, they stripped to the waist and got somebody to keep an eye on their things till they were through. The man they got was a fire-breathing young arch-conservative Jew named Saul, who was there because he thoroughly approved of what they were doing.[6]

Christ's brave ambassador died a terrible death! Yet in that death there was also an awesome beauty:

> *But Stephen, full of the Holy Spirit, looked up to heaven and saw the glory of God, and Jesus standing at the right hand of God. "Look," he said, "I see heaven open and the Son of Man standing at the right hand of God." (vv. 55-56)*

The Scriptures uniformly picture Jesus as seated, but on this occasion he was "*standing* at the right hand of God." Christ came to his feet with arms open to welcome the first martyr home. Beautiful!

Stephen describes Jesus as the "Son of Man," a title referring to the Incarnation. Our Savior continues to bear the marks of Calvary in heaven, and Stephen, himself a martyr, recognized Jesus' martyred body. He knew Jesus understood his servant's pain and felt it along with him. Saviour and saint were one in experience and heart!

Stephen lived the last day of his life with remarkable Christlikeness, and he died the same way. "While they were stoning him, Stephen prayed, 'Lord Jesus, receive my spirit'" (v. 59). He was just like Jesus, who had said from the cross, "Father, into your hands I commit my spirit" (Luke 23:46). What grace! What power! What wisdom! He was like the Lord even in death.

Verse 60 goes on, "Then he fell on his knees and cried out, 'Lord, do not hold this sin against them.' When he had said this, he fell asleep." Like Jesus, he prayed for his executioners. This was an overflow of grace — God's unmerited, unconditional favor. Stephen lived out Christ's power — the power to *do* and to *be* what God wanted him to do and be.

He heeded not reviling tones
Nor sold his heart to idle moans,
Tho 'cursed and scorned and bruised with stones.
But looking upward, full of grace,
He prayed, and from a happy place
God's glory smote him on the face.

—*Tennyson*

Death will ultimately reveal what each of us truly is. Stephen lived his last hours as Christ would and did. He spoke his last words as Christ would and did. He died a martyr's death as Christ would and did. He stood tall through the matchless grace of God! If today were our final day, what would others write about us?

Was it worth it? Stephen would say yes.

The soul that on Jesus hath leaned for repose,
I will not, I will not desert to his foes;
That soul, though all hell should endeavor to shake,
I will never, no never, no never forsake!

Was it worth it? The Apostle Paul would say so because it was the memory of Stephen that tormented him and refused to let go. This is what Jesus was referring to when he said on the Damascus Road, "Saul, Saul, why do you persecute me? It is hard for you to kick against the goads" (26:14). Stephen's death kept goading the persecutor Saul, nudging him toward the throne of grace.

PRAYER

O God, help us to live, to speak, and to die the way Christ would and did. Help us to look beyond the enemies, the obstacles, the problems and perils, to see the Savior who died for us and who now stands with open arms waiting to welcome us home. Help us to stand tall by divine grace. In Jesus' name, Amen.

13

God's Way

ACTS 8:1-25

The book of Acts opens with Christ's final earthly words to his disciples — a remarkable blueprint for world evangelization:

> *"But you will receive power when the Holy Spirit comes on you; and you will be my witnesses in Jerusalem, and in all Judea and Samaria, and to the ends of the earth." (1:8)*

However, the outreach of the church might never have reached beyond Jerusalem if it had not been for Stephen's death and the intensifying persecution it precipitated. Following the church through Acts is like following a wounded deer through a forest. Drops of blood mark the trail. The opening verses of chapter 8 portray the persecution of the early church:

> *And Saul was there, giving approval to his [Stephen's] death. On that day a great persecution broke out against the church at Jerusalem, and all except the apostles were scattered throughout Judea and Samaria. Godly men buried Stephen and mourned deeply for him. But Saul began to destroy the church. Going from house to house, he dragged off men and women and put them in prison. Those who had been scattered preached the word wherever they went. (vv. 1-4)*

This hateful opposition was brutal. The word behind Paul's "ravaging" (v. 3, NASB; NIV, "destroy") suggests sadistic cruelty, like a wild boar tearing a victim's body apart. Paul later described himself as having been a graceless, vindictive man: "I persecuted the followers of this Way to their death, arresting both men and women and throwing them into prison" (22:4). To the Galatians he explained:

> *For you have heard of my previous way of life in Judaism, how intensely I persecuted the church of God and tried to destroy it. (1:13)*

Paul, the relentless hunter, brought death and misery to the church! But amidst the horrors of the waves of persecution against Christ's followers, two especially wonderful things took place: the gospel invaded Samaria, thus fulfilling the second step in Christ's blueprint, and it went out with amazing spiritual power, just as Christ also had promised.

As we study the spread of the gospel into Samaria, we see that many people experienced spiritual power, some became channels of it, and others sought it but were denied. In telling the thrilling story of revival in Samaria, Luke shows us how to acquire and continue to experience the power of the Holy Spirit.

THE EXHIBITION OF SPIRITUAL POWER (vv. 5-17)

The power of God first brought about the miracle of Samaritan conversions:

> *Philip went down to a city in Samaria and proclaimed the Christ there. When the crowds heard Philip and saw the miraculous signs he did, they all paid close attention to what he said. With shrieks, evil spirits came out of many, and many paralytics and cripples were healed. So there was great joy in that city. (vv. 5-8)*

The miracle began with Philip. This is not Philip the apostle but Philip the deacon, one of the seven Greek-speaking men (including Stephen) appointed to serve the widows in Jerusalem (see 6:6). As a Hellenistic Jew, he was not particularly welcome in Jerusalem, and as a Christian he was doubly unwelcome. So when the persecution began, he fled to Samaria. There he "preached the word wherever [he] went" (literally, "evangelized") and "proclaimed" (or heralded) Christ to the people (see vv. 4-5). He may have been unaware of the incredible strides he was making in presenting Christ to an alien and hostile culture. The Holy Spirit was breaking new ground.

The other side of the miracle lay in the Samaritans' amazing acceptance of Philip and his message. History records intense animosity between the Samaritans and Jews that had lasted hundreds of years. In 721 B.C. the Assyrians took the inhabitants of Israel, the northern kingdom, off to Assyria, where the Jews intermarried with the Assyrians and Cuthites. In

587 B.C. the people of the southern kingdom, Judah, were taken captive into Babylon. But in Babylon there was no intermarriage. So when those Jews came back to their homes, they were of unadulterated Jewish blood, unlike the inhabitants of the northern kingdom.

To the Jews, the Samaritans were a mongrel nation of half-breeds. The Jewish rabbis said, "Let no man eat the bread of the Cuthites (the Samaritans) for he who eats their bread is as he who eats swine's flesh." A popular prayer in those days said, ". . . and, Lord, do not remember the Samaritans in the resurrection." You can be sure the Samaritans felt the same way about the Jews.

So why was Philip's preaching so successful? He was a Hellenistic, Jewish Christian. The Hellenistic Jews were tolerated but not accepted by Hebrew-speaking Jews, and as Christians they were sometimes disowned or neglected, as we saw in Acts 6. This fostered a feeling of kinship between the formerly dispossessed Samaritans and the recently dispossessed Christian Hellenists.

Further, Philip's Christ-centered message discounted the importance of the Jerusalem temple, which the Samaritans hated. Also, the Samaritans, who were looking for a prophet like Moses, were naturally sympathetic with Philip's announcement that Jesus was the fulfillment of Deuteronomy 18:15, Moses' prophesy that "The LORD your God will raise up for you a prophet like me." Socially and theologically the Samaritans were open to Philip. He fared far better than the apostles would have. The Holy Spirit chose just the right man for the task at hand.

Primarily, however, Philip preached with power because he loved Jesus. He was not an apostle. He was not a big shot. He was, in fact, a refugee in a hostile environment. He was not in Samaria by choice — persecution drove him there! He probably would have liked to remain in Jerusalem. But once in Samaria, he was so full of love for Christ that he could not stop telling others about Jesus. His power came from a heart-love for Christ. And before he knew it he had a revival on his hands.

> *When the crowds heard Philip and saw the miraculous signs he did, they all paid close attention to what he said. (v. 6)*

Miraculous power was his.

> *With shrieks, evil spirits came out of many, and many paralytics and cripples were healed. (v. 7)*

The result? "So there was great joy in that city" (v. 8). The prodigals had returned, and the Lord brought out the best robes, the most expensive rings, and the finest sandals! There was laughter in Samaria. There was vibrant spiritual power in the Samaritan miracle!

This power was especially evident in its effect upon Simon the sorcerer.

> *Now for some time a man named Simon had practiced sorcery in the city and amazed all the people of Samaria. He boasted that he was someone great. (v. 9)*

Simon was probably a known expert in the occult. Some surmise that he was a renegade Jew. As a profit-motivated enchanter, his style was a combination of theosophical rubbish, profitable eclecticism, and a dominating personality — a first-century combination of Harry Houdini and Madam Blavatsky. Perhaps he wore saffron robes marked with the signs of the zodiac and made theatrical entrances. Whatever his style, he had immense power.

> *And all the people, both high and low, gave him their attention and exclaimed, "This man is the divine power known as the Great Power." They followed him because he had amazed them for a long time with his magic. (vv. 10-11)*

Simon held tremendous sway over the city. Gustaf Dalman believed that he claimed to be God Almighty.[1] The people followed him, rationalizing to themselves, "What this man does is supernatural. Simon — the Great Power of God!" And Simon loved it. How different he was from the truly great servants of God. As Paul said to the Corinthians:

> *When I came to you, brothers, I did not come with eloquence or superior wisdom as I proclaimed to you the testimony about God. For I resolved to know nothing while I was with you except Jesus Christ and him crucified. I came to you in weakness and fear, and with much trembling. (1 Corinthians 2:1-3)*

Simon was a man of immense power, but Philip's power was greater. As a result, Simon lost his followers.

> *But when they believed Philip as he preached the good news of the kingdom of God and the name of Jesus Christ, they were baptized, both men and women. (v. 12).*

Simon was eclipsed by the Jewish refugee. His star was fading fast. What could he do? Simon got a brilliant idea! "If you can't beat 'em, join 'em."

> *Simon himself believed and was baptized. And he followed Philip everywhere, astonished by the great signs and miracles he saw. (v. 13)*

Simon could not get over what he was seeing. Fascinated, he made a public profession of faith and was publicly baptized, but it was not a genuine conversion of the heart. Subsequent history and legend portray Simon as the arch-villain of the early church. Irenaeus (A.D. 180) speaks of him as the father of Gnosticism. What we have here is the devil joining the church. And it is no wonder, for as Paul says:

> *Satan himself masquerades as an angel of light. It is not surprising, then, if his servants also masquerade as servants of righteousness. (2 Corinthians 11:14-15)*

Simon's "conversion" made a vast impression on the Samaritans. Philip's gospel power had broken the spell of the sorcerer upon the people, and many of them found new life in Christ. The story of Simon leaves us in no doubt of the pulsating, overwhelming power of the Word of God.

Soon afterwards, a direct display of apostolic power through Peter and John accomplished a further miracle.

> *When the apostles in Jerusalem heard that Samaria had accepted the word of God, they sent Peter and John to them. When they arrived, they prayed for them that they might receive the Holy Spirit, because the Holy Spirit had not yet come upon any of them; they had simply been baptized into the name of the Lord Jesus. Then Peter and John placed their hands on them, and they received the Holy Spirit. (vv. 14-17)*

When the apostolic leadership in Jerusalem heard about the amazing happenings in Samaria, they sent two front-office apostles to check things out. When they arrived, they found everything as it had been described. The believers were genuine, except that they had not received the indwelling of the Holy Spirit. So, laying hands on them, Peter and John imparted the Spirit. This apostolic bestowal confirmed that the Samaritans were not second-class believers.

To Simon the sorcerer, this was a dazzling, irresistible display of power. And remember, power had been this man's consuming narcotic — life's magic elixir. He had spent long nights dreaming and scheming his way to the top. He had to have this new power at any price!

THE APPROPRIATION OF SPIRITUAL POWER (vv. 18-24)

> *When Simon saw that the Spirit was given at the laying on of the apostles' hands, he offered them money and said, "Give me also this ability so that everyone on whom I lay my hands may receive the Holy Spirit." (vv. 18-19)*

Instead of asking for the Holy Spirit, Simon asked for the *power* to bestow the Spirit. He actually thought he could buy the authority to bestow spiritual power on others (undoubtedly for a price). We may laugh at Simon for being so ignorant, but many Christians have believed exactly this. In church history it is called "simony," after this very man. W. A. Criswell has written about this:

> The church became a part of the state at the time of Constantine's conversion. Simony was already practiced but it increased in the buying of ecclesiastical office and benefits. A bishop's office could be bought for so much money. The same was true of an archbishop's office, a cardinal's hat, an ecclesiastical living in parishes and in monasteries. Simony finally gave rise to the Reformation when all over Europe indulgences were sold in order to get money to build St. Peter's Cathedral in Rome.[2]

We could, no doubt, point to much of the same today but should mainly check our own hearts. We would be wrong to suppose this does not apply to us simply because we have not offered money for spiritual power. Simon tried to obtain spiritual power in order to promote himself, and anytime we seek spiritual power or abilities to put ourselves forward we make the same error. Preaching to gain recognition or status is simony. Serving with an eye to advancement in the church's power structure is simony. Seeking spiritual gifts for the promotion of oneself is simony. Even seeking to be godly so others will think we are godly is a type of simony.

I heard about a pastor and his wife who wanted to buy a house. They found a home they liked and went over to make an offer. The people who were selling the residence said, "We would like to give you the house," then explained that since the buyers were in the ministry, they believed that if they gave them the house, they would ensure themselves a place in Heaven. To the credit of the buyers, they said, "It does not work that way," then sat down and led the couple to Christ. Interestingly, the couple did give them the house anyway, but the point is, money cannot buy spiritual favor or ability.

> Money will buy luxuries, but it will not buy spiritual power. Money will buy advancement and preferment, but it will not buy the recog-

> nition of God. Money will buy sycophantic, fawning favor and accolades, but it will not buy soul-respect. Money will buy libraries, but it will not buy poetic fire or insight or wisdom. Money will buy a prostitute, but it cannot buy love. Money can buy diamonds, but it cannot buy the sparkle and light in the eye. Money can buy pleasure and entertainment, but it cannot buy happiness. Money can buy a suit, but it cannot buy a physique. Money can buy medicine, but it cannot buy health. Money can buy a house, but it cannot buy a home.[3]

Simon should have realized that God does not belong to the magician's union. Peter's response to Simon's request was firm, but he told him the truth: "May your money perish with you, because you thought you could buy the gift of God with money!" (8:20). An older translation says: "But Peter said to him: The silver of thee with thee may it be into perdition." But Peter's answer ended with grace as he explained that Simon had a heart problem:

> *"You have no part or share in this ministry, because your heart is not right before God." (v. 21)*

> *"For I see that you are full of bitterness and captive to sin." (v. 23)*

"Full of bitterness" suggests wretchedness. "Captive" suggests that Simon was a prisoner of sin. Seeing that the man was in desperate need, Peter went all-out for his soul:

> *"Repent of this wickedness and pray to the Lord. Perhaps he will forgive you for having such a thought in your heart." (v. 22)*

Unfortunately, Simon may have never repented. His reply was insipidly lame: "Pray to the Lord for me so that nothing you have said may happen to me" (v. 24). Only slightly moved by Peter's stern rebuke, he did not pray for forgiveness but rather asked Peter to do it for him. He did not repent as he was enjoined to do. So now his name lives in infamy.

A FINAL WORD

What do we learn from all this? We learn that the gospel has astonishing effects! God can use a layman like Philip to influence a whole culture for Christ. Through the gospel, healing can come wholesale to a needy people, so that there is "great joy" in their land. Men and women can become fountains of divine power right where they are.

We learn too that spiritual power cannot be bought. The pursuit of God, not power, is what counts. Philip's great power came from the fact that he loved Jesus, pure and simple. Alexander Maclaren put it this way: "A heart right in the sight of God is the indispensable qualification for all possession of spiritual power, or of any blessings which Jesus gives."

> *"Now this is eternal life: that they may know you, the only true God, and Jesus Christ, whom you have sent." (John 17:3)*

> *I want to know Christ and the power of his resurrection. (Philippians 3:10)*

> *My soul thirsts for God, for the living God. (Psalm 42:2)*

We taste thee, O Thou Living Bread,
And long to feast upon Thee still:
We drink of Thee, the Fountainhead
And thirst our souls from Thee to fill.

PRAYER

O Lord, help us see any points of self-seeking in our lives — any way we are seeking your power for wrong reasons. Help us to seek you only, and not merely your gifts. Search our hearts today. Purge us and strengthen us. Use us to touch our community, our culture, our nation with the name of Jesus — to point many to fullness of life and joy through the Savior. In Jesus' name, Amen.

14

Philip: The Touch of God

ACTS 8:26-40

Reading Acts for the first time, none of us would have guessed when we came to the dawn of Philip's ministry in chapter 6 that he would ascend to such spiritual heights in chapter 8. Philip's ministry began as a lay-deacon humbly doling out the widow's portions in the Jerusalem church. But it soared to unimagined heights when persecution hit. Though he was not a "pro," God's power coursed through him to the despised Samaritans, and large numbers of them believed the good news and were saved.

In the last half of Acts 8 Philip's ministry is still at its zenith. However, instead of the vast multitudes of Samaria, the transforming touch of God now comes through Philip to one man in a desert place far from the teeming city. God valued that individual as much as the multitudes, and he used Philip to touch his life.

But the Master comes, and the foolish crowd
Never can quite understand
The worth of a soul and the change that's wrought
By the touch of the Master's hand.[1]

Each of us, like Philip, can bear the gracious touch of God to others.

IN TOUCH WITH THE SPIRIT (vv. 26-29)

When Philip was installed as deacon, he was "full of the Holy Spirit" (6:3). That means he exhibited the fruit of the Spirit — love, joy, peace, patience, kindness, goodness, faithfulness, gentleness, self-control —

and that he had a melody in his heart (cf. Galatians 5:22-23; Ephesians 5:18ff.).

Being in touch with the Holy Spirit, Philip was open to the Spirit's direction. This sensitivity to divine guidance was a major factor in his becoming the touch of God to others. We must all beware of rigid suppositions as to how the Holy Spirit works or leads. We cannot assume that since God directed men in a certain way in the past, that is the way he will do it for anyone who is truly Spirit-led today. For example, some preachers have looked down on me for developing my sermons beforehand and thus not being subject to the Spirit's guidance while preaching. (The other side of the coin is the story of the preacher who told his congregation one Sunday morning, "I have had a terrible week and have not been able to prepare, so I am going to have to depend on the Holy Spirit. But let me assure you, this will never happen again!") We must never confine the Spirit's guidance to the box of past experience. He just will not fit!

Philip had enough spiritual understanding not to resist the unfolding guidance of the Holy Spirit. The Spirit first directed Philip through persecution to leave his ministry in Jerusalem and go to Samaria for a much wider ministry. Philip knew by experience that God directs by *difficulties*, but he did not believe that is the *only* way God leads.

Next Philip was led by an *angel*. As Philip was busy ministering in Samaria, "an angel of the Lord said to Philip, 'Go south to the road — the desert road — that goes down from Jerusalem to Gaza.' So he started out, and on his way . . ." (vv. 26-27a). Hebrews 1:14 tells us that angels are "ministering spirits sent to serve those who will inherit salvation." All of us, all the time, are being touched by the ministry of angels, though we usually do not see them. The point is, God guided Philip in a new way, and Philip was enough in touch to respond.

As we read on, we see Philip's continued openness to the Spirit's unique direction:

> *So he started out, and on his way he met an Ethiopian eunuch, an important official in charge of all the treasury of Candace, queen of the Ethiopians. This man had gone to Jerusalem to worship, and on his way home was sitting in his chariot reading the book of Isaiah the prophet. The Spirit told Philip, "Go to that chariot and stay near it." (vv. 27-29)*

Philip obeyed *the subjective inner voice of the Holy Spirit*. He remained open as to how God would lead him.

When we are in touch with the Holy Spirit, we will be sensitive to his guidance — sometimes through difficulties, sometimes through an inner voice, maybe even through angels — and thus we will be the touch of God to others.

Philip was so in touch with the Spirit that he was not only flexible as to *how* the Holy Spirit would lead, but as to *where* the Spirit would use him. And he was obedient. Put yourself in Philip's place. You are not one of the Twelve or the Big Three, but you really have something going in the Samaritan crusade. Simon the magician has been defeated. The entire town thinks your message is God's truth and knows you are from God. It is a happy time — a marvelous revival, and suddenly the Lord tells you to take a hike to, of all places, the desert! Philip went from an exciting city and a growing congregation to a lonely desert road and a congregation of one. It would have been so easy to be discouraged. "Lord, do you really want me to go to the desert? There is nothing there but lizards. Have I not proved myself worthy of a broader ministry? I have been faithful in the small things — I even waited on the widows. And now the desert? Lord . . . !"

But that is not how Philip responded. He was ready to serve anywhere anytime. This is a great example to emulate. Over the years I have encountered individuals who are absolutely blah until they are in front of a crowd of several hundred, and suddenly they were ministers who were excited, charming, full of power! The refreshing reverse of this happened when I recently met Billy Graham. Almost the first thing he said was, "Do not call me Dr. Graham. I do not have an earned doctorate. I am just Billy." Then he went on to ask questions about me, my wife, my children. Humble submission to the Spirit of God is essential for joyful living and effective service.

Philip was so in touch with the Spirit that he became the touch of God anywhere and in any way and to anyone that God asked him to be. He was flexible and sensitive to the Spirit's direction. These are wonderful qualities, but the transcending element of Philip's divine touch was his obedience to the Lord: "And he arose and went" (v. 26); "Philip ran up to the chariot" (v. 30). Why did God use Philip? Were not there other laymen who could have served just as well? Maybe not. Perhaps his obedient spirit was unique at that time.

The text presents two perspectives on the Ethiopian eunuch's coming to Christ. From above we see the sovereign God working in a man's heart in such a way that after making a pilgrimage to Jerusalem he remains spiritually hungry. While reading a scroll of Isaiah as he is borne across the desert in a chariot, he encounters a Spirit-sent ambassador of Christ, Philip, who leads him to the Savior.

From ground level we see the role of human obedience. Would the eunuch have been saved even if Philip had disobeyed? The question is irrelevant. God chooses to use human obedience to carry out his plan. Exactly whom he uses or how is incidental. As Lloyd Ogilvie says, "The Lord of all creation has ordained that he would do his work through us. Our seeking the Spirit's guidance and obeying what he wants us to do and say is the way he works to bless the world."[2] *God's sovereign work plus man's obedience brings the touch of God to needy human lives*. Put another way, there are all kinds of "chance" meetings ready to take place in a life that is sensitive and obedient to God's leading.

Ian Thomas tells of getting on an airplane and being so tired that he planned to just curl up and sleep. But then he heard a "psssst" and then another "psssst." Looking in the direction of the sound, he heard a man say, "I am reading in the Bible about Nicodemus in John 3, and I do not understand it. Do you know anything about the Bible?"

Once when I was flying back from a hectic missions conference in California, I was looking forward to reading Lewis's *Letters to Malcolm.* But as I got on the plane I prayed, "Lord, if you want me to share Christ with someone, I am willing." As I sat down, the seat next to me was already occupied by a young man reading an Isaac Asimov novel. I took out my Lewis and said, "Are you enjoying the book?" I do not even remember the jet taking off or the meal being served, but I do know I had the opportunity to share Christ with a young man who lived within five blocks of my former California residence. I was so caught up in my divine appointment that I left my *Letters to Malcolm* on the plane!

Divine appointments await us if we are obedient to God's leading. That was Philip's experience, and it can be ours.

IN TOUCH WITH THE GOSPEL (vv. 30-38)

Imagine how Philip's heart jumped when he saw the Ethiopian's entourage out there in the desert. It must have been an impressive caravan because the man was the secretary of the treasury for the Candace Dynasty of the kingdom of what was then known as Ethiopia (between the Egyptian city of Aswan and the Sudanese city of Khartoum, corresponding to the modern region called Nubia). The eunuch was a black man and therefore a Gentile. He had just completed a thousand-mile religious pilgrimage to Jerusalem and had a searching heart. Evidently while in Ethiopia he had come under the influence of Judaism and had gone to Jerusalem to become either a proselyte or a near proselyte. Most commentators feel he was probably a full proselyte because he had a copy of the Scriptures, which were then difficult to obtain.

In any event, he was a noble man on a noble search. As he traveled along in his chariot, he was reading Isaiah 53:7-8 aloud (as was the universal practice in the ancient world). And suddenly there stood Philip, God's hitchhiker. "Have Spirit, will travel."

Philip was so much in touch with the Spirit and God's Word that what followed came naturally.

> *The Spirit told Philip, "Go to that chariot and stay near it." Then Philip ran up to the chariot and heard the man reading Isaiah the prophet. "Do you understand what you are reading?" Philip asked. "How can I," he said, "unless someone explains it to me?" So he invited Philip to come up and sit with him. The eunuch was reading this passage of Scripture: "He was led like a sheep to the slaughter, and as a lamb before the shearer is silent, so he did not open his mouth. In his humiliation he was deprived of justice. Who can speak of his descendants? For his life was taken from the earth." The eunuch asked Philip, "Tell me, please, who is the prophet talking about, himself or someone else?" Then Philip began with that very passage of Scripture and told him the good news about Jesus. (vv. 29-35)*

Note that final phrase: "Philip began with that very passage of Scripture and told him the good news about Jesus." There is perhaps no better place in the Old Testament from which to preach Jesus. No doubt Philip took the man through all twelve verses of Isaiah 53, describing his royal lineage, the Incarnation, the vicarious atonement. "We all, like sheep, have gone astray, each of us has turned to his own way; and the LORD has laid on him the iniquity of us all." I am sure Philip explained about the suffering and resurrected Messiah — and what he said was absolutely revolutionizing. Dr. Longenecker says, "A doctrine of a suffering Messiah was unheard of and considered unthinkable in first-century Jewish religious circles."[3] Undoubtedly Philip quoted other Scriptures as well (Psalm 22; 34; 69; 118; Isaiah 42 — 44; 49; 50), and the two men examined them together. Only the angels know how long they rode in the chariot. But we know that the Ethiopian was convinced and marvelously converted!

The principle here is clear: all of us are called to be in touch with the Spirit and with the gospel. All of us should be able to explain Christ from the Scriptures. Unfortunately, too few can do so.

Meanwhile, the eunuch was not only convinced — he wanted to take the next step.

> *As they traveled along the road, they came to some water and the eunuch said, "Look, here is water. Why shouldn't I be baptized?" Philip said, "If you believe with all your heart, you may." The official answered, "I believe that Jesus Christ is the Son of God." And he gave orders to stop the chariot. Then both Philip and the eunuch went down into the water and Philip baptized him. (vv. 36-38)*

As a proselyte or near proselyte, the Ethiopian knew that baptism was the expected external symbol for a Gentile's repentance and conversion. Maybe Philip even ended his explanation of the gospel with an appeal for baptism like Peter did at Pentecost. For whatever reason, a memorable baptismal service took place in that ancient desert setting while the eunuch's dark-hued attendants looked on. Luke concludes that narrative in verses 39-40:

> *When they came up out of the water, the Spirit of the Lord suddenly took Philip away, and the eunuch did not see him again, but went on his way rejoicing. Philip, however, appeared at Azotus and traveled about, preaching the gospel in all the towns until he reached Caesarea.*

The result of Philip's Samaritan ministry was "great joy" (v. 8), and here the Ethiopian "went on his way rejoicing" (v. 39). The touch of God produces genuine joy! Philip disappeared, but he was not missed, for the black man now had Christ! Irenaeus says this man became the first missionary to the Ethiopians, and it may well be true. He certainly would not have been able to keep his merriment to himself!

IN TOUCH WITH PEOPLE

Reportedly a man stood up in one of D. L. Moody's meetings and said, "I have been for five years on the Mount of Transfiguration." "How many souls have you won to Christ?" was the sharp question that came from Moody in an instant. "Well, I do not know." "Have you won any?" persisted Moody. "I do not know that I have," answered the man. "Well," said Moody, "sit down then. When a man gets so high that he cannot reach down and save others, there is something wrong." It does little good to be in touch with the Spirit and the Word if we are not in touch with people.

If Philip had not loved people with Christ's love, he would never have reached across the substantial barriers between Samaritans and Jews. It was the same with the Gentile Ethiopian. Philip loved Jews, Samaritans, Gentiles, whites, blacks — it made no difference. He was in touch with people and genuinely cared about them.

George MacDonald wrote:

> *I said: "Let me walk in the field."*
> *He said: "No, walk in the town."*
> *I said: "There are no flowers there."*
> *He said: "No flowers, but a crown."*

I said: "But the skies are black;
There is nothing but noise and din."
And he wept as he sent me back —
"There is more," he said;
"There is sin."

I said: "But the air is thick,
And fogs are veiling the sun."
He answered, "Yet souls are sick,
And souls in the dark undone!"

I said: "I shall miss the light,
And friends will miss me, they say."
He answered: "Choose tonight
If I am to miss you or they."

I pleaded for time to be given.
He said: "Is it hard to decide?
It will not seem so hard in Heaven
To have followed the steps of your Guide."

I cast one look at the fields,
Then set my face to the town;
He said, "My child, do you yield?
Will you leave the flowers for the crown?"

Then into his hand went mine;
And into my heart came He;
And I walk in a light divine,
The path I had feared to see.

God's path leads to people!

The book of Acts gives us a glimpse of the dawn of Philip's ministry and a rather extended look at the great high noon of his service for Christ. It also provides us with a brief peek at his life near sunset.

> *Leaving the next day, we reached Caesarea and stayed at the house of Philip the evangelist, one of the Seven. He had four unmarried daughters who prophesied. (21:8-9)*

Twenty years have now passed, and Philip's stellar ministry has faded from prominence but not from obedience and faithfulness. His four gifted daughters are testimonies to that. As the shadows lengthened with the years, Philip the deacon remained in touch with the Spirit, in touch with the Word, and in touch with people and so continued to be the touch of God to others. Paul and Luke found rest and restoration under his favored roof.

> *The righteous will flourish like a palm tree, they will grow like a cedar in Lebanon; planted in the house of the LORD, they will flourish in the courts of our God. They will still bear fruit in old age, they will stay fresh and green. (Psalm 92:12-14)*

To bring a touch of the Master's hand to those around us, we must:

1. *Daily yield to the Spirit's guidance*, remembering that he guides in many different ways.
2. *Understand and proclaim the gospel* — the old, old story of God's gracious rescue of repentant sinners.
3. *Love people with God's love.*

PRAYER

O Lord, may we each be full of the Spirit, full of the gospel, full of your compassion for people — sinners who need a Savior. May we each bear your touch today and in days to come! Please help us to be channels of your grace to all those around us. Thank you for your willingness to use us to reach others. In Jesus' name, Amen.

15

Saul: The Hunter Hunted

ACTS 9:1-18

Richard Connell, in his famous story *The Most Dangerous Game*, tells about the adventure of his hero, Sanger Rainsford, one of the world's most celebrated big-game hunters. Rainsford accidentally falls from his speeding yacht at night while en route to a hunting expedition along the coast of South America. He is a strong swimmer and manages to beach himself on a foreboding island. Rainsford knows the island is inhabited because he has heard shots during the night. To his complete amazement he finds a palatial chateau inhabited by a Russian nobleman, General Zaroff, and his servant. The general recognizes his visitor's name and welcomes him warmly because he too is a big-game hunter. Rainsford is pleased with his good fortune — until the formal dinner that evening when during the conversation the general announces that he is hunting a "new animal" on the island.

When Rainsford inquires as to the identity of this "new animal," the general answers, "It supplies me with the most exciting hunting in the world. No other hunting compares with it for an instant. Every day I hunt, and I never grow bored now, for I have a quarry with which I can match my wits."

When Rainsford's face shows great bewilderment, the general explains, "I wanted the ideal animal to hunt. So I said: 'What are the attributes of an ideal quarry?' And the answer was, of course, 'It must have courage, cunning, and, above all, it must be able to reason.'"

"But no animal can reason," Rainsford protests.

"My dear fellow," the general responds, "there is one that can."

"But you cannot mean —" Rainsford exclaims.

"And why not?"

"I cannot believe you are serious, General Zaroff. This is a grisly joke."

"Why should I not be serious? I am speaking of hunting."

To his growing horror, Sanger Rainsford, the great hunter, learns that *he* is Zaroff's intended game.[1] *The hunter has become the hunted.*

On an infinitely higher level, that is what Acts 9 is all about. There too the pursuer became the prey. Saul, a fierce persecutor of the church of Christ, discovered first to his horror and then to his eternal delight that he, the hunter, was also the hunted. For all of us who are Christ's, the story in Acts 9 is a picture of how we came to be his. As we study Saul's experience, we will learn how the divine hunt is conducted. We will see the interior workings of God's providence and will be filled with hope and joy.

HUNTING THE HUNTER (vv. 1-2)

The story begins with a description of the hunter and his prey:

> *Meanwhile, Saul was still breathing out murderous threats against the Lord's disciples. He went to the high priest and asked him for letters to the synagogues in Damascus, so that if he found any there who belonged to the Way, whether men or women, he might take them as prisoners to Jerusalem. (vv. 1-2)*

The hunter's quarry, according to our text, were those "who belonged to the Way" — believers who long before they were called Christians were called "the Way." This was beautifully fitting because Christ had said, "I am the way and the truth and the life" (John 14:6). These early followers of the Lord Jesus Christ were the hunted — targets of Saul's murderous hatred!

Saul, the hunter, was a brutal, implacable, bloody man. His goal was nothing short of the complete extermination of the Way! Verse 1 ("breathing out murderous threats against the Lord's disciples") literally reads, "*breathing in* threats and murder." "Threatening and slaughter had come to be the very breath that Saul breathed, like a warhorse who sniffed the smell of battle."[2] He was a frightening, violent enemy. Paul later described his behavior to Agrippa by saying:

> *"I too was convinced that I ought to do all that was possible to oppose the name of Jesus of Nazareth. And that is just what I did in Jerusalem. On the authority of the chief priests I put many of the saints in prison, and when they were put to death, I cast my vote against them. Many a time I went from one synagogue to another to*

have them punished, and I tried to force them to blaspheme. In my obsession against them, I even went to foreign cities to persecute them." (26:9-11)

He was a callous, self-righteous, bigoted murderer set on a full-scale inquisition. Soon Jerusalem could not hold him. He sought and received extradition papers from the Sanhedrin so he could go to Damascus and ravage the growing Christian community there as well. It was 150 miles to Damascus (about a week's travel), but he would have traveled a month for the privilege. Saul the hunter! Saul the man of blood! Yet this persecutor, by the grace of God, became an apostle of Jesus Christ.

The story of Saul's spiritual transformation ought to remind us never to write anyone off as being beyond the love of Christ. We may do so with relatives whom we know have heard the Word for years without response, or a sinner who has gone to a crass level of depravity, or someone who has gone into a cult or is propagating false doctrine. But Scripture is clear — God can reach anyone!

The workings of the divine hunter are subtle and profound. As Saul set out on his bloodthirsty hunt, he, unknowingly, was the hunted. The Hound of Heaven was tracking him down just as surely as the persecutor was tracking down God's saints. God was still at work.

We know from Acts 26 that Jesus said to Saul at the time of his conversion, "It is hard for you to kick against the goads" (v. 14). A goad was a stick with which one poked an ox to get him moving. Sometimes an ox would kick up its heels at the stick — a futile endeavor. Jesus was saying, "Saul, your kicking against the interior workings of the Spirit of God is pointless." These goads included Stephen who prayed for his murderers — "Lord, do not hold this sin against them" — and the men and women who bravely refused to deny their Lord, suffering imprisonment and even death instead. Such goads kept poking the persecutor, and in moments of honesty he must have wondered whether his attacks on the Church were indeed just. "How can people suffer and die like this if they are believing and preaching a lie?" But Saul would kick against the goads and push the thoughts away. He knew something was wrong but was unwilling to examine himself or repent. He was oppressed by guilt but silenced his conscience by giving himself even further to his terrible pursuit.

That fateful day on the Damascus Road it was midday, the time for the traditional Middle-Eastern siesta. But Saul was so bent on destruction that he had no time for a nap. He had no idea of what was about to occur: the hunter was being hunted, and the interior assaults of God's grace were softening him for the final onslaught. The Hound of Heaven was at hand.

CAPTURED BY CHRIST (vv. 3-9)

Saul's destiny was about to change as he approached Damascus, a beautiful white city on a green plain. There was a blinding flash, and suddenly Saul was quivering and lying in the dirt. "Saul, Saul, why do you persecute me?" The voice began with the traditional formal double intonation of his name. But Saul did not know who was speaking to him. He did not know what was going on. "Who are you, Lord?" (*Lord* was a term of respect — "Who are you, sir?") The voice's response hit home like a bolt of lightning: "I am Jesus, whom you are persecuting" (v. 5). Jesus' words triggered an ongoing explosion within the young persecutor.

At least two things burst on Saul's conscience. First, *Jesus Christ was alive!* Verse 17 of our text, as well as 1 Corinthians 15:8, indicates that Saul actually saw Christ. Later he would present this vision as part of his apostolic credentials. Everything in Saul's life had opposed this, but now he knew Christ was alive, and if Christ were alive . . .

Second, Saul now knew he was not merely attacking those belonging to the Way — *he was persecuting Christ.* He now understood the spiritual unity between the Savior and the saints. This truth was at once terrible and wonderful, but Saul was at first overwhelmed by its terror.

While Saul lay prostrate, the voice instructed him, "Now get up and go into the city, and you will be told what you must do" (v. 6). Luke goes on to describe the situation:

> *The men traveling with Saul stood there speechless; they heard the sound but did not see anyone. Saul got up from the ground, but when he opened his eyes he could see nothing. So they led him by the hand into Damascus. For three days he was blind, and did not eat or drink anything. (vv. 7-9)*

The great hunter who was going to wreak havoc on the Damascus church entered Damascus led by the hand — blind, weak, impotent. Saul was frightened and in despair. This was the midnight of his soul. His physical blindness paralleled his spiritual sightlessness.

Though he was blind, he had seen Christ, and as he saw Christ he also saw himself for the first time. His life was utterly wrong. He was a criminal before God. As he wrote later, "Nothing good lives in me" (Romans 7:18). As Christ's enemy, he had drawn blood, and now darkness was everywhere, especially within his own soul. The hunter had been hunted down. There was no escape.

What do we learn from all this? Primarily that *Christ is always the initiator.* He still seeks sinners today, just as in preparatory grace he exposed

Saul to the faith and courage of Stephen and the Way. We can never be sure in whom this grace is working, but we know that God always makes the first move. We search for him only in response to his prior advance. Jesus orchestrated the Damascus confrontation, and he directs our encounters as well.

Francis Thomson's early life was one dead end after another. He studied for the priesthood but did not complete the course. He studied medicine but failed. He joined the military but was released after one day. He finally became an opium addict in London. But he could not get away from God's persistent love for him. In the midst of his despondency Thomson was befriended by an associate who saw his poetic gifts, and eventually Thomson was able to share his experience in verse. His famous poem is, of course, *The Hound of Heaven*, which Coventry Patmore has called one of the finest odes in the English language. Many of us have experienced the truth of Thomson's powerful words:

I fled Him, down the nights and down the days;
I fled Him, down the arches of the years;
I fled Him, down the labyrinthine ways
Of my own mind; and in the mist of tears
I hid from Him, and under running laughter.
Up vistaed hopes, I sped;
And shot, precipitated
Down Titanic glooms of chasmed fears,
From those strong Feet that followed, followed after.

Christ is always the Hunter and the initiator. He brings us to our knees, acknowledging how desperately we need him. If there was ever anyone who had come to the end of himself, who was truly "poor in spirit," it was Saul. "But whatever was to my profit I now consider loss for the sake of Christ" (Philippians 3:7).

Have we been brought to the end of our resources? Have we ever been completely helpless unless the Lord intervened? Have we ever given up and given in to Christ? Our Damascus Roads are generally less dramatic than Saul's, but they are meant to have the same effect — to break our compulsive independence and arrogance and to bring us to Christ for salvation or reconsecration. Our Damascus Roads are meant to convey our emptiness and the greatness of Christ. Have we gotten the message?

Furthermore, *the Hunter chooses us!* The Lord told Ananias, "This man [Saul] is my chosen instrument to carry my name" (9:15), and Saul would gladly proclaim Christ for the rest of his life. He marveled at the splendors of God's grace, and so do we.

> *He chose us in him before the creation of the world to be holy and blameless in his sight. In love he predestined us to be adopted as his sons. (Ephesians 1:4-5)*

Lewis saw this clearly in his own conversion:

> I did not then see what is now the most shining and obvious thing; the Divine humility which will accept a convert even on such terms. The Prodigal Son at least walked home on his own feet. But who can duly adore that Lord which will open the high gates to a prodigal who is brought in kicking, struggling, resentful, and darting his eyes in every direction for a chance of escape? The words *compelle intrare*, compel them to come in, have been so abused by wicked men that we shudder at them; but, properly understood, they plumb the depth of the Divine mercy. The hardness of God is kinder than the softness of men, and his compulsion is our liberation.[3]

That final line is my favorite: "The hardness of God is kinder than the softness of men, and his compulsion is our liberation." The inner workings of God's preparatory grace touch our lives in ways we are sometimes not even aware of — appropriate words spoken here and there, pressures or lack of pressures, joys, sorrows — subtle workings orchestrated by the divine Hunter. Finally our vistas are opened, and we see! He brings us to the end of ourselves, and we have the joy of being the Hunter's prize.

CARED FOR BY THE HUNTED (vv. 10-19)

Those traveling with Saul finally gained their composure and led Saul by the hand into Damascus, where an amazing thing happened. The hunted do not usually minister to the hunter. Normally that would be as crazy as Peter Rabbit caring for Mr. McGregor or Golda Meir nursing Adolf Eichmann. But this is exactly what happened in Saul's case.

> *In Damascus there was a disciple named Ananias. The Lord called to him in a vision, "Ananias!" "Yes, Lord," he answered. The Lord told him, "Go to the house of Judas on Straight Street and ask for a man from Tarsus named Saul, for he is praying. In a vision he has seen a man named Ananias come and place his hands on him to restore his sight." (vv. 10-12)*

I can imagine Ananias listening to the Lord and responding affirmatively, then asking a question or two. "Go to Straight Street . . . Okay, Lord

. . . A man from Tarsus? Fine . . . Saul? *The* Saul? The guy who has been tearing up the church? Lord, are you sure . . . ?"

> *"Lord," Ananias answered, "I have heard many reports about this man and all the harm he has done to your saints in Jerusalem. And he has come here with authority from the chief priests to arrest all who call on your name." (vv. 13-14)*

This believer's fears were understandable, but the Lord's answer was good enough for him:

> *"Go! This man is my chosen instrument to carry my name before the Gentiles and their kings and before the people of Israel. I will show him how much he must suffer for my name." (vv. 15-16)*

Spiritual usefulness and honor go hand in hand with suffering. Both were part of the Hunter's plan for Saul — and for us. Ananias probably left his house with trepidation, but to his credit he obeyed. And as had happened with Philip the deacon, Ananias' obedience made him party to a great work of God.

"Then Ananias went to the house and entered it. Placing his hands on Saul, he said, 'Brother Saul . . .'" (v. 17). The angels must have sung when they heard these words of forgiveness. Ananias probably knew some young women who had been widowed by Saul. Perhaps some of his friends had been orphaned by Saul's bloodbath or had been killed themselves. But Ananias (whose name means "God is gracious") forgave him. Because the two men were brothers in Christ, they were parts of the same body. With his hands on Saul, Ananias said:

> *"Brother Saul, the Lord — Jesus, who appeared to you on the road as you were coming here — has sent me so that you may see again and be filled with the Holy Spirit." Immediately, something like scales fell from Saul's eyes, and he could see again. He got up and was baptized. (vv. 17-18)*

Ananias is one of the obscure heroes of the Church. We never hear of him again, though he did a great work. Who remembers who led D. L. Moody to Christ? Who knows the name of the person who pointed Jim Elliot to the Way? How many know the name of the one who led Billy Graham to the Lord? The Hunter knows, and that is enough.

The physical scales falling to the ground mirrored Saul's spiritual transformation — all things had become new. The eyes of Saul's heart had been enlightened. The one who had persecuted Christ by hating his people now belonged to Christ — forever.

JOINING THE HUNT (vv. 20-22)

> *At once he began to preach in the synagogues that Jesus is the Son of God. All those who heard him were astonished and asked, "Isn't he the man who raised havoc in Jerusalem among those who call on this name? And hasn't he come here to take them as prisoners to the chief priests?" Yet Saul grew more and more powerful and baffled the Jews living in Damascus by proving that Jesus is the Christ. (vv. 20-22)*

Saul was now a mighty hunter for God! Instead of exhaling threats and murder, he helped men and women find life in Jesus Christ. Instead of incarceration, he brought liberation. What a miracle!

When we read about Sanger Rainsford's discovery that he, the celebrated hunter, was now the hunted, our skin crawls at the horror of such a discovery. Not so with the divine Hunter, for his is a joyous, life-giving hunt. On our own we would never have found peace or purpose. But praise God, he brought others along to minister his grace to us. And now he gives us the privilege of participating in the Great Hunt to reach others.

All around us miracles are waiting to happen. We must never write anyone off. We must be like Ananias, willing to be the life-giving ambassadors of God. We must be like Saul-become-Paul, pursuing the world for the Lord Jesus Christ.

PRAYER

> *O Lord, thank you for hunting us down and bringing us into your kingdom. And thank you that now we can hunt others, showing them their desperate need because of their sin, and telling them the good news of forgiveness and salvation and life through Jesus Christ. Thank you for the miracle that has happened in our lives and for the miracles that are about to happen all around us. In Jesus' name, Amen.*

16

Saul's Preparation for Ministry

ACTS 9:19-30

Once Saul had done a 180-degree turnabout, instead of persecuting Christ, he began proclaiming him.

> *Saul spent several days with the disciples in Damascus. At once he began to preach in the synagogues that Jesus is the Son of God. (vv. 19-20)*

Saul did not know much Christian theology, but one thing he knew for sure: "Jesus is the Son of God."

> *All those who heard him were astonished and asked, "Isn't he the man who raised havoc in Jerusalem among those who call on this name? And hasn't he come here to take them as prisoners to the chief priests?" (v. 21)*

The people were "ecstatic" — the literal translation of the word "astonished" (*ekstasis*) in verse 21. The characteristic glow of fresh conversion radiated from Saul, and it was (as it always is) a thrilling wonder to behold. "Come hear Dr. Saul of Tarsus — the great Gamaliel's protégé. Converted Pharisee tells all!" His immense intellect, his razor-sharp lawyer's mind, and his Pharisee's knowledge of the holy scrolls made him, though a novice, a formidable enemy. "Saul grew more and more powerful and baffled the Jews living in Damascus by proving that Jesus is the Christ" (v. 22).

Every Christian goes through three stages: "This is easy!" — "This is difficult!" — "This is impossible!" Saul was in the first stage. If we had been there in Damascus, we would probably have told him, "Saul, you are the hottest thing to hit Damascus since Alexander the Great. So get going!

We will be praying for you." But Saul was not yet ready for front-line ministry. In fact, the Lord had a long program of preparation in store for him — longer than he or we would have ever imagined. Saul's impressive abilities and background, even combined with a dramatic conversion experience, did not qualify him for ministry. God still had some work to do to get him ready for what lay ahead.

More or less the last half of chapter 9 shows us how God prepared Saul for service, highlighting three essentials of that preparation — and thus illustrating how he prepares us as well. The first step is found between verses 22 and 23 — *between* because in Galatians 1:15-18, which covers the same period as Acts 9, Paul tells us that he went away for three years immediately after his conversion:

> *But when God, who set me apart from birth and called me by his grace, was pleased to reveal his Son in me so that I might preach him among the Gentiles, I did not consult any man, nor did I go up to Jerusalem to see those who were apostles before I was, but I went immediately into Arabia and later returned to Damascus. Then after three years, I went up to Jerusalem to get acquainted with Peter and stayed with him fifteen days.*

Most interpreters believe that this three years in Arabia and Damascus came between verses 22 and 23 because the opening phrase of verse 23, "After many days had gone by," seems to be a reference to that period of time.

PREPARING FOR SERVICE BY SPENDING TIME ALONE WITH GOD (vv. 22-23)

The first step in God's preparation of Saul was a lonely stint in the Arabian wilderness. Specifically, this was the Sinai wilderness.

> What associations the place must have had for Saul! Under the shadow of Sinai the great lawgiver of the people to whom he also belonged, had spent forty years of preparation for service. . . . Moreover, it was from that same district that the next outstanding figure in the history of the people, Elijah the prophet, had suddenly appeared. These two, Moses and Elijah, the great lawgiver and the great reformer, had spoken upon the mount with Jesus . . . and these men had received the training of the desert for their ministry among the multitudes.[1]

There is divine poetry here. At Sinai Moses received the Law. Now at Sinai Saul learns about grace. The first step in Saul's preparation took place on the backside of the desert. The usual approach today is to promote a famous convert's testimony, not to send him off for in-depth spiritual grounding.

A number of years ago, when I was a youth pastor, word came to me from one of the large churches in my area that the last living member of the Bonnie and Clyde gang, Big Jim Harrington, had been giving his testimony to standing-room-only crowds with amazing results. So I made the arrangements for him to speak at our church. I arranged for special music, had several thousand handbills printed and distributed at the local high schools, and enlisted counselors. The night arrived, and it went beyond our expectations — a sea of teenagers.

Big Jim was unbelievable — an imposing man about eighty years old with tattoos on the back of his hands and an indentation atop his bald head from an old bullet wound. For two hours he regaled us with powerful stories of his wasted life with Clyde Barrow. He poignantly exhorted us not to waste our youth and urged us to commit our lives to Christ. Everyone was thrilled. The elders who had been reticent congratulated us on the service. I was very satisfied and a little smug — until two days later when I received a call from Big Jim's agent, who told me he had just learned that Big Jim was an imposter, that in fact he was a well-meaning alcoholic who lived with his daughter out in the desert and suffered delusions about his uneventful past. Gulp! I learned a major lesson from that experience!

The promotion of famous converts is not infrequent. Sometimes it works out, as in the case of Charles Colson. Sometimes it does not. In 1 Timothy 3:6 Paul warns about promoting a new believer to a position of responsibility: "He must not be a new convert, or he may become conceited [literally, "become wrapped up in smoke" — with his own glory] and fall under the same judgment as the devil." The natural plan for Saul would have been *promotion*. God's plan was *seclusion*.

Saul's time in Arabia is shrouded with mystery, but we can reasonably ascertain something of what transpired. His two questions as he lay on the Damascus Road often accompany new faith: "Who are you, Lord?" — "What shall I do, Lord?" (Acts 22:8, 10). In answering these questions we find out who God is and, by implication, who we are and what we are meant to do. Saul undoubtedly received divine instruction along these lines during his time with Christ.

The first thing Saul learned was *who Jesus is*. He was already convinced that Jesus Christ is the Son of God, but in Arabia the depth of that truth undoubtedly broke over his soul in wave after refreshing wave. Jesus had prayed in his high-priestly prayer, "Now this is eternal life: that they may know you, the only true God, and Jesus Christ, whom you have sent" (John 17:3). Now that prayer was being answered for Saul. Saul's experience of knowing Christ filled him with such a thirst for more that he later wrote, "I want to know Christ and the power of his resurrection and the fellowship of sharing in his sufferings, becoming like him in his death" (Philippians 3:10).

Jesus, I am resting, resting
In the joy of what Thou art;
I am finding out the greatness
Of Thy loving heart.

Christ's explicit declaration, "I am Jesus, whom you are persecuting," had brought Saul to a new understanding. Christ so identified with his people that when they were persecuted, *he* was persecuted. He was a vulnerable God. This made the cross more understandable to Saul. Jesus truly did suffer for the world's sins at Golgotha. Saul's heart soared in responsive love.

The second thing Saul learned was *who he was*. Whenever we truly see God, we truly see ourselves, just as Isaiah did when he saw the thrice holy God "seated on a throne, high and exalted, and the train of his robe filled the temple" (6:1). He cried in response, "Woe to me! I am ruined! For I am a man of unclean lips" (6:5). He saw himself as he was, as God saw him. Saul needed the same experience. He needed to get over being Saul.

He was named after King Saul, Israel's very first king. He was proud of being a Benjamite because they were always the tribe that went into battle first. A frequently used battle cry was, "After you, O Benjamin!" Saul was also "a Hebrew of Hebrews" (Philippians 3:5) — a Pharisee and the son of a Pharisee. Because he had outdistanced his contemporaries, he was a proud man. He needed to get over that, and he did.

As we follow Saul's life we see that he preferred the name Paul (*Paulos*), which means "small." He was now yoked to Christ for service, and Christ had said, "Take my yoke upon you and learn from me, for I am gentle and humble in heart" (Matthew 11:29). Saul learned the humility of Christ's yoke. Alan Redpath once said, "When God wants us to do an impossible task, God takes an impossible man and crushes him," and that is what happened to Saul-become-Paul. God always takes us to the end of ourselves before he uses us!

The third thing Saul learned is *what God wanted him to do*. He learned that he was chosen to be a mighty hunter for God — a supreme missionary mastermind and an apologist par excellence. However, Saul would not only climb mountains but also endure pain. Jesus had told Ananias that he would show Saul "how much he must suffer for my name" (v. 16). "Who is weak, and I do not feel weak? Who is led into sin, and I do not inwardly burn?" (2 Corinthians 11:29).

Saul was prepared for effective service through the time he spent alone with God. If we want to serve God, we too must spend time with him. God may not ask us to seclude ourselves for years or even months of preparation, but we must be with him one on one. Moses spent forty years learning to think he was someone, forty more years learning who he really was (in the same desert where God later discipled Saul), and only then forty years serving profitably. Jesus spent eighteen years preparing for three years of ministry, and at the beginning of the three years, forty days alone with the Father. We need to retreat regularly — often daily — to commune with God and be prepared by him to accomplish his purposes for us.

We must remember that preparation for service does not happen overnight. It takes time to brew good coffee — and to grow to maturity. The Lord is never in a hurry. He is building us for eternity. Sometimes he has to bench us. Such times can be lonely and painful, but they can also lead to greater service. As Lloyd Ogilvie has commented:

> When I look to those times out of the mainstream of what I thought the Lord was doing, I can see that I was being better prepared for fast-moving currents which later carried me on the high seas of adventure and effectiveness. The Lord will not use us until he has made us ready. Then we thank him for knowing what he is doing.[2]

Saul had now received his D.D. (Dr. of the Desert) and was moving toward effective service. But there were more steps in his preparation.

PREPARING FOR SERVICE BY A DOSE OF MINISTERIAL REALITY (vv. 23-25)

> *After many days had gone by, the Jews conspired to kill him, but Saul learned of their plan. Day and night they kept close watch on the city gates in order to kill him. But his followers took him by night and lowered him in a basket through an opening in the wall.*

Saul's ministry in Damascus met such resistance that the Jews, in league with their Arab governor (as 2 Corinthians 11:32 tells us), hid at the city gates in ambush. Saul escaped only because someone in the church had a home on the city walls, so that he could be let down the walls in a basket in the dead of night.

Though in a way this may have been exciting for Saul (as Churchill once said, "Nothing is so exhilarating as to be shot at without result"), it was also humiliating. In 2 Corinthians 11:30-33 Saul associates this experience with weakness:

> *If I must boast, I will boast of the things that show my weakness. The God and Father of the Lord Jesus, who is to be praised forever, knows that I am not lying. In Damascus the governor under King Aretas had the city of the Damascenes guarded in order to arrest me. But I was lowered in a basket through a window in the wall and slipped through his hands.*

Saul blew into town after being one-on-one with God in Sinai like some spiritual Rip Van Winkle (see Galatians 1:17). He had spent plenty of quality time with the Lord, he was rarin' to go, and yet his ministry almost immediately met with stiff resistance. Damascus did not lie down before him ready for revival, and Saul (who had been one of the seventy top rulers of Israel) had to vamoose in a basket! It was humiliating. What happened? Why did this happen to Saul at this time?

Apart from the fact that the Jews in Damascus were just plain ornery and the gospel is offensive, constant success would have made Saul insufferable, especially at the beginning of his ministry. If goals had been reached too easily, he would have never written marvelously encouraging passages like, "We have this treasure in jars of clay to show that this all-surpassing power is from God and not from us" (2 Corinthians 4:7).

I once had a great plan. I shared it with a number of people, and everybody told me it sounded great. So I put it to work, and it failed miserably. Everybody knew that it had failed, and I was humiliated. So I called a friend and asked him if we could talk. We met in a restaurant, and he said to me, "I am glad this happened to you. If you had succeeded in this, you would have become impossible. You would have gone around and told everybody else how to do it. You would have probably franchised it!" Those were the wounds of a friend (see Proverbs 27:6)!

Someone has wisely said, "God ruthlessly perfects those he royally elects." This is true without exception! Our humiliating failures can become marvelous preparation for greater service, if we let God use them in that way.

PREPARING FOR SERVICE THROUGH OTHER BELIEVERS' CARE FOR US (vv. 26-30)

> *When he came to Jerusalem, he tried to join the disciples, but they were all afraid of him, not believing that he really was a disciple. (v. 26)*

This was perfectly understandable, but it must have been crushing for Saul. A glorious conversion and three years of preparation, then ministerial frustration, and now, even worse, rejection by the mother church. What next!

"But Barnabas . . ." (v. 27). Barnabas saved the day.

> *But Barnabas took him and brought him to the apostles. He told them how Saul on his journey had seen the Lord and that the Lord had spoken to him, and how in Damascus he had preached fearlessly in the name of Jesus. So Saul stayed with them and moved about freely in Jerusalem, speaking boldly in the name of the Lord. (vv. 27-28)*

Barnabas, "the son of encouragement," threw caution to the wind, sought Saul, heard him out, and was convinced of the genuineness of his faith. This was the beginning of a lifelong friendship. The Greek implies that Barnabas took Saul by the hand and led him among the apostles. "Hey, men, he's for real! It's all right, Philip — you can come out from under the bed." Barnabas was an interceder, a reconciler, an enabler. He was able to forgive and put aside the past — to trust Saul despite his past sins and dangers. Sometimes we Christians are evangelical in our theology and yet distrust others. But not Barnabas! He believed the best of others.

I had the privilege of working under a man for ten years who never said anything bad or critical about anyone else. I was once in his office when he had been grievously slandered by someone, and I let him know what I thought about the person who did it. To my amazement he began to quietly defend the person — "She's been under a lot of strain. I do not think she understood the situation." How wonderful and God-honoring is the Barnabas syndrome. May his tribe increase!

The result of Barnabas' care, according to Galatians 1:18-19, was that Saul got to know James, the Lord's brother, and spent two weeks at Peter's place. Just think of the healing and encouragement that came out of this. We are often prepared for effective service by the counsel and care of other believers.

How beautiful is the ministry of Barnabas — giving a word of encouragement, confirming others' gifts, reconciling believers with believers, taking a risk for Christ in human relationships, promoting the ministry of others, rejoicing in another's success. God mightily uses men and women like Barnabas for his glory!

Verses 28-30 tell us how Saul's ministry was relaunched, and once again it was not smooth sailing.

> *So Saul stayed with them and moved about freely in Jerusalem, speaking boldly in the name of the Lord. He talked and debated with the Grecian Jews, but they tried to kill him. When the brothers learned of this, they took him down to Caesarea and sent him off to Tarsus.*

During Paul's ministry years, sometimes there were successes, sometimes there were failures, and sometimes there were quiet times. We do not hear from Saul again for eight to ten years — until Barnabas comes to Tarsus to ask him to help with the work in Antioch. But the foundation for ministry was well-laid, and Saul would eventually shake the world.

There are at least three applications from all this. First, *God does everything possible to do away with the energy of our human flesh in order to teach us that without him we can do nothing.* Whether this happens through a professional job situation, a death in the family, or some other failure or burden, we all come to the end of ourselves from time to time. God loves to renew and re-enable the person who comes to such a point. Dead end today — unlimited vistas tomorrow!

Second, *in the service of Christ no one is indispensable.* We may think we are the only ones who can fill a certain hole (pastoring a particular church, teaching an adult Sunday school class, directing a kids' program, training others for door-to-door evangelism, or whatever). A friend of mine used to say, "When you think you are indispensable, go stick your hand in a pail of water, then pull it out and see what kind of hole is left." The church will go on fine without you or me, and God sometimes lets us know that by putting us on the shelf for a while as he prepares us for further (and even greater) service.

Third, *it takes time to build a life that is eminently usable in the program of God.* Do not undervalue times out of the mainstream, times to recharge or rest or become further trained. In such times God prepares us for fast-moving currents that will take us to high seas of effectiveness.

PRAYER

> *O God, prepare us as you did Saul. May we accept with joy a similar work in our own lives, willingly allowing our Father in heaven to teach us, prepare us, mold us, protect us, humble us, and continually remind us how much we need him without whom we can do absolutely nothing. In Jesus' name, Amen.*

17

Peter's Preparation for Greater Ministry

ACTS 9:32 — 10:23

Nicolo Paganini, the great concert violinist, stood before a packed house, surrounded by a full orchestra. He played a number of difficult pieces, then came to one of his favorites, a violin concerto. Shortly after he was underway, as the Italian audience sat in rapt attention, one of the strings on his violin snapped. Relying on his genius, he improvised and played on the next three strings. Shortly thereafter a second string broke on his instrument. He again began to improvise and continued playing the piece. Almost at the end of the magnificent concerto, a third string snapped! Amazingly, he finished the piece on one string.

The audience stood to its feet and applauded until their hands were numb. They assumed the concert was over. But Paganini proceeded to play an encore with the full orchestra. He made more music out of one string than many violinists ever could on four. Paganini took what appeared to be a most difficult situation and turned it into a triumph. His attitude made all the difference.

No matter what we pursue in life — music, athletics, education, business, homemaking, politics — attitude is key. Nowhere is this more important than in the spiritual life. It is possible for dynamic events to occur in our lives only to have them neutralized by a wrong attitude about something or someone. Our perceptions and misconceptions, what we view as possible and impossible, our prejudices or lack of them, make an awesome difference.

This was certainly true in the life of the Apostle Peter. Having begun his spiritual pursuits full of well-intentioned but self-sufficient presumption ("Lord, though all forsake you, I will never forsake you. I will lay down my life for you"), Peter plunged to the depths of despair when he denied his

Lord three times the night before the crucifixion. But this resulted in spiritual progress because Peter learned firsthand the emptiness of fleshly dependence and the necessity and sufficiency of being filled with the Spirit. However, Peter was still by no means perfect, and one of his biggest imperfections was his attitude toward Gentiles.

Peter was heir to a strong tradition of prejudice that went clear back to Abraham and was exemplified in men like Jonah, who resisted bearing witness to the Gentiles and was actually angry with God when the Ninevites repented and escaped judgment. During Peter's time, Jewish midwives were forbidden to aid a Gentile woman in childbirth, for they would thereby help propagate Gentile scum. The tradition-minded Hebrew called Gentiles *goyim* ("the nations") and spat that word out with intense contempt. This attitude even permeated the Hebrew-Christian community.

Jesus had commissioned his disciples to go into all the world and preach the good news. His final words had instructed them to be witnesses "in Jerusalem, and in all Judea and Samaria, and to the ends of the earth." But somehow in running all this through their Jewish grids, they missed the point. Maybe some of them saw the mandate as meaning that the gospel would go to the Jews wherever in the world they might be. At any rate, six years after the cross the Christian movement remained distinctly Jewish.

In Peter's case, despite all of his love and devotion for Christ, his unfortunate attitude could have strangled his ministry and could have reduced Christianity to just another sect of Judaism. God could not allow that, so he began to help Peter develop a proper attitude toward the world — the *whole* world. This text has as much to say to us as it did to Peter and the apostles. The stakes are just as high today. How we look at those around us is crucial.

PREPARED BY PERSONAL EXPERIENCE (9:32-43)

Peter had two very positive ministry experiences that helped to turn his attitude around. The first, according to verses 32-35, was in the town of Lydda (today called Lod, at the site of the modern Tel Aviv airport) and involved a paralytic named Aeneas who had been a quadriplegic for eight years. Aeneas was fully familiar with the attendant problems of paralysis — the discomfort, the social restriction, the hygienic difficulties, the emotional depression. Evidently a believer, he made the acquaintance of Peter, who one day felt called to heal him, saying, "Aeneas, Jesus Christ heals you. Get up and take care of your mat" (v. 34). And Aeneas got up and made his bed! Charles Swindoll has said, "This was really power! Some of us for years have been saying, 'Arise and make your bed,' to our teenagers with no result!'" It was a great miracle. There is no other explanation.

The second miracle, described in verses 36-42, involved a woman in the nearby seaside town of Joppa (about ten miles from Lydda). Her Hebrew name was Tabitha, which means "gazelle," as does the Greek equivalent, Dorcas. Evidently the name fit her because she was a lovely, graceful, giving person who made garments for the needy. Her busy hands carried out the plans of a loving heart. But suddenly Dorcas became ill and died. Hoping for a miracle, the grieving church sent to Lydda for Peter, and they were not disappointed. Peter came, and with a prayer and a few words — "Tabitha, get up" (v. 40) — he presented her alive.

Peter had wonderfully positive ministry experiences back to back, and they became significant factors in shaping his attitude toward the world because these great successes occurred in Gentile settings. The miracles were performed on Jews among Jews, but the environments of the commercial centers of Lydda and Joppa were generally Gentile. God's power was operative through Peter in a pagan environment, among the *goyim*.

Interestingly, these successes were essentially duplicates of miracles Jesus had performed. The healing of Aeneas' paralysis was similar to that of the paralytic at Bethesda to whom the Savior said, "Get up! Pick up your mat and walk" (John 5:8). Regarding Dorcas' healing, Peter may have learned the procedure from Jesus' raising of Jairus' daughter as recorded in Mark 5 because when Peter arrived the people were making a commotion, just as others had done in Jairus' home. The apostle shut them all out of the room, just as Christ had done, and then said, "*Tabitha kumi*" ("Tabitha, get up"), which if you change one letter is the duplicate of Christ's words, "*Talitha kumi*" — "Little girl, get up" (Mark 5:41).

All of this taken together had a wonderfully softening effect on Peter's prejudice. He was doing Christ's work away from Jerusalem and in the midst of the defiling grit of Gentile culture. Positive experiences can go miles in rearranging attitudes. We have all seen a basketball team fall behind but suddenly get a couple of quick baskets and reverse the momentum. Spiritually too, key experiences can change our lives dramatically.

After this final miracle "Peter stayed in Joppa for some time with a tanner named Simon" (v. 43). The significance of this is that a tanner's place of business was anathema to a fastidious Jew. It was highly unpleasant and smelly, and animals were slain there. Tanners were ostracized and had to live fifty cubits outside of town. Rabbinical law stated that if a betrothed woman discovered that her fiancé was involved in tanning, she could break the engagement. However, Peter had met a Jewish tanner who loved Jesus, and he was willing to associate with him. God was at work in the impulsive apostle's heart. The old biases were wearing thin.

God has a way of softening our prejudices if we are the least bit willing to learn. Peter's attitude toward the world was mellowing. But a bigger change was still to come.

CHANGED BY PERSONAL REVELATION (10:1-23)

> *At Caesarea there was a man named Cornelius, a centurion in what was known as the Italian Regiment. He and all his family were devout and God-fearing; he gave generously to those in need and prayed to God regularly. (vv. 1-2)*

As a "centurion," Cornelius was a noncommissioned officer of the Roman army. Centurions were not high-ranking, but they did most of the work and were the backbone of the Roman legion, commanding from 300 to 600 men. Our text says Cornelius was "devout and God-fearing . . . and prayed to God regularly." As a typical Roman he had been exposed to the Roman gods — Jupiter, Augustus, Mars, Venus, etc. — but found they were not real and could do nothing for him. While stationed in Palestine, he had been exposed to the enlightened concepts of Judaism and had become devoutly monotheistic. As a result, he, a Roman soldier, gave offerings to benefit those in need among the Jewish people.

Was he a sinner? Yes. Outside the covenant? Certainly. A swine? No. He was a noble and spiritual-minded Roman army officer who was longing for the true God — "he and all his family." In response to the deep yearnings of this centurion's heart, God met Cornelius in a vision.

> *One day at about three in the afternoon he had a vision. He distinctly saw an angel of God, who came to him and said, "Cornelius!" Cornelius stared at him in fear. "What is it, Lord?" he asked. The angel answered, "Your prayers and gifts to the poor have come up as a memorial offering before God. Now send men to Joppa to bring back a man named Simon who is called Peter. He is staying with Simon the tanner, whose house is by the sea." (vv. 3-6)*

Cornelius' long service as a soldier had trained him to obey. So he immediately summoned his trusted servants and sent them to Joppa. What happened as a result was memorable, for God had divinely choreographed everything in his own unique way.

> *About noon the following day as they were on their journey and approaching the city, Peter went up on the roof to pray. He became hungry and wanted something to eat, and while the meal was being prepared, he fell into a trance. (vv. 9-10)*

The sun was reflecting off the Mediterranean Sea, and perhaps Peter's thoughts traveled across the sea as he wondered about the remotest parts of the earth. He fell into a "trance," and just as he did so, Cornelius' messengers came to the outskirts of town. What Peter saw in the vision was bizarre and inscrutable.

> *He saw heaven opened and something like a large sheet being let down to earth by its four corners. It contained all kinds of four-footed animals, as well as reptiles of the earth and birds of the air. Then a voice told him, "Get up, Peter. Kill and eat." "Surely not, Lord!" Peter replied. "I have never eaten anything impure or unclean." The voice spoke to him a second time, "Do not call anything impure that God has made clean." This happened three times, and immediately the sheet was taken back to heaven. (vv. 11-16)*

Among the variety of animals Peter saw were approved animals such as oxen, sheep, and doves, but also livestock forbidden to his people (the creatures in both categories are listed in Leviticus 11). Undoubtedly there were swine and perhaps a buzzard, an owl, a seagull, reptiles, lobsters, and four-footed winged insects. Peter found the picture all revolting — and the command to kill and eat shocked him even more, for he had always observed the basic dietary laws God had given to his people. Since Peter had never eaten anything that was not kosher, he balked at such an unholy smorgasbord! His protest was understandable in the light of his upbringing. Any serious Jew would have reacted in the same way.

Within the boundaries of the vision, it is doubtful that Peter understood the significance of the heavenly explanation: "Do not call anything impure that God has made clean." How could things that had been unclean for thousands of years suddenly be clean? Twice more the grotesque sheet descended, compounding Peter's misery and perplexity. We have all experienced the helpless horror of a nightmare. Imagine what this bizarre scene meant to this devoted apostle!

The four corners of the sheet in the vision correspond to the four points of the compass — north, south, east, and west. The sheet's contents indicate the swarming millions that populate the earth. Cornelius, all his soldiers, all his servants, all the Roman people, all other nations on the face of the earth — all mankind were bound up together in one loathsome bundle. And Peter was standing above them, surveying them all and spitting out revulsion and rejection.

Peter was about to see in living color his cold attitude toward the world — or at least toward non-Jews. Teeming millions were stone-blind spiritually, and yet Peter's callous reply was, "Surely not, Lord!" But once he really understood what it all meant, Peter would never forget this strange vision! In fact, he spoke of it over and over again.

It is easy to see what this attitude, left unchecked, would have done to the spread of the gospel. Large areas of the world would have been written off as beyond God's grace. All of us who are Gentile believers would still be without Christ! Dr. H. A. Ironside said that when his father died, this passage was running through his father's mind, and he kept repeating, "A great sheet and wild beasts, and . . . and . . . and . . ." When he could not get the words out, he started over but stalled once more at the same place. Finally a friend bent over and whispered, "John, it says, 'creeping things.'" "Oh yes," he said, "that is how I got in. Just a poor, good-for-nothing creeping thing, but I got in."[1] Without a change in apostolic attitudes, none of us would have heard the gospel of the love of Jesus Christ.

How does Peter's experience apply to us? No one has given a better answer than the peerless Alexander Whyte to his vast congregation at Free St. George's in Edinburgh:

> All so like ourselves. For, how we also bundle up whole nations of men and throw them into that same unclean sheet. Whole churches that we know nothing about but their bad names that we have given them, are in our sheet of excommunication also. All the other denominations of Christians in our land are common and unclean to us. Every party outside our own party in the political state also. We have no language contemptuous enough wherewith to describe their wicked ways and their self-seeking schemes. They are four-footed beasts and creeping things. Indeed, there are very few men alive, and especially those who live near us, who are not sometimes in the sheet of our scorn; unless it is one here and one there of our own family, or school, or party. And they also come under our scorn and our contempt the moment they have a mind of their own, and interests of their own, and affections and ambitions of their own.[2]

We too write off whole churches simply by what we have heard about them. We too shut out whole ethnic groups because of a bad experience with one person or family. We too mentally excommunicate those who do not agree with us on one secondary issue or another. Our sheets easily fill with educational, racial, cultural, and spiritual rejects, and we cry, "By no means, Lord — they are not my type!" The result, of course, is a Christianity that grows solely on homogeneous lines. We then only seek to win our own kind, and thousands never come to grace who, humanly speaking, would have if they were given the chance.

The tragedy is compounded by the fact that, like Peter, we can have these unacceptable attitudes even while generally being in fellowship with Christ. Remember, Peter was praying when he had this vision. He had a beautiful attitude toward God but a lousy one toward the world! If we do not respond to Christ's prodding and let him change our heart attitudes, our relationships with people will suffer — and eventually our relationship with God as well.

Peter was at a crossroads, but he came through beautifully.

> *While Peter was wondering about the meaning of the vision, the men sent by Cornelius found out where Simon's house was and stopped at the gate. They called out, asking if Simon who was known as Peter was staying there. While Peter was still thinking about the vision, the Spirit said to him, "Simon, three men are looking for you. So get up and go downstairs. Do not hesitate to go with them, for I have sent them." Peter went down and said to the men, "I'm the one you're looking for. Why have you come?" The men replied, "We have come from Cornelius the centurion. He is a righteous and God-fearing man, who is respected by all the Jewish people. A holy angel told him to have you come to his house so that he could hear what you have to say." Then Peter invited the men into the house to be his guests. (vv. 17-23)*

The angels must have watched Simon the tanner's home carefully that night. How would the apostle respond to the heavenly vision? Hallelujah — he obeyed! He took a glorious first step and invited the visitors in. The Jewish phase of the church thus came to an end, and a new attitude began to sweep the church.

Do we see those around us as potential heirs of grace? Do we view those who are different from us and who do things we do not approve of as candidates for the kingdom? Our attitude makes all the difference. If we are anti-Semitic, we will never lead a Jew to Christ. If we have written off a relative, he or she may be written off for eternity. If we are elitists, most of the rest of the world will never experience grace through us. I like C. S. Lewis's statement: "Next to the blessed sacrament, your neighbor is the holiest object presented to your senses."

Peter's attitude changed that day. To be sure, there were still a lot of rough edges. Sometimes — for example, later in Antioch — he regressed. But it is also true that Peter died in Rome — the center of Gentile power. He never sheltered himself among his own people or homeland again. God changed him, and he can change us!

If we are resisting God's overtures in this regard, we need to hear the words of Alexander Whyte:

> It would change your whole heart and life this very night if you would take Peter and Cornelius home with you and lay them both to heart.

> If you would take a four-cornered napkin when you go home, and a Sabbath-night pen and ink, and write the names of the nations, and the churches, and the denominations, and the congregations, and the ministers, and the public men, and the private citizens, and the neighbors, and the fellow-worshippers — all the people you dislike, and despise, and do not, and cannot, and will not, love. Heap all their names into your unclean napkin, and then look up and say, "Not so, Lord, I neither can speak well, nor think well, nor hope well, of these people. I cannot do it, and I will not try." If you acted out and spake out all the evil things that are in your heart in some such way as that, you would thus get such a sight of yourselves that you would never forget it.[3]

Do we dare write down the names of individuals and groups to which we have in effect said, "By no means, Lord"? Only God can give us the grace to love them, and he will do exactly that if we ask him.

PRAYER

> *O God, please forgive me for not allowing your great love to flow through me to others, for refusing to love and win those whom I deem dangerous or dirty or unworthy — those who have hurt me or whom I consider beneath me. I confess that I am the worst of sinners. How could anyone be lower than me? Impossible! May your grace burst through my walls of pride and prejudice, and may your love conquer my selfishness and others' sinful rebellion, so that in me and in them your name will be extolled and exalted. In Jesus' name, Amen.*

18

Opening the Church's Arms

ACTS 10:23 — 11:18

When God told Peter, "Do not call anything impure that God has made clean," God was confronting Peter's prejudice. Peter had bound all the peoples of the world, except for his own race, into one loathsome bundle. God used a vision to bring a radical change in the attitude of the leading apostle of the early church, and it is a good thing he did. Otherwise, Christianity would have been reduced to a narrow sect of Judaism, and you and I would have never heard the good news. Those whom we reject and scorn will also be excluded from Christ — as far as *our* Christian outreach and ministry is concerned.

Mahatma Gandhi shares in his autobiography that in his student days in England he was deeply touched by reading the Gospels and seriously considered becoming a convert to Christianity, which seemed to offer a real solution to the caste system that divided the people of India. One Sunday he attended church services and decided to ask the minster for enlightenment on salvation and other doctrines. But when Gandhi entered the sanctuary, the ushers refused to give him a seat and suggested that he go elsewhere to worship with his own people. He left and never came back. "If Christians have caste differences also," he said to himself, "I might as well remain a Hindu!"

Some draw a circle that shuts men out;
Race and position are what they flout;
But Christ in love seeks them all to win,
He draws a circle that takes them in!
—Edwin Markham, adapted

Peter's attitude suffered a decisive blow in two areas — his unfortunate racial prejudice and his resistance to change.

That must have been quite a night at Simon the tanner's house. Just as Peter's vision concluded, the three Gentile messengers from Cornelius came to the door. Peter, under the leadership of the Holy Spirit, invited them in, and they spent the night. No doubt this caused quite a stir among the local brethren. "Simon has three *goyim* staying at his home. Next thing you know, the whole block will be overrun with them." Furthermore, that night Peter agreed to go with the men to Caesarea and to share Christ with Cornelius.

PETER'S ENLARGING COMPLETED (10:23-48)

"The next day Peter started out with them, and some of the brothers from Joppa went along" (v. 23). According to Acts 11:12, six Christian brethren from Joppa accompanied Peter and his new friends. William Barclay says this was because they and Peter were seven witnesses, the number of witnesses necessary to validate a case.[1] So the party of ten began the thirty-five-mile trek to Caesarea on the Sea. There must have been some animated conversations along the way. When they arrived at Caesarea, they received an extraordinary reception.

> *The following day he arrived in Caesarea. Cornelius was expecting them and had called together his relatives and close friends. As Peter entered the house, Cornelius met him and fell at his feet in reverence. But Peter made him get up. "Stand up," he said, "I am only a man myself." Talking with him, Peter went inside and found a large gathering of people. (vv. 24-27)*

Cornelius' response was astounding! The Greek word translated "fell at his feet in reverence" (*proskuneo*) literally means "to kiss toward" and is used for offering homage to deity and angels and sometimes men. This leader of the oppressive military occupation force fell at Peter's feet! This was the perfect opportunity for Peter to put his old prejudices into high gear. "The Big Fisherman is here. You may kiss my ring."

But that was no longer Peter's style! God had changed his heart. "But Peter made him get up. 'Stand up,' he said, 'I am only a man myself.'" The house was packed out with Cornelius' family and close friends. Everyone was there — Mom, the children, the grandparents, his military associates and servants. They did not know it, but they were about to have the first-ever cross-cultural home Bible study.

Cornelius was so spiritually hungry that he put away his own racism and reached out to Peter. He could have said, "I'm a Roman centurion. How fitting it is that you, a peasant preacher and fisherman, have come at my command," but he did not. Instead, he groveled before a Jew in front of his whole family. He desperately wanted to hear the truth not only for himself but for his family and friends.

Interestingly, the Scriptures consistently present centurions in a good light. It was to a Roman centurion that Jesus said, "I have not found anyone in Israel with such great faith" (Matthew 8:10). It was a centurion at the cross who cried, "Surely he was the Son of God!" (Matthew 27:54). It was a centurion who deferred to Paul and spared the prisoners when they were shipwrecked on Malta (Acts 27:42-43). No one really knows why they received such good press, but it may have been because they were the real working officers of the Roman army and because the pressures of their position made them more willing to face their own inadequacy and need.

The apostle and the centurion had an exciting exchange in front of the whole household. Peter spoke first, and he appeared a little uneasy and self-conscious. Perhaps "old tapes" of Jewish prejudice were still playing despite his new understanding.

> *He said to them: "You are well aware that it is against our law for a Jew to associate with a Gentile or visit him. But God has shown me that I should not call any man impure or unclean. So when I was sent for, I came without raising any objection. May I ask why you sent for me?" Cornelius answered: "Four days ago I was in my house praying at this hour, at three in the afternoon. Suddenly a man in shining clothes stood before me and said, 'Cornelius, God has heard your prayer and remembered your gifts to the poor. Send to Joppa for Simon who is called Peter. He is a guest in the home of Simon the tanner, who lives by the sea.' So I sent for you immediately, and it was good of you to come. Now we are all here in the presence of God to listen to everything the Lord has commanded you to tell us." (vv. 28-33)*

Few preachers have ever had a more receptive audience than the apostle on that day. Peter was prepared, the people were prepared, and the Holy Spirit was in control from beginning to end. It was the first time the gospel had ever been preached to Gentiles!

Peter's sermon was a concise summary of the apostolic *kerygma* (preaching) that he had given at Pentecost (2:14-36) and before the Sanhedrin (3:12-26). After a brief introduction (vv. 34-37), Peter reviewed Christ's life (v. 38), his death (v. 39), his resurrection (vv. 40-41), his return as Judge (v. 42), and his offer of salvation (v. 43). The sermon concluded with Peter's statement in verse 43: "All the prophets testify about him that *everyone who believes in him receives forgiveness of sins through his name.*" "Everyone" — not only Jews, but "everyone."

Verses 44-46 describe the amazing response:

> *While Peter was still speaking these words, the Holy Spirit came on all who heard the message. The circumcised believers who had come with Peter were astonished that the gift of the Holy Spirit had been poured out even on the Gentiles. For they heard them speaking in tongues and praising God.*

The apostle only spoke for a few minutes before there were results. (Acts 11:15 tells us that when he "*began* to speak, the Holy Spirit came on them.") Peter laid down the major points, mentioned some outstanding facts, and was interrupted by a special working of the Holy Spirit! Cornelius and his household heard that "everyone who believes in him receives forgiveness of sins," and they responded in faith. No altar call! No invitation! They simply believed and were born again on the spot!

Peter and his six friends were amazed that God gave the Romans the ability to glorify him in other languages just as he had done for the Jews at Pentecost. It was crucial for the Jews to understand that Gentiles and Jews were on equal ground. There was no denying that fact now. Seven witnesses had seen it, including an apostle!

> *Then Peter said, "Can anyone keep these people from being baptized with water? They have received the Holy Spirit just as we have." So he ordered that they be baptized in the name of Jesus Christ. (vv. 46b-48a)*

Cornelius and his family and friends had perhaps never seen a baptism. They were not Jews. Old conventions were being broken right and left. The day when Cornelius and others came to faith held more than one surprise for Israel's sons. A spiritual continental divide had been breached.

"Then they asked Peter to stay with them for a few days" (v. 48b). Peter was having a great time — the first Gentile baptism, the first Gentile church service, the first Gentile follow-up class. During this time with the Gentiles he began to see that they were human, that they felt much as he did, that they loved Jesus. Experience is a wonderful teacher. Allan Emery, in his book *Turtle on a Fencepost*, tells how as a wealthy man at age forty-five he sold his family business and went to work for ServiceMaster. He says:

> My first assignment was to work for two weeks as a houseman at a large metropolitan hospital. I was to mop corridors, empty trash containers, and clean ashtrays. While not in the best condition for this work, I completed the day's schedule. The shock was not in the work but in the general rejection of me as a person because of my green uniform and the kind of work I was doing. Not a single person responded to my "Good Morning" except others in the Housekeeping Department. I had never before experienced the caste system.[2]

Nothing helps one's perspective like spending some time with those we view as beneath us. Peter was a changed man with an enlarged heart.

Peter's story takes seventy-seven verses to tell and repeats his vision twice. God wanted to make sure we did not miss the point. God had enlarged Peter by positive reinforcement when he performed great miracles in a Gentile environment, then by a vision of his narrowness, and now by fruitful ministry with Gentiles. Peter now understood that Christ was for everyone! He was optimistic about what the gospel could do for all who believe.

> *He himself bore our sins in his body on the tree, so that we might die to sins and live for righteousness; by his wounds you have been healed. (1 Peter 2:23)*

I once had the wonderful privilege of leading a collegian to Christ. He began to blossom and developed a great concern for his father and his family. His father was an intimidating man, and when I met him I felt like I was on military inspection. One day my young friend asked, "Would you tell my dad how to know Christ?" So, my heart pounding, I visited that man's home. It took me forty-five minutes to get around to what I wanted to say. But as I shared the good news of Jesus Christ, tears began to course down his face, and he said, "Do you think God could save an old sinner like me?" He trusted Christ that day and went on to become a very outspoken Christian.

If we do not believe the gospel is inclusive, if we are not optimistic about what it will do, if we are not a little aggressive about sharing it, people will not come to Christ.

> *I am not ashamed of the gospel, because it is the power of God for the salvation of everyone who believes: first for the Jew, then for the Gentile. (Romans 1:16)*

There is no one whose life God cannot turn inside out. The Lord can even change an entire family. There is power in the blood!

PETER'S ENLARGING COMMUNICATED (11:1-18)

Bad news travels fast, and soon the Christians in Jerusalem called Peter on the carpet for fraternizing with the Gentiles.

> *The apostles and the brothers throughout Judea heard that the Gentiles also had received the word of God. So when Peter went up to Jerusalem, the circumcised believers criticized him and said, "You went into the house of uncircumcised men and ate with them." (vv. 1-3)*

These Jewish Christians were not unhappy because the Gentiles received grace but because Peter had associated with them!

Peter had his hands full, but he answered admirably. Verses 4-18 record his defense, which was so good that in the end, according to verse 18,

> *When they heard this, they had no further objections and praised God, saying, "So then, God has granted even the Gentiles repentance unto life."*

What produced such a dynamic response? *Peter had a vision, and he shared it* (see vv. 5-10)! God brings change and enlargement through men and women who have a vision — through those who see themselves and others as God sees them and act accordingly. That is the way it was with St. Francis and John Wesley and William Carey and Amy Carmichael and William Booth and Corrie ten Boom, and that is the way it is today with Billy Graham and Tony Evans and Joni Eareckson Tada and Luis Palau. When such ambassadors of Christ impart their vision, the horizons of those around them are widened.

Peter was able to promote this broadening change because his experience proved his vision to be true. The seven witnesses had seen the Holy Spirit fall on the Gentiles. "As I began to speak, the Holy Spirit came on them as he had come on us at the beginning" (v. 15).

Peter's vision was in agreement with Scripture. When Peter saw the Gentiles receive the Spirit, he thought back to something else.

> *"Then I remembered what the Lord had said: 'John baptized with water, but you will be baptized with the Holy Spirit.' So if God gave*

> *them the same gift as he gave us, who believed in the Lord Jesus Christ, who was I to think that I could oppose God?"* (vv. 16-17)

Any change that God brings about will be consistent with his holy Word. As we see in Peter's case, vision, experience, and the Word working together constitute an irresistible force.

> *When they heard this, they had no further objections and praised God, saying, "So then, God has granted even the Gentiles repentance unto life."* (v. 18)

A giant step in enlarging the church's attitude was accomplished. Praise God!

A FINAL WORD

Our attitude toward the world — those who do not know God — is supremely important. That is thrust of the book of Jonah. It was the prophet's bad attitude toward the world that landed him in the belly of the great fish. God was saying to him, "Jonah, this is what I think of your self-will, your prejudice, your elitism. Take a good look."

In Christ there is no basis for discrimination of any kind. Prejudice or elitism on the lips of a believer is an obscenity — whether it be racial, national, cultural, or social. James says, "My brothers, as believers in our glorious Lord Jesus Christ, don't show favoritism" (2:1). If only there had been more love and less bias in that usher's heart when he met Gandhi. The future world leader had read the New Testament and had even seriously considered Christianity, but his conclusion was, "I like the New Testament, I like your Christianity, but I do not like your Christians."

What a difference it makes when we look at others with attitudes that are inclusive, open-armed, optimistic, and lovingly and courteously aggressive. Peter's story reminds us that God wants to instill in us his attitude toward the world.

The gospel never changes. But we can become unchangeable, inflexible, and thus unusable. What are our attitudes toward others? Exclusive — pessimistic — passive? Or concerned — hopeful — actively loving? We need to regularly consider Peter's vision and its meaning and implications for us today.

PRAYER

> *Our gracious Lord, we want to have hearts that are inclusive and optimistic. We desire a blessed, merciful aggressiveness like Jesus'.*

Enlarge the circle of our lives, we pray, whatever the cost. Help us to be open to your leading and to not see ourselves as above those you want us to reach. May your love for everyone *overflow from our hearts and draw others to the Savior who died for them as much as he died for us. In Jesus' name, Amen.*

19

The First Christians

Acts 11:19-30

This passage records the final step of the gospel's beginning to be proclaimed to Gentiles — specifically, the formation of a Gentile church in the city of Antioch in Syria.

Apparently so many people came to Christ in Antioch that the local populace coined a new name for Christ's followers: "The disciples were called Christians first at Antioch" (v. 26). This nickname probably came from the (Gentile) townspeople, because believers would have been reticent to describe themselves with a term built on Christ's holy name. Besides, they already had several long-used self-designations such as "the disciples," "the saints," "the believers," and "the brethren." Moreover, the Jews would never have named them "Christians" because Christ is the Greek word for Messiah; to call them *Christ*ians, followers of the Messiah, would have been unthinkable.

The people of Antioch observed this vibrant spiritual movement (though to them it appeared narrow-minded and suspicious). Seeking a new term to describe it, they took the Greek name for Messiah and added a Latin suffix, producing a hybrid word we pronounce today in English as "Christian."[1] The people of Antioch composed a label for the new vessels into which the new wine of salvation had been poured. The name was wonderfully true, though also derogatory and costly.

We live in a time when the term *Christian* has become one of the vaguest epithets in the English language. During the British colonial era it became synonymous with "Englishmen" in India — it did not make any difference how godly or perverted the man was. In our own century "Christian" nations have engaged in two world wars. Some people think that everyone who is not a Jew or a Muslim is a Christian.

Dr. Harry Ironside once handed a gospel booklet to a man on a train, and the man turned to him and asked, "What did you give me that book for?" Dr. Ironside replied, "I thought you might be interested; and, may I ask, are you a Christian?" "Well," he replied indignantly, "take a good look at me — do I look like a Jew or a Chinaman?" "You look like an American." "Then," he responded, "that is your answer."[2] Even today many people are willing to say, "I am a Christian" but would balk at saying they are "believers" or "disciples." They are cultural Christians who have not experienced saving commitment to Jesus Christ.

Antioch was situated on the Orontes River, about 300 miles north of Jerusalem and twenty miles east of the Mediterranean, at the convergence of the Taurus and Lebanon mountains where the Orontes breaks through on its way to the sea. During the first century it was the third-largest city in the world, behind Rome and Alexandria. It was the melting pot for at least five cultures — the Greek, Roman, Semitic, Arab, and Persian. The Jews made up one-seventh of the city's population and had legal sanction to follow their own laws in their own neighborhoods. Antioch was famous for its chariot racing and for its deliberate pursuit of pleasure — Las Vegas on the Orontes.

Antioch was most famous for its worship of Daphne, whose temple stood five miles outside town in a laurel grove. Apollo's famous pursuit of Daphne there was reenacted night and day by the men of the city and by the priestesses, who were in fact ritual prostitutes. Throughout the world "the morals of Daphne" was a euphemism for depravity. The Roman Juvenal aimed one of his sharpest barbs at his own decadent Rome when he said the Orontes had flowed into the Tiber, flooding the city with wickedness (*Satirae* 3.62).

Amazingly, it was in this city, with all its sensuality and immorality, that "the disciples were called Christians first." Antioch was also the birthplace of foreign missions (see 13:2) and had the greatest preachers — in the first century Barnabas, Paul, and Peter; in the second Ignatius and Theophilus; in the third and fourth Lucian, Theodore, Chrysostom, and Theodoret. God's light can shine in the darkest pit. God's flowers can blossom in the most putrid bog.

Why were the believers first called Christians in Antioch?

GROUND-BREAKING PREACHING (vv. 19-21)

Now those who had been scattered by the persecution in connection with Stephen traveled as far as Phoenicia, Cyprus and Antioch, telling the message only to Jews. Some of them, however, men from

Cyprus and Cyrene, went to Antioch and began to speak to Greeks also, telling them the good news about the Lord Jesus. (vv. 19-20)

Persecution thrust two kinds of believers into other parts of the world. The first shared the good news only with fellow Jews. The second was willing to share the gospel with both Jews and Gentiles because they were Hellenized (Greek-speaking Jews) and were not so attached to Jewish prejudices. Merely verbalizing the indwelling witness of Christ in their hearts, they were not aware they were doing anything radical. These unnamed Jews from the island of Cyprus and Cyrene (in North Africa) — with no official direction, no human instruction, no precedent to follow, nothing but a burning love for Christ — took the message to Antioch without realizing the revolutionary greatness of their act. They were the first believers to bring the explosive light of Christianity into the midnight of paganism.

Antioch was evangelized not by apostles but by average members of Christ's Body who were willing to share their faith. Wherever these fugitives landed, they kindled a blaze. Sharing Christ was to them as natural as tears to sorrow or a smile to happiness. Everyday believers empowered by the Holy Spirit of God blew away the hold of paganism on needy souls. What an example!

The result was a great harvest in Antioch: "The Lord's hand was with them, and a great number of people believed and turned to the Lord" (v. 21). No apostles — no deacons — no ecclesiastical structure! Just "the Lord's hand" and a tremendous number of new believers.

A heavenly vitality now burned in the midst of the materialistic and spiritual darkness of Antioch. This was so foreign to its bleak environment that it would alter the vocabulary of the city — and indeed of the entire world. A similar thing happened to George Fox and his followers in 1640 when he stood before a certain Justice Bennet and "bid him to tremble at the word of the Lord." In response the justice called Fox and his followers "Quakers." Elton Trueblood comments: "One of the best evidences that the image which Fox and his associates conveyed to their contemporaries was a dynamic one, is that provided by the nickname Quaker . . ."[3] The same thing happened to the Methodists, who were so named because of their systematic, methodical pursuit of holiness.

If a spiritual dynamic operated among us causing people to reach for a new word to describe us, what would the word be? What words do they use now? When God's people live for Christ in such depth and power that those around them have to strive for a new term to describe what they see — that is awesome!

Before long the Jerusalem church heard what was going on in Antioch and decided to send Barnabas to check things out.

A DELEGATED INVESTIGATION (vv. 22-24)

Raised on the island of Cyprus, Barnabas was a Hellenistic Jew. He probably had personal friends among some of those evangelizing in Antioch because some of them were from Cyprus too. He was highly respected by the Jerusalem church for his piety and generosity. He had sold his property on Cyprus and laid it at the apostles' feet (4:36-37). Barnabas was a proven encourager and reconciler, the one who brought Saul and the Jerusalem church together. He was cheerful, big-hearted, loving. He was a perfect choice.

> *When he arrived and saw the evidence of the grace of God, he was glad and encouraged them all to remain true to the Lord with all their hearts. (v. 23)*

Barnabas "saw the evidence of the grace of God." He could easily have seen the situation in a different light. These people were new, untaught Christians. They still carried the mire of Antioch with them. Some of them had miles to go in their language and relationships and ethics. But Barnabas "saw the evidence of the grace of God." He could see Christian grace and charm in their lives — the fruit of the Spirit: "love, joy, peace . . ." — and "he was glad." So he simply "encouraged them all to remain true to the Lord with all their hearts," to meditate on him, to make him *everything*!

In this way Barnabas helped them focus on that which would cleanse them of the defilement of Antioch. His advice is appropriate for all Christians, whether in beginning stages or well along the path. Maclaren rightly warned, "Many of us are so busy thinking about Christianity that we have lost our hold of Christ."[4]

Barnabas saw grace, rejoiced, then tenderly encouraged God's people. How was he able to do this? "He was a good man, full of the Holy Spirit and faith" (v. 24). The refreshing water of the Spirit flowed from Barnabas' innermost being. His faith produced spiritual desire, expectation, and dependence. Can you think of anyone like that? Why not be such a person?

The church was a holy but disconcerting presence in the dark city of Antioch. The church became even more vital and, to the pagan mind, more perplexing as the goodness and fullness of the Holy Spirit and faith seen in Barnabas began to reproduce in that young church. "And a great number of people were brought to the Lord" (v. 24).

The ministry in Antioch was going so well that it was too much for Barnabas. He was a fine man, but he knew his limitations. Perhaps Barnabas lay awake one night, burdened, tired, exploring his options. In the last three days he had led ten Bible studies, conducted five baptisms, and shared the gospel countless times. *I need some help! I cannot keep this up.* Then he thought about Paul and immediately began praying for God's guidance.

A TIMELY RECRUITMENT (vv. 25-26)

When Barnabas and Paul had seen each other last — eight to ten years earlier, the church in Jerusalem had sent Paul to Tarsus for safety (9:30), and there he had remained. A lot of water had gone under the bridge since Paul's conversion, and he was now a well-seasoned servant of Christ. Commentator Richard Longenecker believes that many events that cannot be fitted into the known chronology of Paul's life happened during those years. Certainly Paul continued preaching during that time. Perhaps this is when he received the five sets of thirty-nine stripes at the hands of synagogue officials and underwent other persecutions (see 2 Corinthians 11:23-27). Probably this is when he experienced the loss of all things (Philippians 3:8) and was disinherited by his family. Perhaps the ecstatic experience of being caught up to the third heaven (2 Corinthians 12:1-4) happened during those years as well.[5] Paul was no longer a neophyte. His theology had crystallized and matured. He was full of Christ.

> *I have been crucified with Christ and I no longer live, but Christ lives in me. The life I live in the body, I live by faith in the Son of God, who loved me and gave himself for me. (Galatians 2:20)*

We have seen Barnabas' goodness expressed in his generosity to the church (4:36-37) and in his sticking his neck out to commend Paul to the apostles (9:27). But here we find something even more beautiful because Barnabas would soon yield his preeminence to Paul. Barnabas was older, more respected, and in many ways more experienced. But when he asked Paul to help in Antioch (v. 25) and when they later commenced a missionary journey together, Paul began to play a greater role than Barnabas. The story began "Barnabas and Saul," but it soon became "Paul and Barnabas," and it stayed that way to the end.[6] Barnabas to Paul was like John the Baptist to Christ — "he must become greater; I must become less" (John 3:30). May his tribe increase!

When Paul traveled with Barnabas to heathen Antioch, they were a dynamic duo! They complemented one another beautifully, thanks to the expert orchestration of the Spirit of God. Barnabas was sensitive, empathetic, gracious. Paul had a brilliantly honed, razor-sharp lawyer's intellect. Together, with the Spirit's power working through them, they were unconquerable.

A FINAL WORD

Cosmopolitan, sordid, voluptuous Antioch could not fit this new people into any of its categories, so a new name was born. Perhaps there was a jesting and mocking edge to the nickname, perhaps even a bit of rage, because these people were such a contradiction to the ethos of Antioch. The new term was a mongrel name (part Greek and part Latin), but it said it all: *Christ-ians* — followers of Christ! Christ was so much on these believers' lips, they lived so like Christ, that no other name would do. *Christian* is a wonderful name — a name of which we should seek to be worthy.

Alexander the Great once learned that in his army was a namesake, another Alexander, who was a notorious coward. "Alexander the Great, who conquered the world when he was just twenty-three, called the soldier before him and said, 'Is your name Alexander and are you named for me?' The trembling coward said, 'Yes, sir. My name is Alexander and I was named for you.' The great general said, 'Then either be brave or change your name!'"[7] Fortunately, Christ does not say that to us, but he does exhort us to be who we are — to live out our calling in faithful, obedient service.

PRAYER

O God, help us to be loyal, brave, committed followers of Christ who refuse to turn back — who dare to stand firm and to make Christ's name known to all around us — who desire, with your divine enabling, to shine the light of the gospel upon a dark world, winning others to you. In Jesus' name, Amen.

20

Getting Acquainted with Our Power

ACTS 12:1-24

Acts 1 — 11 portrays the river of God's grace growing wider and wider in fulfillment of Acts 1:8 — "you will be my witnesses in Jerusalem, and in all Judea and Samaria, and to the ends of the earth." The river of grace threatened to jump its banks when Philip preached to the Samaritans, and it made noticeable ripples when he shared Christ with the Ethiopian eunuch. It dramatically overflowed with the conversion of Cornelius and his household. A worldwide flood of grace began when the good news was preached in Antioch. And from the end of Acts 12 on, attention turns to the Gentile world. Antioch became the center instead of Jerusalem, all subsequent missionary journeys going out from there.

However, before completely redirecting our focus to the Gentile ministry, Luke takes the opportunity in chapter 12 to present two final glimpses of God's working on behalf of the church in Jerusalem. Specifically, he records Peter's miraculous deliverance from prison and the death of Herod. Luke does this so that the Jerusalem church, and the subsequent readers of Acts, will not imagine that God's care for the Jerusalem church had diminished. The interventions recorded here were meant to acquaint, or perhaps reacquaint, the church with its authority and power. This account was reassuring for the surrendered, beleaguered church then and remains so today.

Chapter 12, set in a context of mounting persecution, opens with the apparent inability of God's people to do anything to deliver themselves but then depicts an amazing display of strength among seemingly helpless Christians and reveals the source of that strength.

THE ABSENCE OF STRENGTH IN GOD'S PEOPLE (vv. 1-5)

To understand the persecution cited in this text, we need to understand what King Herod was like. His father, Aristobulus, had been murdered by his own father, Herod the Great, the ruler who had ordered the slaughter of innocent babies at Christ's birth. After the death of Aristobulus, the Herod of Acts 12 was sent to Rome to be educated, and there he grew up as a close friend of the imperial family. He was something of a playboy, and in A.D. 23 he fled to Palestine to escape his creditors. In Palestine he lived in humility and poverty under his uncle, Herod Antipas.

Upon his return to Rome, he was imprisoned by the Emperor Tiberius for some critical remarks he had made. His life had hit bottom. But then Tiberius died, and Herod's childhood friend, Caligula, came to power — not only freeing him from prison, but giving him a gold chain weighing as much as his iron fetters in prison. Soon Herod was named ruler of some Palestinian provinces. When another childhood friend, Claudius, succeeded Caligula, Herod became ruler of Judea and Samaria. Murder and intrigue had been the currency of his entire life.

Herod was preeminently a politician. When he was with the Romans, he did as the Romans did. Though he was Jewish only by race and not by conviction, when he was with the Jews he acted like a Jew. *The Mishnah* records that during the annual procession bearing the firstfruits to the temple, "when they reached the temple Mount, Agrippa the king [Herod] would take his basket on his shoulder and enter as far as the Temple Court."[1] He would do *anything* to maintain his popularity with the Jewish people. However, he saw Jewish Christians as divisive and believed their activities would disturb the people. And he was not finished yet.

> *It was about this time that King Herod arrested some who belonged to the church, intending to persecute them. He had James, the brother of John, put to death with the sword. When he saw that this pleased the Jews, he proceeded to seize Peter also. This happened during the Feast of Unleavened Bread. After arresting him, he put him in prison. (vv. 1-3)*

James was executed with the sword because, according to *The Mishnah* (Sanhedrin 9:1), the sword had to be used for murderers and apostates. This action ingratiated Herod even further with the Jews. James, the Apostle John's brother, was dead, and Peter was in prison, destined for the same end. God's people appeared utterly powerless in this grim situation.

This must have been especially difficult for the Apostle John. As we see in the Gospels, he and James were always together. They were the two for whom their mother tried to get special thrones at Jesus' side in the Kingdom. Jesus affectionately called them "Sons of Thunder" (Mark 3:17) — apostolic buccaneers. Now with the sudden word of a mad despot, James was gone. That must have shaken John terribly. And the church was certainly in shock as well. The believers had not expected this to happen to one of their leaders.

The authorities imprisoned Peter too. As soon as the Feast of Unleavened Bread was over (executions were not permitted during the Passover), there would undoubtedly be a mock trial and Peter would join James in death!

The beleaguered Jerusalem church seemed overwhelmed and helpless. There was *nothing* they could do. Their despair undoubtedly moved to even darker levels because it was Passover week, the same week Christ had been earlier murdered. Grim associations inevitably flooded their minds.

Their apparent weakness was underlined by the fact that all they could do was pray (v. 5). Sometimes Christians today feel the same way about situations they face — cancer in a loved one, unemployment and an inability to find a good job, trying to turn a straying son or daughter back to the Lord, seeking to reverse the tides of evil in our land (abortion, murder, open immorality). Does anything look more ridiculous to oppressors than a ragtag, harried group of believers praying for God's help in the midst of oppressive darkness? To those outside the family of God, this is terminal weakness. The Christians should have been planning a terrorist reprisal or a kidnapping. What good would this effeminate praying do?

Nevertheless, God's people continued to pray — and rightly so! "The church was earnestly praying to God for him." The Greek word translated "earnestly" comes originally from a word that means "to stretch" or "to strain." They were straining in prayer![2] — praying "with agony," as G. Campbell Morgan says. If one of our closest brothers or sisters in Christ were awaiting execution, we would pray fervently too.

What fools they were, their opponents thought, to pray about the situation. After all, Herod's power was irresistible. The axe had fallen once, and it would fall on the helpless neck of another of their leaders. Who were God's people to dare to believe anyone or anything could help them now?

THE DISPLAY OF STRENGTH IN GOD'S PEOPLE (vv. 6-11)

Zero hour was at hand. Passover was complete, and now Herod and his staff could kill Peter — the victim of a kangaroo court. Verse 6 begins the description of that final night:

The night before Herod was to bring him to trial, Peter was sleeping between two soldiers, bound with two chains, and sentries stood guard at the entrance.

Peter was "sleeping" — quite soundly sleeping in fact. He did not have some kind of martyr complex. His restfulness simply meant he was at peace with himself and with God. He probably shared Christ as best he could with his captors, had a time of prayer, and fell asleep resting in Jesus.

Herod wanted to make sure his dangerous prisoner did not somehow escape. Verse 4 tells us that Peter was guarded by four quarternions (squads with four soldiers each). Roman soldiers stood guard in three-hour shifts. So there were always four soldiers guarding Peter. Extraordinary precautions were also taken by chaining him to two soldiers instead of one as usual (compare Seneca, Epistulae, 5:7). The other two soldiers kept watch outside the cell.

Verse 11 indicates that everyone in Jerusalem figured Peter was through. No one was prepared for the display of power that was soon to come. Sometimes we miss the drama of these situations by relegating them to a distant time and setting. It is imperative that we see the powerful significance of this important account.

Why were the believers not prepared for God's intervention? They had forgotten about his army of angels.

Suddenly an angel of the Lord appeared and a light shone in the cell. He struck Peter on the side and woke him up. "Quick, get up!" he said, and the chains fell off Peter's wrists. (v. 7)

With the appearance of "an angel of the Lord," five things happened: 1) The angel brought some light, or perhaps he simply glowed. 2) He struck Peter. Being sound asleep, Peter probably did not appreciate that! 3) The angel told him to "Quick, get up!" 4) Peter's chains fell off. 5) Peter must have been groggy, because the angel had to tell him how to get dressed: "Put on your clothes and sandals. . . . Wrap your cloak around you and follow me."

Peter obeyed, but he was probably in disarray — sandals on the wrong feet, his tunic hanging loosely, his hair uncombed. He needed his morning coffee. Peter was dazed and bewildered, like a sleepwalker who is not quite sure where he is or why.

Peter followed him out of the prison, but he had no idea that what the angel was doing was really happening; he thought he was seeing a vision. (v. 9)

He was confused, but there was a dawning awareness of reality, and as he rubbed his eyes, the reality must have staggered him:

> *They passed the first and second guards and came to the iron gate leading to the city. It opened for them by itself, and they went through it. When they had walked the length of one street, suddenly the angel left him. Then Peter came to himself. (vv. 10-11)*

His chains fell away, he walked right on by the two guards chained to him, he walked right past the two sentries, and the iron gate swung open! Incredible! The Greek word translated "by itself" is *automáte*. The gates opened automatically — a sight Peter had never seen before! Sleepy or not, he probably felt the goose bumps and adrenaline now. Then *poof!* — the angel was gone, and there stood Peter on the streets of Jerusalem, rubbing his wrists and eyes, stifling a yawn.

Do you get the picture? Those ragtag, beleaguered Christians possessed greater power than Herod's hordes! The legions of Rome barred the door, but it only took one of God's secret agents to liberate the captive!

Peter's experience reacquainted the embattled church with the true nature of her strength: no matter how grim life might appear, God and his angels are present and ministering, and he can deliver us anytime he sees fit!

God taught Jacob this same truth when, after the scheming patriarch-to-be had deceived Esau and stolen the blessing and fled for his life, he lay down on a stone pillow in utter despondency. Jacob was miserable, homesick, and overwhelmed with loneliness. But God loved him, rascal that he was. So God gave him a marvelous vision (Genesis 28:12) of a ladder reaching into Heaven and angels ascending and descending. Although Jacob appeared to be abandoned by God and man, there was angelic traffic between Heaven and earth on his behalf. Jacob's response? "Surely the Lord is in this place, and I was not aware of it" (v. 16). That day he anointed his stone pillow with oil and called the place "Bethel" — "the house of God." There was a connection between Heaven and earth for Peter too. His jail cell was the very house of God. It is the same for us in the dilemmas that threaten us. We are not alone.

A missionary friend of mine who spent over fifty years on the mission field beginning in China and Tibet, Mrs. Carol Carlson, once told me her husband, Edwin, was protected by angels when "he had gone through a lonely mountain area where bandits were known to be, and he came to the little village where their headquarters were located." Amazingly, he met with no mishap or trouble. Why? He was escorted by "people in white, as usual." Another day in the dull, prosaic life of a pioneer missionary to Tibet!

Then Peter came to himself and said, "Now I know without a doubt that the Lord sent his angel and rescued me from Herod's clutches and from everything the Jewish people were anticipating." (v. 11)

"Hey, that was an angel!" Peter had believed before, but now he really believed!

Jesus said, "I tell you the truth, you shall see heaven open, and the angels of God ascending and descending on the Son of Man" (John 1:51). He meant, "I am the ladder. I control the highway between Heaven and earth." Hebrews 1:14 adds, "Are not all angels ministering spirits sent to serve those who will inherit salvation?" Hebrews 12:22-23 states, "But you have come to Mount Zion, to the heavenly Jerusalem, the city of the living God. You have come to thousands upon thousands of angels in joyful assembly, to the church of the firstborn, whose names are written in heaven. You have come to God, the judge of all men, to the spirits of righteous men made perfect."

Furthermore, Philippians 3:20 reminds us, "Our citizenship is in heaven. And we eagerly await a Savior from there, the Lord Jesus Christ." We are citizens of Heaven. There is movement and communication between Heaven and earth on our behalf. The Lord Jesus Christ is the ladder, and through him we may interact with myriads of angels. No matter how grim, perplexing, and difficult our situation is, God and his angels are present to minister to us. He can deliver anytime, anywhere, anyplace. If we ever think God does not understand or cannot or will not help, we have bad theology. If we could have our eyes opened right now, wherever we are or whatever is going on around us, we would say, "God is in this place! This is Bethel, the house of God."

THE SOURCE OF STRENGTH IN GOD'S CHILDREN (vv. 12-17)

Peter knew some of the old gang would be at John Mark's house, and he knew what they would be doing when he got there.

When this had dawned on him [i.e., that the angel had rescued him], he went to the house of Mary the mother of John, also called Mark, where many people had gathered and were praying. (v. 12)

John Mark's family was evidently wealthy and had a large home, so there were a lot of people inside. Probably some of them were praying that Peter would have the courage to die a proper death. Others were undoubtedly praying that he would be a witness to those around him — soldiers, government officials, maybe even fellow prisoners. Certainly there were also a few who dared to pray, "God, you delivered Daniel from the lions' den, and you delivered David from Saul. Now deliver Peter. Do not let him die like James." We can be sure they were praying fervently. Just then Peter knocked at the front door. What follows is a story of confusion and joyful humor.

> *Peter knocked at the outer entrance, and a servant girl named Rhoda came to answer the door. When she recognized Peter's voice, she was so overjoyed she ran back without opening it and exclaimed, "Peter is at the door!" (vv. 13-14)*

The name Rhoda means "rose." From the way she was treated it would seem that she was rather young. The poor little rose answered the door and became so befuddled at Peter's voice that she ran to announce his arrival without even opening the door! Their response has become famous:

> *"You're out of your mind," they told her. When she kept insisting that it was so, they said, "It must be his angel." But Peter kept on knocking, and when they opened the door and saw him, they were astonished. (vv. 15-16)*

Rhoda was not easily intimidated. At first the others said she was crazy, and then they switched to the theory that Peter was dead and it was his angel or spirit. "Rhoda! Shhh! Can't you see we're praying? Don't bother us with the answer we're asking for!" We pray fervently for the conversion of a relative, and when it happens we say, "Amazing!" What is amazing is our slowness to believe God's ability and willingness to answer our prayers. The power of fervent, even if doubting, prayer is greater than that of kings!

In late 1964 Communist Simba rebels took over the town of Bunia in Zaire and began arresting and executing anyone they considered "enemies of the revolution." One of their victims was a pastor, Zebedayo Idu. The day following his arrest was to be a great political holiday, and as part of the celebration great crowds were gathered in front of the monument to Patrice Lumumba, the spiritual leader of the revolution. There were to be speeches by dignitaries from the provincial capital, Stanleyville, and a large number of prisoners were to be executed in front of the monument.

The prisoners were taken from their cells and herded onto a truck to be taken to the plaza, but for some mysterious reason the engine refused to start. The prisoners were finally unloaded and compelled to push the truck to get it started. When they finally arrived in front of the angry police commissioner's office, the furious official wanted no further delay, so he lined the prisoners up and ordered them to count off—"one, two, one, two"! The number twos were marched back to prison. The commissioner then ordered all of the number ones to march double-time to the monument, where they died a few minutes later. In their cells the twos could hear the sound of gunfire. They wondered why they had been spared and what the future held for them. Pastor Zebedayo shared with them his hope of Heaven and eternal life, and eight people found the Lord that day. Hardly had the pastor finished ministering the Word to them when a very excited messenger came panting to the door with an order. The pastor had been arrested by mistake. They were to release him at once.

Pastor Zebedayo bade farewell to the remaining prisoners and returned to his home next to the chapel, where he discovered that a crowd of believers had gathered in the house of God and were on their knees praying earnestly for his safety and release. Great was their rejoicing when the answer to their prayers walked into the building. The prayer service became a praise service for God's faithfulness. The God of Peter still lives!

If we are not seeing similar power working among us, why not? James 4:2 says, "You do not have, because you do not ask God." God can do anything he wants, but there are some things he gives only in answer to prayer. Ray Stedman has stated, "As a result of their intercession God was 'free' to act in unusual and remarkable ways."[3]

Peter went on to reacquaint the Christians in Jerusalem with God's sufficiency for every situation.

> *Peter motioned with his hand for them to be quiet and described how the Lord had brought him out of prison. "Tell James and the brothers about this," he said, and then he left for another place. (v. 17)*

Peter's deliverance became one of the favorite stories of the early church, along with the account of the interrupted prayer meeting. I am sure this always brought some laughs, and sometimes some tears. Some lives were changed that night as the church in Jerusalem was reacquainted with its power and God's provision. It is awesome to truly believe that regardless of the circumstances God can deliver us anytime he chooses. It is transforming to truly believe in the ministry of angels. It is life-changing to pray fervently.

A FINAL WORD

God wants his people to rest in the assurance of his unchanging, constant power. In subsequent months God would again underline this truth for the Jerusalem church by dealing with Herod in an unforgettable way. As a result of Peter's deliverance, Herod had the apostle's guards executed and left town himself for Caesarea, perhaps because of embarrassment. Verses 20-23 tell us what happened next:

> *He had been quarreling with the people of Tyre and Sidon; they now joined together and sought an audience with him. Having secured the support of Blastus, a trusted personal servant of the king, they asked for peace, because they depended on the king's country for their food supply. On the appointed day Herod, wearing his royal robes, sat on his throne and delivered a public address to the people. They shouted, "This is the voice of a god, not of a man." Immediately, because Herod did not give praise to God, an angel of the Lord struck him down, and he was eaten by worms and died.*

The Jewish historian Josephus wrote of this same event. On a festival day Herod presented himself in the theater in Caesarea to make a speech dressed in a beautiful robe woven of silver. As he moved in the sun, the brilliant flashing at times blinded the people. When, pleased with his speech, the people cried, "The voice of a God and not of a man!" this incredibly twisted king received their worship and immediately was "struck" by an angel (v. 23). There is divine poetry here because the same Greek word was used when the angel "struck" Peter to arouse him (v. 7)! Possibly it was even the same angel, though the results were far different! Herod suffered a terrible death. Remember, Luke was a medical doctor and thus knew the facts and understood the malady. The medical description of such a death is too unpleasant to read.

> *My days are in yellow leaf;*
> *The flower and fruits of love are gone;*
> *The worm, the canker, and the grief*
> *Are mine alone!*

Fitting but startling words because they were the last poetic lines Lord Byron ever wrote.[4]

Some of us need to be reacquainted with our position and power in Christ. Once-dear realities have faded, and as life passes by we feel like leaves in the wind. Difficulties have eased our grasp of spiritual realities, and our lives seem askew. The truth is, we are God's children, and God's children will never be orphans! God is in control! He has promised to never abandon us or leave us to our resources (see John 14:18; Hebrews 13:5). His angels are sent to minister to us. Prayer brings amazing power into our lives.

The question is, do we believe God is in control? Do we believe in the ministry of angels to the elect? Do we believe that prayer brings untold power?

> Just before World War II in Itasca, Texas, there was a school fire that took the lives of 263 children. It was a horrifying tragedy. After the war Itasca built a new school with the finest sprinkler system in the world. Never again would the citizens of Itasca be caught with such a tragedy on their hands. Honor students were selected to take citizens of the community on tours through the new school, to show them the finest sprinkler system ever assembled. The town continued to grow, and seven years after the new school was built an addition was needed. As the new construction began, it was discovered that the sprinkler system was never connected.[5]

Some of us need to come into better connection with the Source, and this happens only through a growing faith and honest prayer.

PRAYER

> *God, we believe with all our hearts that you can deliver us anytime from anything. Our Master, we believe in the ministry of angels. Lord, we believe in the power of prayer to bring these things about in and through our lives. Thank you for reacquainting us with our position and power in you. In Jesus' name, Amen.*

21

Realities of the Church Militant

ACTS 13:1-13

Acts 12 gives the account of Peter's amazing deliverance from prison. But as encouraging as that chapter is, it is a parenthesis in the flow of the story of Acts, and chapter 13 takes up where chapter 11 leaves off. Chapter 11 tells the exciting story of the birth of the Gentile church in Antioch and ends with the believers there doing a very beautiful thing for the mother church in Jerusalem.

> *The disciples, each according to his ability, decided to provide help for the brothers living in Judea. This they did, sending their gift to the elders by Barnabas and Saul. (11:29-30)*

The last verse of chapter 12 adds to the story: "When Barnabas and Saul had finished their mission, they returned from Jerusalem, taking with them John, also called Mark." After having the joy of delivering the offering to the Jerusalem church, and probably hearing the great story of chapter 12, Barnabas and Saul returned to Antioch, taking along with them Barnabas' young cousin (see Colossians 4:10), John Mark.

These great men and their young friend did not know it, but the greatest chapter in the church's history was about to open. The church at Antioch would receive its orders and go on the march — and face the difficulties of the church militant.

We are all familiar with Murphy's Law. #1: Nothing is as easy as it looks. #2: Everything takes longer than you think. #3: If anything can go wrong, it will! Whoever you are — rich, poor; young, old; pious, impious — you will encounter hardships! The only time troubles will cease is when you are in the grave (and then if you are not a believer, your troubles are just beginning). Let me take this a step further: life is continually difficult for the Christian. "Accept Christ and everything will be fine!" sounds good but is simply not true. We have all met fine Christians who are going through tough times. Some are battling disease, some gut-wrenching family problems, others financial straits. Accepting Christ is no guarantee against calamity.

No matter what your level of involvement in Christian activity or ministry, you will be subject to difficulties and trials. Friends will sometimes forsake you. Families will fail you. Heartache will be a regular part of your life. In fact, dedication to Christ often brings us face to face with more problems than if we lived for ourselves. If some of the great Christians in the history of the church had aimed lower, they would not have experienced such an incredible variety of sorrows — and would not have been used mightily by God.

How we view the war makes a vast difference in our conduct and even our longevity, just as it did with Paul, the great missionary general, and John Mark, the first missionary casualty.

THE COMMISSION OF THE CHURCH MILITANT (vv. 1-3)

> *In the church at Antioch there were prophets and teachers: Barnabas, Simeon called Niger, Lucius of Cyrene, Manaen (who had been brought up with Herod the tetrarch) and Saul. While they were worshiping the Lord and fasting, the Holy Spirit said, "Set apart for me Barnabas and Saul for the work to which I have called them." So after they had fasted and prayed, they placed their hands on them and sent them off. (vv. 1-3)*

This church was amazingly heterogeneous. It included Barnabas, a native of Cyprus, and a black man named Simeon (his other name, "Niger," is Latin for "black"). Another Gentile named Lucius may also have been black because he was from Cyrene or North Africa. Also in this church was Manaen, who had been reared as part of King Herod's household. Finally, there was Rabbi Saul.

This was the church staff at Antioch — a racially integrated group of go-getters who, Luke says in verse 1, were "prophets and teachers." Antioch was certainly where the action was — teachers teaching, prophets prophesying — the original church militant! The perfect profile for a missionary church was exhibited there at Antioch. They were in microcosm what the church would become in the world. This was no accident, but rather a deliberate work of God!

Notice that the Holy Spirit's commission — "Set apart for me Barnabas and Saul for the work to which I have called them" (v. 2) — came while they worshiped God (v. 2 — "While they were worshiping the Lord and fasting, the Holy Spirit said . . .'").

"Fasting" is always a mark of deep spiritual concern, indicating that a person is willing to set aside the normal demands of life in order to concentrate for a time on what God wants. It appears that the entire Antioch church was joined in this pursuit. They were "worshiping the Lord," and during that time the call of the Holy Spirit came upon them. Worship and service go together and should never be separated. If we try to work for the Lord without worshiping him, we will settle for legalistic, self-centered service. And if we worship and never work, we will end up with a form of godliness but no power.

While God alone did the commissioning, he did it through the church, through the laying on of hands. Some have surmised that this was a kind of ordination to the Gentile ministry, but actually it was an expression of the church's identification with Barnabas and Saul as they began a work of world evangelization. Just as in the Old Testament the offerer placed his hands on the sacrifice, expressing his identification with it, so now the assembled church of Antioch laid their hands on these two ambassadors for Christ. They were saying in effect, "Brothers, we are with you in this great enterprise. As you go, we go. We are part of you."

Barnabas and Saul left on their journey with the full identification and support of the church. The missionary church at Antioch is a great example for us.

THE MISSION OF THE CHURCH MILITANT (vv. 4-5)

> *The two of them, sent on their way by the Holy Spirit, went down to Seleucia and sailed from there to Cyprus. When they arrived at Salamis, they proclaimed the word of God in the Jewish synagogues. John was with them as their helper. (vv. 4-5)*

It was clear where their orders came from — they were "sent on their way by the Holy Spirit." They were divinely enabled and had a remarkable willingness to bravely follow. As they set sail, the Lord was the captain of their ship and of their souls. This was radically different from the arrogant pride exemplified in William Ernest Henley's classic poem "Invictus":

Out of the night that covers me,
Black as the Pit from pole to pole,
I thank whatever gods may be
For my unconquerable soul.

In the fell clutch of circumstance
I have not winced nor cried aloud.
Under the bludgeonings of chance
My head is bloody, but unbowed.

Beyond this place of wrath and tears,
Looms but the Horror of the shade,
And yet the menace of the years
Finds and shall find me unafraid.

It matters not how strait the gate,
How charged with punishments the scroll.
I am the master of my fate:
I am the captain of my soul.

Paul and Barnabas were not the masters of their fate or the captains of their souls. Christ was! And because he was, he produced an incredible bravery in them (compare 2 Corinthians 11). As they sailed out of Seleucia, it was Saul and Barnabas *contra mundum* — God's ambassadors standing against the world.

Because they allowed Christ to be the captain of their souls, they modeled a willingness to follow the Savior that should be ours as well. From here on they remained open to the Spirit's redirection at a moment's notice. I have done, at God's leading, things I had said I would never do. Never say, "Never, God!" Rather say, "God, I would love to go to the Sahara . . . I would love to go to Alaska." What models of willingness we see in Barnabas and Saul. If God is speaking to us, we must go!

The course of their first mission was quite simple. They set sail from Seleucia, the port city near Antioch, for Salamis, the port city of the island of Cyprus. It was an easy 130-mile voyage. The ancient world regarded Cyprus very much like we regard Hawaii or the Bahamas. William Barclay says it was called Markaria or "Happy Isle" because its climate was so perfect and its resources so abundant.[1] For some it was a place in the sun or a "Fantasy Island." But it was also a needy place, the crossroads of the Mediterranean, and a natural place to go to first because Barnabas was a Cypriot himself. Upon arrival, their method was simple — travel the island from east to west, from Salamis to Paphos, a distance of about ninety miles, preaching the gospel first in the Jewish synagogues but also to the Gentiles.

The realities of the spiritual war now began to show themselves. Little happened at first. They traveled about ninety miles preaching to Jews and Gentiles, but nothing notable happened — not even in Salamis, the largest city of the island.

Verse 5 tells us they had brought along John Mark as their "helper." Some see him as the first ministerial intern. According to Colossians 4:10, he was Barnabas' young cousin. He evidently came from a well-to-do family in Jerusalem and had been privy to the great goings-on in the Holy City. He would later author the Gospel of Mark. I believe, considering what happened later, that he was enamored with the romance of the venture. In his mind he saw himself accompanying Barnabas and Saul as they conquered the world. He probably expected to see the miracle of the Antioch church duplicated elsewhere. There was also the appeal of a cruise to "Happy Isle," where the olive trees glistened in the sun.

But once on the missionary journey, reality quickly set in. They all became tired, even exhausted. The accommodations were not always the best, and soon the romance was gone. Mark began to wonder why he had come on this trip.

OPPOSITION TO THE CHURCH MILITANT (vv. 6-8)

> *They traveled through the whole island until they came to Paphos. There they met a Jewish sorcerer and false prophet named Bar-Jesus, who was an attendant of the proconsul, Sergius Paulus. The proconsul, an intelligent man, sent for Barnabas and Saul because he wanted to hear the word of God. But Elymas the sorcerer (for that is what his name means) opposed them and tried to turn the proconsul from the faith. (vv. 6-8)*

When the trio came to the capital of the island, they encountered two men. One was the Roman governor of Cyprus, Sergius Paulus, whom Luke describes with the highly complimentary adjective *sunétos* ("intelligent"), indicating he was a man of great understanding. He was evidently weary of materialism and idolatry and was looking for a higher, more genuine spiritual reality. This accounts for the presence of the wizard Elymas, also known as Bar-Jesus. Sergius Paulus had been consulting him for help and was under his sway. Bar-Jesus means "son of Jesus" or "son of salvation," perhaps because he claimed to be a spiritual descendant of Jesus and thus an heir to his magical powers. At any rate, this sorcerer was claiming to know the way of salvation. Elymas (an Arabic word) means "skillful one," and this, no doubt, he was. He was a man of immense power, having a controlling influence over the ruler of Cyprus.

A major battle was inevitable. Spiritual warfare is not a fantasy of over-imaginative theologians or novelists. It happens today, and it happened to Paul, Barnabas, and John Mark then — a bare-knuckle, heart-thumping confrontation. The truth is, life is difficult, and sometimes even more so when you choose to follow Christ. Corrie ten Boom would never have ended up in the concentration camp at Ravensbruck if she and her family had not chosen to consistently obey Christ by sheltering fellow human beings from genocide. G. Campbell Morgan would never have cried out, "During these two years, I have known more of visions fading into mirages, of purposes failing of fulfillment, of things of strength crumbling away in weakness than ever in my life before" if he had not obeyed Christ and pastored Westminster Chapel, the great "White Elephant" of Congregationalism.

There is a cost to sincere service for Christ. Never share your faith and you will never look like a fool. Never stand for righteousness on a social issue and you will never be rejected. Never walk out of a theater because a movie or play is offensive and you will never be called a prig. Never practice consistent honesty in business and you will not lose the trade of a not-so-honest associate. Never reach out to the needy and you will never be taken advantage of. Never give your heart and it will never be broken. Never go to Cyprus and you will never be subjected to a dizzy, heart-convulsing confrontation with Satan. Seriously follow Christ and you will experience a gamut of sorrows almost completely unknown to the unbeliever. But of course you will also know the joy of adventure with the Lord of the universe and of spiritual victory as you live a life of allegiance to him.

For Saul and Barnabas, the battle was on.

THE VICTORY OF THE CHURCH MILITANT (vv. 9-12)

Verse 9 tells us that Paul fixed his gaze on Elymas, the wizard. What a stare that must have been. Then the apostle spoke:

> *"You are a child of the devil and an enemy of everything that is right! You are full of all kinds of deceit and trickery. Will you never stop perverting the right ways of the Lord?" (v. 10)*

This does not sound Christian. How could Paul talk that way to anyone? He was "filled with the Holy Spirit" (v. 9). It was through the discernment that the Spirit gives that Paul saw the state of Elymas' heart. The Holy Spirit also fills his children with love. Paul loved God, and he loved Paulus, but "The spirit of love is a Spirit of fire."[2]

> *"Now the hand of the Lord is against you. You are going to be blind, and for a time you will be unable to see the light of the sun." Immediately mist and darkness came over him, and he groped about,*

> *seeking someone to lead him by the hand. When the proconsul saw what had happened, he believed, for he was amazed at the teaching about the Lord. (vv. 11-12)*

Interestingly, archaeology has confirmed Luke's report. Sir William Ramsay reports that inscriptions bearing Sergius Paulus' name have been found on Cyprus confirming that he was a Christian and that his entire family became Christians.[3]

How did all this affect John Mark? "From Paphos, Paul and his companions sailed to Perga in Pamphylia, where John left them to return to Jerusalem" (v. 13). The realities of missionary life were too much for John Mark. He had inwardly romanticized the ministry they were undertaking, but reality had smashed his dreams. First came the disappointment in the seeming ineffectiveness of the initial ministry. Then there had been a convert, but what a battle for that one soul! Now they were setting sail from the sunny shores for the ominous cliffs of Perga, 175 miles away.

There may also have been sickness along the way, because Paul did not preach in Pamphylia but in Galatia. He wrote in Galatians 4:13, "As you know, it was because of an illness that I first preached the gospel to you." Scholars conjecture that he caught malaria in Pamphylia (which was notorious for the ailment) and moved to the safer climate of Galatia. All of this, combined with John Mark's privileged upbringing, was simply too much for the young man. So he went home. Later he would beautifully redeem himself (compare 2 Timothy 4:11), but for the time being Paul considered him a deserter.

John Mark was a wonderful young man, but at this point in his life he was the victim of his own uninformed, idealistic expectations. He did not understand the realities of war. But later he would understand, and Paul would say, "Get Mark and bring him with you, because he is helpful to me in my ministry." We too sometimes draw back from a commitment we have made, but there is hope — God loves to give us another chance.

Let's face it — Murphy's Law is alive and well in the Church. Life is difficult even for Christians. Any teaching otherwise is at best misinformed and at worse an outright lie.

Joy and woe are woven fine,
A clothing for the soul divine,
Under every grief and pine
Runs a joy with silken twine.
It is right it should be so;
Man was made for joy and woe;

And when this we rightly know,
Through the world we safely go.
—William Blake

Life is quite often difficult for the militant Christian. If you truly and fully follow Christ, you will open yourself to a diversity of troubles scarcely known by the self-serving nonbeliever.

The sad reality is, many of us are too soft! We think, "This cannot be God's will — it is too hard! I know it is not God's will — it hurts!"

The bright reality, such a part of Paul's life, is that there is no trial or difficulty Christ cannot see us through. This same Paul wrote the triumphant words, "We are more than conquerors through him who loved us" (Romans 8:37). With Christ there is room for vast optimism!

We are called to war! Onward, Christian soldiers!

> Some years ago there was a great missionary rally in the Royal Albert Hall in London, England, and a clergyman turned to the Duke of Wellington (the "Iron Duke," whose armies had defeated Napoleon) and asked, "My lord Duke, do you believe in missions?" "What are your marching orders?" asked the Duke. "Of course, the Bible says to 'go into all the world,'" answered the clergyman. "Then you have nothing to say about it. As a soldier you are to obey orders."[4]

Let us not go to war with glorified expectations. War is difficult, but through Christ we are more than conquerors!

PRAYER

O Lord, left to ourselves, we all will turn back — dismayed because we expected greater results and greater emotional highs, afraid because the enemies are too much for us, discouraged because physical trials slow us down. Each of us, in our hearts, is at times a deserting John Mark. Help us, O God, to excel in Spirit-led ministry for Christ, to persevere and triumph through our reigning Lord. In Jesus' name, Amen.

22

Sticking to the Task, Regardless

ACTS 14:1-28

One night in 1945 Captain Terry Simeral brought his crippled B-29 in for a safe landing amidst waiting fire engines and red flares, unloaded the plane, and entered the group headquarters tent. His face was white. He seemed to be in a state of shock, and it was several minutes before he could talk. An incredible feat had been accomplished as Captain Simeral piloted his Pathfinder plane toward the enemy coast in order to drop phosphorus smoke to mark the mission's target.

On B-29s it was the radio operator's job to release the bomb through a narrow tube. On this particular night Sgt. Henry Erwin received the routine order, triggered the flare, and dropped it down the tube. But there was a malfunction, and the bomb exploded and bounced back into Erwin's face, blinding both eyes and searing off an ear. Burning phosphorus melts metal like butter, and the bomb was now at Sgt. Erwin's feet and eating rapidly through the deck of the plane toward a full load of incendiaries. He was alone because the navigator had gone to the transparent dome atop the plane to make some celestial computations.

Not having the luxury of time to analyze his situation, Erwin picked up the white-hot bomb in his bare hands and stumbled forward toward the cockpit, groping along with elbows and feet. The navigator's folding table was down and latched, blocking the way. Sgt. Erwin hugged the blazing bomb under one arm as it burned the flesh over his ribs, unfastened the latch, and lifted the table. He stumbled on, a walking torch. His clothing and hair were ablaze. Dense smoke filled the plane, and Simeral had opened the window beside him to clear the air.

"I could not see Erwin," says Simeral, "but I heard his voice right at my elbow. He said, 'Pardon me, sir,' and reached across the window and tossed the bomb out. Then he collapsed on the flight deck." Amazingly, Sgt. Erwin survived and went on to regain the use of his hands and partial vision in one eye. Sgt. Henry Erwin is one of our country's Congressional Medal of Honor winners, receiving it from General Curtis LeMay while still in a Pacific hospital.[1]

The story of Sgt. Henry Erwin and the blazing bomb is one of the most amazing accounts of valor I have ever read. It is a tribute to the human spirit. Yet there is a bravery that exceeds even that. It is not as dramatic, not as conspicuous, and not as likely to be remembered. It is the bravery that is called forth by consistent devotion to a course or ideal. Consider the bravery of a young mother as she devotes herself to the care of a handicapped child, or the gallantry of men and women who endure the world's scorn as they pour out their lives for the abolition of a social evil.

The supreme Christian examples come to us from the early church. Acts 14 shows us the consistently courageous attitude of the apostles in their loyalty to Christ through thick and thin. Specifically, the first missionaries bravely held to their purpose of preaching Christ despite extreme temptations. Their valiant and consistent attitude is a great model for us.

Paul and Barnabas had already demonstrated their bravery on their first missionary journey. Paul and Barnabas against the world! On Cyprus they gallantly preached the gospel, with no response except indifference. In Paphos they finally had a convert, but only after a fierce battle with a wizard. In brave obedience they set sail for Asia Minor, but it was all too much for John Mark, who returned home. In Pisidian Antioch they again ministered the Word with great effect (13:42-52), which brought great persecution, so that finally they shook the dust off their feet and headed for Iconium. Through thick and thin they maintained an unflinching devotion and singleness of purpose in following Christ. Chapter 14 depicts Paul and Barnabas completing their first missionary journey, traveling through Iconium, Lystra, and Derbe, and returning to home base in Antioch in Syria.

Words like *gallantry*, *loyalty*, and *devotion* sound like nineteenth-century anachronisms — vestiges of Victorian rhetoric. Actually, however, we all long for these qualities in ourselves and in others, as evidenced by the popularity of the stories of such persons as Eric Liddell, told in the award-winning movie *Chariots of Fire*.

Having been booted out of Pisidian Antioch, Paul and Barnabas now headed elsewhere. They went southeast some eighty miles on the famous Via Sebaste through rolling countryside, then past the snow-capped peaks of Sultan Dag, until they came to a beautiful plateau surrounded by fertile plains and verdant forests — Iconium.

ICONIUM (vv. 1-7)

Iconium was an ancient city that claimed to be older than Damascus. In the dim past it had a king named Nannacus, and the phrase "since the days of Nannacus" was proverbial for "from the beginning of time."[2] There were no large Roman garrisons in Iconium, so it remained more Greek in attitude and was somewhat resistant to Roman authority. They were governed by an assembly of citizens called the *Demos*, which held itself aloof from the Roman representative.

Here the missionaries met with immediate success and immediate opposition. We see the success in verse 1:

> *At Iconium Paul and Barnabas went as usual into the Jewish synagogue. There they spoke so effectively that a great number of Jews and Gentiles believed.*

This was no bland, empty gospel. It hit the locals like a ton of bricks, and many believed! But trouble followed.

> *But the Jews who refused to believe stirred up the Gentiles and poisoned their minds against the brothers. So Paul and Barnabas spent considerable time there, speaking boldly for the Lord, who confirmed the message of his grace by enabling them to do miraculous signs and wonders. (vv. 2-3)*

When their enemies stirred up hatred against them, what did Paul and Barnabas do? They stayed around for a long time and continued to speak boldly. They had just been run out of Pisidian Antioch, but they were not about to run at the first sign of trouble.

Such pluck and spunk has always been true of God's warriors. John Wesley once encountered a village bully when their carriages met upon a narrow road. The bully knew Wesley and disliked him and would not give him any leeway, staying in the middle of the road. John Wesley cheerfully gave the man the entire road, even though he had to turn into the ditch. As they passed, the bully said, "I never turn out for fools," and Wesley — all five foot two of him — retorted, "I always do." In 2 Corinthians 4:8-9 Paul wrote of himself and his kind:

> *We are hard-pressed on all sides, but we are never frustrated; we are puzzled, but never in despair. We are persecuted, but we are never deserted; we may be knocked down but we are never knocked out! (*Phillips*)*

Paul and Barnabas were always brave, always gallant. Finally, however, it appeared that it was wise to leave:

> *The people of the city were divided; some sided with the Jews, others with the apostles. There was a plot afoot among the Gentiles and Jews, together with their leaders, to mistreat them and stone them. But they found out about it and fled to the Lycaonian cities of Lystra and Derbe and to the surrounding country, where they continued to preach the good news. (vv. 4-7)*

Their enemies finally divided the *Demos*, the town council, and decided to do what they never would have attempted if the Roman rule had been strong enough — they wanted to stone God's missionaries! Paul and Barnabas were brave but not foolish. They were born-again, not born yesterday. The Lord protects his children, but he wants us to use common sense. So the missionaries departed.

They had now been booted out of two cities back-to-back, but they kept serving Christ and proclaiming his gospel. Undoubtedly they felt some discouragement. Some of the things that were said to them hurt. They may have worried about leaving some baby Christians behind. Yet, when we read Paul's life accounts we also find an underlying sense of anticipation and joy. Paul was a realist but also an optimist. One preacher described an optimist as an eighty-five-year-old man who marries a thirty-five-year-old woman and moves into a twelve-room house next to an elementary school. An optimist does not allow the "facts" that surround him to take away his belief that great things can happen. Remember Paul's words from the Philippian jail?

> *I know what is to be in need, and I know what is to have plenty; I have learned the secret of being content in any and every situation, whether well fed or hungry. I can do everything through him who gives me strength. (Philippians 4:12-13)*

So Paul and Barnabas moved another twenty-six miles out into the wilds to a place called Lystra. Now the action became intense.

LYSTRA (vv. 8-20)

Though little is known of the origin of Lystra, we do know it was a frontier outpost. Caesar Augustus had made it a Roman colony in 6 B.C., establishing it as the easternmost of the fortified cities of Galatia. I imagine it had a sort of "old-west" flavor and ethos. Most of the populace were uneducated

Lycaonians who had their own language. The people were half-barbarous. The Romans ruled the land, the Greeks controlled the commerce, and the Jews had little influence. In fact, there was no synagogue there.

The ministry got off to a flying start in Lystra with the healing of a cripple.

> *In Lystra there sat a man crippled in his feet, who was lame from birth and had never walked. He listened to Paul as he was speaking. Paul looked directly at him, saw that he had faith to be healed and called out, "Stand up on your feet!" At that, the man jumped up and began to walk. (vv. 8-10)*

As Paul preached publicly, he observed a lame man whose interest and willing gaze indicated a work of grace within. Those who preach understand what Paul experienced. Dr. Barnhouse put it this way:

> There have been numerous times in my own ministry when, while I was speaking from the pulpit, I have seen a response on some particular face in the audience, and I knew that the Holy Spirit had begun a work of grace in that person. Frequently, after the meeting was over that person would come to me and tell me that at that precise moment he knew — just knew — that Christ had died and risen again for him and that he was truly born again.[3]

Paul saw this man's response and, following the impulse of the Holy Spirit, healed him without warning. Paul had everyone's undivided attention as the ex-cripple (whom *everyone* knew) danced in front of the people and cried out, "Is it really true? I have never walked in my life before! Look, Mom — no cane!" Now Paul could give them the goods — a little on the doctrine of man, the story of the Incarnation, the atoning work of the cross, the necessity of faith. A great harvest followed!

There was just one complication: these half-wild Lycaonians had an ancient legend that Zeus and Hermes had once come to the hill country disguised as mortals seeking lodging. Though they asked a thousand homes, no one would take them in. Finally, at a humble cottage of straw and reeds, a poor elderly couple, Philemon and Baucis, freely welcomed them and feasted them with what meager means they had. In appreciation, the gods transformed the cottage into a temple, making the couple priest and priestess. And when they died, they were immortalized as a great oak and a great linden tree. The inhospitable homes, however, were destroyed.[4] These poor Lycaonians were determined not to make the same mistake again.

> *When the crowd saw what Paul had done, they shouted in the Lycaonian language, "The gods have come down to us in human form!" Barnabas they called Zeus, and Paul they called Hermes because he was the chief speaker. The priest of Zeus, whose temple was just outside the city, brought bulls and wreaths to the city gates because he and the crowd wanted to offer sacrifices to them. (vv. 11-13)*

Barnabas evidently had a more noble presence, so they called him Zeus, the chief god. Since Paul was the spokesman, they naturally called him Hermes, the messenger of the gods. Poor Paul and Barnabas did not know what was going on because when the people became excited they began to speak Lycaonian. The devil was having a banner day! What had started out with such promise was about to be ruined.

When the priest came with sacrificial oxen with garlands on their horns, Paul and Barnabas were horrified. Now they understood what was happening! "But when the apostles Barnabas and Paul heard of this, they tore their clothes and rushed out into the crowd, shouting . . ." (v. 14). Tearing one's robe was the traditional Hebrew way of responding to sacrilege. "Hey, fellow-mortals, we are just like you! Look — five fingers, five toes — count 'em yourself!"

Next Paul tried to preach a sermon. It was good as far as he got. He used a simple argument, for untaught people, based on what they could see of nature. If the apostle had been able to continue, he would have gone on to the gospel, but that was not to be. Verse 18 tells us the crowds persisted in their intended homage: "Even with these words, they [Paul and Barnabas] had difficulty keeping the crowd from sacrificing to them." This was terrible! The apostles had been locked out of Pisidian Antioch and Iconium as heretics, and now they were being deified in Lystra! It is difficult to say which was worse — having stones thrown at them or this blasphemous attempt to worship them as gods.

Satan was giving them his best shot — manipulation at its worst! The Lystrans' misplaced praise kept Paul and Barnabas from presenting the full truth. These people wanted to know this new God only on their own terms. Paul and Barnabas never got to explain the Incarnation because the people were determined to keep them within the boundaries of their religious presumptions. Today too Christ is often made such a captive of men's presuppositions (what they think he ought to be or what they want him to be) that they do not really understand him. Lloyd Ogilvie has put it this way:

> When Jesus was born there was no room at the inn. But today we not only have room at our inn, but a penthouse suite away from reality.

> Jesus is a V.I.P. to be honored but not believed or followed. In America, he is a custom but not the true Christ; a captured hero of a casual civil religion, but not Lord of our lives.[5]

This is idolatry. We cut Christ down to our size and squeeze him into the straitjacket of one of our little gods. That way he is safe and always at a distance.

When Jesus came triumphantly into Jerusalem on the colt of a donkey on Palm Sunday 2,000 years ago, the people were delirious with praise, singing their loud hosannas. But when he spoke of his coming death, they began to cool. The cross did not fit their preconceptions of the Messiah. Finally they shouted, "Away with him. Crucify him!"

It is the same today. Almost everyone will receive him as the greatest man who ever lived. Just leave it there and everything will be fine. Enlightened circles are comfortable with calling him the supreme psychologist of history. He is safe as the most important person of all time. The safe, sweet Jesus, meek and mild — sentimental, impotent, distant — is no threat. The world will do anything for a Christ who is limited by our own perspectives. What it will not do is allow him to put forth his own claims. The world will not receive him as Lord! We all sometimes wear blinders as we read the Bible, seeing what we think supports our preconceived system and missing those things that do not fit. It is only with God's help that such a serious error can be avoided or changed.

The story of Lystra also exposes another of our weaknesses: we find it easy to exalt the messenger instead of the message. We want to make men and women, rather than God, our sense of security. So we have our own Christian pantheon — our own Christian matinee idols. We must, with God's help, honestly examine our hearts to see whom we are truly worshiping. Ourselves? Our favorite preacher or writer or Christian entertainer? Or do we worship and serve the Lord Jesus Christ?

What a temptation this was for Paul and Barnabas, and Satan knew it. It would have been so easy for the apostles to rationalize, "We will accommodate these poor savages and then point them to God. This sure beats stoning!" It is to their eternal credit that they did not receive worship by men for even a split second. But now they were in definite trouble! Hell hath no rage like a worshiper scorned! If the people could not fit Paul and Barnabas into their neat little idolatrous preconceptions, they would do away with them.

Notice how quickly the crowd changed:

> *Then some Jews came from Antioch and Iconium and won the crowd over. They stoned Paul and dragged him outside the city, thinking he was dead. (v. 19)*

A stoning was a horrible, bloody thing! As the rocks crashed against Paul's skull, I wonder if his mind flashed back to Stephen's execution, in which he had participated. Soon there he lay — a blood-spattered, broken frame beneath the rubble of Lystra. Maybe this is when he experienced the ecstasy of being caught up into the third heaven as described in 2 Corinthians 12:1-4. To the Galatians he would later write, "Finally, let no one cause me trouble, for I bear on my body the marks of Jesus" (6:17). As he lay there, the disciples stood around deciding what to do with his body. Tears streamed down their faces. "What a pity — he was in the prime of his ministry. If only he could have lived longer." Suddenly Paul popped one eye open, then the other. "It's all right, brothers and sisters! No funeral today! Let's get out of here!"

"He got up and went back into the city" (v. 20). What supreme bravery! What a witness! This had more effect than a thousand sermons. Paul, caked with blood and dirt, must have been quite a spectacle. Dave Howard, in his book *The Power of the Holy Spirit*, tells about a fearless pastor he ministered with in Colombia named Lupercio Taba. One Sunday Taba was preaching from his pulpit when a man appeared at a side window of the church, aimed a pistol at him, and ordered him to stop preaching. The congregation, seeing the danger, dove to the floor and hid under the pews. Taba, however, went right on preaching the gospel. The man then fired four shots at him. Two shots went past the preacher's head, one on one side, one on the other, and lodged in the wall behind him. Two shots went past his body, one under one arm, one under the other, and also lodged in the wall. The would-be assassin then dropped his gun and fled. Taba, still unmoved, continued his sermon.[6]

Nothing could deter Paul and Barnabas from bravely preaching Christ! What an example! Interestingly, Lystra was the city from which Paul would recruit Lois and Eunice and their young grandson/son Timothy.

The courage of the apostles continued as they kept up their itinerant preaching, then revisited all the cities that had thrown them out.

> *They preached the good news in that city [Derbe] and won a large number of disciples. Then they returned to Lystra, Iconium and Antioch, strengthening the disciples and encouraging them to remain true to the faith. "We must go through many hardships to enter the kingdom of God," they said. (v. 21)*

Paul comments on experiences like this in 2 Timothy 3:11-12:

> *. . . persecutions, sufferings — what kinds of things happened to me in Antioch, Iconium and Lystra, the persecutions I endured. Yet the*

> *Lord rescued me from all of them. In fact, everyone who desires to live a godly life in Christ Jesus will be persecuted.*

Jesus said the same thing: "If the world hates you, keep in mind that it hated me first" (John 15:18). Knowing this and serving Christ anyway calls for bravery, which can only come about with heavenly assistance.

After installing elders in the churches, the apostles finally headed home.

> *After going through Pisidia, they came into Pamphylia, and when they had preached the word in Perga, they went down to Attalia. From Attalia they sailed back to Antioch, where they had been committed to the grace of God for the work they had now completed. On arriving there, they gathered the church together and reported all that God had done through them and how he had opened the door of faith to the Gentiles. (vv. 24-27)*

With old Barnabas the encourager alongside, Paul said, "Do you remember when you laid your hands on us here in Antioch? Then we went across to Cyprus, where we preached from Salamis to Paphos. We fought for the soul of the proconsul there, Sergius Paulus, and Christ won him over. We went to Asia Minor, and I was sick and ill in Perga and Pamphylia. We went to Iconium, and they booted us out. We went to Lystra and were stoned." What a story!

Barnabas probably interjected and gave the Antioch Christians some further details. "Then we went on to Derbe, then back through the cities and back down the coast and preached to Perga, and now we are back here, brothers and sisters."

Their example and personal call to commitment is reminiscent of the sentiment expressed so beautifully by Winston Churchill:

> It is not the critic who counts, not the man who points out how the strong man stumbled or where the doer of deeds could have done them better. The credit belongs to the man who is actually in the arena, whose face is marred by dust and sweat and blood, who strives valiantly, who errs and comes short again and again, who knows the great enthusiasm, the great devotions, and spends himself in a worthy cause, who at the best knows in the end the triumph of high achievement, and who at the worst, if he fails, at least fails while daring greatly, so that his place shall never be with those cold and timid souls who know neither victory nor defeat.[7]

PRAYER

Our Father, we are elevated by human gallantry, especially in your cause. Father, we love the words gallant, brave, devoted, true *and ask that you would help us be all of that, for your honor and praise. Lord, we pray that some of what was in Paul and Barnabas would be in our lives today and in days to come. In Jesus' name, Amen.*

23

Grace Alone

ACTS 15:1-35

After Paul and Barnabas' first missionary journey, they gave the church at Antioch a missionary report:

> *They gathered the church together and reported all that God had done through them and how he had opened the door of faith to the Gentiles. (14:27)*

The river of God's saving grace had overflowed its banks. One of the early root ideas behind "grace" was that of "charm," and there was a graciousness among the early believers that attracted others to Christ.

Things were going well — too well for the enemy's taste, and the inevitable satanic counterattack soon came.

> *Some men came down from Judea to Antioch and were teaching the brothers: "Unless you are circumcised, according to the custom taught by Moses, you cannot be saved." (15:1)*

Good-bye, free grace! Good-bye, joy! These men — Judaizers — did not deny salvation by grace per se. They simply said salvation came by "grace plus . . ." — specifically "grace plus circumcision." These were the kind of ecclesiastical wet blankets who can listen to the testimony of a new convert and say, "Well, that is okay, but there is something more that you must do before you have the whole package." The Judaizers did not know the joy of pure grace — God's divine favor freely given.

This was upsetting, to say the least. "This brought Paul and Barnabas into sharp dispute and debate with them" (v. 2a). There was passionate argument, perhaps even some shouting. No doubt the Judaizers claimed front-office support from Jerusalem, and Paul and Barnabas said those men had no such thing. The result was division among the brethren. This was tragic. It seemed that the only solution was to send Paul and Barnabas up to Jerusalem to meet with the leaders (v. 2). So the dynamic duo set out for the Holy City. En route they spread great joy to other believers as they shared what God had been doing among the Gentiles (v. 3). However, when they got to Jerusalem, they found that the Judaizers were well entrenched.

> *When they came to Jerusalem, they were welcomed by the church and the apostles and elders, to whom they reported everything God had done through them. Then some of the believers who belonged to the party of the Pharisees stood up and said, "The Gentiles must be circumcised and required to obey the law of Moses." (vv. 4-5)*

Some of the Pharisees who had been converted to Christ were insisting on their version of Christianity. To become a Christian, according to them, one must go through a procedure very much like becoming a Jewish proselyte. The apostles were faced with a huge problem, a problem compounded by the fact that these Pharisaic Christians were not intrinsically evil. If they had worn horns, it would have been so much easier. They had genuinely come to know Christ, and their faith had cost them dearly. But they were also the product of their upbringing. Lloyd Ogilvie put it this way:

> Think of the stability of the Pharisee's training and Hebraism, his immersion in Mosaic Law and tradition, his pride in being part of the chosen people of God. Live in his shoes as we relive the steps of his rigorous education and joyous participation in Israel's customs. Feel the loving arms of parents and family as he is circumcised on the eighth day; catch the awe and wonder he felt sitting at the feet of the elder Pharisees studying the Scripture; identify with the pride he felt when he became a son of the Law at his bar mitzvah. Become one with him as he grew to full manhood and earned the revered status of a Pharisee, and consider how he must have burst with satisfaction as he put on the dignified robes of a leader of Israel.[1]

Into the Pharisees' neat, well-ordered life came the claims of Christ, and with that an agonizing civil war within. Then came conversion — new life from above. Of course, they gained so much by knowing Christ, but parents, other relatives, and friends would consider them dead. They lost everything because of their association with the Savior. It was natural for some of them to find it difficult to make a clean break with their past as Pharisees. Though Christians, they could not bring themselves to give away centuries of distinctives that had set their people apart from the world. So with good intentions they thrust those distinctives and traditions onto others.

> If Jesus was the Hebrew Messiah, anyone wanting his salvation would have to become a Hebrew first! How else could he know the full meaning and purpose of God? The Pharisee Christians banded together to make sure no one slipped by Mount Sinai on the way to Calvary![2]

They were not bad people at this point. But given time, their views, tightly held, would pull them so far away from the doctrine of grace that they would become apostate. We all are influenced by our backgrounds. Each of us has experienced some doctrinal or practical distortion because of past experience or environment. The challenge is to identify those points of error or misemphasis before we drift too far away from Christ.

Nevertheless, the future of the church of Christ and the doctrine of the way of salvation were at stake. History and experience have proven that anything made a co-requirement with faith soon shoves faith aside and becomes the means of salvation. If the apostles had capitulated, there would soon have been a "Christian" doctrine of "salvation by circumcision" and "The First Church of the Circumcision." Similarly, today we must withstand false doctrines of baptismal regeneration and salvation through sacraments.

I once had the privilege of leading a rewarding ministry with an exciting college group. When it came time to move on, I happily turned the work over to a man who I had every reason to believe would do a good job. He was a graduate of the same seminary as myself, had spent several years working with a fine Christian organization, and had an exceptional wife. However, it wasn't long after he began his ministry that alarming reports began to come my way. He believed that through meditation God could give him special spiritual understanding that went beyond the clear meaning of Scripture. Because according to him godly women should cover their ankles and hair, the young ladies in his inner circle began wearing bonnets and dresses that touched their shoes. Likewise, young men in the inner circle would not wear garments of mixed fibers, in keeping with Old Testament laws. The good news of Christ was reduced to a list of do's and don'ts. In a short time this man led numerous lives astray, including some who have yet to recover. He even became the leader of a cult and divorced his wife. He toppled grace and faith from their proper position — a serious error we must all take care to avoid.

Theologically, the truth of the gospel was at stake in Jerusalem. And relationally the stakes were just as high. A wrong decision in Jerusalem and gracious openness would be replaced with jaundiced exclusiveness.

Fortunately, the Jerusalem Council followed Christ, and in doing so they gave us a basis upon which to build grace into our theology and our relationships.

PETER'S SPEECH (vv. 7-11)

By verses 6 and 7 the Council has convened, and there has been much debate. No doubt some of the hotter heads had said some things for which they were already sorry. Perhaps there were even times of chaos before Peter rose to speak. Knowing Peter, he probably could not sit still any longer. First, he recalled his experience with the Gentiles:

> *"Brothers, you know that some time ago God made a choice among you that the Gentiles might hear from my lips the message of the gospel and believe. God, who knows the heart, showed that he accepted them by giving the Holy Spirit to them, just as he did to us. He made no distinction between us and them, for he purified their hearts by faith." (vv. 7-9)*

He was referring to his ministry years earlier in seeing the Gentile Cornelius and his entire house receive Christ and the Holy Spirit through faith. The conclusion? "[God] made no distinction between us and them." Then came Peter's stunning pronouncement:

> *"Now then, why do you try to test God by putting on the necks of the disciples a yoke that neither we nor our fathers have been able to bear? No! We believe it is through the grace of our Lord Jesus that we are saved, just as they are." (vv. 10-11)*

Peter affirmed his perplexity as to why the Judaizers would saddle anyone with the Law. They themselves could not bear it, so why heap it upon others? God had given them the Law as a schoolmaster to lead them to Christ by demonstrating at every turn they were sinners in need of mercy (see Galatians 3:23-25; Romans 3:19-20). They transgressed the basic commandment to love God with all their heart, soul, mind, and strength and their neighbor as themselves daily. The conclusion of all this? Grace alone! "We believe it is through the grace of our Lord Jesus that we are saved, just as they are." Every person — the Ph.D. and the least-taught child — comes into God's family the same way — solely by the undeserved kindness of a forgiving God!

With the conclusion of Peter's speech a turning point came, as evidenced in verse 12 by the multitude's silence. We learn when we listen. During that silence, Barnabas and Paul seized the moment and verified what Peter had said by relating the signs and wonders that God had done through them among the Gentiles. The miracles of their first missionary trip were recited, and the Council was awestruck.

JAMES'S SPEECH (vv. 13-21)

After some time Barnabas and Paul finished, and James stood up. If there had been silence before, there was absolute silence now, for James was the Lord's earthly half-brother. After the Resurrection Jesus had visited him personally (1 Corinthians 15:7). Called "James the Just" because of his piety, he was ascetic and scrupulous. When he died, his knees were allegedly callused like those of a camel because of his many hours of prayer. He was a pillar of the church (Galatians 1:19; 2:9) and the moderator of the assembly now considering an all-important dispute. Some call him the first bishop of Jerusalem.

The hopes of the Pharisaic sect rocketed as James stood to speak. Surely he would set Peter and Paul and Barnabas right. They were undoubtedly surprised at the apostle's response, for James first showed how the conversion of Gentiles was in accord with the Old Testament Scriptures.

> *"Simon has described to us how God at first showed his concern by taking from the Gentiles a people for himself. The words of the prophets are in agreement with this, as it is written: 'After this I will return and rebuild David's fallen tent. Its ruins I will rebuild, and I will restore it, that the remnant of men may seek the Lord, and all the Gentiles who bear my name, says the Lord, who does these things' that have been known for ages." (vv. 14-18)*

Through this combination of passages taken largely from Amos 9:11-12, James was saying that according to the Old Testament prophets God's people would consist of two concentric groups. At the core would be Israel ("the tabernacle of David," NASB), and gathered around them would be the Gentiles ("the rest of mankind," NASB), who would share the messianic blessings without becoming Jewish proselytes.[3] Thus, everything that was happening was just as the Scriptures prophesied.

Then came James's pronouncement, the heart of the whole scene:

> *"Therefore it is my judgment that we do not trouble those who are turning to God from among the Gentiles, but that we write to them that they abstain from things contaminated by idols and from fornication and from what is strangled and from blood." (vv. 19-20)*

James had some advice for both groups. To the pharisaical Jewish believers he said, "Lay off these new Gentile Christians — do not trouble them."

To the Gentile believers, he gave three restrictions:

1. Stay away from anything that has to do with idols.
2. Avoid fornication.
3. Do not partake of meat that has been strangled or has blood in it.

There was to be no idolatry because there is only one true God, and only he is to be worshiped. Fornication was forbidden in all cases[4] because fornication was at that time rampant among the Gentiles. Why the third restriction? "For Moses has been preached in every city from the earliest times and is read in the synagogues on every Sabbath" (v. 21). In other words, Jewish communities existed in nearly every city, and the Gentile converts were not to do anything that would offend the Jews' religious scruples.

James gives us two complementary principles for grace-filled living. First: *as those under grace we are not to make non-Biblical requirements of others* — specifically, those that come from secondary cultural traditions. In that day this meant not foisting a Jewish lifestyle on Gentiles. Today this means we are not to make areas of our lifestyle that are not spelled out in Scripture normative for others if they are to be "good" Christians — for example, how we dress, how we run our church, the standards of living we think proper, personal tastes, musical preferences (including in a worship service), etc. If we thrust any of these on others as necessary to a life of grace, we repeat the sin of the Judaizers!

We so easily push our preferences on others. We assume they will either do things our way or they are unspiritual. We too often put others through the paces of our own heritage before we fully accept them as brothers and sisters. Sadly, sometimes a church will radiate more of this than the gospel!

One of the reasons (though not the only one) we are not to do this is because of what it does to us. Winston Churchill told of a British family that went out for a picnic by a lake. In the course of the afternoon the five-year-old son fell into the water. Unfortunately, none of the adults could swim. As the child was bobbing up and down and everyone on the shore was in panic, a passerby saw the situation. At great risk to himself, he dove in fully clothed and managed to reach the child just before he went under for the third time. He was able to pull him out of the water and present him safe and sound to his mother. Instead of thanking the stranger for his heroic efforts, however, the mother snapped peevishly at the rescuer, "Where's Johnny's cap?" Somehow in all of the commotion the boy's cap had gotten lost. Instead of rejoicing in her son's deliverance, the woman found something about which to be critical!

It is so easy for us to be like that woman — especially as we relate to our brothers and sisters in Christ. Somehow others are never quite right. There is always something more that is needed before they measure up. Such an attitude is not only bad for us — it is deadly to the church.

Dr. Howard Hendricks has remarked that he grew up in a legalistic home where the use of fingernail polish was enough to condemn one to Hell. He said, "I repudiated legalism intellectually and theologically in 1946, but in 1982 I am still wrestling with it emotionally."[5] Extra-Biblical restrictions take their toll. Perhaps even more serious, they block the proclamation of God's grace (divine favor — free and undeserved) to a dying world.

So much for the first principle. The second is: *because we are under grace, we gladly restrict our freedom for the sake of others*. There was not anything intrinsically wrong with eating a rare steak, but James said to boil it or eat it well-done for the sake of fellowship with the Jews. Paul states the same principle in 1 Corinthians 9:19-21:

> *Though I am free and belong to no man, I make myself a slave to everyone, to win as many as possible. To the Jews I became like a Jew, to win the Jews. To those under the law, I became like one under the law (though I myself am not under the law), so as to win those under the law. To those not having the law I became like one not having the law (though I am not free from God's law but am under Christ's law), so as to win those who not having the law.*

James's magnificent pronouncement carried the day! Who could take issue with the most scrupulous of all the Hebrew Christians — a man whose piety was admired by the most orthodox, a man who led a life of such exemplary self-denial?

THE COUNCIL'S PROCLAMATION (vv. 22-29)

The apostles and elders drafted a letter and sent it along with Paul and Barnabas and their friends, Silas and Judas Barsabbas, to take back to Antioch. The letter's conclusion was almost word for word as suggested by James:

> *It seemed good to the Holy Spirit and to us not to burden you with anything beyond the following requirements: You are to abstain from food sacrificed to idols, from blood, from the meat of strangled animals and from sexual immorality. You will do well to avoid these things. Farewell. (vv. 28-29)*

The Council's proclamation has been called one of the most courageous documents in the annals of history because its authors declared the truth even though they knew it would fully antagonize the Jewish establishment. From this time on, Christian work in Jerusalem became very difficult. While still trying to carry on a ministry to the Jewish nation, the apostles heroically refused to do or say anything to impede the progress of the gospel among the Gentiles. Brave men!

> *The men were sent off and went down to Antioch, where they gathered the church together and delivered the letter. The people read it and were glad for its encouraging message. (vv. 30-31)*

Why were they encouraged? The letter imposed some dietary restrictions. Why were they happy about that? A letter that a coed wrote to her parents humorously points out the reason.

> Dear Mom and Dad,
>
> Just thought I'd drop you a note to clue you in on my plans. I have fallen in love with a guy called Jim. He quit high school after grade eleven to get married. About a year ago he got a divorce.
>
> We have been going steady for two months and plan to get married in the fall. At any rate, I dropped out of school last week, although I'd like to finish college sometime in the future.

On the next page the letter continued:

> Mom and Dad, I just want you to know that everything I have written so far in this letter is false. NONE of it is true.
>
> But, Mom and Dad, it *is* true that I got a C- in French and flunked Math. And it *is* true that I am going to need some more money for my tuition payments.

News that may not sound particularly good sounds terrific if seen from a different perspective. For the believers in Antioch, a few minor restrictions in relation to their Hebrew brothers were nothing compared to the burden of the Law. Compared with what the Jerusalem Council could have insisted upon, the final recommendation was a great relief.

What does this mean to us today? First, *we must preach grace alone.*

> *For it is by grace you have been saved, through faith — and this not from yourselves, it is the gift of God — not by works, so that no one can boast. (Ephesians 2:8-9)*

Thy grace alone, O God,
To me can pardon speak;
Thy power alone, O Son of God,
Can this sore bondage break.

Second, like James the Just, *we must tolerate nothing else!* Grace is risky and can be abused but must not be rejected. Giving our kids the car keys is always a risk, but because we love them we do it. God allows us to choose, even wrongly. His continuing grace sustains and empowers us daily.

PRAYER

O Lord, help us to see any way we are mixing law with your grace, any false standards we are imposing on others, any conditions we are placing on our acceptance of them. Forgive us, cleanse us, shower us once again with your grace and love and mercy. In Jesus' name, Amen.

24

God's Guidance

ACTS 15:36 — 16:10

Paul and Barnabas returned home victoriously from the Council of Jerusalem, bringing with them the wonderful news that Gentile believers did not have to be circumcised or adopt a Jewish lifestyle to be saved. If the decision had gone the other way, evangelism of the Gentiles would have ended. But now the great apostle could not wait to get going again.

His plan was to retrace those memorable steps of his first missionary journey — from Antioch to the island of Cyprus, transversing it from Salamis to Paphos, then sailing to Asia Minor and Pamphylia and traveling up into Galatia, visiting Iconium, Lystra, Perga, and Attalia. These were worthy plans, and he and Barnabas were a great team. They expected to follow up on the new believers — to reprove false doctrine, teach more about God's grace, share the results of the Jerusalem Council, build up the leadership in each church. Paul and Barnabas were not willing to make the mistake so often made in modern-day evangelism — that of allowing converts to go their own way without follow-up.

However, to Paul's lasting amazement, soon after he began, he found himself taking an unexpected leap across the Dardanelle Straits from Asia to Europe in obedience to a special call to Macedonia. So important was this redirecting of Paul's life that the Pauline scholar Richard Longenecker says, "Authentic turning points in history are few, but surely among them that of the Macedonian vision ranks high."[1] They were momentous days when Columbus set sail from Spain, or when Vasco da Gama discovered the sea route to the West Indies, but those were of little significance compared with this great event! Something happened that completely redirected Paul's ministry, keeping it in line with God's hidden agenda.

How was Paul was directed from point A in Antioch, with his neatly ordered plans for follow-up, to point B in Europe? The answer does not fit some of the neat little formulas we sometimes hear on how to know God's will. Paul did not fully understand what was going on until he and Luke sat down for a chat after it was all over. But in retrospect Paul's experience is a marvelously revealing tapestry.

DIRECTION FROM CONFLICT AND FAILURE (15:36-41)

> *Some time later Paul said to Barnabas, "Let us go back and visit the brothers in all the towns where we preached the word of the Lord and see how they are doing." (v. 36)*

This was a natural proposal. Paul and Barnabas had worked well together. Ever since Barnabas had retrieved Paul from Tarsus to help with the ministry in Antioch, their teamwork had been charmed with grace. Barnabas' relational gifts coupled with Paul's immense mastery of the Law and his brilliant intellect produced dramatic results. Moreover, the vicissitudes of that first missionary journey had produced a profound exchange of soul between these two men of God. Sharing not only wounds but vision, they were soul brothers. To be sure, they had disagreements and even occasionally disappointed one another, but never ever did they dream of being separated, except perhaps by death. Certainly the two missionaries did not expect what was about to happen.

> *Barnabas wanted to take John, also called Mark, with them, but Paul did not think it wise to take him, because he had deserted them in Pamphylia and had not continued with them in the work. They had such a sharp disagreement that they parted company. Barnabas took Mark and sailed for Cyprus, but Paul chose Silas and left. . . . (vv. 37-40a)*

We cannot be sure why John Mark originally left them in Pamphylia. Most likely it was a combination of things — the realities of missionary life with its ongoing conflicts and discomforts, sickness in Pamphylia, Paul's growing ascendancy over Barnabas, a pampered upbringing, homesickness. Whatever the reason, Paul considered it desertion! Barnabas, who was John Mark's cousin (Colossians 4:10), saw the situation much differently. He saw a change in John Mark, who obviously wanted another chance, and Barnabas resented Paul's rejection of the young man. The result was what verse 39 translates "a sharp disagreement." The Greek word, *paraxusmos*, is the word from which we derive our English word *paroxysm*, which denotes violent action or emotion. This was not a mild gentlemen's disagreement but an intense and passionate conflict!

As to who was to blame, that is not an easy question. Scholars have had paroxysms over it. I feel for Barnabas, and yet Paul is the greatest of the apostles. Perhaps they were both right. No one can rightly blame Barnabas for wanting to give his cousin a second chance, nor can we fault Paul for fearing to trust him again. Our judgment goes with Paul, but our hearts go with Barnabas. According to verse 40, the church sided with Paul, and perhaps that is where we should leave it.

It was a miserable predicament. Recollections of similar events in our experience put us in touch with the smothering cloud that descended on the two missionaries. At that moment there were no two unhappier brothers in all of Antioch. I chuckle when I read Morgan's comment on this: "I am greatly comforted whenever I read this . . . if I had never read that . . . Paul and Barnabas had a contention, I should have been afraid."[2] They were not angels — they were men!

The truth is, even the best Christians do not always agree. Sometimes good Christians intensely disagree! When two believers disagree over an important issue, at least one of them must have something wrong in his life — if not in his walk, at least in his viewpoint. All Christians walk with limps. We all rely on the grace of our Lord.

Some of the church's greatest leaders have been difficult people. Luther in a famous self-evaluation said, "I am rough, boisterous, stormy, and altogether war-like, fighting against innumerable monsters and devils. I am born for the removing of stumps and stones, cutting away thistles and thorns, and clearing wild forests."[3] This was a rather sober evaluation, but Luther was not exaggerating. He could indeed be a difficult man. If you doubt it, read his *Table Talk*. He was also one of God's princes. Similar things could be said of George Fox, John Wesley, and other Christian leaders.

So the unthinkable happened, and Paul and Barnabas agreed to disagree and went their separate ways of ministry for Christ.

> *Barnabas took Mark and sailed for Cyprus, but Paul chose Silas and left, commended by the brothers to the grace of the Lord. He went through Syria and Cilicia, strengthening the churches. (vv. 39b-41)*

This is the last glimpse Luke gives us of Barnabas, one of the noblest figures in the New Testament. In leaving Paul, Barnabas was separating himself from the greatest servant of Christ of all time. And Paul was losing the man to whom he owed more than any other human being. When

Barnabas sailed away with John Mark to his native Cyprus, he sailed into further fruitful ministry, but out of history. In contrast, the continuing ministry of Paul and Silas is well-known. The point here, however, is that the relationship between two great men of God had failed. Nowhere in the account does it say that the two prayed and that it seemed good to them and the Holy Spirit for Mark to remain or for the two of them to double their ministry by going in different directions. The omission of a harmonious conclusion indicates the unstated but undeniable failure of two of the greatest souls the church has ever known.

What does this reveal about how God directs his servants? While God did not cause the disagreement or the fateful separation, he used it to guide both men into increased fruitfulness and service. There were now two missionary teams instead of one. Moreover, Silas brought to Paul's ministry some ingredients that Barnabas did not have. He was a Roman citizen (16:37). He was a prophet (15:32). He probably spoke Greek (compare 15:22, 32). And he served as Paul's stenographer (1 Thessalonians 1:1; 2 Thessalonians 1:1; compare 1 Peter 5:12). Though Barnabas was a great loss, Silas was a great gain.

It is often through our difficulties and failures that God leads us to increased creativity and productivity. Phillips Brooks, one of the greatest preachers America has ever produced, failed miserably as a schoolteacher. He did not like his students, and they did not like him. Brooks wrote when he was fired, "I do not know what will become of me and I do not care much. . . . I wish I were fifteen years old again. I believe I might become a stunning man: but somehow or other I do not seem in the way to come to much now."[4] Anyone who has seen his statue in front of Holy Trinity in Boston knows that spiritual greatness came out of his personal failure as he yielded to God's redirection in his life.

Though there is nothing wrong with desiring success per se, it is from our failures that we learn the most. We sometimes experience what we discern as failure and cannot see the hand of God's guidance any more than Paul could when he set out heartsick on his second missionary journey with his new companion. At such times we need to accept God's direction and entrust our lives anew to him. We should not seek failure or excuse it, but we can learn from it and grow through it.

As Barnabas sailed to Cyprus, Paul began traveling around the northeast end of the Mediterranean by the Gulf of Issus and on through the Syrian Gates, a narrow road between steep rocks and the sea, and then inland past Tarsus and over Mt. Taurus and finally to the churches of Galatia, where he and Barnabas had ministered on his first journey and where he would now discover Timothy.

DIRECTION DISCERNED IN THE ENLISTMENT OF TIMOTHY (16:1-5)

> *He came to Derbe and then to Lystra, where a disciple named Timothy lived, whose mother was a Jewess and a believer, but whose father was a Greek. The brothers at Lystra and Iconium spoke well of him. Paul wanted to take him along on the journey, so he circumcised him because of the Jews who lived in that area, for they all knew that his father was a Greek. (vv. 1-3)*

When Paul came to Lystra, he was much impressed by a young man (probably a teenager) named Timothy. Though his father was an unbeliev-ing Gentile, Timothy had a godly upbringing under his mother Eunice and his grandmother Lois (compare 2 Timothy 1:5; 3:15). Evidently Timothy had come to Christ during Paul's first missionary trip and had demonstrated remarkable spiritual growth. So Paul now circumcised him, and young Timothy began his missionary career.

Some have suggested that this circumcision was a compromise of the principle of the Council of Jerusalem. Actually it was not. Paul had strongly resisted circumcision in the case of Titus, a pure Greek (Galatians 2:3, 5) because the principle of Gentile liberty was at stake. But Timothy was both Jew and Greek and, uncircumcised, would continually offend the Jews, with no advantage to the cause of freedom. So Timothy voluntarily removed the stumbling block.

How Paul loved Timothy! This was the birth of a rare and beautiful friendship. Paul even came to call him his son (1 Corinthians 4:17).

God's guidance is a multifaceted jewel. Lystra was where Paul had ear-lier been stoned and tossed on the refuse heap, and it was in Lystra that Paul now found and received Timothy. How had Timothy become a disciple of Christ? Probably in the same way Paul had been influenced toward the gospel by the stoning of Stephen. At Lystra Paul had gone through Stephen's experience — though not to death, and Timothy saw it and was drawn to the Christ for whom Paul was willing to suffer.

Undoubtedly during this time the apostle reflected much on the misery of the stoning in Lystra and the recent separation from his beloved Barnabas. Both experiences had brought him disappointment and pain. But God loves to bring joy and hope during times of trial, and now it was Paul and Silas and Timothy — coworkers for Jesus Christ. Ever since Golgotha, Christianity has transmuted hardship and failure into holiness and honor to God.

Being half Gentile and half Jew, Timothy could bridge both cultures. Perhaps if John Mark had been along, they could not have taken on another young trainee. The sovereign God makes excellent use of even the most trying circumstances.

> *As they traveled from town to town, they delivered the decisions reached by the apostles and elders in Jerusalem for the people to obey. So the churches were strengthened in the faith and grew daily in numbers. (vv. 4-5)*

Paul's missionary policy was working. However, all was not smooth sailing because the little trio was about to run into some closed doors.

DIRECTION THROUGH RESTRAINT (16:6-7)

> *Paul and his companions traveled throughout the region of Phrygia and Galatia, having been kept by the Holy Spirit from preaching the word in the province of Asia. When they came to the border of Mysia, they tried to enter Bithynia, but the Spirit of Jesus would not allow them to. (vv. 6-7)*

When Paul finished his ministry in Galatia, he decided to go south and minister in Asia (not the continent of Asia, but a small province called Asia, where Ephesus was located). But something stopped him. Then he tried to go north into Bithynia so he could minister in the prosperous cities around the Black Sea. But again he was hindered. The overall effect was to funnel him directly west toward the Dardanelle Straits and into Europe. He was actually driven west by closed doors.

Specifically how did the Holy Spirit restrain them? Through the bestowing or removing of a subjective sense of peace? Possibly. That is often how he directs us in our day-to-day lives. Or possibly it was through difficult circumstances, such as transportation problems or illness. Personally I think, although I will not be dogmatic, that it was illness, because Luke, a physician, joined them right after this time, as is shown in verse 10 when Luke changes the narrative from "they" to "we." By any estimation their missionary work was not smooth sailing. As Paul experienced these closed doors, he faced driving cross currents and inscrutable difficulties.

What kept Paul going despite estrangement, sickness, disappointment, and closed doors? His simple faith that God was in control of his life. Later while in a Roman jail, as his detractors took advantage of his imprisonment to build up their own following, he said, "Now I want you to know, brothers, that what has happened to me has really served to advance the gospel" (Philippians 1:12). God rules! To the Corinthians he wrote, "We are hard pressed on every side, but not crushed; perplexed, but not in despair" (2 Corinthians 4:8). He kept trusting in God!

Paul refused to indulge himself with "what ifs." "If only we had never taken John Mark along in the first place . . . if only John Mark had not asked to go again . . . if I did not always get sick . . . if I were smarter . . . if I had stayed home." It would have been so easy to pity himself, but instead he kept trusting and following Christ. Later he would write to Timothy:

> *You then, my son, be strong in the grace that is in Christ Jesus. And the things you have heard me say in the presence of many witnesses entrust to reliable men who will also be qualified to teach others. Endure hardship with us like a good soldier of Christ Jesus. (2 Timothy 2:1-3)*

Paul succeeded where we so often fail in our attitude and approach to life — he maintained loyalty to the Lord and faith in the guidance of the Holy Spirit.

> *He leadeth me; O blessed thought!*
> *O words with heavenly comfort fraught!*
> *What'er I do, where'er I be,*
> *Still 'tis God's hand that leadeth me.*

Finally the tiny band arrived at Troas, at the mouth of the Dardanelles, between the land masses of Europe and Asia and the great waterways of the Aegean and Black Seas. New Illium on the site of ancient Troy was just four miles to the north.

GUIDANCE THROUGH REVELATION (16:8-10)

Paul now received a vision.

> *So they passed by Mysia and went down to Troas. During the night Paul had a vision of a man of Macedonia standing and begging him, "Come over to Macedonia and help us." (vv. 8-9)*

Some say Paul saw a sudden appearance by Dr. Luke and heard his plea for Paul to cross the channel. Some even conjecture that this was a vision of Alexander the Great, the archetype of Macedonia, speaking for his lost race. Whatever the vision encompassed, its meaning was clear: Europe was calling for help — the people of Europe needed the gospel of Christ.

The result is recorded in verse 10:

After Paul had seen the vision, we got ready at once to leave for Macedonia, concluding that God had called us to preach the gospel to them.

The word translated "concluding" is an old Greek verb that means "to bring together," "to coalesce or knit together." As Luke and Paul and company considered the vision in the context of all that had gone before, it all came together and they knew God was calling them to Europe![5]

This was one of the great turning points of history, and we should thank God for it, for as a result the gospel has come to us in the West. Nothing makes a person strong like hearing someone cry for help! You can be walking down the street completely fatigued so that you would like to lie down on the curb and go to sleep, but then you hear a cry — someone is in trouble! — and you completely forget your weariness. Paul and his associates moved forward in the power of Christ's strength.

A FINAL WORD

What are the abiding lessons we see in all of this? First, they all succeeded for Jesus — Barnabas and Paul and their companions. Silas was an effective partner in Christian ministry. Timothy was a good soldier for Christ. Two of Paul's letters were addressed to him, and six of Paul's letters include Timothy in the salutation. Timothy served heroically in Ephesus during days of strife. He went with Paul on his last visit to Jerusalem. Timothy was even with him in prison. He was his son, his comrade in battle.

John Mark got back on track under Barnabas' loving care. He was a great help to Peter (1 Peter 5:13). And at the sunset of his life Paul himself wrote, "Only Luke is with me. Get Mark and bring him with you, *because he is helpful to me in my ministry*" (2 Timothy 4:11). John Mark wrote the Gospel of Mark — the Gospel that presents Christ as the perfect Servant. Something wonderful had happened to this tender man who had so miserably failed in service — and to his relationship with the Apostle Paul. There was healing between Paul and Barnabas as well (compare 1 Corinthians 9:6).

God can use unhappy, perplexing failures to bring fresh purpose and direction to our lives. He can restore the years the locusts have eaten — with abundance (see Joel 2:25-27)! Even when we are at fault, God will use our failures to bring greater blessing!

God will lead us according to his own perfect plan for our lives and ministries. We must be careful not to box God in by our prior experience. The most important thing by far is our attitude. Why God directs us west when we want or expect to go north, we do not know. Why he did not give Paul a vision at the beginning instead of the end, we cannot fully explain.

But this we know: God directs us through every situation, the apparently good and the apparently bad. We need to yield to his caring hand. In G. Campbell Morgan's words, "It is better to go to Troas with God, than anywhere else without Him."[6]

PRAYER

O God, forgive us for those times when we refuse to walk or minister in harmony with our fellow servants. We thank you that you so graciously use our failures to bring increased fruit in character and service. And we thank you that your redirection is always best, your plan always superior to ours. Help us to walk before you humbly, eagerly yielding to your will as you reveal it to us step by step. In Jesus' name, Amen.

25

Beachhead in Europe

ACTS 16:11-40

After experiencing the famous vision of "a man of Macedonia" imploring him to bring help to Europe, Paul and his companions undoubtedly reflected on their journey thus far. They had been driven west by crosswinds of failure and rejection, and they interpreted this correctly as God's loving direction. God was leading them to Europe.

> *From Troas we put out to sea and sailed straight for Samothrace, and the next day on to Neapolis. From there we traveled to Philippi, a Roman colony and the leading city of that district of Macedonia. And we stayed there several days. (vv. 11-12)*

That they "sailed straight for Samothrace" is quite revealing, because this is a nautical expression that means the wind was at their backs. So perfect were the winds that they sailed the 156 miles in just two days, whereas returning the other way at a later time (20:6) it took five days. They were surely conscious that God's forces of nature were propelling them forward with the message of grace.

The first night they laid over at the storied island of Samothrace under the towering presence of Mt. Fengari Poseidon, 5,500 feet high. It was on this island that the famed statue of the Winged Victory was discovered in 1863. From there it was smooth sailing to Neapolis, the port city of Philippi, and then an eight-mile walk into Philippi itself.

Philippi was an ancient town, having been renamed in 356 B.C. by Philip II of Macedon after himself. With the expansion of the Roman Empire, it became a Roman possession in 167 B.C. But its greatest fame came from the fact that it happened to be the place where the armies of Mark Antony and Octavian defeated Brutus and Cassius in the decisive battle of the second Roman civil war in 42 B.C. It was from this event that Philippi derived its character in Paul's day because for its part in the battle it was awarded the status of a Roman colony that answered directly to the Roman emperor. Roman soldiers were encouraged to retire there, and its citizens were exempt from provincial taxes. Paul and company were now in for a complete cross-cultural missionary experience!

Rome did not know it, but the flag of Christianity was unfurled in the Empire that day, and the reigning Christ was about to win many to himself. G. Campbell Morgan wrote:

> How little the world knows of the Divine movements. Rome had small idea that day, that the van of the army of its ultimate Conqueror had taken possession of one of its frontal defences. On the day when Paul hurried from Neapolis, over the eight miles up to Philippi — and came into the city and made arrangements for his own lodging . . . the flag was planted in a frontier colony of Rome, which eventually was to make necessary the lowering of her flag, and the change of the world's history.[1]

This section of Acts gives us valuable insights for waging effective warfare for Jesus Christ.

THE GOSPEL'S POWER WHEN PROCLAIMED (vv. 13-15)

> *On the Sabbath we went outside the city gate to the river, where we expected to find a place of prayer. We sat down and began to speak to the women who had gathered there.* (v. 13)

The missionary quartet (Paul, Silas, Timothy, Luke) went to the riverside on the Sabbath instead of a synagogue because there was no synagogue in Philippi. According to Jewish tradition, there had to be a quorum of at least ten male heads of households before a synagogue could be formed. If these requirements could not be met, the faithful were to meet under the open sky near a river or sea. So Paul and company walked outside the city on the Sabbath, probably to the Gangites River, looking for some fellow Jews. They discovered a small group — all women — who met to recite the Shema and pray the Shemoneth Esreh and read the Law and Prophets.[2] This was a divine appointment!

One of those listening was a woman named Lydia, a dealer in purple cloth from the city of Thyatira, who was a worshiper of God. The Lord opened her heart to respond to Paul's message. When she and the members of her household were baptized, she invited us to her home. "If you consider me a believer in the Lord," she said, "come and stay at my house." And she persuaded us. (vv. 14-15)

Evidently Lydia took her name from her native province — Thyatira's ancient name was Lydia. Because she was "a worshiper of God" — a Gentile who saw truth in Judaism and wanted it, she came under the influence of the Jews. The majority of those accompanying this wealthy woman were probably family and servants. Lydia had been divinely prepared for an encounter with the gospel, and as she listened, "the Lord opened her heart." The man of the Macedonian vision turned out to be a woman! Paul's pharisaical prejudices, which in pre-Christian years had taught him to pray, "God, I thank you that I am not a Gentile, or a slave, or a woman," had been sharply altered by Christ and his growth in faith. Later he would write:

There is neither Jew nor Greek, slave nor free, male nor female, for you are all one in Christ Jesus. (Galatians 3:28)

As Lydia placed her faith in Christ, she experienced the wonderful sensation of her sins being borne away. Joy welled up within and flowed over to her companions. Her entire household believed. They were all baptized right on the spot in the Gangites River. What an astounding spiritual success! God opened the heart of one woman in a colonial extension of Rome, and that city became a mighty beachhead for God. We cannot assess a situation by the numbers. One woman's heart in Philippi doomed the flag of Rome.

Dear Lydia then twisted the evangelists' arms so they would stay at her home. The word translated "persuaded" in verse 15b is the exact word used to describe how the disciples prevailed upon Jesus to stay with them after their encounter on the road to Emmaus.

Philippi was destined to become one of Paul's most beloved congregations.

I thank my God every time I remember you. (Philippians 1:3)

Moreover, as you Philippians know, in the early days of your acquaintance with the gospel, when I set out from Macedonia, not one church shared with me in the matter of giving and receiving, except you only. (Philippians 4:15)

The apostles now had the wind at their backs. They were not sailing — they were hydroplaning! God's grace produced Christlike spirits and sacrificial giving. Blown from the coasts of Troas to Samothrace to Neapolis, they now breezed right into Lydia's heart and home. It was experiences such as this that caused Paul to write in Romans 1:16:

> *I am not ashamed of the gospel, because it is the power of God for the salvation of everyone who believes: first for the Jew, then for the Gentile.*

At this point it may have looked like all their trouble was behind them. But from experience Paul knew better.

THE GOSPEL'S REMARKABLE POWER OVER DEMONS (vv. 16-18)

God was graciously working, but Satan was at work too.

> *Once when we were going to the place of prayer, we were met by a slave girl who had a spirit by which she predicted the future. She earned a great deal of money for her owners by fortune-telling. This girl followed Paul and the rest of us, shouting, "These men are servants of the Most High God, who are telling you the way to be saved." (vv. 16-17)*

Was this girl a Christian believer? What she was saying was absolutely true. Wherever the missionaries went, she attracted attention to their work. But actually this was an insidious satanic attack. The original Greek behind the phrase "had a spirit" reveals the horror with which she was involved, literally reading "had a Pythian spirit" or "had a spirit of Python." According to myth, Python was a snake that guarded the Temple of Apollo and was eventually killed by Apollo. Later the word *python* came to mean a demon-possessed person through whom Python spoke.

The poor girl was "demonized," filled with a demon or demons who revealed the future to her clients. She was a clairvoyant owned by spiritual pimps who sold her metaphysical powers. Satan's strategy was obvious: to derail the gospel by infiltrating it, by forming an apparent alliance with Christ's work — for his own ends, of course. He loves to distort the gospel just enough to twist it into a deadly heresy.

This approach is difficult to resist. The missionary team could easily have reasoned, "She's telling the truth. Why not let her speak? We would never get crowds like this on our own. Besides, maybe as she associates with us, she will see the light." Whatever their initial inclinations, they did not fall for the devil's bait. Perhaps they remembered that every time a demon confirmed that Christ was the Son of God, Jesus rebuked it — every time! He always silenced them and ordered them to leave.

Satan kept the pressure on for several days. It was his first and best approach. But Paul responded decisively.

> *She kept this up for many days. Finally Paul became so troubled that he turned around and said to the spirit, "In the name of Jesus Christ I command you to come out of her!" At that moment the spirit left her. (v. 18)*

What a great moment in the life of the Pythoness. She was restored to her right mind and, we presume, received Christ. Again God's power had worked a miracle! The populace of Philippi was now completely galvanized. The apostle and his coworkers had met some headwinds and conquered them, and the wind was again at their backs.

THE GOSPEL'S POWER IN PERSECUTION (vv. 19-34)

Now winds of violence began to assail God's ambasadors:

> *When the owners of the slave girl realized that their hope of making money was gone, they seized Paul and Silas and dragged them into the marketplace to face the authorities. They brought them before the magistrates and said, "These men are Jews, and are throwing our city into an uproar by advocating customs unlawful for us Romans to accept or practice." The crowd joined in the attack against Paul and Silas, and the magistrates ordered them to be stripped and beaten. (vv. 19-22)*

Paul and Silas were in trouble because they had exorcised the girl's owners' source of income. Whenever the preaching of the gospel touches the economic structure of the powers that be, opposition is bound to come. Richard Collier, the historian of the Salvation Army, says:

> Persecution was great from the beginning. . . . Gangs frequently hurled mud and stones through the windows at the preaching and the crowd. The liquor dealers worked hard to have Booth kicked out of East London. The police were no help; in fact, they often broke up outdoor meetings and accused Booth's followers of being the cause of all the trouble. . . . Beatings were not uncommon: in 1889, at least

> 669 Salvation Army members were assaulted — some were killed and many were maimed. Even children were not immune; ruffians threw lime in the eyes of a child of a Salvation Army member. The newspapers ridiculed Booth. PUNCH referred to him as "Field Marshal von Booth."[3]

Paul had touched the profiteers' hearts. The problem was, their hearts were in their wallets. In the ensuing melee, false charges and racial innuendo were arrayed against Paul and Silas, and their arrest followed. Apparently Timothy and Luke escaped because they were Gentiles. Note how quickly the devil changed tactics. When subterfuge did not work, he tried outward persecution. Both are effective, though the latter sometimes backfires. "The blood of martyrs is the seed of the church." The forces of darkness were not at their smartest when they turned so quickly to persecution.

> *After they [Paul and Silas] had been severely flogged, they were thrown into prison, and the jailer was commanded to guard them carefully. Upon receiving such orders, he put them in the inner cell and fastened their feet in the stocks. (vv. 23-24)*

The officials who punished Paul and Silas were called *lictors* in Latin. This is where the expression "getting your licks" came from. The evangelists' backs were reduced to a sticky, swollen mass of lacerated skin and dried blood. The jailer perhaps went a step further than necessary, brutally putting them in the stocks. They could not lie down without tearing up their backs even worse. If that had been us, we might have wallowed in self-pity or plotted revenge or cursed our enemies. But victorious gospel power resounded in that inner cell!

> *About midnight Paul and Silas were praying and singing hymns to God, and the other prisoners were listening to them. (v. 25)*

This was even more dramatic than the earthquake that would soon follow! Songs from the bowels of that miserable, vermin-infested pit? Yes, because those men's heart realities exceeded their miserable circumstances. What glory this brought to God!

These men of God had no reason to expect a miracle. Yes, God had delivered Peter, but Stephen and James had been martyred. These faithful witnesses did not know what was going to happen, but they sang God's praises anyway. Why? They passionately believed God could deliver them anytime and from any place if he so desired. Their assurance resembled that of the three young Jews who stood before Nebuchadnezzar:

> *Shadrach, Meshach and Abednego replied to the king, "O Nebuchadnezzar, we do not need to defend ourselves before you in this matter. If we are thrown into the blazing furnace, the God we serve is able to save us from it, and he will rescue us from your hand, O king. But even if he does not, we want you to know, O king, that we will not serve your gods or worship the image of gold that you have set up." (Daniel 3:16-19)*

Paul and his gospel companions sang because they knew God had called them across the expanse of Asia Minor. They sang because they believed rightly that they were prisoners of Christ and not of Rome. Paul felt the same way in all of his imprisonments. "Silas, this is great! We have a captive audience." They sang because they knew that if they survived they would be better men afterwards.

> *For it has been granted to you on behalf of Christ not only to believe on him, but also to suffer for him. (Philippians 1:29)*

The participles in Acts are continuous: they were *continually* praying and singing. Everyone in jail heard the gospel singers. A. T. Robertson says, "It was a new experience for the prisoners and wondrously attractive entertainment to them."[4]

Then came outward power! God's heart was blessed by his servants' praise, and he chose to respond with power.

> *Suddenly there was such a violent earthquake [Greek,* seismos*] that the foundations of the prison were shaken. At once all the prison doors flew open, and everybody's chains came loose. (v. 26)*

One Easter Dr. Elam Davies was preaching at Fourth Presbyterian in downtown Chicago. Just as he dramatically called out, "And the last enemy to be conquered is death!" a huge slab of ice loosed itself from the steeple and crashed into the roof of the church, shaking the whole building. Davies looked up and said, "Thank you, Lord, for the sound effects." In Philippi, Europe's first sacred music concert brought down the house. The power of the gospel was changing lives in Europe!

> *The jailer woke up, and when he saw the prison doors open, he drew his sword and was about to kill himself because he thought the pris-*

oners had escaped. But Paul shouted, "Don't harm yourself! We are all here!" The jailer called for lights, rushed in and fell trembling before Paul and Silas. He then brought them out and asked, "Sirs, what must I do to be saved?" They replied, "Believe in the Lord Jesus, and you will be saved — you and your household." Then they spoke the word of the Lord to him and to all the others in his house. (vv. 27-32)

Awakened by the noise, the poor turnkey rushed in and found all the cells open — not an encouraging sight for a jail keeper. Assuming the prisoners had fled, he prepared to fall on his sword rather than suffer execution according to the Code of Justinian (9, 4.4). But Paul's gracious cry stopped him. Confused, trembling with fear, the jailer then asked a compelling question: "Men, what must I do to be saved?" He had heard the testimony of the Pythoness, had handled Paul and Silas' incarceration firsthand, and had heard their songs in the night. His question was sincere and earnest, and he received an answer that has resounded through the ages: "Believe in the Lord Jesus, and you will be saved — you and your household." Paul did not suggest a system, no organization or religion to join. He simply urged faith in Jesus Christ.

Bishop John Taylor Smith, honorary chaplain to Queen Victoria and the chaplain general of the British Army during World War I, was "Everybody's Bishop" — jovial, saintly, a favorite at Keswick conferences. Bishop Smith used to ask all the candidates for the chaplaincy one question:

> "Now, I want you to show me how you would deal with a man. We will suppose I am a soldier who has been wounded on the field of battle. I have three minutes to live and I am afraid to die, because I do not know Christ. Tell me, how may I be saved and die with the assurance that all is well?" If the applicant began to beat about the bush and talk about the true Church and ordinances and so on, the good Bishop would say, "That will not do. I have only three minutes to live. Tell me what I must do." And as long as Bishop Smith was Chaplain-General, unless a candidate could answer that question, he could not become a chaplain in the Army.[5]

Bishop Smith was right — a gospel that cannot save a dying man is no gospel. A gospel that initially requires more than faith alone is no gospel. The Philippian jailer was saved that night by faith. If his life extended over many months and years, he discovered that the Christian life demands all. But he always knew that his salvation came through faith in the Lord Jesus

Christ alone! What a glorious thing it is to offer salvation to all by trust in Christ plus nothing!

Not only was the jailer saved, but so was his family.

> *At that hour of the night the jailer took them and washed their wounds; then immediately he and all his family were baptized. The jailer brought them into his house and set a meal before them; he was filled with joy because he had come to believe in God — he and his whole family. (vv. 33-34)*

Possibly the man and his family were baptized at the same well where the jailer, a new man in Christ, had just washed the missionary prisoners' wounds. As they all sat down to breakfast, they sat down as brothers and sisters in Christ. God's power had effected the conversion and forgiveness of guilty sinners!

THE GOSPEL'S POWER FOR THE CHURCH (vv. 35-39)

> *When it was daylight, the magistrates sent their officers to the jailer with the order: "Release those men." The jailer told Paul, "The magistrates have ordered that you and Silas be released. Now you can leave. Go in peace." But Paul said to the officers: "They beat us publicly without a trial, even though we are Roman citizens, and threw us into prison. And now do they want to get rid of us quietly? No! Let them come themselves and escort us out." The officers reported this to the magistrates, and when they heard that Paul and Silas were Roman citizens, they were alarmed. They came to appease them and escorted them from the prison, requesting them to leave the city. (vv. 35-39)*

Paul could be tough! He refused to be dealt with summarily because he did not want the idea that he and Silas were lawbreakers to stand. A public escort from jail by the ruling magistrates would publish their innocence, and that would bring protection to Lydia and her house church as well.

So, after some hemming and hawing, here came the magistrates, hats in hand. "Mr. Paul, sir, and Mr. Silas, sir, we have made a grave error. We would appreciate it if you would not think badly of us. We meant no harm."

> *After Paul and Silas came out of the prison, they went to Lydia's house, where they met with the brothers and encouraged them. Then they left. (v. 40)*

A FINAL WORD

Some meeting! Imagine the joy at Lydia's as Paul and his associates in the gospel recounted the events of the previous night. There were undoubtedly tears and maybe even some riotous laughter. Maybe they sang a few prison songs and acted out the *seismos*. Whatever the agenda, it culminated in praise.

Some church! Lydia the merchant princess, the ex-Pythoness, the Philippian jailer, and probably a few ex-inmates made up the first European church. The rich and the poor, the slave and the free, male and female were all one in Christ. The flag of the gospel was unfurled on a continent that needed it desperately!

Some life! Through thick and thin, despite the whirlwinds of Satan's opposition, the wind of the Spirit was always at the backs of Paul and his companions. Wherever they were — skimming the Aegean, preaching by the river, delivering souls from demons, taking their licks, singing in the night while the world shook away, or praying with a trembling man for his soul — they were serving an awesome God.

Some gospel!

> *I am not ashamed of the gospel, because it is the power of God for the salvation of every one who believes: first for the Jew, then for the Gentile. (Romans 1:16)*

PRAYER

> *O Lord, help us to unfurl the flag of your Son wherever you desire to use us as your witnesses today and in days to come. Help us to know with whom you want us to share the gospel of life, and to do so wisely and skillfully. Help us not to be mute because of fear, but to praise you always, even in the most difficult circumstances. May your presence in us draw others, even our enemies, to your salvation, found only in your Son. In Jesus' name, Amen.*

26

God's Nobles

ACTS 17:1-15

Many believe that though the church of Jesus Christ has had numerous princes, the Apostle Paul stands above them all — that Paul is the greatest son of the church — the noblest servant she has ever produced. His words in Philippians 3:10 — "I want to know Christ and the power of his resurrection and the fellowship of sharing in his sufferings, becoming like him in his death" — are as forceful an expression of love as any in the Scriptures. This was the driving force of Paul's noble life.

His life was one of ongoing bravery and determination. The list of Paul's sufferings in 2 Corinthians 11 is mind-boggling. If anyone questioned the apostle's sincerity, he could point to the scar tissue on his face and back. He was willing to suffer for Christ and for others because he loved them. Regarding his people, the Jews, he said, "For I could wish that I myself were cursed and cut off from Christ for the sake of my brothers" (Romans 9:3). To some of his converts he wrote, ". . . my brothers, you whom I love and long for, my joy and crown" (Philippians 4:1). He loved deeply and royally.

We marvel too at the massive intelligence that could write the closely reasoned pages of Romans and the lyrical thirteenth chapter of 1 Corinthians. Permeating all was his supreme passion for the Lord Jesus Christ. Paul put everything he had into living (and dying) for Christ. He was alive for Christ!

John Powell in his best seller *Fully Human Fully Alive* says:

> Fully alive people are those who are using all of their human faculties, powers, and talents. They are using them to the full. These indi-

> viduals are fully functioning in their external and internal sources. They are comfortable with/and open to the full experience and expression of all human emotions. Such people are vibrantly alive in mind, heart, and will. There is an instinctive fear in most of us, I think, to travel with our engines at full throttle. We prefer, for the sake of safety, to take life in small and dainty doses.[1]

Paul was fully alive with interest compounded! We can learn the secrets of a noble life from the lives of Paul and his coworkers and thus elevate our Christian lives.

Paul and Silas and Timothy did not leave Philippi with their tails between their legs. They left at their own pace, saying good-bye to a marvelous new church that contained, among others, the wealthy Lydia and her family, the Philippian jailer and his household, and the ex-Pythoness clairvoyant.

"When they had passed through Amphipolis and Apollonia, they came to Thessalonica, where there was a Jewish synagogue" (v. 1). This was at least a three-day journey of about 100 miles. When they arrived, they found a thriving city of about 20,000. Unlike Philippi, there was a synagogue, where they went to minister first.

> *As his custom was, Paul went into the synagogue, and on three Sabbath days he reasoned with them from the Scriptures, explaining and proving that the Christ had to suffer and rise from the dead. "This Jesus I am proclaiming to you is the Christ," he said. (vv. 2-3)*

Paul's public ministry was three-pronged. First, he "reasoned with them from the Scriptures." The Greek word translated "reasoned" is the root for our English word dialogue. There was exchange, questions and answers. He dialogued with them "from the Scriptures." They would together take up the vellum and parchment copies of the popular Greek Septuagint, and Paul would select a passage and submit it for give and take.

Further, there was "explaining," as verse 3 indicates. This word literally means "opening." A very strong word, Luke used it to describe the opening of the womb in Luke 2:23 (NASB) and in the twenty-fourth chapter for spiritual openings on the road to Emmaus:

> *Then their eyes were* opened *and they recognized him, and he disappeared from their sight. They asked each other, "Were not our hearts burning within us while he talked with us on the road and* opened *the Scriptures to us?" (vv. 31-32)*

Paul opened the Scriptures with clarity and simplicity — a priceless virtue that is not always appreciated. A freshman student once remarked after hearing a sermon by the great George W. Truett, "So that is George Truett, is it? Huh, he didn't use one word I couldn't understand." Simplicity can make all the difference between communication and confusion. "Hence from my sight — nor let me thus pollute mine eyes with looking on a wretch like thee, thou cause of my ills; I sicken at thy loathsome presence" is fine, but in some situations "Scram!" works better. We have the greatest message on earth, but sometimes the gospel is hid to those who are perishing simply because of our verbiage. Not so with Paul.

The third prong of his method is stated as "giving evidence" (NASB; "proving," NIV), which means "to place beside" or "to set before." "Have you considered the testimony of Hosea? Then there's the story of Abraham and Isaac . . ." He was proving his case, preaching to lead his hearers to a particular verdict. The message was that Christ (the Messiah) had to suffer. No doubt Paul took them to many Scriptures, including Psalm 22 and Isaiah 53.

> *But he was pierced for our transgressions, he was crushed for our iniquities; the punishment that brought us peace was upon him, and by his wounds we are healed. (v. 5)*

He undoubtedly taught that Christ had to rise from the dead and surely showed them Psalm 16:10 — "For Thou wilt not abandon my soul to Sheol; neither wilt Thou allow Thy Holy One to undergo decay" (NASB margin).

Paul exhibited great patience and care, taking the time to complete his three-pronged attack and to call for a heart response. Our text indicates that Paul was in the synagogue for three Sabbaths, and he probably ministered in that area for much longer than that. This was not a one-shot approach.

Paul was particularly noble in that he treated the people with respect and dignity. He did not demand that they swallow what he said simply because he said it. Em Griffin in his book *The Mind Changers*, in a chapter entitled "An Ethic for the Christian Persuader," states:

> Simply stated, [the standard] is this: Any persuasive effort which restricts another's freedom to choose for or against Christ is wrong.[2]

In sharing our faith we must give others room to move and think. The gospel dialogued, opened, and placed before others will always stand on its own!

Paul's approach was also noble because it cost him. His persistence and honest integrity in dialogue and sharing made him terribly vulnerable, so that he often encountered agonizing opposition. In 1 Thessalonians 2:1-2 he reminds the believers:

You know, brothers, that our visit to you was not a failure. We had previously suffered and been insulted in Philippi, as you know, but with the help of our God we dared to tell to you his gospel in spite of strong opposition [literally, "much agony"].

The apostle was also willing to work hard so he could share the gospel with others.

We loved you so much that we were delighted to share with you not only the gospel of God but our lives as well, because you had become so dear to us. Surely you remember, brothers, our toil and hardship; we worked night and day in order not to be a burden to anyone while we preached the gospel of God to you. (1 Thessalonians 2:8-9)

Paul mended tents just to maintain the privilege of sharing the Word of God with the Thessalonians. Paul was one of God's great princes. What an example! And in time his work began to bring notable results.

Some of the Jews were persuaded and joined Paul and Silas, as did a large number of God-fearing Greeks and not a few prominent women. (v. 4)

A few Jews believed, along with an impressive number of God-seeking Greeks, including a number of prominent women. A spiritual nobility was beginning to form in Thessalonica. But as usual, that meant trouble was on the way.

THE PRINCE AND THE IGNOBLE (vv. 5-9)

But the Jews were jealous; so they rounded up some bad characters from the marketplace, formed a mob and started a riot in the city. They rushed to Jason's house in search of Paul and Silas in order to bring them out to the crowd. (v. 5)

Some of the Jews rejected Paul and, having become inflamed with a misplaced zeal, went to the center of town and recruited a mob. Our text calls them "wicked men" (NASB), and the *King James Version* says, "lewd fellows of the baser sort." I like A. T. Robertson's rendering — "bums."[3]

Soon Thessalonica was in an uproar, and these unruly men descended on the home of Jason like flies on meat. Luke goes on in verse 6: "But when they did not find them [Paul and Silas], they dragged Jason and some other brothers before the city officials." Paul and Silas were gone, giving the lynch mob an opportunity to pay them an unwitting but immortal compliment:

> "These men who have caused trouble all over the world *have now come here, and Jason has welcomed them into his house. They are all defying Caesar's decrees, saying that there is another king, one called Jesus." (vv. 6-7)*

In effect these critics of Christianity were saying, "These men have turned the world upside-down." In one sense, what they said was true, though in its natural state the world is already upside-down. The world was turned wrong-side-up at the Fall and has being going in reverse ever since. So when men and women in Thessalonica were turned around by Christ, everyone else saw them as upside-down. A believer lives right-side-up in a topsy-turvy world.

The rulers caved in to the mob because they were well aware of Emperor Claudius' edict that all Jews had to leave the city of Rome.[4] God's nobleman had run into some "bad characters," and as a result he and his coworker had to flee the city by night (v. 10). This must have been disheartening for the zealous ambassadors of Christ. A short time later Paul wrote the believers there, "But, brothers, when we were torn away from you for a short time (in person, not in thought), out of our intense longing we made every effort to see you" (1 Thessalonians 2:17). I think the apostle's sentiment was not unlike that of the China Inland Mission missionary who wrote as he fled the Communists' burning of Shanghai:

Tonight Shanghai is burning
And I am dying too.
But there's no death more certain
Than death inside of you.
Some men die of shrapnel
While some go down in flames.
But most men die inch by inch
While playing at little games.

So Paul left for Berea — and a much nobler crowd.

THE PRINCE AND THE NOBLE (vv. 10-12)

> *As soon as it was night, the brothers sent Paul and Silas away to Berea. On arriving there, they went to the Jewish synagogue. Now the*

Bereans were of more noble character than the Thessalonians . . . (vv. 10-11a)

Some might surmise that the Bereans were more nobly disposed than the Thessalonians because they were off the beaten track and had not fallen prey to the vices of metropolitan living. "We who live in cities can come to some strange conceits."[5] But verse 11 gives us the true secret of a noble life:

> *Now the Bereans were of more noble character than the Thessalonians,* for they received the message with great eagerness and examined the Scriptures *every day to see if what Paul said was true.*

Their "eagerness" carries the idea of rushing forward.[6] They could not wait to receive God's message! Eagerness makes all the difference in the flavor, quality, and nobility of our Christian lives. J. I. Packer says:

> John Owen and John Calvin knew more theology than John Bunyan or Billy Bray, but who would deny that the latter pair knew their God every bit as well as the former? (All four, of course, were beavers for the Bible, which counts for far more than a formal theological training.)[7]

The Bible says, "Faith comes by hearing the message, and the message is heard through the word of Christ" (Romans 10:17). George Müller read the Bible over 200 times, and that certainly is a primary reason he was such a man of faith. All of us should be constantly reading, digging, cross-referencing, comparing — rushing with eagerness to feed on the Word of the Lord!

The Bereans were "noble" because they "examined the Scriptures every day to see if what Paul said was true." They eagerly but cautiously listened, then compared everything to the touchstone of Scripture. Acceptance of teachings without discernment is not a Christian virtue. Luke congratulated the Bereans because they avoided predigested food, choosing to hunt it out for themselves. If we listen uncritically to only one preacher or read only one author (even if he is C. S. Lewis), we are in danger! We cannot afford not to "examine the Scriptures every day."

Though the Bereans were cautious, they also remained open. No one has ever had a silver tongue who did not have a golden ear. Some of the Jews in Thessalonica did not listen, but the Bereans did. The exchange of ideas in modern society has been called "the dialogue of the deaf." In contrast, God's nobles hear! Consider the mind-set of the noble Jonathan Edwards:

> Resolved, therefore, that if ever I live to years I will be impartial to hear the reason of all pretended discoveries, and receive them, if rational, how long soever I have been used to another way of thinking.[8]

The Christian life can be most stimulating if we allow ourselves to be open to learning and growth, continually immersing ourselves in the Scriptures. God's Word will keep us in touch with the fundamental issues of life and so keep us alive and growing — honorable ambassadors of Jesus Christ!

The outcome of all this was predictable: "Many of the Jews believed, as did also a number of prominent Greek women and many Greek men" (v. 12). A new royalty was born in Berea!

The noble life had been turned upside-down, or, more accurately, right-side-up. God's princes and princesses had their lives revolutionized. They kissed the doctrines they once despised and now saw themselves and life as it really is. Once their thoughts were devoted to this world, but now they looked upward.

> *Since, then, you have been raised with Christ, set your hearts on things above, where Christ is seated at the right hand of God. (Colossians 3:1)*

> *. . . while we wait for the blessed hope — the glorious appearing of our great God and Savior, Christ Jesus. (Titus 2:13)*

Old pleasures had taken on new meaning. New pleasures had come to the surface. The Word of God had come alive. They rushed to taste it, and it satisfied their souls.

This can come to pass anywhere! It even happened among the less-than-noble Thessalonians. Listen to the opening sentences of 1 Thessalonians, written a short time later:

> *You became a model to all the believers in Macedonia and Achaia. The Lord's message rang out from you not only in Macedonia and Achaia — your faith in God has become known everywhere. Therefore we do not need to say anything about it.*

And in 2 Thessalonians 1:4 Paul said:

> *Therefore, among God's churches we boast about your perseverance and faith in all the persecutions and trials you are enduring.*

A pastor friend of mine was in a nice restaurant one day. When the waitress came over to the table, he said, "Have you made the wonderful discovery of knowing Christ personally?" In the conversation she indicated that she had not and began to make excuses — she could not get to church on Sunday because she worked, she would be more comfortable with a Bible in her own language (Romanian), and so on. Since there were not very many people in the restaurant, my friend reached for a copy of the tract *Four Steps for Peace with God*, but discovered he did not have any with him. So he took a napkin, wrote out the steps, and gave it to her. He went on his way but later dropped off a Romanian Bible for her.

At a later date he came back to the restaurant, now very busy. Across the restaurant the waitress saw him and came over to tell him that she was reading the Bible. In fact, she had sometimes read it all night long! Better yet, she had come to know Christ. Then she pulled the napkin out of her pocket, now almost in tatters, and said, "Would you write that down for me again? I have showed this so many times, my napkin is coming apart." The power of the Word of God had turned another life upside-down.

May the Word of God dwell richly
In my heart from hour to hour.

PRAYER

O God, help us understand who we are — your nobles, your royalty — and to maintain behavior in keeping with who we are. Grant us a continuing hunger for spiritual truth. Make us ever thirsty for the feasts in your precious Scriptures. Please deliver us from ever accepting teaching about you without examining the Word to see if the things we have read or heard are in fact so. Please watch over your children, who so easily stray and misunderstand. In Jesus' name, Amen.

27

Paul versus Athens

ACTS 17:16-34

G. K. Chesterton, in his book *The Ball and the Cross*, tells the story of two Englishmen's unsuccessful attempts to stage a duel. One is a volatile atheist named Turnbull who edits a paper appropriately named *The Atheist.* The other is Evan MacIan, a devout Roman Catholic. Their disagreement and attempts at dueling develop when Turnbull publishes an offensive article about the Virgin Mary and MacIan responds by tossing a brick through the newspaper's window.

The remainder of the story is a humorous account of their fantastic dash back and forth across the British Isles in attempted combat. Somehow, no matter how hard they try, they are again and again thwarted. After all, civilized men do not fight over such insignificant matters. Soon they become the number-one fugitives of society, and upon their inevitable capture both are judged mad and are put into an asylum. What becomes apparent is that it is not they who are insane, but their captors and, indeed, society itself.

Chesterton's point is not that men should resort to physical combat over the truth of Christianity. Rather, he is saying that a culture that prides itself on its detached approach to the central issues of life and regards those who approach them otherwise as uncivilized or insane is itself under delusion.

Today it is commonly held that it is fine to be a Christian as long as one does not take it too seriously. "Christianity has produced some of the world's greatest minds. Some of her doctrines are fascinating for intellectual exercise. But to take them seriously — to base one's life on them? Surely you cannot be serious!"

That not only describes the attitudes we commonly face, but what the church has historically encountered and what Paul faced in Athens. Paul, one of the most passionate and fiery Christians who ever lived, collided head-on with the dispassionate intellectualism of Athens. The story of "Paul versus Athens" can set our hearts on fire.

Paul left Berea and made the 200-mile trip down to Athens, leaving Silas and Timothy behind. He was alone in the glorious Athens of Socrates, Plato, Aristotle, Epicurus, and Zeno. Though it had been some 400 years since the golden age of Pericles, Paul found the city's glory and prestige intact. Athens was the intellectual center of the world (much like Oxford in the nineteenth century), and scholars from all over the inhabited earth made her their adopted home.

Even though the Romans conquered Athens in 146 B.C. Athens retained her supremacy, because the Romans loved everything Greek and so did not change her status as a free city. Despite all her glory, Athens was empty because she was living on the memories of the past. In philosophy she simply repeated the echoes of men long gone. Her art was no longer innate overflow but a lingering reflex. It was to such a city that the apostle came — proud, glorious to the eye, but dead. What a contrast between the apostle and the metropolis.

THE PRELUDE OF THE ATHENIAN ADDRESS (vv. 16-24)

> *While Paul was waiting for them in Athens, he was greatly distressed to see that the city was full of idols. (v. 16)*

The word translated "beholding" (NASB; NIV, "see") is the same word from which we derive *theater*. The apostle stared long and hard at what he saw, for the city was truly "full of idols." Pausanius, who visited Athens fifty years later, said it was easier to meet a god or goddess on the main street of Athens than to meet a man. This was statistically true because the population was about 10,000, but there were 30,000 statues of gods. The streets lined with idols of false deities, framed by the architectural magnificence of the Parthenon and the Acropolis, were dazzling to the eye.

No doubt Paul appreciated much of the city's beauty, being a man of culture. Nevertheless, "he was greatly distressed." The Greek literally means this was a paroxysm (see the notes on 15:39). He was angry about a lie. As a Jewish monotheist, he would have been disturbed, and as a Christian apostle he was even more enraged! Every idol demonstrated the Athenians' hunger for God, but it also testified to their spiritual emptiness. Ignorant of the true God, the Athenians were lost!

Paul felt desperate concern for the spiritual need before his eyes. As had happened with Jeremiah (Jeremiah 20:9), an urge to speak came like a burning fire, and the apostle could not hold it in. As believers, our hearts should ache and our eyes blur at what we see around us — ignorant souls denying the one God and giving allegiance to false deities. If we experience no inner paroxysms, we either have not truly been redeemed by Jesus Christ or we have become apathetic to the things of God.

Paul could not be indifferent or detached. So he jumped right in, raging heart and all.

> *So he reasoned in the synagogue with the Jews and the God-fearing Greeks, as well as in the marketplace day by day with those who happened to be there. A group of Epicurean and Stoic philosophers began to dispute with him. (vv. 17-18)*

Paul began dialoguing with anyone who would talk, and he found three groups of hearers — those who were religious ("the Jews and the God-fearing Greeks"), street-variety pagans, and intellectual philosopher-types called "Epicurean and Stoic philosophers." The latter two groups represented the competing philosophies of the day. The Epicureans believed that everything happens by chance, and death is the end — extinction with no afterlife. They believed there are gods, but those gods have nothing to do with the world. They were practical agnostics who believed pleasure is the chief end of man and that a simple lifestyle is the most pleasurable. The Stoics were pantheists, believing that everything is god and that whatever happened to them was their destiny. Consequently, they sought to live with apathy and detachment — fatalistic resignation. Together, these two philosophies represented the popular pagan alternatives for dealing with the plight of humanity apart from Christ. Epicureanism? Simple lifestyle. Stoicism? Apathy. Both were highly intellectual, and both lacked divine validation.

How would they respond to the gospel Paul preached?

> *Some of them asked, "What is this babbler trying to say?" Others remarked, "He seems to be advocating foreign gods." They said this because Paul was preaching the good news about Jesus and the resurrection. (v. 18)*

They wrapped their response with clever ironic sarcasm. The word translated "babbler" is literally "seedpicker." Originally used to describe birds picking up seeds and grain, over the years the word came to mean one who peddled others' ideas as original without understanding them — a plagiarist, a chirping gutter sparrow who went around peeping borrowed ideas! This was undoubtedly a very "in" word with this crowd: "seedpicker . . . gutter sparrow . . . ignorant babbler."

In verse 21 Luke gives his evaluation of the Athenians:

All the Athenians and the foreigners who lived there spent their time doing nothing but talking about and listening to the latest ideas.

They were the babblers!

The Athenian University was the home of dilettantism and of the cool, cultivated, critical intellect, which had tried all things and found all wanting; and in it there were few hearers and no open door for new teaching.[1]

The Athenian mind-set was always in pursuit of the *nouveau*, the dazzling, the sensational, the whims of the hour. So now the crowd brought Paul before the Areopagus — the Council of Ares (or as the Latin has it, Mars). If the speech was given at Mars Hill, as many believe, then before Paul lay the Theseum, the wonderful Doric temple. On his right was the upper city — the Acropolis and then the matchless Parthenon. Around him loomed thousands of statues and altars in gold, silver, and bronze. Paul stood amidst the symbols of departed greatness, with the gods of Greece staring down at him. Immediately before him sat the most exclusive philosophical review board in the world!

What a face-off! On one side stood Paul — divinely empowered, a man who had staked everything he had on his message. On the other side stood the Areopagus — sophisticated but indifferent. Paul stood before this intimidating group of powerful philosophers absolutely alone! What would the seedpicker say? Paul was about to give what F. F. Bruce has rightly called "a masterpiece of communication."

THE PROCLAMATION OF THE ATHENIAN ADDRESS (vv. 22-20)

Paul then stood up in the meeting of the Areopagus and said: "Men of Athens! I see that in every way you are very religious. For as I walked around and looked carefully at your objects of worship, I even found an altar with this inscription: TO AN UNKNOWN GOD. Now what you worship as something unknown I am going to proclaim to you." (vv. 22-23)

Paul's approach was brilliant. As courteous and conciliatory as possible, he complimented them on being "in every way . . . very religious." Paul was undoubtedly eager to protest their idolatry and point them to the truth, but he restrained himself and gave a genuine compliment first. He met them where they were. "In my stroll around your famous city I found an altar to an unknown god. Let me tell you about the one who you are worshiping." Paul established common ground.

His message also made brilliant application, for he pointed directly to the problem. The word translated "unknown" is the root from which we get *agnosticism*, which means "without knowledge." The Athenians were supposed to know everything, and they did, almost. But on the most important truth they came up short — they did not know God. Paul did not say this — they did ("TO AN UNKNOWN GOD"). Many of them probably grasped the apostle's irony.

Having established the bridge, Paul now began giving the Athenians doses of spiritual truth — first about God and then about themselves. Truth about God always helps us understand ourselves.

> *"The God who made the world and everything in it is the Lord of heaven and earth and does not live in temples built by hands. And he is not served by human hands, as if he needed anything, because he himself gives all men life and breath and everything else." (vv. 24-25)*

The fundamental truth about God is that he is the Creator: "the God who made the world and everything in it." That may not sound earth-shaking to us, but it challenged their whole theology. The Stoics were pantheists and the Epicureans practical atheists. Paul's declaration denied the premises of both groups. The accompanying statement in verse 25 that God is the Lifegiver — "he himself gives all men life and breath and everything else" — drove the truth home even further, for it directly attacked the Epicureans' belief that God was absent and the Stoics' belief that he was in everything. As the giver of life, God is actively here, but he is not contained in creation.

The final great truth about God is that he is not only the Creator and the Lifegiver, but he seeks us out.

> *"From one man he made every nation of men, that they should inhabit the whole earth; and he determined the times set for them and the exact places where they should live. God did this so that men would seek him and perhaps reach out for him and find him, though he is not far from each one of us." (vv. 26-27)*

Practically, Paul was saying that they were not living in Athens as a result of some cosmic accident. Rather, God had structured their lives in order to attract them to him. Great truths about God led to the truth about themselves: they were specially created by God, and he was seeking a personal relationship with them.

> *"'For in him we live and move and have our being.' As some of your own poets have said, 'We are his offspring.' Therefore since we are God's offspring, we should not think that the divine being is like gold or silver or stone — an image made by man's design and skill." (vv. 28-29)*

The apostle explained that as God's creatures, the Athenians had intrinsic dignity. Paul was a master communicator! He quoted a couple of their own poets in order to maintain rapport and keep their interest. The first part of verse 28, "For in him we live and move and have our being," is from the work of Epimenides. The final line in verse 28, "We are his offspring," is from the writings of Aratus:

> All ways are full of Zeus and all meeting places of men; the sea and the harbours are full of him. In every direction we all have to do with Zeus; for we are also his offspring.[2]

The apostle's point was that as creatures of intrinsic dignity, having been created by God, men ought to refrain from false worship. Since we are made in the image of God, it is insulting to God and degrading to us to make an idol of him.

Paul may have stumbled in his presentation. It may have been delivered "in weakness and fear, and with much trembling" (see 1 Corinthians 2:3). But we can be sure it was passionate. It came from the depths of his soul. He spoke with directness — "we should not think . . ." He rightly made the message personal.

THE PLEA OF THE ATHENIAN ADDRESS (vv. 30-31)

> *"In the past God overlooked such ignorance, but now he commands all people everywhere to repent. For he has set a day when he will judge the world with justice by the man he has appointed. He has given proof of this to all men by raising him from the dead." (v. 30)*

Men are to "repent." Of what? Idolatry. If men set anything above God as the object of their time, thought, energy, or life, they are worshiping the work of their hands and are thereby degrading God and themselves. They must repent because judgment is coming! Mankind is not moving toward extinction (as the Epicureans thought), nor toward absorption in the cosmos (as the Stoics supposed). But mankind is moving toward divine judgment. Moreover, our Judge is a resurrected man. The Areopagites did not like this at all. Five hundred years earlier Aeschylus had written, "When the dust has soaked up a man's blood, once he is dead, there is no resurrection," and this was a popular Greek sentiment in Paul's day.

This confronting call for decision was not what these cultured dilettantes were looking for. The famous Spanish philosopher Miguel de Unamuno comments:

> This admirable account plainly shows how far Attic [Greek] tolerance goes and where the patience of the intellectual ends. They all listen to you, calmly and smilingly, and at times they encourage you, saying: "That is strange!" or, "He has brains!" or, "That is suggestive!" or, "How fine!" or, "Pity that a thing so beautiful should not be true!" or, "This makes one think!" But as soon as you speak to them of resurrection and life after death, they lose their patience and cut short their remarks and exclaim, "Enough of this! We will talk about this another day!"[3]

Everything is fine as long as we remain theoretical, but when we call for action, men begin to shift their posture and look at their watches. Seeing their accountability to the true God makes many uncomfortable.

THE PRODUCT OF THE ATHENIAN ADDRESS (vv. 32-34)

> *When they heard about the resurrection of the dead, some of them sneered, but others said, "We want to hear you again on this subject." At that, Paul left the Council. A few men became followers of Paul and believed. Among them was Dionysius, a member of the Areopagus, also a woman named Damaris, and a number of others. (vv. 32-34)*

Paul's sermon had three results — mockery, delay, and belief. The first two responses show that many did not care about truth. Some said, "Seedpicker . . . what a waste of time!" When the discussion went beyond fun and games, they cut it off. Others said, "We want to hear you again," but they cared little whether they actually did or did not, and they never did hear him again. Verse 33 and the opening verse of chapter 18 tell the story: "Paul left the Council. . . . After this, Paul left Athens." Praise God — some truly believed and came to faith. But most apparently rejected the apostle's message and the Savior he proclaimed.

When men were angry with him, Paul argued with them. When he was persecuted, he returned again to the place of persecution. But for intellectual flippancy and moral dishonesty he had no stomach.

A FINAL WORD

Despite the prevalence of mockery and rejection that day, a man and a woman gave their lives to Jesus Christ. The man's name was Dionysius, and he was one of the elite — a member of the Areopagus. The woman was called Damaris. We know nothing else about them, but we do know they listened to Paul's words with all their hearts.

If we are believers, if we truly know Christ, we must never hear or read God's Word in a detached manner. We must pay attention to God with all our being. We must never give way to a cerebral detachment when it comes to divine things. We must always respond. Jesus stated the principle beautifully in Matthew 13:12:

> *"Whoever has will be given more, and he will have an abundance. Whoever does not have, even what he has will be taken from him."*

When truth comes, we must interact with it and appropriate it. One of the great sins of the church today is the dispassionate hearing of God's Word. Because of this, there are many who are spiritually ill, unable to comprehend the truths they once held dear. Only God can deliver his children from such apathy!

PRAYER

> *O God, help us not to consider your Word in a casual, unfeeling way. May our hearts burn with sacred truth — flames of the Holy Spirit that cannot remain within us but must overflow to others, drawing them into personal relationship with the Lord Jesus Christ. May our grief over the idolatry all around us move us to speak and live the gospel, so that others will come into your precious kingdom. In Jesus' name, Amen.*

28

Rejuvenating God's Servants

ACTS 18:1-17

The greatest description of Christian zeal that I know of was given by the famous nineteenth-century Anglican bishop J. C. Ryle in his book *Practical Religion.*

> A zealous man in religion is pre-eminently a man of one thing. It is not enough to say that he is earnest, hearty, uncompromising, through-going, whole-hearted, fervent in spirit. He only sees one thing, he cares for one thing, he lives for one thing, he is swallowed up in one thing; and that one thing is to please God. Whether he lives, or whether he dies, whether he has health, or whether he has sickness, whether he is rich, or whether he is poor, whether he pleases man, or whether he gives offence, whether he is thought wise, or whether he is thought foolish, whether he gets blame, or whether he gets praise, whether he gets honour, or whether he gets shame, for all this the zealous mans cares nothing at all. He burns for one thing; and that one thing is to please God, and to advance God's glory. If he is consumed in the very burning, he cares not for it; he is content. He feels that, like a lamp, he is made to burn; and if consumed in burning, he has but done the work for which God appointed him . . . This is what I mean when I speak of "zeal" in religion. (p. 130)

Paul was such a man, and he made a brilliant contrast to the pagan philosophers of Athens with their studied, philosophical detachment. For a man like Paul, burning with prophetic unction, smug complacency in his hearers was too much to bear. So he left Athens in search of more receptive fields. So eager was Paul to get out of Athens that he did not even wait for

Silas and Timothy, then en route. Paul must have felt at least a little dejected as he walked the fifty miles to Corinth. Since coming to Europe, he had suffered a terrible beating in Philippi, civil rejection in Thessalonica and Berea, and indifference in Athens.

To put it in today's terms, Paul may have felt like a football that had taken the right bounces and refused to be fumbled, and yet every time his team scored he was spiked to the turf mercilessly and then kicked the length of the field. In fact, the better he performed, the more he was spiked and kicked! The last punt from Athens, though apparently voluntary, was particularly grievous to his passionate heart. No one likes to be called a seed-picker — a hayseed. We get a glimmer of how Paul felt when he arrived in Corinth in the opening verses of chapter 2 of his first letter to the Corinthians:

> *And when I came to you, brothers, I did not come with eloquence or superior wisdom as I proclaimed to you the testimony about God. . . . I came to you in weakness and fear, and with much trembling. (vv. 1-3)*

The last line suggests a man who had been through the wringer. However, when Paul arrived in Corinth, some encouraging things happened. To begin with, he met Aquila and Priscilla.

> *After this, Paul left Athens and went to Corinth. There he met a Jew named Aquila, a native of Pontus, who had recently come from Italy with his wife Priscilla, because Claudius had ordered all the Jews to leave Rome. Paul went to see them, and because he was a tentmaker as they were, he stayed and worked with them. Every Sabbath he reasoned in the synagogue, trying to persuade Jews and Greeks. (Acts 18:1-4)*

There had recently been an anti-Semitic stir in Rome, and this dynamic couple, Aquila and Priscilla, was forced to move their business to Corinth. *Aquila* means "eagle." *Priscilla* is a diminutive form of Prisca, which is the name of one of the great families of Rome. She was probably related to this family in some way. Whatever the connection, she must have been a gifted woman, for in half the occurrences of their names she is mentioned first, which is highly unusual. Somehow they had both come to Christ and into Paul's life (which was first, we cannot be sure). They were a great encouragement to the apostle. In the final chapter of Romans Paul calls them his "fellow workers in Christ Jesus," saying that they "risked their lives" for him (16:3). They were close friends — towers of strength.

Silas and Timothy now arrived from Berea.

When Silas and Timothy came from Macedonia, Paul devoted himself exclusively to preaching, testifying to the Jews that Jesus was the Christ. (v. 5)

The apostle's associates brought two things with them — good news about the Thessalonian church (their faith and love were standing firm, 1 Thessalonians 3:6-10) and a missionary offering from Philippi (2 Corinthians 11:9; Philippians 4:14-15), so that Paul was free to "hold himself to the word" (literal translation). All this was in addition to the blessing of reunion with faithful Silas and Timothy, whom Paul often called "my son."

Furthermore, the gospel of Christ began to bear fruit in Corinth.

Crispus, the synagogue ruler, and his entire household believed in the Lord; and many of the Corinthians who heard him believed and were baptized. (v. 8)

Paul had substantial reasons to be encouraged: Priscilla and Aquila, Silas and Timothy, financial help, a full-time ministry, encouraging results (though he also faced opposition, v. 6). In the midst of all this, he fell prey to fear and discouragement. We know this is so because God gave him a vision to encourage him (vv. 9-10).

What was getting the apostle down? Like the Old Testament prophet Elijah, Paul had been under excruciating tension for a long time, and he was losing his ability to rebound. Elijah took a nosedive after the heart-thumping tension of his encounter with the priests of Baal followed by Jezebel's threats, and Paul was similarly reeling from his multiple encounters in recent months. He probably had not had sufficient time to recover from his beating. He was tired. And he now faced the depressing moral ambience of Corinth.

For 500 years the verb *korinthiozesthai*, "to Corinthianize," meant to be sexually immoral. Corinth was the Vanity Fair of the ancient world. Every night a thousand prostitutes descended the Acrocorinth to ply their trade in worship of Aphrodite. One could buy anything in Corinth if he had the money. Homosexuality was rampant. When Paul wrote Romans 1:26-28 he was describing what he saw in Corinth. What a contemporary ring this has:

Because of this, God gave them over to shameful lusts. Even their women exchanged natural relations for unnatural ones. In the same way the men also abandoned natural relations with women and were inflamed with lust for one another. Men committed indecent acts with

> *other men and received in themselves the due penalty for their perversion. Furthermore, since they did not think it worthwhile to retain the knowledge of God, he gave them over to a depraved mind, to do what ought not to be done.*

There had been culture shock in Athens, and now Paul experienced moral shock in Corinth. Its sweat and perfume and grit smothered Paul's righteous soul, and he became depressed. Remembering his past experiences, he knew what could happen to him in Corinth, and the apostle, as great a servant of Christ as he was, became discouraged, fearful, insecure. Even though there were some spiritual bright spots in Corinth, he needed a lift.

In the midst of Paul's despondency, God ministered to him through a vision bearing words of refreshment — great words for those who are beginning to wonder if they should give up the battle. When we feel the unrelenting persistence of evil, when we sense that the forces of darkness are sending troops to defeat us, when we feel that our finest hour is about to give way to our lowest, there is an antidote for our hopelessness. What did God tell Paul?

> *"Do not be afraid; keep on speaking, do not be silent. For I am with you, and no one is going to attack and harm you, because I have many people in this city." (vv. 9-10)*

This marvelous message from heaven can bring rejuvenation to our souls.

FEAR NOT (v. 9)

The Lord began by saying, "Do not be afraid." Paul had given way to fear and discouragement even though he was experiencing spiritual success. That may seem rather strange until we realize that success is what he feared. After all, past successes had led to persecution — in Pisidian Antioch, Lystra, Philippi, Thessalonica, Berea, and, in its own way, Athens. Now in Corinth when the apostle told the Jews, "Your blood be on your own heads! I am clear of my responsibility. From now on I will go to the Gentiles" (v. 6), moved next door to the home of Titius Justus, and led Crispus, the head rabbi of the synagogue, to Christ (v. 8), he just knew he was headed for trouble!

From Paul's perspective, the immediate future was perfectly predictable. Soon there would be a riot, and he would be spiked and punted. The diabolical pattern was quite clear. He was like a boxer who knows what is coming when he answers the bell.

Poor Paul was worrying about troubles he was not facing yet, a terrible habit in which we all engage.

> When Lincoln was on his way to Washington to be inaugurated, he spent some time in New York with Horace Greeley and told him an anecdote which was meant to be an answer to the question which everybody was asking him: Are we really to have Civil War? In his circuit-riding days Lincoln and his companions, riding to the next session of court, had crossed many swollen rivers. But the Fox River was still ahead of them; and they said one to another, "If these streams give us so much trouble, how shall we get over the Fox River?"
>
> When darkness fell, they stopped for the night at a log tavern, where they fell in with the Methodist presiding elder of the district who rode through the country in all kinds of weather and knew all about the Fox River. They gathered about him and asked him about the present state of the river. "Oh yes," replied the circuit rider, "I know all about the Fox River. I have crossed it often and understand it well. But I have one fixed rule with regard to the Fox River — I never cross it till I reach it."[1]

That is a good rule — easy to remember, not so easy to keep.

> Today if you visit Thomas Carlyle's famous home in London, they will show you an almost soundproof chamber that Carlyle had built so the noise of the street could be shut out and he could work in silence. One of his neighbors, however, kept a rooster that several times in the night and in the early morning gave way to vigorous self-expression. When Carlyle protested to the owner of the rooster, the man pointed out to him that the rooster crowed only three times in the night, and that after all could not be such a terrible annoyance. "But," Carlyle said to him, "if you only knew what I suffer waiting for that rooster to crow!"[2]

Many of us are pros at borrowing trouble. We feel harassed as we wait for something disastrous and unpleasant to happen. We just know the social event is going to be a flop. What if it rains on our picnic? We are sure So-And-So will put the wrong interpretation on our words. So we go through a thousand tribulations we are never meant to undergo — and probably never will.

The vision and its opening words — the fact that God made the effort to encourage Paul not to fear — meant that God loved and cared for his ambassador. This assurance ministered to Paul's heart, just as 1 John 4:18

teaches us: "There is no fear in love. But perfect love drives out fear." The simple words in the vision filled Paul's heart with God's love, and fear was put to flight. Time and time again the Scriptures tell us to fear not — to stop worrying about tomorrow, to stop borrowing trouble — because we are divinely loved, and God's love is enough!

KEEP MINISTERING

Next God told Paul to "keep on speaking, do not be silent" (v. 9). Paul's fear had made him afraid to speak, and the Lord knew that such silence would imprison his fear, while boldness would overcome it. It is to Paul's eternal credit and our ongoing edification that Paul obeyed and kept ministering.

Actually, as Paul later wrote, his weakened condition prepared him for the perfection of God's power within him.

> *I came to you in weakness and fear, and with much trembling. My message and my preaching were not with wise and persuasive words, but with a demonstration of the Spirit's power. (1 Corinthians 2:3-4)*

Lloyd Ogilvie writes:

> I have learned this repeatedly in my own life. When my strength is depleted, when my rhetoric is unpolished by human talent, when I am weary, the Lord has a much better tool for empathetic, sensitive communication. The barriers are down. When I know I can do nothing by myself, my poverty becomes a channel of his power. More than that, often when I feel I have been least efficient, people have been helped most effectively. It has taken me a long time to learn that the lower my resistances are and the less self-consciousness I have, the more the Word of God comes through.[3]

Weakness is the secret strength of God's most effective servants and the indispensable element of potent preaching. If you are feeling weak and fearful, praise God! Now is the time to speak and not be silent, relying on him to make his power perfect in your weakness (see 2 Corinthians 12:9-10). Then whatever you do, whatever is accomplished for Christ, all the glory will go to God.

RECEIVE PROMISED PROTECTION

The Lord next promised protection and care. The first facet of this jewel was his presence: "For I am with you" (v. 10) — a precious promise for the fearful. Sometimes I recite to myself the comforting words of Hildebert of Lavardin:

> God is over all things; outside all; within but not enclosed; without but not excluded; above but not raised up; below but not depressed; wholly above, presiding; wholly beneath, sustaining; wholly within, filling.[4]

This truth bears unending practical applications. He is here! He is under me! He is over me! He is inside me! But he is not shut in! God says, "Do not fear — keep going — I am with you!" John Wesley's dying words, his very last words, were: "The best of all is, God is with us!"

The second facet of the promised protection was, "No one is going to attack and harm you." No hurt would come to Paul in Corinth. This had not been true in previous months, for Paul had suffered terribly. And it would not be true in the future. But for a particular window of time it was true, because God had promised.

Some years back I was watching *Monday Night Football*, and the camera zeroed in on Otis Sistrunk, the great defensive tackle of the Oakland Raiders. He had taken his helmet off his shaved head, and steam was rising from him. The sight reminded me of Sears Tower! No quarterback could survive if it were not for the pocket formed by equally gigantic offensive linemen. Because God's big boys watch over us — Michael and Gabriel and other angels — we are safe. No one can touch anyone on God's team unless he allows it.

In Corinth nothing and no one could do ultimate harm to the Apostle Paul, and it is the same with us. God's protection does not mean we will be free from difficulties, but God will never allow us to face more than we can bear. Not only that, but no eternal damage can befall us.

RECOGNIZE THAT YOUR WORK WILL NOT BE IN VAIN

God assured his apostle, "I have many people in this city." Those were encouraging words. Paul's work would not be fruitless. Some of the Corinthians were tired of Tinsel Town. The fleshly pleasures had lost their attraction. Some were suffering deep guilt and an awful emptiness of soul. They were ready to receive Christ. These people, according to Paul's other writings, included Erastus, Gaius, Stephanos, Fortunatus, and Achaicus.

According to verses 11-18, Paul stayed in Corinth for eighteen months. For him that was like putting down roots! It was not long before there were many believers, perhaps hundreds. Persecution did come, just as Paul had expected, when the Jews took him before the proconsul Gallio (the famous

Seneca's brother) and charged him with introducing an illicit religion. However, that opposition backfired, and for a time Paul and his followers enjoyed more freedom than before.

Some of us may be discouraged and fear an uncertain future. Some of us are seeing encouraging things happen but are afraid they will not last and hard times will return. The Lord has a message for us:

> "Do not be afraid. Stop borrowing trouble. Look to me! I love you. Keep ministering. Keep caring. Keep speaking my name. Inactivity will only imprison your fears. Believe that I am with you and that I will give you all the protection you need. Believe that your life will bear fruit — I promise."

According to an ancient story, when Leonides, the noble hero of the Spartans who defended Greece from the Persians, was in battle against thousands of invaders, one of his men said to him, "General, when the Persians shoot their arrows, there are so many of them that they darken the sky." Leonides replied, "Then we will fight in the shade." Paul continued serving the Lord and fighting the battle, regardless of his feelings, no matter what circumstances he saw on the horizon. We must do the same.

PRAYER

O God, help us not to turn aside because of fear, but rather to have courage through the Holy Spirit. Help us to keep serving, fighting, hoping, proclaiming, no matter what obstacles the enemy might put in our way. Help us to recognize and claim the protection you have provided, knowing that whatever happens to us, no real harm can befall us, for we are shielded by your eternal love and faithfulness. Help us to remember that what we do for you will indeed bear fruit, for your glory and exaltation. In Jesus' name, Amen.

29

The Missing Ingredient

ACTS 18:22 — 19:7

John Wesley's early life suggested that he would certainly become a man of God. He was the son of a clergyman, Samuel Wesley, and the unusually godly and dedicated Susanna Wesley. After a privileged upbringing John attended Charterhouse and Oxford and became double professor of Greek and logic at Lincoln College. He also served as his father's assistant and was ordained by the church.

While at Oxford he was a member of the "Holy Club," a group so nicknamed by the other students because they seriously attempted to cultivate their spiritual lives. Finally he even accepted an invitation from the Society for the Propagation of the Gospel to become a missionary to the American Indians in Georgia, *where he utterly failed.* Forced to return to England he wrote, "I went to America to convert the Indians; but, oh, who shall convert me?"

Not all was lost, however, because in his earlier travels to America he had encountered some Moravians whose living faith deeply impressed him. So upon his return to London he sought out one of the leaders and, to use Wesley's words, was "clearly convinced of unbelief, of the want of that faith whereby alone we are saved." On the evening of May 24, 1738, Wesley wrote in his journal:

> In the evening I went very unwillingly to a society in Aldersgate Street where one was reading Luther's preface to the Epistle to the Romans. About a quarter before nine, while he was describing the change which God works in the heart through faith in Christ, I felt my heart strangely warmed. I felt I did trust in Christ, Christ alone, for salvation; and an assurance was given me, that he had taken away my sins, even mine, and saved me from the law of sin and death.

John Wesley's "warming" was the regenerating work of the Holy Spirit. Amazingly, until Aldersgate, John Wesley, a man who knew more theology and was more dedicated than most believers, did not know Christ or the saving power of the Holy Spirit. He was in the church but was condemned!

Acts 18:22 — 19:7 deals with the same phenomenon — religious people who have not personally experienced the reality of Jesus Christ. "Did you receive the Holy Spirit when you believed?" Paul asked (19:2). As we preach the Word, we have no way of discerning if our hearers truly have the Holy Spirit. Hundreds of thousands of people profess some type of belief in Christ, display a reverence for God, go to church on Sundays, contribute to the offering, sit at the Lord's Table, and admire the ethical teachings of the Lord — but are as lost as John Wesley before Aldersgate. They have no fire, no passion, no life because they do not have Christ. They are "icily regular, splendidly empty."[1] They do not have the life and warmth of the Holy Spirit. This is a life and death issue.

Acts 18:22 — 19:7 depicts three religious profiles that are still present today. First, those who have not received the Holy Spirit, who have not been baptized into Christ, and are therefore not Christians. Second, those who have received the "washing of rebirth and renewal by the Holy Spirit" (Titus 3:5) and are genuine believers. Third, those who are true believers and have received the Spirit, but give little evidence of the life of the Spirit. Whatever our state, we can here learn how to appropriate and maintain the vitality of the Holy Spirit. This is an antidote for a sterile, lifeless Christianity.

Dr. Luke provides insight into this matter through the case studies of Apollos of Alexandria and of twelve unnamed Jewish disciples. While in Corinth, Paul had taken a Nazirite vow that had now ended. So he cut his hair in Cenchrea and set out for Jerusalem to offer his hair in the temple. He took Priscilla and Aquila along with him and left them in Ephesus (probably to prepare the way for his return ministry on a third missionary trip) and continued on to Jerusalem (18:18-23). While Paul was in either Palestine or Asia Minor, Apollos of Alexandria came to the synagogue in Ephesus on a self-styled preaching mission.

CASE STUDY #1 IN SPIRITUAL VITALITY: APOLLOS (18:24-28)

Luke pictures Apollos *before*, *during*, and *after* the reception of the life of the Holy Spirit. We will first look at the *before*:

> *Meanwhile a Jew named Apollos, a native of Alexandria, came to Ephesus. He was a learned man, with a thorough knowledge of the Scriptures. He had been instructed in the way of the Lord, and he*

spoke with great fervor and taught about Jesus accurately, though he knew only the baptism of John. (vv. 24-25)

Apollos was the kind of man who stood out in any gathering. He knew the Scriptures — the Old Testament — thoroughly. John Broadus (one of the founders of the Southern Baptist Seminary and the author of the most influential book on preaching ever written in America) was lecturing his class just nine days before he died when he paused and said:

> Gentlemen, if this were the last time I should ever be permitted to address you, I would feel amply repaid for consuming the whole hour endeavoring to impress upon you these two things: true piety, and, like Apollos, to be men "mighty in the Scriptures."

Broadus then paused and stood for a moment with his piercing eyes fixed upon the class. Over and over he repeated in that slow but wonderfully impressive style that was distinctly his, "Mighty in the Scriptures, mighty in the Scriptures, mighty in the Scriptures."[2]

Apollos knew the Word. He was also unusually learned. Alexandria, the place of his birth, rivaled Athens's reputation for knowledge. The greatest library in the world was in Alexandria. That city was the home of Euclid, Porphyry, Plotinus, and Philo. The Septuagint was accomplished there. Apollos represented an amazing synthesis of Greek and Hebrew learning.

Not only this, but he was "an eloquent man" (NASB). He had no doubt read Aristotle's *Rhetoric*, he reveled in the messages of the Old Testament prophets, and he could hold a crowd in the palm of his hand. Perhaps he was like Alexander Whyte of Edinburgh, whom A. J. Gossip once went to hear but sat where he could see the faces of those watching Whyte. When Whyte frowned, they frowned. When he smiled, they smiled. They were so absorbed in the message, so one with him, that they acted unconsciously as a perfect mirror of his every mood.[3]

Part and parcel with this, Apollos was passionate — "he spoke with great fervor." Literally the word means "burning" or "boiling hot." He exemplified Lloyd-Jones's definition of preaching: "logic on fire." Apollos was a superior man. He was in the forefront wherever he went — and yet he did not fully know Christ! He "taught about Jesus accurately, though he knew only the baptism of John." He had been a disciple of John the Baptist, he had obediently been baptized into repentance, and he was looking for the coming Messiah. But he did not know the meaning of the cross. He was not familiar with the fact of the Resurrection or the outpouring of the Holy Spirit at Pentecost.

He was a superb man who had a burden for the scattered Jews of the ancient world. He wanted them to be ready for the coming of the Messiah. That is what he was like *before* receiving the life of the Spirit. What happened to Apollos *during* the reception of the Spirit?

> *He began to speak boldly in the synagogue. When Priscilla and Aquila heard him, they invited him to their home and explained to him the way of God more adequately. (18:26)*

Priscilla and Aquila recognized some deficiencies in Apollos' understanding, but they did not correct him in public. There was no scorn, criticism, or rejection. They did not embarrass him. Only God's grace makes us like this. When I was eighteen years old, I spent a summer studying the doctrine of the sovereignty of God. It was a theological springtime for me, and I wanted everyone to understand what I had found — and to express it in the same way! I was so fervent that I would actually approach speakers after conference messages and tell them that their message would be more complete with some teaching on God's sovereignty. Gasp!

Priscilla and Aquila had none of this nit-picking mentality. Their method was beautifully life-giving. They took the young man aside and ministered Christ to him. Maybe they washed his feet and gave him a good Sabbath supper. They certainly lovingly completed his theological picture. Apollos of Alexandria at this time became born again — baptized with the Spirit. This godly couple's attitude made all the difference. The Holy Spirit can work with or without us, but he has elected to work most often through his people. From ground level, it appears that Apollos would not have come to life in the Spirit had Priscilla and Aquila not been such gentle channels of divine grace. Life in the Spirit spreads through people like this.

Though erudite and polished, Apollos humbly sat at the feet of these tentmakers. "Apollos is the patron saint of those who find that religion is not enough."[4] And he found life! The truth of Christ and life in the Spirit come to those who are humble enough to listen and to be taught. Such an attitude is essential for life and ongoing growth in the Spirit. Every time we open the Word, we should be willing to hear and heed it.

What happened to Apollos *after* the reception of the life of the Spirit?

> *When Apollos wanted to go to Achaia, the brothers encouraged him and wrote to the disciples there to welcome him. On arriving, he was a great help to those who by grace had believed. For he vigorously refuted the Jews in public debate, proving from the Scriptures that Jesus was the Christ. (vv. 27-28)*

Apollos became a superbly effective minister of the gospel. John

Wesley's conversion began a movement that historians rank with the French Revolution and the Industrial Revolution as one of the great historical phenomena of the nineteenth century. Wesley's preaching may have even saved England from a revolution similar to that of France.[5] Apollos' ministry too became supremely effective in its historical context. Apparently some who knew both Paul and Apollos preferred Apollos, though both men rejected such foolishness. Paul commented on this, saying:

> *What, after all, is Apollos? And what is Paul? Only servants, through whom you came to believe — as the Lord has assigned to each his task. I planted the seed, Apollos watered it, but God made it grow. (1 Corinthians 3:5-6)*

Apollos became one of God's great ambassadors. Perhaps he was even the author of Hebrews, as Luther thought. Apollos' life shows us that we can lift others only to the level on which we ourselves live. Apollos — a Jew, an Alexandrian, learned, mighty in the Scriptures, fervent in spirit, accurate in his teaching, bold in his preaching — could only take the people as far as he had come himself, and not one step further. Do we want people to overflow with the Holy Spirit? Then we must be full ourselves (see Ephesians 5:18; Galatians 5:22ff.).

While Apollos was in Corinth watering what Paul had planted, Paul came to Ephesus on his third missionary journey.

CASE STUDY #2 IN SPIRITUAL VITALITY: THE TWELVE DISCIPLES OF JOHN (19:1-7)

Interestingly, in Ephesus Paul discovered some men who had the same problem as Apollos.

> *While Apollos was at Corinth, Paul took the road through the interior and arrived at Ephesus. There he found some disciples and asked them, "Did you receive the Holy Spirit when you believed?" They answered, "No, we have not even heard that there is a Holy Spirit." So Paul asked, "Then what baptism did you receive?" "John's baptism," they replied. (vv. 1-3)*

During the latter part of the eighteenth century many colonists left Virginia and started through the mountains to settle the valleys that lay far to the west. Fear of Indians, the death of a horse, or the breaking down of a wagon forced many to stay in the mountains. For over twenty years these settlers saw no white men at all, until a group of travelers straggled into the neighborhood. Naturally there was much conversation about the outside world. The travelers asked the mountaineers what they thought of the new republic and the policies of the Continental Congress. The others answered, "We have not so much as heard of a Continental Congress or a Republic." They thought of themselves as loyal subjects of the British king and had not even heard of George Washington or the Revolutionary War.[6]

After coming into contact with the teaching of John the Baptist, these men in Ephesus had become spiritual Rip Van Winkles. Their reply, "No, we have not even heard that there is a Holy Spirit," does not mean they knew nothing about the Holy Spirit, for the Holy Spirit came on Jesus when he was baptized, and John taught that the Messiah would baptize believers with the Spirit and with fire. These men simply did not know that the promised Spirit had come.

Paul knew just what to do — he preached Christ!

> *Paul said, "John's baptism was a baptism of repentance. He told the people to believe in the one coming after him, that is, in Jesus." On hearing this, they were baptized into the name of the Lord Jesus. When Paul placed his hands on them, the Holy Spirit came on them, and they spoke in tongues and prophesied. There were about twelve men in all. (vv. 4-7)*

This was a mini-Pentecost. We see the Pentecost experience four times in the book of Acts: to *Jewish* believers in Jerusalem, to the *Samaritans* through Philip, to the *Gentiles* by Peter, and here to *dispersed Jews* through Paul.

This was a time of ecstasy and emotional release. They praised God in other languages. Tears flowed freely. Some cried aloud for joy. They "prophesied." The word *prophecy* comes from two words — *pro*, "before," and *phaino*, "to shine." Ephesus, the city with everything, had never seen anything like this. This was springtime in the church.

What transpired inside these men? The Holy Spirit convicts the world of sin, righteousness, and judgment (see John 16:8-11), and now, thanks to the Spirit's illumination, they saw themselves and the world as they really were. As a result, they were flooded with assurance and security. The Spirit of God bore witness with their spirits that they were indeed children of God (see Romans 8:16). They sensed the presence of One coming alongside to help — the *Paraclete*, the Holy Spirit of God. There was an overflow of joy and praise.

> *Jesus stood and said in a loud voice, "If a man is thirsty, let him come to me and drink. Whoever believes in me, as the Scripture has said,*

> *streams of living water will flow from within him." By this he meant the Spirit. (John 7:37-39)*

These men praised God, which is always a sign that the Holy Spirt is at work. They exalted Jesus Christ, because the Spirit does not promote himself but Christ. These men could not stop talking about Jesus. Like Apollos, they made a difference in their world. The remainder of the chapter shows that Ephesus now became a sounding board for the gospel in Asia Minor. Ultimately the presence of these Spirit-energized believers so undermined idolatry that many idols were burned.

CASE STUDY #3 IN SPIRITUAL VITALITY: OUR OWN

What do we need in order to appropriate and maintain the life of the Holy Spirit within us? The Holy Spirit releases his fullness in our lives through genuine, ongoing faith. In fact, the Holy Spirit is initially given when a person exercises trust in the Lord Jesus Christ for salvation and new life. That is what Paul had in mind in 1 Corinthians 12:13:

> *For we were all baptized by one Spirit into one body — whether Jews or Greeks, slave or free — and we were all given the one Spirit to drink.*

Belief releases the ever-fresh power of the Holy Spirit within us. Colossians 2:6 says, "Just as you received Christ Jesus as Lord, continue to live in him." That is, "You received him by an act of humble believing, so now keep on believing in him, so you will demonstrate the life of the Holy Spirit." When there is no evidence of the working of the Holy Spirit in our lives — no power, no joy, no grace — we are not believing in him.

We may have believed in Christ five years ago or twenty years ago or . . . But perhaps today there is no vitality. Our life has a bedrock of faith, but because of unbelief there is no freshness. We need to come back to square one — the foot of the cross — and again cast everything on Jesus. Believing is receiving! The church of Jesus Christ desperately needs vitality today.

There are three kinds of people in our churches. There are *non-Christians* — individuals who have not received Christ or the Holy Spirit, though they may have some degree of intellectual belief. They may, like John's disciples, have even manifested a willingness to repent, but they have not yet met the resurrected Christ. Such individuals need to receive him by opening their heart to him, believing on him as their sole hope for salvation. He will then give them the Spirit, and they will know it!

There are also *committed Christians* who need to keep on believing. Continually believing in Christ means continually receiving the Holy Spirit's grace and power.

There are also *Christians who used to believe*. Such persons need the advice given by Christ to the church of the Ephesians when they left their first love and, a natural consequence, lost the vitality of the Holy Spirit: "Remember the height from which you have fallen! Repent and do the things you did at first" (Revelation 2:5). Remember — repent — return.

The church today needs a new appropriation of the vitality and life of the Spirit of God.

PRAYER

O God, please work in each of our hearts. Help those who are yet outside your grace to come to believe in the Lord Jesus Christ as Savior and so to receive the Spirit as well. Help your people to keep believing and serving and worshiping, giving your Son preeminence day by day. Help others to come back to the place of truly believing the message with overflowing joy. We constantly need your sustaining, enabling mercy and power. Please open our hearts anew to receive all you wish to do in and through us. In Jesus' name, Amen.

30

Assaulting the Castle Dark

ACTS 19:8-20

During the Battle of Waterloo, England waited silently for news of the outcome. If Wellington could not defeat Napoleon, England had a frightening future. Finally, from the top of Winchester Cathedral, trained eyes read the semaphore signals:

W-E-L-L-I-N-G-T-O-N-D-E-F-E-A-T-E-D

Just then fog set in, and no further transmission was possible. "Wellington Defeated" was relayed throughout England. Despair reigned as people prepared for the worst. What would happen to their beloved land? But later the fog lifted, and the full message was revealed:

W-E-L-L-I-N-G-T-O-N-D-E-F-E-A-T-E-D-T-H-E-E-N-E-M-Y

How different history would be without those final two words. And how different the Church would be if through the haze of history all we could see were the words:

P-A-U-L-D-E-F-E-A-T-E-D

But that is sometimes how the situation appeared, until the smoke finally settled and the message read:

P-A-U-L-D-E-F-E-A-T-E-D-T-H-E-E-N-E-M-Y

These words could well be written across Acts 19:8-20 — the extraordinary account of Paul's early triumph over the powers of darkness in Ephesus.

Ephesus' strategic position made her the "Treasure House of Asia" and the mother of materialism and ambition. She was the site of the Temple of Artemis (or Diana), one of the seven wonders of the ancient world. One hundred and twenty-seven marbled pillars rose sixty feet to support the gorgeous ceiling, many of them inlaid with gold and rare gems. The temple's huge canopy, covering an area 425 feet in length and 200 feet in width, housed the multi-breasted image of Artemis, supposed to have fallen from the stars. This temple was the center for a thriving cult of fertility worship.

Ephesus became a collecting place for superstition and the dark arts — a cesspool of the occult. Aware of this, Paul wrote to the Ephesian believers:

> *For our struggle is not against flesh and blood, but against the rulers, against the authorities, against the powers of this dark world and against the spiritual forces of evil in the heavenly realms. (6:12)*

Ephesus was the waterhole for every kind of magician, witch, clairvoyant, and criminal. Con artists, murderers, and perverts all found the climate of Ephesus unusually agreeable. That city was the Dark Castle of Asia Minor.

DARKNESS UNDER ATTACK (vv. 8-12)

Paul's assault on the evil powers of Ephesus began with aggressive teaching.

> *Paul entered the synagogue and spoke boldly there for three months, arguing persuasively about the kingdom of God. But some of them became obstinate; they refused to believe and publicly maligned the Way. So Paul left them. He took the disciples with him and had discussions daily in the lecture hall of Tyrannus. (vv. 8-9)*

As always, Paul started in the synagogue, and in Ephesus he had one of his longest hearings — three months. His method was "reasoning" (NASB) or literally "dialoguing" — exchange, question and answer, give and take. Some were persuaded by Paul's reasoning, and "some of them became obstinate." When persecution set in, Paul and his followers made arrangements to continue the dialogue in a rented hall belonging to a local philosopher named Tyrannus, which literally means "tyrant." Concerning this name, Richard Longenecker notes:

Since it is difficult (except in certain bleak moments of parenthood) to think of any parent naming his or her child "Tyrant," the name must have been a nickname given by the man's students.[1]

On the surface, this move to the halls of Tyrannus does not seem very significant. But this change shows Paul's aggressiveness and determination in assaulting the powers of darkness. The Western text says Paul rented Tyrannus' quarters "from the fifth hour to the tenth" — that is, from 11 A.M. to 4 P.M. That was when the people of Ephesus took their midday siesta. The workday began at 7, broke at 11, and continued from 4 until about 9:30 at night. Evidently Paul made tents during the morning hours, taught between 11 and 4, and then went back to work. Paul says in 20:34, "You yourselves know that these hands of mine have supplied my own needs." Paul kept a killer schedule! Religion was big business in Ephesus, and Paul was determined to keep himself free from any suspicion that he was in it for the money.

Paul both paid his own way *and* taught five hours a day, six days a week, fifty-two weeks a year for two years — 3,120 hours of lecture. This is equivalent to 130 days of lecturing continuously for twenty-four hours a day. Paul was a determined man who at great personal cost made a relentless assault for Christ against the fortresses of evil. This aspect of the apostle's character dominates his assault as seen in verses 8-12.

The apostle's attack on the citadels of darkness brought remarkable spiritual advances.

This went on for two years, so that all the Jews and Greeks who lived in the province of Asia heard the word of the Lord. God did extraordinary miracles through Paul, so that even handkerchiefs and aprons that had touched him were taken to the sick, and their illnesses were cured and the evil spirits left them. (vv. 10-12)

Luke tells us that everyone in Asia (the area around modern-day Turkey) "heard the word of the Lord." It was during this time that the seven churches named in Revelation 2 — 3, as well as many others, came into being. By any estimate, what happened in those two years is amazing.

This advance of the gospel was accompanied by unusual miracles. The Greek says, "miracles not of an ordinary kind." Some were *direct*, coming through the hands of Paul. Others were *indirect*, being somehow mediated through articles of Paul's clothing that, when applied to the ill, brought healing.

This and similar accounts have suffered disgraceful abuse in the hands of opportunists. I once received a colored brochure that featured pictures of an "evangelist" (I am using his word) designed to show what a versatile man of God he was — praying by a waterfall, praying with his hands placed on a pile of letters, holding a baby (he liked children), shaking the hand of a poor man (he knew poor people). But what really got my attention was the offer of a specially blessed handkerchief that had been dipped in the Jordan River and that, if prayerfully applied, would bring healing — at a cost of only 15 dollars.

Paul was not selling his handkerchiefs or socks or aprons to the local faithful. They were "borrowing" them and applying them to the sick. And God, at this critical juncture in the church's history, being a God of incredible patience and grace, met these people on their own level with bona fide miracles, accommodating himself to their uninstructed faith.

The full meaning of these indirect miracles ties in with God's view of Paul's costly, determined labor for Christ. The Greek word translated "handkerchiefs" in verse 12 was a Latin loanword carrying the root meaning of sweat.[2] These "handkerchiefs" were the cloths Paul used to wipe away sweat while working. Moreover, the "aprons" were those he wore while making tents and working with leather. The hankies and aprons were "symbols which God chose to employ in order to underscore the characteristic of the apostle which made him a channel of the power of God. In the same way, Moses' rod was a symbol. Cast on the ground, the rod became a serpent; lifted over the waters, it rolled them back. There was nothing magic about the rod itself; it was the symbol of something about Moses which God honored. So these sweatbands and trade aprons were symbols of the honest, dignified humility of heart, the servant-character which manifested and released the power of God."[3]

The power of God is released through a man or woman whose heart is so utterly committed that he or she is ready to invest diligent labor to make the gospel available, even if they need to stoop to a lowly trade. In contrast, my wife once conversed with a collegian who told her that he and his fiancée were going into a ski ministry because they liked the outdoors and loved to ski. While it is true that God often calls us to ministries compatible with our interests and abilities, one's own comfort and pleasure should never be the primary factor for entering a given ministry.

Certainly this was not the case with Jesus when he ministered to the Samaritan woman at the well (John 4). Jesus sent the disciples into town for groceries because he was tired and needed some time alone. The Greek text suggests that he plopped himself down the way a tired man does at the end of a tough day. Jesus was always expending himself for others. A glance at the Gospels reveals that he could hardly find two minutes to rub together. He had to sneak away to avoid the crowds or the disciples' constant questions and needs. Our Lord was often weary in his ministry to sin-ravaged hearts, and yet he kept ministering his love to them.

As he reclined by the well, it is very possible that our Lord had his eyes closed when he heard the approaching footfalls. He looked up and saw a Samaritan woman. It would have been easy, humanly speaking, to rationalize, "I have been ministering to thousands. I am tired, and she is only one person. I just have to relax!" That option was available to Jesus, but instead he reached out to the heart of this woman and so provided one of the most glorious cases of spiritual aggression in all of Scripture. Jesus' assault on the darkness of her heart was sustained by a conscious determination to do the work of the Father through diligent labor. Jesus not only died for her — he sweat for her!

This truth must be held in balance. Christians need to sleep and take proper care of themselves. Some are on the verge of collapse because they have not been doing that. They need to take a vacation — to get away and relax. But it is also true that none of us will ever accomplish anything in the spiritual battle if we are not willing to labor to the point of exhaustion. Paul later told the Thessalonians:

> *Surely you remember, brothers, our toil and hardship; we worked night and day in order not to be a burden to anyone while we preached the gospel of God to you. (1 Thessalonians 2:9)*

Paul made tents, taught apologetics, pastored, watched over God's people, admonished the erring with tears, went from house to house, evangelized, planted churches, and directed great missionary enterprises. What a man! What a servant of Christ! Truly great athletes learn to train even when they do not feel like it and to play even when hurt. That is especially true in the battle against evil. In this day of "me-ism" and hedonism and leisure, we need tough, muscular Christians like Paul.

DARKNESS IN CONFUSION (vv. 13-16)

Predictably, the gospel's initial success led to others trying to get in on the act.

> *Some Jews who went around driving out evil spirits tried to invoke the name of the Lord Jesus over those who were demon-possessed. They would say, "In the name of Jesus, whom Paul preaches, I command you to come out." (v. 13)*

Exorcism was a common trade, and the best exorcists were thought to know the names of the more powerful spirits. It was also commonly believed that the Jewish priests had access to the secret name of the God of Israel and its pronunciation and thus had special power over the spirit world.[4] So it was very natural for renegade Jewish exorcists to add Jesus' name to their incantations.

But the situation was intolerable, and the Lord decided to purge the bandwagon by providing an unforgettable example.

> *Seven sons of Sceva, a Jewish chief priest, were doing this. The evil spirit answered them, "Jesus I know, and I know about Paul, but who are you?" Then the man who had the evil spirit jumped on them and overpowered them all. He gave them such a beating that they ran out of the house naked and bleeding. (vv. 14-16)*

The seven sons of Sceva thought they would have another quick exorcism and an easy buck — until they intoned the name Jesus. Then the demoniac rolled his frenzied eyes and said, " I know who Jesus is, and I know who Paul is, but who do you think you are?" After that, all they remembered were some rights and lefts, the door opening, and streaking madly for cover! Oh, how the church probably loved to tell that story!

Confusion reigned among the dark powers, now divided. The exorcists had been attacked by an evil spirit who should have been working with them. As Jesus himself stated, "If a house is divided against itself, that house cannot stand" (Mark 3:25). This was the first sign of a crack in the Castle Dark of Ephesus. And it came because of the dogged assault of one man — the courageous Apostle Paul.

DARKNESS IN RETREAT (vv. 17-19)

As the darkness began to retreat, fear came upon the entire populace.

> *When this became known to the Jews and Greeks living in Ephesus, they were all seized with fear, and the name of the Lord Jesus was held in high honor. (v. 17)*

It was not the extraordinary miracles that brought on this healthy fear, but the knowledge that some who tried to use Jesus' name had been judged.

Verse 18 continues the story: "Many of those who believed now came and openly confessed their evil deeds." Through the ministry of Paul, believers became sensitized to their sin. A nine-year-old girl once wrote President Grover Cleveland, admitting to having used two postage stamps a second time because they had not been properly canceled. She asked President Cleveland's forgiveness and enclosed the money for the stamps.

She concluded the letter by writing, "And I will never do it again." Her conscience had been quickened, and she responded with confession and restitution. In Ephesus the church became sensitized to its sin to such a degree that the people confessed their hidden sins to one another and abandoned known evils.

Also, unbelievers came to saving faith.

> *A number who had practiced sorcery brought their scrolls together and burned them publicly. When they calculated the value of the scrolls, the total came to fifty thousand drachmas.* (v. 19)

Terror undoubtedly gripped those in the dark castles of Ephesus as a fortune in cultic goods went up in flames in the center of the town. *Darkness was in retreat.* The connection is undeniable: when the church seriously cleanses itself, some on the outside find it irresistible.

What would be burned today if the Spirit's conviction swept the church? I think some magazines would be quietly removed from out-of-the-way desk drawers or certain novels from the family bookshelves. Perhaps some television channels would be boycotted. Some people would ask others to pray that they would be set free from whatever is dragging them down. And many would come to Christ for forgiveness of sin and deliverance from the eternal wrath of God.

A FINAL WORD

Verse 20 contains a parenthetical summary of Paul's initial victory over the Castle Dark. It is parenthetical because the evil forces regrouped for a vicious counterattack (we will study this in the next chapter). But at this point Paul experienced great victory in his gospel ministry.

Why was this so? He ministered the Word of God in the power of the Holy Spirit and prayer, which is always the way we are to assault the forces of evil. And, second, he worked up a sweat as he served God and man. We are all called to live like Paul — to abide in the Word and to labor, even to exhaustion. We must always do our best to proclaim and teach the gospel with whomever we can. We should give our all wherever we serve — at home, on a church committee, with our young people, in the marketplace.

The Danish philosopher Søren Kierkegaard is often very difficult to read. But his parable of the wild duck is a splendid illustration of how the soul declines from its ideals and becomes satisfied with lower standards. Flying northward across Europe with his friends one spring, a certain duck landed in a Danish barnyard where there were tame ducks. Enjoying some of their corn, he stayed for an hour, then a day, then a week, then a month.

Finally, relishing the good fare and safety of the barnyard, he stayed all summer. One autumn day when his wild-duck friends were winging their way southward again, they passed over the barnyard, and the duck heard their cries. He felt the thrill of joy and delight, and with a great flapping of wings he rose in the air to join his old comrades in their flight.

But he found that his good fare had made him so soft and heavy, he could rise no higher than the eaves of the barn. So he dropped back again to the barnyard and said to himself, "Oh well, my life is safe here, and the food is good." Every spring and autumn when he heard the wild ducks honking, his eyes would gleam for a moment and he would begin to flap his wings. But finally the day came when the wild ducks flew over him and uttered their cry, but he paid not the slightest attention to them.

If God is calling us, whether for salvation or for increased service, by all means we ought to respond *now*. Perhaps he is asking us to say, "I am willing to spend and be expended." Or perhaps he is calling us to lay aside some personal goals, some entertainments, or even some vices. We must respond with a life-giving, "Yes, Lord!" while we can still hear his voice.

PRAYER

O God, may we not be intimidated by the darkness all around us, may we not believe the enemy's lies about how invincible he is, but may we rather worship you, the all-powerful God. Help us to walk in your strength, not in our weakness. Make us bold with truth, aggressive in our walk, generous with your light. May darkness retreat around us as we proclaim and live the gospel of your Son, the Lord Jesus Christ. In Jesus' name, Amen.

31

When the Leaves Fall Away

ACTS 19:21-41

Dr. Donald Grey Barnhouse, pastor of Tenth Presbyterian Church in Philadelphia, was one of the most powerful preachers our nation has ever known. His strengths lay in his theological brilliance and his mastery of illustration. One of Dr. Barnhouse's stories has helped many Christians understand the workings of the life of Christ within the human soul. Its mystic, dreamlike air is beautiful and inspiring.

> Shortly after the Armistice of World War I, Dr. Barnhouse visited the battlefields of Belgium. In the first year of the war the area around the city of Mons was the scene of the great British retreat; in the last year of the war it was the scene of the greater German retreat. For miles to the west of the city the roads were lined with artillery, tanks, trucks, and other materials of war which the Germans had abandoned in their hasty flight.
>
> It was a lovely day in spring; the sun was shining; not a breath of wind was blowing. As Dr. Barnhouse walked along examining the German war material, he noticed that leaves were falling from the great trees that arched above the road. He brushed at a leaf that had blown against his chest; it became caught in the belt of his uniform. As he picked it out he pressed it in his fingers and it disintegrated. Dr. Barnhouse looked up curiously and saw several other leaves falling from the trees. It was not autumn. There was no wind to blow them off. They were the leaves that had outlived the winds of autumn and the frosts of winter.
>
> Now they were falling, seemingly without cause. Then he realized that the most potent force of all was causing them to fall. It was

> spring; the sap was beginning to run; the buds were beginning to push from within. From down beneath the dark earth, the roots were taking life and sending it along trunk, branch and twig, until that life expelled every bit of deadness that remained from the previous year. It was, as a great Scottish preacher termed it, "the expulsive power of a new affection."[1]

I know of no clearer or more beautiful illustration of how the new life of Christ expels the old. As the seasons of life roll past and we try to shake off the old leaves, some hold fast. But as the new life of the gospel of the Lord Jesus Christ grows within us, those leaves will quietly and surely drop away. This is precisely what happened in Ephesus when, through the persistent labors of Paul, the church began to repent of its dead leaves, so that believers "came and openly confessed their evil deeds" (v. 18). Their lives took on such an authenticity that many other townspeople came to Christ and fueled a great bonfire with their idols.

The continuation of the story reveals what happens when the leaves fall away. What should we expect when the Holy Spirit fills us and we truly repent of our sins?

WHEN THE LEAVES FALL AWAY, WE CAN EXPECT PERSECUTION

With the greening of the church in Ephesus, Paul felt he could move on to other fields.

> *After all this had happened, Paul decided to go to Jerusalem, passing through Macedonia and Achaia. "After I have been there," he said, "I must visit Rome also." He sent two of his helpers, Timothy and Erastus, to Macedonia, while he stayed in the province of Asia a little longer. (vv. 21-22)*

Paul felt a sense of accomplishment and well-deserved satisfaction. Soon he would be on his way to other locales and other promising opportunities for gospel ministry. However, his reverie was not to last long because violence was brewing. Luke gives us a blow-by-blow description:

> *About that time there arose a great disturbance about the Way. A silversmith named Demetrius, who made silver shrines of Artemis, brought in no little business for the craftsmen. He called them together, along with the workmen in related trades, and said: "Men, you know we receive a good income from this business. And you see*

and hear how this fellow Paul has convinced and led astray large numbers of people here in Ephesus and in practically the whole province of Asia. He says that man-made gods are no gods at all. There is danger not only that our trade will lose its good name, but also that the temple of the great goddess Artemis will be discredited, and the goddess herself, who is worshiped throughout the province of Asia and the world, will be robbed of her divine majesty." (vv. 23-27)

Prior to the fresh growth of the church, the local artisans had a good thing going — big business! The epicenter of Artemis worship was a black meteorite that either resembled or had been fashioned into a grotesque image of a woman. The lower part was wrapped like a mummy, and the image was covered with round objects that Sir William Ramsay said were the ova of bees. The idol was covered with breasts, symbolizing fertility.[2]

The economy of Ephesus was dependent upon the industry of idolatry. Enter Demetrius, president of Silversmith Local 666, and, thanks to him, persecution! Demetrius was a clever antagonist. In his speech he mentioned the economic implications, but he was careful to couch his attack in pious terms about how poor Artemis would be defamed. It was the old "god, mother, country" routine.

The persecution was economically motivated. The greening of the church had touched the most sensitive part of people's anatomy — their pocketbooks. And this persecution was sure to end in violence.

When they heard this, they were furious and began shouting: "Great is Artemis of the Ephesians!" Soon the whole city was in an uproar. The people seized Gaius and Aristarchus, Paul's traveling companions from Macedonia, and rushed as one man into the theater. Paul wanted to appear before the crowd, but the disciples would not let him. Even some of the officials of the province, friends of Paul, sent him a message begging him not to venture into the theater. The assembly was in confusion: Some were shouting one thing, some another. Most of the people did not even know why they were there. The Jews pushed Alexander to the front, and some of the crowd shouted instructions to him. He motioned for silence in order to make a defense before the people. But when they realized he was a Jew, they all shouted in unison for about two hours: "Great is Artemis of the Ephesians!" (vv. 28-34)

Demetrius did not have any trouble getting a crowd together because they were celebrating the Artemis festival (called "Artemesia"), a month of debauchery during which pilgrims came from everywhere to participate in athletic contests, drink, carouse, and have a ritual fling with prostitutes. Achilles Tatius, an eyewitness to one of these festivals, left this description: "It was the festival of Artemis, and every place was full of drunken men, and all the market-place was full of a multitude of men through the whole night."[3]

Demetrius' friends began a ritual chant, "Great is Artemis of the Ephesians!" and soon multitudes poured into the Arcadian Way, the magnificent boulevard that ran straight through the city, connecting the harbor with the great 24,000-seat amphitheater. Confusion reigned and continued for two solid hours. Can you imagine chanting "Great are the Forty-niners of San Francisco!" or "Great are the Rolling Stones" or "Great is the President of the United States" for two hours without a break! It was a wild event. If someone had made the first move, a thousand hands would have torn the apostle and his companions limb from limb. It was a terrifying scene.

Paul and the Ephesian church were assaulted because dead leaves were giving way to new life and repentance, and consequently people's approach to life changed, even the way they spent their money. They were transformed by "the expulsive power of a new affection." This was a positive change, but the change brought trials because whenever Christianity is perceived to hurt vested financial interests, persecution is sure to follow.

In the latter half of the nineteenth century in England, an ostensibly Christian nation, the Salvation Army underwent terrible persecution because their Christianity touched the pocketbooks of society. Richard Collier, historian of the Salvation Army, says the attacks were led by publicans and brothel-keepers, and these antagonists organized the "Skeleton Army."

> When the Skeleton opened subscription lists, brewers and publicans weighed in generously . . . one saloon keeper offered £1,000. They took their name from the skull-and-crossbones banners they adopted, inscribed with strange legends — gorillas, rats, even Satan himself.[4]

If the professing Christian church today were to undergo the repentance and new life experienced by the Ephesian church and faithfully live out the implications of such faith, the wrath of this world would soon fall upon it. Why? True Christianity calls for a spirit of sacrifice, even financially, but our pleasure-seeking, hedonistic economy rests on a hoped-for profit margin, even if it is only a single percentage point. Monetary gain is seen as the highest good, and when that is threatened by commitment to Christ . . .

Imagine what would happen if because of repentance and the urging of the Holy Spirit Christians stopped watching certain television programs. The pollsters would detect the rating decline and convey the findings to the sponsor, and that would be the end of those programs. Then would come the Demetrius-like rage of prominent TV producers. Or imagine what would happen if 10 or 20 percent fewer Christians attended R-rated movies. Money is the bottom line!

Today the Christian church is clothed with dead leaves of materialism and sensuality. A majority of Christian believers have been desensitized to the lures and poisons of the world, the flesh, and the devil. Multitudes within the professing church are not only thoroughly infatuated with the charms of Mammon but are practicing sensualists who enjoy the most degrading entertainment without any remorse whatsoever.

Today many believers' witness is anemic and corrupted. Much of the church is clamoring to get on the world's bandwagon. Christianity sells — so give people a gospel Grammy, or add a gospel number to the concert to balance out the repertoire and appease Christian critics. But it is impossible to be filled with the Spirit *and* set our minds on things below. It is impossible to be filled with the Spirit *and* live for the dollar. It is impossible to be filled with the Spirit *and* watch a drama that feeds the base appetites of the flesh.

Though Paul and the others were not afraid to attack the Ephesians' idolatrous lifestyle, this was not their primary approach. The town clerk stated in their defense (v. 37) that they had "neither robbed temples nor blasphemed our goddess." What was being manifested was simply the positive, expulsive force of the indwelling Spirit. These men and women were so full of love for Christ that they repented and thus brought on themselves persecution.

WHEN THE LEAVES FALL AWAY, WE CAN EXPECT PEACE AND COURAGE

Paul and the raging mob — what a contrast!

> *Soon the whole city was in an uproar. The people seized Gaius and Aristarchus, Paul's traveling companions from Macedonia, and rushed as one man into the theater. Paul wanted to appear before the crowd, but the disciples would not let him. Even some of the officials of the province, friends of Paul, sent him a message begging him not to venture into the theater. (vv. 29-31)*

In Lystra after Paul was revived following his stoning, he got up and started walking right back into the city. In Philippi he was so miserable after his beating that he began to sing! Now here in Ephesus he was like an immovable rock in a stormy sea — peace in the midst of hateful turmoil. Paul stood in the tradition of Daniel — scratching the lions' tummies until daybreak — and of David — "Who is this uncircumcised Philistine that he should defy the armies of the living God?"

How did Paul and his friends display such amazing peace? Their hearts were pure and their consciences clean. Inward purity is the key to power and peace amidst spiritual conflict. When there are no walls between you and God, you can rest assured that God is standing with you. They also had peace because they trusted in God.

I once experienced something of this with my family, though in a much lesser way. We were on Cape Cod for the final week of vacation. As we were driving to the beach, I realized that I had locked my keys in the cottage. When I went to the real estate office, I discovered that the cottage we were staying in was the only rental for which they did not have a duplicate set of keys. Worse, it also dawned on me that when I left the cottage I had put my wallet on top of the station wagon, and it had fallen off somewhere along the way. We searched diligently but could not find my wallet. Vacation was not going as we had planned.

However, in the midst of all this my wife and I chose to just trust the Lord, and we experienced peace and rest despite our circumstances. Why? Because trusting God brings peace. There was even a happy ending, for when I called my church office the next day, my secretary told me that a man who lived ten miles from where we were staying had found my wallet and called the church office. He was a graduate of Gordon Conwell Seminary!

Though stories do not always turn out as well as this, rest and trust in God always come when we give the Holy Spirit free rein in our hearts. Isaiah 26:3 promises, "Thou wilt keep him in perfect peace, whose mind is stayed on thee: because he trusteth in thee" (KJV). The *New International Version* reads, "You will keep in perfect peace him whose mind is steadfast, because he trusts in you." Any way you say it, it is true. The Hebrew for "perfect peace" is "*shalom shalom.*" "You will keep him in *shalom shalom* — double peace!"

When the Holy Spirit causes us to repent of old leaves, changing our life so that we are out of sync with the world's agenda and maybe even undergo some persecution, he also supplies perfect *shalom*. Some of God's people, though they hear much great preaching and read the Scriptures often, are worriers. But anxiety makes for poor company. They need to reclaim their God-given peace and just trust in him.

WHEN THE LEAVES FALL AWAY, GOD ASSURES US OF HIS PROVIDENTIAL CARE

The city clerk quieted the crowd and said: "Men of Ephesus, doesn't all the world know that the city of Ephesus is the guardian of the temple of the great Artemis and of her image, which fell from heaven?

Therefore, since these facts are undeniable, you ought to be quiet and not do anything rash. You have brought these men here, though they have neither robbed temples nor blasphemed our goddess. If, then, Demetrius and his fellow craftsmen have a grievance against anybody, the courts are open and there are proconsuls. They can press charges. If there is anything further you want to bring up, it must be settled in a legal assembly. As it is, we are in danger of being charged with rioting because of today's events. In that case we would not be able to account for this commotion, since there is no reason for it." After he had said this, he dismissed the assembly. (vv. 35-41)

Our amazing God was in control all the time! He would have been in control even if Paul and his friends had perished. While all the shouting was going on, God was moving the local officials like checkers. At the perfect psychological moment, when the crowd had shouted itself out, a pagan city official, a stickler for law and order, brought the mob to its senses. A simple accomplishment if you are God!

When we are brimming with the Holy Spirit so that the old leaves are falling off, we experience a special personal assurance that God is in control.

A FINAL WORD

How is our spiritual life going? Is it perpetual winter? Have we become desensitized to sin? Are we doing some things that we once abhorred? Do we smile (even laugh) at some things that break God's heart? Are we indistinguishable from our decaying culture? Are we useless spiritually?

Or is it springtime in our soul? Is the sap running? Are the buds pushing from within so that life is traveling through every limb, expelling the deadness of the past? Is our life making a difference? Are we sometimes at odds with the world not because we are difficult or priggish, but because we are so full of Christ that our lifestyle has changed — even the way we spend our time and money?

If you long for the expulsive power of new life, you should do the following, in God's strength:

1. Yield to the Holy Spirit's promptings. Surrender daily to him.
2. Confess specific sins (agree with him that the matters he is convicting you of are wrong). Name them. Materialism? Sensuality? Idolatry? Pride? Lying? Bitterness? Coldness of heart?
3. Ask God to give you the strength to turn back to him. Tell him you can truly repent only by his enabling grace.
4. Do whatever he tells you to do in his precious Word.
5. Rest in him.

PRAYER

O God, thank you for the new life you have created within us through your Son, Jesus Christ. We thank you that when we turned to you, you made us new from the inside out. Help us, O God, to faithfully follow and obey you, even when opposition or trials come. Help us to be courageous and to experience your sustaining peace. Help us to never lose sight of your providential care over us. May we be your victors today and tomorrow and in the days to come, until that day when we will enjoy eternal triumph in Heaven with you forever. In Jesus' name, Amen.

32

Falling Asleep in Church

ACTS 20:1-16

Many of us are familiar with James Russell Lowell's oft-quoted phrase, "Truth forever on the scaffold / Wrong forever on the throne." Acts 20 relates Paul's broken-field running as he eluded those who wanted to put him on the scaffold. Verses 1-6 tell us that after the riot in Ephesus Paul crossed the Aegean to Macedonia, where he encouraged struggling churches, then continued down into Greece, doing the same. His intent was to sail from Corinth to Jerusalem with an offering for the beleaguered mother church. However, when he learned of a plot to do away with him at sea, he eluded his foes by traveling back up through Macedonia and crossing the Dardanelles to Troas — the city where several years before he had experienced the vision of the man of Macedonia imploring him to "Come over to Macedonia and help us."

Troas, adjacent to ancient Troy, was the peaceful setting for the remarkable Communion service described in verses 7-12. When Paul arrived, there was a joyous time of reunion because his traveling companions had gone on ahead and were eagerly awaiting his arrival. Luke tells us that among them were Sopater of Berea, Aristarchus and Secundus of Thessalonica, Gaius of Derbe, Timothy, and Tychicus and Trophimus of Asia — a most heterogeneous group! But they were one in Christ! For the next seven days they engaged in team ministry, with Paul as their leader.

> *On the first day of the week we came together to break bread. Paul spoke to the people and, because he intended to leave the next day, kept on talking until midnight. There were many lamps in the upstairs room where we were meeting. (vv. 7-8)*

Scriptural sleuths think we can identify the home in which they met that night because Paul in his final letter from jail in Rome (2 Timothy 4:13) asked Timothy to stop at Troas and pick up the old robe he had forgotten at the home of Carpus. So Acts 20 probably took place in the upper chamber of Carpus' spacious three-story home (see v. 9). This took place on Sunday, the Lord's Day, the day of the Resurrection — not on the Sabbath. The congregants had worked a full day but came together in the evening for a common meal and the commemoration of the death of Jesus. It was a larger gathering than usual, for Paul's presence, coupled with his intended departure at sunrise, had brought out everyone who was able to attend. The room was packed.

Paul was an experienced communicator. He knew how to keep the cookies on the bottom shelf. He fed the sheep as well as the giraffes. He also knew that the mind can absorb no more than the seat. As John Newton said, "When weariness begins, edification ends." But Paul had so much to share, he could not help speaking for a long time. This was his first contact with the infant church of Troas, and possibly his last. With the rising of the sun he would be gone to Jerusalem. He could not bring himself to conclude his sermon. And besides, no one was complaining. What a treat for the church of Troas. The believers hoped it would never end.

At the same time, the situation was uncomfortable. The word for "lamps" in verse 8 is literally "torches." We can easily imagine a stuffy, oppressive atmosphere in that third-story chamber. The Mediterranean heat, the grimy press of the weary crowd just returned from work, the smoke from the torches, the lack of oxygen all made for drowsiness. Finally nature asserted itself.

> *Seated in a window was a young man named Eutychus, who was sinking into a deep sleep as Paul talked on and on. When he was sound asleep, he fell to the ground from the third story and was picked up dead. (v. 9)*

The tenses of the Greek verbs portray poor Eutychus as being gradually overcome despite his struggle to remain awake.[1] The word translated "sleep" is the word from which we derive the English word *hypnosis*. Finally the stifling room and the hypnotic flickering of the flames did their work. Eutychus' eyes shut, he relaxed, and out he went — headlong to the pavement three floors below. The congregation gave a horrified gasp and immediately rushed down the outside stairs to the broken form. Some of them began to shriek a Middle-Eastern death wail.

But they did not mourn for long. Verse 10 gives the happy ending: "Paul went down, threw himself on the young man and put his arms around him. 'Don't be alarmed,' he said. 'He's alive!'" Paul prostrated himself across the boy's lifeless form much as did the prophets Elijah and Elisha — and the young man was revived! It was a miracle! No one was sleepy now. Back up to church they went. Verses 11-12 conclude:

> *Then he [Paul] went upstairs again and broke bread and ate. After talking until daylight, he left. The people took the young man home alive and were greatly comforted.*

They celebrated the Lord's Table, and Paul preached again until the break of day, full of joy.

I feel sorry for Eutychus, first, because he fell asleep on the Apostle Paul, second, because his sleepiness had such unhappy results, and, third, because Luke was there to record the whole thing! This is the first record ever of someone falling asleep in church. There have been thousands of successors, but Eutychus is the one everyone remembers.

THE DANGER OF FALLING ASLEEP IN CHURCH

As a pastor I have again and again been reminded that on any given Sunday there are believers who are in danger of falling asleep in church. I have seen people fall asleep and bump their heads on the pew in front of them. I have been sitting on the platform when one of my associates dozed off and dropped his hymnal! I have heard people awaken with a snort. In one congregation a certain young man sat on the front row and slept every Sunday. As soon as I was through the introduction, his eyes closed and his head tilted. The most memorable, however, was the Sunday both he and his wife fell asleep with their heads propped against one another. I have heard a preacher tell of an elder who fell asleep, and when his wife nudged him during the service, he stood and pronounced the benediction!

I have great sympathy for those who have trouble staying awake in church. Some of us work such trying schedules that when we sit down, it is the first time we have relaxed all week. Others are sometimes victims of medication. Sometimes it is just so warm . . . The truth is, some of the best saints have fallen asleep in church. Eutychus was perhaps an enthusiastic new Christian who, though he was tired, would not miss church for anything. His spirit was willing, but his body was sleepy.

Falling asleep in church really does not concern me. It can happen for any number of reasons, both good and bad. What concerns me are the thousands who warm a pew every Lord's Day with their bodies awake and their *souls* asleep. Some use the church hour to mentally complete the unfinished business of the preceding six days. Some people are more awake attending a garage sale or closing a business deal or even watching TV than they are when they sit with eyes wide open in church. Innumerable churchgoers appear to be perfectly awake but are spiritually asleep.

WHY PEOPLE ARE ASLEEP IN CHURCH

Some people are asleep because *they have never been awake*. I am familiar with that state because I was once in it myself. I attended church, heard God's Word preached, sang the great hymns, listened to others pray — but with no depth of comprehension. I was simply present where others worshiped. I was on the outside. I was not alive to spiritual things. Perhaps you derive some vague comfort from being with religious people and doing Christian things, but inside you understand very little of what is going on. The pity is, it is possible to pass from this life into eternity without recognizing your slumber until it is too late. It is possible to be damned even in the church. As Screwtape, a senior devil, said to his trainee, Wormwood (in the great C. S. Lewis novel *Screwtape Letters*), "The safest road to hell is the gradual one — the gentle slope, soft underfoot, without sudden turnings, without milestones, without signposts."[2] Have you ever been truly awake? Would you like to wake up?

Sin, *a compromising, backslidden state*, is a second reason some are in spiritual slumber. Some people have experienced an awakening and are truly Christians but have slipped into a spiritually comatose state. Sometimes we hear of Christians who have fallen to unimaginable depths although they regularly attended church. Though they seemed to listen, they were spiritually and morally asleep.

Samson is the preeminent example of this in Scripture. He began and ended in the faith but messed up big-time in between. Sin progressively and imperceptibly took such hold of him that he was no longer awake to spiritual realities. In fact, his final doze on Delilah's lap was symbolic of his state. "He awoke from his sleep and thought, 'I'll go out as before and shake myself free.' But he did not know that the Lord had left him" (Judges 16:20). Sin desensitizes us, and we soon fall asleep, even in church. Though externally everything may appear fine, sin makes us indifferent and bored with spiritual things.

Familiarity is a third reason some are spiritual slumberers. C. S. Lewis recognized this danger when he warned a friend who was considering the ministry that the constant familiarity with holy matters could dull him to their significance. Lewis summed it up by saying, "None are so unholy as those whose hands are cauterized with holy things."[3] We can become like the man who directs the trains at the railroad station and has been selling tickets to various towns for years. Though he has never himself traveled at all, he begins to think he has been to all the towns to which he sees other people traveling.[4] Some of us had no children's church when we were growing up but instead lay in our parents' laps. On the way to Never-never Land, we would count the holes in the sanctuary ceiling. We knew all the hymns (and their parodies). We knew the Doxology before we knew our times tables. We became so familiar with it all that we took it for granted. Church can easily become ho-hum. Some, though not damned in the church, are bored in the church.

HOW TO STAY AWAKE IN CHURCH

Each of us should periodically make a personal spiritual assessment. If we have never truly been awake, we must ask the God of grace to help us believe. We must confess our sin, declare our faith in Christ, and ask Christ to make us brand-new — to receive him as our Savior. Church will then become more alive than we ever imagined. If we are already children of God and our slumber is due to sin in our lives, we must repent, do a U-turn, and allow the joy of Christ to refill us. The joy of worship will then flood our souls.

Those of us who suffer the problem of familiarity must consciously and deliberately participate with all our being in the corporate worship of the church. When we sing a hymn, we should shut everything else out and sing it to God, singing not only with the mouth but with the heart and mind. As others lead us in prayer, we should pray along with them — a spiritual concert. When we hear the Scriptures, we must listen, for we are hearing the voice of God. We must listen to God's Word as we would to a love letter, for that is what the Bible is.

Dietrich Bonhoeffer ran a seminary in Nazi Germany that was not approved by the state. He was a critical and intelligent man, but in his homiletics class he always laid down his paper and pencil, opened his Bible, and listened to the students' sermons, no matter how poor or unskilled they were. He felt that the preaching of God's Word ought to be received as if he were listening to God himself. That is how we should listen too.

If we have been born again from our slumber, and if we have confessed our sin, we must consciously, in dependence upon God, wake up to the wonders of worship. Our coming together with other believers should demonstrate that we are awake and alive in Christ! Worship is to be in technicolor, for Christ is with us! That is how to stay awake in church.

A FINAL WORD

Martin Luther had a parable or a dream about how on one occasion the devil sat upon his throne listening to his agents report on the progress they had made in opposing the truth of Christ and destroying the souls of men. One spirit said there was a company of Christians crossing the desert. "I loosed the lions upon them, and soon the sands of the desert were strewn with their mangled corpses."

"What of that?" answered Satan. "The lions destroyed their bodies, but their souls were saved. It is their souls that I am after."

Another reported, "There was a company of Christian pilgrims sailing through the sea on a vessel. I sent a great wind against the ship that drove the ship on the rocks, and every Christian aboard the ship was drowned."

"What of that?" said Satan. "Their bodies were drowned in the sea, but their souls were saved. It is their souls that I am after."

The third came forward to give his report, and he said, "For ten years I have been trying to cast a Christian into a deep sleep, and at last I have succeeded." And with that the corridors of Hell rang with shouts of malignant triumph.[5]

If we are asleep, let us hear God's call today!

> *The night is nearly over; the day is almost here. So let us therefore put aside the deeds of darkness and put on the armor of light. (Romans 13:12)*

> *Awake to righteousness, and sin not. (1 Corinthians 15:34, KJV)*

> *"Wake up, O sleeper, and rise from the dead, and Christ will shine on you." (Ephesians 5:14)*

PRAYER

O God, may we each awake from our sinful slumber and come to life in your Son, the Lord Jesus Christ, and then be ever vigilant as we serve you and do your bidding day by day. Help us, Lord, to not become so familiar with your truths and your plans for us that we consider them commonplace or of little consequence. Open our eyes again and again, so that the wonders of your love and life will carry us to ever greater spiritual heights. In Jesus' name, Amen.

33

Paul's Approach to Ministry

ACTS 20:17-38

The Apostle Paul had embarked on his long-anticipated return to Jerusalem. Several decades had passed since his leaving, and he wanted to be home with the mother church for Pentecost. He was a passenger on a merchant ship slowly making its way down the Aegean toward the Mediterranean, stopping at various centers of trade. As the Lord would have it, the freighter stopped in Miletus, which was very close to Ephesus, a layover that lasted for several days. Though he had not planned on this delay, Paul made use of it and sent word requesting the Ephesian elders to come meet with him for a final chat. Paul knew he would never see them again.

This brief interlude in Paul's stormy life provides us with one of the great farewells of Scripture — equal to, if not surpassing, those of Jacob and his sons, Moses and Joshua, and even Jonathan and David. We can draw upon our own experiences to grasp the pathos of this good-bye — pulling up roots to move to a new city, driving around the block a second time to wave one last farewell, traveling along a trail of tears to a new destination. Good-byes are not only a common part of our experience — they occupy prominent places in history.

Consider General Douglas MacArthur's departure from the Philippines. In his own words:

> On the dock I could see the men staring at me. I had lost 25 pounds living on the same diet as the soldiers, and I must have looked gaunt and ghastly standing there in my old war-stained clothes — no bemedaled commander of inspiring presence. What a change had taken place in that once-beautiful spot! My eyes roamed the warped

> and twisted face of scorched rock. Gone was the vivid green foliage, with its trees, shrubs, and flowers. Gone were the buildings, the sheds, every growing thing. The hail of relentless bombardment had devastated, buried, and blasted. Ugly dark scars marked smouldering paths where the fire had raged from one end of the island to the other. Great gaps and forbidding crevices still belched their tongues of flame. The desperate scene showed only a black mass of destruction. Through the shattered ruins, my eyes sought "Topside," where the deep roar of the heavy guns still growled defiance, with their red blasts tearing the growing darkness asunder. . . .
>
> Darkness had now fallen, and the waters were beginning to ripple from the faint night breeze. The enemy firing had ceased and a muttering silence had fallen. It was as though the dead were passing by the stench of destruction. The smell of filth thickened the night air. I raised my cap in farewell salute, and I could feel my face go white, feel a sudden, convulsive twitch in the muscles of my face. I heard someone ask, "What's his chance, Sarge, of getting through?" and the gruff reply, "Dunno. He's lucky. Maybe one in five."
>
> I stepped aboard PT-41. "You may cast off, Buck!" I said. "When you are ready."[1]

If we read Acts 20:17-38 with a sterile detachment, we deprive ourselves of the life and resulting benefit of the passage. The image called to mind by Paul's meeting with the Ephesian elders is that of a group of soldiers still soiled by the dust and blood of war, drawing together with their revered general for some final wisdom.

THE APOSTLE'S COMMITMENT TO MINISTRY

Verses 18-27 describe four aspects of Paul's approach to ministry. First, Paul's approach was based on *an unshakable commitment to God and his people*.

> *When they arrived, he said to them: "You know how I lived the whole time I was with you, from the first day I came into the province of Asia. I served the Lord with great humility and with tears, although I was severely tested by the plots of the Jews." (vv. 18-19)*

Commitment means different things to different people. Consider the young man who waxed eloquent as he poured out his heart's devotion in a letter to the girl of his dreams, saying, "My dear, I would climb the highest mountain, swim the widest stream, cross the burning desert, die at the stake for you. P.S. I will see you on Saturday if it doesn't rain." Paul was not like that! Totally committed to his fellow believers, he was determined to seek their best "the whole time."

Moreover, he so identified with his people that it hurt.

> *"So be on your guard! Remember that for three years I never stopped warning each of you night and day with tears." (v. 31)*

This was typical of Paul wherever he served. To the Thessalonians he wrote:

> *We were gentle among you, like a mother tenderly caring for her little children. We loved you so much that we were delighted to share with you not only the gospel of God but our own lives as well because you had become so dear to us. (1 Thessalonians 2:7-8)*

Paul was an all-weather promise keeper! His commitment to them was driven by the conviction that in serving people he was serving God: "You know how I lived the whole time I was with you. . . . I served the Lord with great humility and with tears, although I was severely tested by the plots of the Jews."

The second aspect of Paul's approach to ministry was *a commitment to sharing God's Word.*

> *"You know that I have not hesitated to preach anything that would be helpful to you but have taught you publicly and from house to house. I have declared to both Jews and Greeks that they must turn to God in repentance and have faith in our Lord Jesus." (vv. 20-21)*

Sharing God's Word presupposes *knowing* God's Word. Henrietta Mears has testified that one of the major influences in her life was Dr. William Evans, the father of Louis Evans, Sr., honored pastor of Hollywood Presbyterian in Hollywood, California. She stated that "Dr. William Evans had the complete Bible memorized in the *King James Version* and the New Testament also in the *American Standard Version*. The young people would delight in giving him passages from either version to quote from memory."[2] Similarly, F. W. Robertson memorized the entire New Testament in English and most of the Greek New Testament. Campbell Morgan's ministry began to prosper after he sequestered himself for two years with his Bible. Is it any wonder these men had such in-depth impact on the lives of others?

Paul too was immersed in the Word of God. More than that, he was dauntless in its proclamation. "I have not hesitated to proclaim to you the whole will of God" (v. 27). Because he could not be intimidated, he "did not shrink from declaring to you anything that was profitable" (v. 20, NASB). He majored on the themes of "repentance toward God and faith in our Lord Jesus Christ" (v. 21, NASB). Paul did not preach an easy-believism but rather the necessity of faith in Christ for salvation, which results in a changed life. Paul's ministry was based on the intrepid proclamation of the whole counsel of God, regardless of the consequences.

The third aspect of Paul's approach was *a commitment that transcended his concern for self.*

> *"And now, compelled by the Spirit, I am going to Jerusalem, not knowing what will happen to me there. I only know that in every city the Holy Spirit warns me that prison and hardships are facing me. However, I consider my life worth nothing to me, if only I may finish the race and complete the task the Lord Jesus has given me — the task of testifying to the gospel of God's grace. Now I know that none of you among whom I have gone about preaching the kingdom will ever see me again." (vv. 22-25)*

Whether or not it was the Lord's will for Paul to go to Jerusalem, he felt he *had* to go, even though he knew there was going to be trouble that might even cost him his life. A commitment to Christ that superseded self-interest had been the pattern of his life ever since his Damascus conversion when Christ told Ananias, "I will show him how much he must suffer for my name" (9:16).

This same commitment was beautifully evident in the life of James Calvert, a young pioneer missionary to the cannibals of the Fiji Islands. En route the ship captain, a humane man, tried to dissuade him, finally crying in desperation, "You will lose your life and the lives of those with you if you go among such savages." Calvert calmly replied, "We died before we came." Karl Marx's remark that "a Communist is a dead man on reprieve" is simply a base parody of this primal Christian principle.

We should be determined to finish the course whatever the cost. A man or woman who never does anything except what can be done easily will never do anything worth doing at all. Think of what such an attitude means to the church! Think of what it means to the missionary enterprise! Undoubtedly cheeks began to flame and eyes to gleam as Paul's comrades-in-arms listened to his gospel passion.

The fourth plank in Paul's approach was *a commitment that produced a sense of well-being and a clear conscience.*

> *"Therefore, I declare to you today that I am innocent of the blood of all men. For I have not hesitated to proclaim to you the whole will of God." (vv. 26-27)*

This is amazing! Paul had been accused of being a craven coward, a freeloader, a blatant opportunist and everything in between. And yet he could say, "I am free from the misery of a guilty conscience. Nobody's blood is on my hands!" How many of us can say that?

THE APOSTLE'S ADVICE TO FELLOW SOLDIERS

Paul's initial advice was to be *vigilant in ministry.*

> *"Keep watch over yourselves and all the flock of which the Holy Spirit has made you overseers. Be shepherds of the church of God, which he bought with his own blood. I know that after I leave, savage wolves will come in among you and will not spare the flock. Even from your own number men will arise and distort the truth in order to draw away disciples after them. So be on your guard! Remember that for three years I never stopped warning each of you night and day with tears." (vv. 28-31)*

Ephesus was at that time a healthy church, but Paul gave a much-needed warning. In fact, some thirty-five years later the risen Lord Jesus told them:

> *Yet I hold this against you: You have forsaken your first love. Remember the height from which you have fallen! Repent and do the things you did at first. If you do not repent, I will come to you and remove your lampstand from its place. (Revelation 2:4-5)*

Paul recommended a three-pronged vigilance. First, we must be on guard for *perils within our own hearts*: "Keep watch over yourselves." In Lewis's words, "The true Christian's nostril is to be continually attentive to the inner cesspool."[3] We must never suppose that we have risen above some particular sin or have attained immunity to various temptations but must always be on our guard.

Second, we must be on guard for *perils from without*: "savage wolves will come in among you." Heretics, cults, secularists, and other spiritual enemies attack healthy churches, not weakened and obsolete ones.

Third, we must be on guard for *perils from within the flock* — "Even from your own number men will arise and distort the truth." Satan loves to subvert from within. Vigilance is ever the price of liberty.

We must not develop a fortress mentality, assuming all to be well, for enemies are to be found both outside and inside the flock of God. History proves this to be true.

Paul also advised the Ephesian elders to *live their lives by the grace of God.*

> *"Now I commit you to God and to the word of his grace, which can build you up and give you an inheritance among all those who are sanctified." (v. 32)*

We are to focus on the heart of God's Word, "the word of his grace." Paul was commending the simple gospel — the doctrine of God's love and undeserved kindness. We must focus on grace!

> *'Tis grace has brought me safe thus far,*
> *And grace will lead me home.*

Paul's final advice was to approach the ministry with *a giving attitude*:

> *"I have not coveted anyone's silver or gold or clothing. You yourselves know that these hands of mine have supplied my own needs and the needs of my companions. In everything I did, I showed you that by this kind of hard work we must help the weak, remembering the words the Lord Jesus himself said: 'It is more blessed to give than to receive.'" (vv. 33-35)*

Notice that Paul's last recorded words to the Ephesian elders were a quotation from the Lord Jesus: "It is more blessed to give than to receive." Beautiful!

This summarizes everything Paul said to his fellow warriors. In a nutshell, their ministry was to be one of giving. Paul gave himself to God and his people. He gave himself to the ministry of the Word. He gave himself with such intensity that he forgot himself. "It is more blessed to give than to receive."

> *When he had said this, he knelt down with all of them and prayed. They all wept as they embraced him and kissed him. What grieved them most was his statement that they would never see his face again. Then they accompanied him to the ship. (vv. 36-38)*

Paul sailed off to keep giving his life to Christ, thus providing us with an example of how we should approach life and ministry.

PRAYER

> *O God, help us each to fully understand how to know and serve you, how to be faithful no matter what the cost, how to remain on our guard against the enemies of truth and of our souls. May our commitment not be one merely of words, but of heart resolve and unswerving love for you and your Son and your Spirit. May we emulate the apostle even as he emulated the Lord Jesus Christ. In Jesus' name, Amen.*

34

Man's Word or God's Word?

ACTS 21:1-16

On April 14, 1521 Martin Luther was on his way to the Diet of Worms. The emperor had forbidden the sale of all the reformer's books and ordered them to be seized. Luther's life was in great danger. Luther's devoted friend and confidant, George Spalatin, had sent word through a special messenger not to come to Worms lest he suffer the same fate as John Hus. Luther comforted his fearful friends, saying, "Though Hus was burned, the truth was not burned, and Christ still lives." Then he sent Spalatin the now famous message, "I shall go to Worms, though there were as many devils as tiles on the roofs."[1]

On April 16 Luther entered Worms in a Saxon two-wheeled cart preceded by an imperial herald. Although it was the dinner hour, 2,000 people were present to observe his entrance. On the following day at four o'clock Luther stood before "Charles, heir of a long line of Catholic sovereigns — of Maximillian the romantic, of Ferdinand the Catholic, of Isabella the orthodox — scion of the house of Hapsburg, lord of Austria, Burgundy, the Low Countries, Spain, and Naples, Holy Roman Emperor, ruling over a vaster domain than any save Charlemagne, symbol of the medieval unities, incarnation of a glorious if vanishing heritage."[2] Most men of God would have been intimidated.

After an exchange between the Archbishop of Trier, Johann Eck, and Martin Luther, the Augustinian monk, overwhelmed by the immensity of what he was doing, requested and received the night for prayer and consideration. We can be sure Luther really prayed that night.

> How frail and sensitive is the flesh of men, and the devil so powerful and active through his apostles and the wise of the world! . . . O Thou,

> my God, my God, help me against the reason and wisdom of all the world! Do this! Thou must do it, Thou alone! For this cause is not mine but Thine. For myself I have no business here with these great lords of the world. Indeed, I too, desire to enjoy days of peace and quiet and to be undisturbed. But Thine, O Lord, is this cause. And it is righteous and of eternal importance. Stand by me, Thou faithful, eternal God! I rely on no man. . . .
>
> O God, stand by me in the name of Thy dear Son, Jesus Christ, who shall be my Protector and Defender, yea, my mighty Fortress, through the might and strengthening of Thy Holy Spirit.[3]

On April 18 a larger hall was chosen but was so crowded that scarcely any save the emperor could sit down. Finally came this famous dialogue:

> ECK: Martin, how can you assume that you are the only one to understand the sense of Scripture? Would you put your judgment above that of so many famous men and claim that you know more than they all? You have no right to call into question the most holy orthodox faith, instituted by Christ the perfect lawgiver, proclaimed throughout the world by the apostles, sealed by the red blood of the martyrs, confirmed by the sacred councils, defined by the Church in which all our fathers believed until death and gave to us as an inheritance, and which now we are forbidden by the pope and emperor to discuss lest there be no end of debate. I ask you, Martin — answer candidly and without horns — do you or do you not repudiate your books and the errors which they contain?
>
> LUTHER: Since then Your Majesty and your lordships desire a simple reply, I will answer without horns and without teeth. Unless I am convicted by Scripture and plain reason — I do not accept the authority of popes and councils, for they have contradicted each other — my conscience is captive to the Word of God. I cannot and I will not recant anything, for to go against conscience is neither right nor safe. God help me. Amen.[4]

It was the greatest moment in the modern history of the world! How did Martin Luther come to such heroics — standing alone before the world, risking his life for the sake of God's truth? *He knew God's will.* He knew through the examination of God's Word while a monk in Wittenberg and through his subsequent encounter with God in Bologna and on his knees in Pilate's staircase in Rome that "The just shall live by faith." He knew that it was God's will for him to go to Worms and declare the truth to the world regardless of the consequences. Furthermore, Martin Luther *did* God's will, and this is what set him apart from ordinary men.

The Apostle Paul too was a man who knew and did God's will, which in this instance was to go to Jerusalem and minister to the church there even though such service would bring him into bonds and afflictions. Not everyone agrees on how to interpret Acts 21. Some might title this section of Scripture "Paul's Bravery," while others call it "Paul's Mistake," arguing that Paul went against the Spirit's direction when he went to Jerusalem. Certainly Paul was human and made mistakes, but here I believe he is a great example for Christian believers today.

Some of us are wrestling with crucial or thorny decisions. We may wonder what God's will for us is, or we may think we know God's will but are not sure we can do it. The story of Paul's struggle offers us helpful insights in how not to be derailed in following God's directions for us.

Paul had just experienced a tearful farewell with the Ephesian elders — tearful because tough times lay ahead for the apostle. "What grieved them most was his statement that they would never see his face again" (20:38). The Holy Spirit had told Paul that "prison and hardships" (20:23) were awaiting him in Jerusalem. It was a wrenching good-bye. "After we had torn ourselves away from them . . ." (21:1) — this was a traumatic, emotional experience. And yet Paul did not proceed toward his difficult date with destiny reluctantly — he sprinted to meet it! Like Luther, he gave God's plan for him higher priority than anything or anyone else. Such joyful abandon to the divine will would go neither unchallenged nor unrewarded.

PRESSURE TO TURN FROM GOD'S WILL

Verses 1-3 describe Paul's hurried journey.

> *After we had torn ourselves away from them, we put out to sea and sailed straight to Cos. The next day we went to Rhodes and from there to Patara. We found a ship crossing over to Phoenicia, went on board and set sail. After sighting Cyprus and passing to the south of it, we sailed on to Syria. We landed at Tyre, where our ship was to unload its cargo.*

In summary, he endured a routine journey filled with time-consuming stops on the way to the port of Patara, then booked passage on a nonstop 400-mile voyage until he landed in the port of Tyre, Syria. Danger lay ahead, but he wanted to be home for Passover when he could have the biggest effect. Trusting God, he did not fear the consequences. Once in Tyre, Paul came under some unexpected pressure to alter his plans.

Finding the disciples there, we stayed with them seven days. Through the Spirit they urged Paul not to go on to Jerusalem. But when our time was up, we left and continued on our way. All the disciples and their wives and children accompanied us out of the city, and there on the beach we knelt to pray. After saying good-by to each other, we went aboard the ship, and they returned home. (vv. 4-6)

Tyre was a major port, and the trans-Mediterranean merchant ship laid over for seven days delivering and receiving cargo. So Paul did the natural thing — he went looking for some Christian brothers and sisters — "disciples" to encourage. And when he found them, there was immediate rapport. The apostle and these new acquaintances all spoke the language of the heart and immediately became part of each other's lives. We all have had this experience — hardly a word spoken, yet a spiritual oneness. "I'm so glad to be a part of the family of God."

There was only one wrinkle: "Through the Spirit they urged Paul not to go on to Jerusalem" (v. 4b). Did Paul sin by resisting their repeated warnings? I think not. For one thing, Tyre was not the first place in which he had heard such predictions. He had heard them in "every city" (20:23). Second, as Richard Longenecker and others point out, "through the Spirit" means that the Spirit told them that Paul would undergo suffering for Christ, a message that naturally gave the believers deep concern. The Spirit did not tell them to inform Paul he was not to go to Jerusalem. The Spirit predicted persecution against the apostle, and the people's love for Paul caused them to beg him not to go.

This was rough on Paul! He was in Tyre for only seven days, and yet when he left, they "all," along with "their wives and children," escorted him out of the city and knelt with him on the beach for prayer (v. 5b)! They loved him! I would not be surprised if some of those prayers were a bit aggressive. "Lord, we thank you for bringing Paul to us. He has ministered to us mightily. We believe you want him to stay here a while longer. Keep him safe as he goes his own way. We all have our faults, Lord. Overrule the apostle's wrong decision."

Paul must have experienced a confusing emotional mix — already missing his new friends in Christ, but also relieved to get away from their negative messages. But that relief did not last long because he came under more pressure in Caesarea, as seen in verses 7-12.

We continued our voyage from Tyre and landed at Ptolemais, where we greeted the brothers and stayed with them for a day. Leaving the next day, we reached Caesarea and stayed at the house of Philip the evangelist, one of the Seven. He had four unmarried daughters who prophesied. After we had been there a number of days, a prophet named Agabus came down from Judea. Coming over to us, he took Paul's belt, tied his own hands and feet with it and said, "The Holy Spirit says, 'In this way the Jews of Jerusalem will bind the owner of this belt and will hand him over to the Gentiles.'" When we heard this, we and the people there pleaded with Paul not to go up to Jerusalem.

After a day in Ptolemais, Paul arrived in Caesarea, the port city of Jerusalem. He could now enter Jerusalem anytime he wished but wanted to wait until Pentecost. Philip the evangelist, his gracious host, was the man who first took the gospel to Samaria and then baptized the Ethiopian eunuch. God had blessed him with four gifted daughters, who may have further prophesied of Paul's difficult future.

Agabus now came along with all the drama of a pre-exilic seer. Ezekiel had foretold the Babylonian siege of Jerusalem by assaulting a model of the city (Ezekiel 4:1ff.), and Agabus foretold Paul's imminent future by tying himself up with Paul's belt. Agabus did not interpret the prophecy or say whether Paul should or should not go to the Holy City, but Paul's friends did! "When *we* heard this, *we* and the people there pleaded with Paul not to go up to Jerusalem" (v. 12). "We" — even Dr. Luke was pleading with Paul not to go on to Jerusalem.

The pressure upon Paul must have been unbearable — months, perhaps years of vague prophecies about future persecution; the wrenching farewell to the Ephesian elders; the heart-tugging love in Tyre; Agabus' dramatic prophecy; and now everyone, even trusted Luke, was begging Paul to turn back. The apostle finally cried out, "Why are you weeping and breaking my heart? I am ready not only to be bound, but also to die in Jerusalem for the name of the Lord Jesus" (v. 13).

Paul acknowledged that they were tearing him apart, that what Satan and his forces could not do was happening through his brothers and sisters! But then, like the Lord himself who "resolutely set his face to go to Jerusalem" (Luke 9:51, NASB), the great apostle renewed his resolve and continued on God's path for him, regardless of the potential cost! What a man of God!

Seeing the apostle's determination, his friends acquiesced.

When he would not be dissuaded, we gave up and said, "The Lord's will be done." After this, we got ready and went up to Jerusalem. Some of the disciples from Caesarea accompanied us and brought us to the home of Mnason, where we were to stay. He was a man from Cyprus and one of the early disciples. (vv. 14-16)

"The will of the Lord be done" can be said either with frustration or with conviction. Paul's friends undoubtedly meant both.

So ends the epic third missionary journey of Saul of Tarsus, the Apostle Paul, missionary general of the apostolic church. Refusing to compromise because of coming affliction, he was going to Jerusalem "though there were as many devils as tiles on the roofs."

WHY THE PRESSURE?

Why did Paul encounter such pressure from his friends to go against what he knew to be the will of God? First, *Paul's acquaintances demonstrated the all-too-common inclination of being quick to know God's will for someone else.* We need to avoid making snap judgments or offering spiritual formulas. What matters is God's will for us, not what others think we should do.

Second, *the well-meaning believers were trying to make God's will conform to their preconceptions.* "If Paul goes to Jerusalem, he is going to suffer, and we will be deprived of his ministry. This *cannot* be God's will." This speaks powerfully to our American culture. As Herbert Hendin says, "It is no accident that at the present time the dominant trends in psychoanalysis are the rediscovery of narcissism. The society is marked by self-interest and ego-centrism that increasingly reduces all relations to the question, 'What am I getting out of it?'"[5] We see similar trends in the church. "God wants me to be happy. If I am not happy, I am not in his will." "God does not want me to suffer pain. I am in pain. Therefore I am not in God's will."

Oswald Chambers expresses the proper approach perfectly:

> To choose to suffer means that there is something wrong; to choose God's will even if it means suffering is a very different thing. No healthy saint ever chooses suffering; he chooses God's will, as Jesus did, whether it means suffering or not.[6]

We must not make our understanding of God's guidance conditional on our own happiness or sense of completeness. We are not to preach because we enjoy it, but because it is God's will. We should not serve as elders or deacons because it is always fun, but because God wants us to. We should not work with a special ed Sunday school class because it is fulfilling (though it is), but because God had led us to do so.

Third, *in attempting to turn Paul away from Jerusalem, his friends demonstrated that their spiritual focus was more horizontal than vertical.* Their love and loyalty were commendable — they wanted to preserve Paul.

But their motives, though noble, were shortsighted. These Christians were not seeing God's ultimate purposes. They were looking out for Paul's good but not God's.

To his credit, Paul survived all of this. How did he remain steadfast?

WITHSTANDING THE PRESSURE

Paul was victorious because *he approached life the same way Christ did.* In fact, his going to Jerusalem is remarkably parallel to Christ's: the plots of the Jews, being handed over to the Gentiles, a triple prediction of coming suffering, his steadfast determination, a trusting surrender to God's will.[7]

Paul held firmly to God's revealed will and did it! He had a longstanding inward constraint to go to Jerusalem and suffer if need be, a resolve that went all the way back to his conversion when Christ said, "I will show him how much he must suffer for my name" (9:16). *Paul refused to be deterred from God's revealed will.*

Further, *he was not a man-pleaser.*

> *Am I not trying to win the approval of men, or of God? Or am I trying to please man? If I were still trying to please men, I would not be a servant of Christ. (Galatians 1:10)*

Paul would have loved Eric Liddell — the runner who placed spiritual conviction and loyalty to Christ above Olympic or national glory! Paul played to an audience of One.

Also, *Paul trusted in God's sovereignty.* He believed God knew what he was doing when he sent him to sure persecution in Jerusalem. As Oswald Chambers said so powerfully in his classic devotional *My Utmost for His Highest*:

> God plants His saints in the most useless places. We say, "I should be here because I am so useful." Jesus never estimated His life by the standard of greatest use. God puts His people where they will glorify Him, and we are not capable of judging where that is.[8]

Paul withstood the pressure and followed God's will. May we all do the same!

A FINAL WORD

Regarding knowing God's will, certain classic explanations are very helpful. For example, the "Four Councils" — the councils of God's Word, the

Holy Spirit, conscience, others — taken together, often reveal God's will. A heart that is saved, Spirit-filled, sanctified, submitted to God can know God's will. Augustine's advice, rightly understood, is also pertinent: "Love God and do what you want." Christians who really do want to know God's will, will know it.[9]

In seeking God's will and doing it, a few practical reminders are in order.

Seek good advisers. Be discerning as you choose those from whom you will accept advice.

Spend time with God regularly. A certain young woman, trying to decide God's will regarding a marriage proposal, took a week off work and vacationed with her Bible and her Lord. She was a wise woman.

Realize that God's will may not be what you want. Many of us are like the little girl who wrote an honest thank-you note: "Thank you for your present. I have always wanted a pin cushion, but not very much." This is humorous in children but sad in God's children.

Finally, and most importantly, *if we know what God wants us to do, we must do it.* For most of us, the problem is not that of knowing God's will but of obeying it. There were undoubtedly others in Luther's day who knew God's will, but what made him a great man who changed history is that he *did* it. If you know you should take an ethical stand with your associates, do it! If God wants you to admit you are wrong, do it as soon as possible. When God calls you to give, preach, do volunteer work with the infirmed, or go to the mission field, do not settle for merely knowing his will — *do it*, in his strength and for his glory!

The final words of Richard Baxter say it all: "Lord, what thou wilt, where thou wilt, and when thou wilt."[10]

PRAYER

O God, help us not to assume that we know your will for someone else. Help us to make your desires first always — above our own wishes or suppositions, above the opinions and even the needs of others, above circumstantial pressures. Grant us the courage to do your bidding no matter what our obedience might cost us. May we not warp your directions for us through selfish preconceptions. You first, you always, you ever — our greatest good and our eternal God! In Jesus' name, Amen.

35

A Dangerous Heart

ACTS 21:17-40

When Lou Little was football coach at Georgetown University, he had on his squad a player of average ability who rarely got into the game. But Coach Little was fond of him. He especially liked the way he walked arm-in-arm with his father on campus. One day, shortly before a big game with Fordham, the boy's mother called with the news that his father had died that morning of a heart attack.

The student went home with a heavy heart but was back three days later. "Coach," he pleaded, "will you start me in the game against Fordham? I think that is what my father would have liked most." After a moment's hesitation, Little said, "Okay, but only for a play or two."

True to his word, he put the boy in — but he never took him out. For sixty action-packed minutes that inspired young man ran and blocked like an All-American. After the game the coach praised him. "Son, you have never played like that before. What got into you?"

"Remember how my father and I used to go arm-in-arm?" answered the boy. "Well, he was totally blind, and today was the first time he ever saw me play!"

His desire to please someone he loved, someone not visibly present, made all the difference.

The Apostle Paul lived, fought, and died with the abiding consciousness that he was doing it all for God. Because he served the risen Christ, he did not allow the well-meaning pleadings of his loving friends — arguments that appealed to his desire for self-comfort, even self-preservation — to sidetrack him from obeying God by going on to Jerusalem.

Paul was certainly not perfect. He made mistakes. Though he was an apostle, he sinned. In fact, many consider Acts 21:17 — 22:29 an example of his fallibility. Whether it is or not, we do know that he was wholeheartedly devoted to God. Determined to pursue the salvation of his people, he now engaged in a controversial accommodation to Jewish culture. He was willing to take risks for the sake of the gospel of Jesus Christ.

PAUL'S ENVIABLE RECEPTION (vv. 17-20A)

Paul had been waiting for just the right moment to enter Jerusalem. Now, with the Passover crowd swelling the city to perhaps two million, he made his entrance.

> *When we arrived at Jerusalem, the brothers received us warmly. The next day Paul and the rest of us went to see James, and all the elders were present. Paul greeted them and reported in detail what God had done among the Gentiles through his ministry. When they heard this, they praised God. (vv. 17-20a)*

After meeting with "the brothers," who greeted Paul and his entourage warmly, they met the following day with the leadership of the Jerusalem church. Some evidence indicates there were seventy elders (patterned after the Sanhedrin). If so, a rather imposing group questioned Paul and his companions. Its leader was the venerable "James the Just," a brother of Jesus and a man famous among all the Jews for his piety. Eusebius said his knees were like those of a camel because of all the time he spent in prayer.

Paul did two things in this interview. First, he shared the amazing things God had done among the Gentiles: the Ephesian riots that came about because of the social impact of the gospel; the power of the gospel in Athens and Corinth; the apostle's escaping his would-be assassins; poor Eutychus' swan dive and miraculous resuscitation during Paul's sermon in Troas. He also presented samples of his work: "Exhibit A" — Trophimus of Asia; "Exhibit B" — Secundus of the Thessalonians.

Second, though Luke does not mention it here, Paul presented the love offering taken among the Gentiles for the poor brethren there. Delivering this gift was Paul's chief motivation for going to Jerusalem, though he feared it would be rejected (see Romans 15:25-31) because of rising Jewish nationalism and the increasing number of legalistic Christians. Paul hoped that the love offering would build solidarity between Jewish and Gentile believers.

What a relief it must have been for Paul when they did accept the love offering. As a result, "they praised God" (v. 20). Everything was going well, so much so that Paul was likely caught off-guard when the elders informed him there was a problem.

THE ELDERS' FATEFUL SUGGESTION (vv. 20B-25)

> *When they heard this, they praised God. Then they said to Paul: "You see, brother, how many thousands of Jews have believed, and all of them are zealous for the law. They have been informed that you teach all the Jews who live among the Gentiles to turn away from Moses, telling them not to circumcise their children or live according to our customs. What shall we do? They will certainly hear that you have come." (vv. 20-22)*

What an amazing reversal! "Paul, thousands of Jewish Christians are Zealots for the Law, but they have been told that you are teaching Jews to forsake Moses! What are we going to do when they find out you are here? This could be trouble!" Some believers in the Jerusalem church believed, mistakenly, that Paul was off-base in his teaching. The church had heard and propagated slanderous hearsay about Paul — misinformation — lies, whether intentional or unintentional.

In an eastern land a woman repeated a bit of gossip about a neighbor, and within a short time the whole town knew the story. The slandered person was deeply hurt and most unhappy. But then the lady responsible for spreading the rumor learned that it was completely untrue, so she went to a wise old sage to find out what she could do to repair the damage. After listening to her problem, he said, "Go to the marketplace, purchase a fowl, and have it killed. Then on your way home pluck its feathers one by one and drop them along the path!" Though surprised by this unusual advice, the woman did as she was told.

The next day she informed the man that she had done as instructed. "Now go and collect all those feathers and bring them back to me," the sage said. The lady followed the same path, but to her dismay the wind had blown all the feathers away. After searching all day long, she returned with only two or three in hand. "You see," said the old wise man, "it is easy to drop them, but impossible to bring them all back. Likewise, it does not take much to spread a false rumor, but you can never completely undo the wrong." We Christians must take this to heart!

Paul, accompanied by non-Jewish believers, was also *persona non grata* because the mother church was slow to accept Gentiles. She had found it difficult to receive the testimony of Peter about the conversion of Cornelius. She was suspicious of the work among the Samaritans. At the Council of Jerusalem, she did not readily give freedom to the Gentile church. On the other hand, she was quick to accommodate Jews and readily received into membership those who had made no break with Judaism. The statement at the end of verse 20 — "all of them are zealous for the law" —

was saying in effect, "We are saved by grace, but we are *kept saved* by the Law."

The mother church was a compromising, prejudiced church, and her sins of lying gossip and spineless accommodation eventuated in Paul's rejection. The elders' suggestion was questionable but predictable:

> *"So do what we tell you. There are four men with us who have made a vow. Take these men, join in their purification rites and pay their expenses, so that they can have their heads shaved. Then everybody will know there is no truth in these reports about you, but that you yourself are living in obedience to the law." (vv. 23-24)*

They asked Paul to pick up the considerable expenses of four men who had taken a Nazirite vow (that is, a vow to abstain from meat and wine and not to cut their hair for thirty days). Paul would have to undergo a seven-day ritual of purification and pay for three animal offerings for each man, plus cereal and drink offerings.[1] Paul was not against Nazirite vows per se, for he seems to have taken one himself in Cenchrea (18:18). So the request does not appear unreasonable.

However, there was more to this than seen at first glance because there was an implicit exchange of favors. "We have accepted this gift from the churches abroad, identifying ourselves with your Gentile mission. Now, Paul, if you will join with these men and identify yourself openly with our nation . . ." They were not asking Paul to compromise his Gentile ministry (see v. 25), but they wanted to portray him as a more scrupulous Jew than he actually was. This was a case of religious politicking!

PAUL'S SUBMISSION TO THE ELDERS' SUGGESTION (v. 26)

This whole idea was surely distasteful to Paul, but he submitted to it.

> *The next day Paul took the men and purified himself along with them. Then he went to the temple to give notice of the date when the days of purification would end and the offering would be made for each of them. (v. 26)*

Was Paul sinning by doing this? Some say no, including the respected and careful scholar F. F. Bruce who says:

> Whether he [Paul] was wise in doing so may well be doubted. . . . But he cannot be fairly charged with a compromise of his own gospel

principles. On the contrary, he was acting in strict accordance with his own stated policy.[2]

That policy is stated in 1 Corinthians 9:19-22:

> *Though I am free and belong to no man, I make myself a slave to everyone, to win as many as possible. To the Jews I became like a Jew, to win the Jews. To those under the law I became like one under the law (though I myself am not under the law), so as to win those under the law. To those not having the law I became like one not having the law (though I am not free from God's law but am under Christ's law), so as to win those not having the law. To the weak I became weak, to win the weak. I have become all things to all men so that by all possible means I might save some.*

Paul was perhaps not in error in any way to participate in the Nazirite ritual.

However, others say Paul was most certainly sinning. They base this conclusion on what he had written long before in his letters to the Galatians and to the Romans regarding Judaizing or adding Law to grace. He most emphatically warned the Galatians:

> *I am astonished that you are so quickly deserting the one who called you by the grace of Christ and are turning to a different gospel — which is really no gospel at all. Evidently some people are throwing you into confusion and are trying to pervert the gospel of Christ. But even if we or an angel from heaven should preach a gospel other than the one we preached to you, let him be eternally condemned! As we have already said, so now I say again: If anybody is preaching to you a gospel other than what you accepted, let him be eternally condemned! (1:6-9)*

In Galatians, Paul also told how he opposed Peter face to face for kowtowing to Jewish legalistic prejudices (imported from Jerusalem) and for refusing to eat with Gentile brothers and sisters (2:11-14). Later he explained that they no longer needed the Law:

> *Before this faith came, we were held prisoners by the law, locked up until faith should be revealed. So the law was put in charge to lead us to Christ that we might be justified by faith. Now that faith has come, we are no longer under the supervision of the law. You are all sons of God through faith in Christ Jesus. (3:23-26)*

In view of all that, they argued, Paul was now walking in error. From their point of view, a tragedy was about to take place. The great defender of Christian freedom through grace was about to make a mockery of grace. This man who wrote, "It is for freedom that Christ has set us free. Stand firm, then, and do not let yourselves be burdened again by a yoke of slavery" (Galatians 5:1) was about to go into bondage once more. How horrible that the Apostle Paul should have come to this! He gave the money for the purification (v. 24) to the very priestly system that had called for the crucifixion of Jesus Christ, in the very temple where the veil had been torn in two when Jesus died — demonstrating that God had made a new way into his presence.[3]

Which view is correct? If Paul was not in error, he was probably dangerously close. Perhaps it is best to reserve judgment.

Why did Paul go along with the Jerusalem elders' advice? The answer is to his credit: he loved the Jewish nation. On another occasion he interrupted a glorious paean of praise for God to state his spiritual burden for his kinsmen:

> *I speak the truth in Christ — I am not lying, my conscience confirms it in the Holy Spirit — I have great sorrow and unceasing anguish in my heart. For I could wish that I myself were cursed and cut off from Christ for the sake of my brothers, those of my own race. (Romans 9:1-3)*

Paul was willing to be damned if it meant that his brethren would be saved. Such a thing is impossible, but that is how Paul felt. This apostle had been "caught up to paradise. He heard inexpressible things, things that man is not permitted to tell" (2 Corinthians 12:4). Yet he would gladly forfeit it all if his people could thus be brought to Christ. What exemplary love! Paul capitulated to the Jerusalem church because he loved people.

He also did this because he yearned for solidarity between the Jewish and Gentile churches. Unity is still a major problem in the church. Two congregations located only a few blocks from each other in a small community decided to become one united, and thus larger and more effective, body instead of two struggling churches. But the merger did not happen because they could not agree on how to recite the Lord's prayer. One group wanted "forgive us our trespasses," while the other demanded "forgive us our debts." Paul's desire for Christian solidarity reflected the heart-cry of Christ in his High-Priestly prayer (John 17:20-23):

> *"My prayer is not for them alone. I pray also for those who will believe in me through their message, that all of them may be one,*

Father, just as you are in me and I am in you. May they also be in us so that the world may believe that you have sent me. I have given them the glory that you gave me, that they may be one as we are one: I in them and you in me. May they be brought to complete unity to let the world know that you sent me and have loved them even as you have loved me."

Paul had a massive vision of solidarity — a church of Jews *and* Gentiles, united, militant, taking the world by storm for Christ — not giving in to legalism like that of the Judaizers! Yet Paul went along with the elders' compromising suggestion. Why? He loved his lost nation more than his own life, and he longed for the evangelistic power that God manifests through a church exhibiting solidarity in Christ.

What do we learn from Paul's experience? First, *in our moments of highest spiritual motivation we need to especially beware of error or bad judgment*. I was once involved in a large evangelistic outreach that about 10,000 were expected to attend. One of our staff arranged for a popular entertainer, who had reportedly become a Christian and is a big box-office attraction today, to participate in the rally. Sadly, after singing only a couple of songs this singer walked backstage and let loose with profanity that faded wallpaper and wilted flowers. The trouble was not that our hearts were wrong, but that our enthusiasm had blurred our judgment.

Second, *we can be pressured toward questionable action by the sins of others*. If the Jerusalem church had defended Paul as it should have and had been catechizing its converts properly, such pressure would never have come upon Paul. We live in a fallen world. Our own sins and the sins of those around us sometimes make it difficult to know what is right. We need to be gracious when our brothers and sisters make what we consider wrong or mistaken decisions, considering not only their actions but their motivations. Paul may have erred in this situation, but if so, it was an error of judgment, not of the heart.

Third, we need, like Paul, to have *hearts that because of a passion for souls and for God's glory are willing to run the risk of unwise decisions*. Some hearts never risk anything. They strive neither for sin nor for sainthood. They desire a temperate zone free from the storms of sin and from the tempests that accompany a life of service. Never burn for the souls of others, and you will avoid rejection. Never suggest a plan to reach the community or the world, and you will never be criticized for it. Never give counsel to someone undergoing the pain of separation or divorce, and you will never give errant advice. But just think of all the heavenly checks you will never cash for yourself or others.

O Lord, give us each a heart like Paul's!

GOD'S OVERRULING OF PAUL'S PREDICAMENT (vv. 27-40)

The situation now worsened, but God sovereignly delivered his apostle.

> *When the seven days were nearly over, some Jews from the province of Asia saw Paul at the temple. They stirred up the whole crowd and seized him, shouting, "Men of Israel, help us! This is the man who teaches all men everywhere against our people and our law and this place. And besides, he has brought Greeks into the temple area and defiled this holy place." (They had previously seen Trophimus the Ephesian in the city with Paul and assumed that Paul had brought him into the temple area.) The whole city was aroused, and the people came running from all directions. Seizing Paul, they dragged him from the temple, and immediately the gates were shut. (vv. 27-30)*

The scene was mayhem, but God was in control and protected his servant (vv. 31-36). Soldiers poured from the adjacent tower of Antonia (more than 200, according to F. F. Bruce, because there was more than one centurion — see 21:32, NASB). They bore Paul away from the murderous crowd and back up the steps of Antonia as the crowd bellowed, "Away with him!" — just as they had done with Christ years before.

Paul then asked for and obtained permission to address the crowd.

> *As the soldiers were about to take Paul into the barracks, he asked the commander, "May I say something to you?" "Do you speak Greek?" he replied. "Aren't you the Egyptian who started a revolt and led four thousand terrorists out into the desert some time ago?" Paul answered, "I am a Jew, from Tarsus in Cilicia, a citizen of no ordinary city. Please let me speak to the people." Having received the commander's permission, Paul stood on the steps and motioned to the crowd. When they were all silent, he said to them in Aramaic . . . (vv. 37-40)*

It is amazing that Paul did this because he had probably been terribly beaten. For that reason, the liberal German theologian Ernst Haenchen believes the story is a fabrication: "A man who has only just been beaten up by a fanatical mob is physically no longer capable of making such a speech. This reason suffices to prove that the speech and the dialogue preparing for it are unhistorical." Haenchen is wrong. For a man with a heart like Paul's, depending as he did on the almighty God of Heaven, such an accomplishment is attainable.

What was it that caused the bleeding and broken apostle to ask for permission to speak? A swelling passion for his people — the desire even to be anathema for their sake, that they might know Christ!

PRAYER

O God, as we seek to know your will, we sometimes are not sure which way to go or what action to take. Please help us not to be so afraid of making a wrong decision that we sit on the sidelines, nor to be over-sure of ourselves and so take a wrong turn or cause brothers or sisters in Christ to do so. May we ever be moved with a burning love for others that will not allow us to hoard the gospel. Whether convenient or costly, may we take full advantage of opportunities to voice the good news of new life in Jesus Christ. In Jesus' name, Amen.

36

Encouraged in the Night

ACTS 22:30 — 23:24

When Henry VIII arranged for his illicit marriage to Anne Boleyn, one of those who opposed him was Sir Thomas More, a saintly man whose life has been dramatized in the magnificent play and movie *A Man for All Seasons*. Once the marriage was accomplished, would Thomas More, a sensible man, give up his passive resistance and attend the coronation ceremony?

> Two Bishops acted as the King's agents, but More declined the invitation, pleading poverty. Promptly they offered to pay for a velvet costume suitable to the ceremony. Again the Lord Chancellor refused. In doing so, he recited a little tale. Once upon a time, it seemed, there was an Emperor who had condemned a maiden to die for some infringement of the law. But the death penalty could not be enforced because she was a virgin and he had previously decreed that no virgin should ever be put to death. His problem was solved by one of his council who said: "Why make you so much ado, my Lord, about so small a matter? Let her first be deflowered, and then after may she be devoured."
>
> "Now, my Lord," said Thomas More to the King's messengers, "it lieth not in my power that they may devour me; but God being my good lord, I will provide that they shall never deflower me."[1]

Sir Thomas More was clearly a man of integrity, and so was Paul. As the apostle prepared to face the angry mob and later the Sanhedrin, he knew they might put him to death, they might make a spectacle of him before the

Jewish nation, but he would not be bullied into even the slightest spiritual compromise.

Paul, bleeding and torn from a terrible beating by his Jewish kinsmen, escaped death only because of Roman intervention, and then, having the commander's permission to address the people, lovingly held forth the Word of Life (22:1-21). The sad result was a further outpouring of hatred from the Jewish mob as they threw off their cloaks, tossed dust into the air, and cried out, "Rid the earth of him! He's not fit to live!" (22:22-23).

Though Paul was spirited away under Roman "protection," he was not out of danger, for the confused Roman tribune ordered that Paul be strung out for scourging with the vicious flagellum (earlier applied to Christ). Paul would probably have either died or been crippled for life, but he escaped when he informed a nearby centurion that he was a Roman citizen.

In a final attempt to get to the bottom of the matter, the tribune called a hasty meeting of the Sanhedrin, the ruling body of the Jews, and shoved Paul before them. The apostle probably expected to be slandered or ridiculed, but he would not back down, no matter what the consequences. As Paul was arraigned before the Sanhedrin, he undoubtedly hoped to convince some of his hearers of the gospel of Christ.

Paul's integrity remained intact throughout his confrontation with the Jewish council. Nevertheless, it was one of the worst days in his life, and he could have conducted himself much more wisely. The hearing began well enough, as 23:1 records:

> *Paul looked straight at the Sanhedrin and said, "My brothers, I have fulfilled my duty to God in all good conscience to this day."*

Paul began by taking a long look at the Sanhedrin (the same word used in Acts 1 for the apostles' gazing toward Heaven as Christ ascended). Paul knew some of these men. Even if he had not been a member of the Sanhedrin in earlier days, he had run in the same social circles. No doubt there was a spark of recognition here and there as he gazed around the room. He addressed them informally — "My brothers." A more formal beginning might have been appropriate, but Paul was familiar with them and he was not intimidated.

Though this was not a disrespectful beginning, "the high priest Ananias ordered those standing near Paul to strike him on the mouth." This order was illegal, for the Jewish law said, "He who strikes the cheek of one Israelite, strikes as it were the glory of God," and "He that strikes a man strikes the Holy One." All this flashed through Paul's mind in an instant, and he in turn called out:

> *"God will strike you, you whitewashed wall! You sit there to judge me according to the law, yet you yourself violate the law by commanding that I be struck!" (v. 3)*

The Jews painted their tombs white as a warning, because to touch a tomb brought defilement. Paul was saying that Ananias, though he looked okay on the outside, was full of decaying filth. This was angry, impulsive retaliation.

Paul had momentarily lost control. His bitter reply was far different from his Lord's, for "when they hurled their insults at him, he did not retaliate; when he suffered, he made no threats" (1 Peter 2:23). God's Word does not touch up its pictures of the lives of the saints. When an apostle or patriarch falls — David's adultery and murder, Jonah's pouting, Peter's violence — his failure is honestly recorded.

Paul's bitter words brought an immediate response.

> *Those who were standing near Paul said, "You dare to insult God's high priest?" Paul replied, "Brothers, I did not realize that he was the high priest; for it is written: 'Do not speak evil about the ruler of your people.'" (vv. 4-5)*

Realizing his error, Paul immediately recanted — a credit to his character. He was human, he made mistakes, and he was the first to admit so.

Did Paul really not know Ananias was the high priest? Edersheim suggests that Ananias was not wearing his robes because he only donned the distinctive dress when participating in public affairs. Others think the situation was due to Paul's poor vision, an infirmity suggested in the book of Galatians (6:11). Moreover, this probably happened during the early morning, and the room was dimly lit with torches. For whatever reason, Paul had made a poor beginning, and it was going to get worse.

Seeing that matters were going badly, Paul began crying out (actually this is the imperfect tense — "continued crying out," v. 6): "My brothers, I am a Pharisee, the son of a Pharisee. I stand on trial because of my hope in the resurrection of the dead." The result was predictable: the Sadducees — anti-supernaturalist liberals of the day — took offense, while the Pharisees applauded Paul.

> *When he said this, a dispute broke out between the Pharisees and the Sadducees, and the assembly was divided. (The Sadducees say that there is no resurrection, and that there are neither angels nor spirits, but the Pharisees acknowledge them all.) There was a great uproar, and some of the teachers of the law who were Pharisees*

> *stood up and argued vigorously. "We find nothing wrong with this man," they said. "What if a spirit or an angel has spoken to him?" (vv. 7-9)*

Paul's ploy accomplished his immediate objective of directing the Sanhedrin's attention away from himself. But it also removed the possibility of his giving further witness to his peers at that time. Later, when Paul stood before Felix, he hinted that his action before the Sanhedrin was a misdeed that he regretted (24:20-21).

> *The dispute became so violent that the commander was afraid Paul would be torn to pieces by them. He ordered the troops to go down and take him away from them by force and bring him into the barracks. (v. 10)*

Just how violent this must have become can be discerned from the fact that the only other place where the word translated "torn" is used is Mark 5:4, where the Gerasene demoniac is said to have torn his chains and shackles apart. Claudius Lysias, the tribune, must have been ready to tear his hair out. Just a few days before, he had rescued Paul from mob violence in the temple. When he allowed Paul to speak, the riot flared up again. Then, about to beat the truth out of Paul, he discovered that he had almost whipped a Roman citizen. Now, before the Sanhedrin, there was nearly another riot!

This was one of the darkest nights of Paul's life. For years he had hoped to give fruitful witness in Jerusalem. But when he arrived, he found a compromising church full of legalistic believers who held him suspect because of his contact with Gentiles. Now his hopes of convincing the leadership of his people had gone up in smoke as well. His dreams of effective testimony to the Jews lay in ashes at his feet, and his vision for successful witness in Rome began to fade too.

Paul's heart ached. He was physically, emotionally, and spiritually tired. Even the most optimistic person can experience a low after a battle (consider Elijah), and Paul was in the depths. As he sat in Antonia he was utterly humiliated — alone, dejected, dispirited. We all sometimes want to curl up with the biggest blanket we can get, thumb in mouth, and forget the world. What would Christ do for Paul in such a valley?

> *The following night the Lord stood near Paul and said, "Take courage! As you have testified about me in Jerusalem, so you must also testify in Rome." (v. 11)*

A DIVINE VISIT AND AN EXHORTATION (23:11)

Once when my boys were small (three and five) I took them along on a college retreat, and one of the college boys, Rick, took them for a walk in the forest. As they were walking along, my boys asked if there were any wild animals there, and Rick answered seriously, "Only the giant tree sloth and the sea behemoth!" My wide-eyed boys grabbed his hands tightly and huddled close. Then Rick said, "But don't worry — you're with me," and my sons relaxed.

The Lord Jesus Christ stood at Paul's side, and that made all the difference! If Steffi Graf teamed up with an average housewife on the tennis court, they would win some doubles matches! If Steve Young is throwing the ball to me, I will score some touchdowns (assuming I can catch the ball)! Christ stood by Paul, not through a *vision* as happened in Corinth (compare 18:9), nor through a *trance* as in the Jerusalem temple (compare 22:17-18), but *physically*. This was a palpable revelation of what is true for all God's faithful servants in a spiritual sense— his sustaining presence.

The experience of the Apostle Paul was similar to that of Shadrach, Meshach and Abednego, who spoke boldly when King Nebuchadnezzar threatened to throw them into the blazing furnace:

> *"The God we serve is able to save us from it, and he will rescue us from your hand, O king. But even if he does not, we want you to know, O king, that we will not serve your gods or worship the image of gold you have set up." (Daniel 3:17-18)*

As Nebuchadnezzar looked into the fiery furnace, he himself observed God's presence with his servants:

> *"Look! I see four men walking around in the fire, unbound and unharmed, and the fourth looks like a son of the gods." (3:25)*

Though Christ is with all his children all the time, he is especially with those who are faithfully serving him. As we follow Christ, he stands with us. Christ's presence made Paul's dungeon flame with light. Comprehending the nearness of his Savior, Paul was revived and revolutionized.

Christ greeted Paul with one word (though our English Bible renders it with two) — "Take courage." How that must have soothed Paul's soul. Only Christ uses this word in the New Testament, and all five instances brought wonderful comfort. He called to the bedridden paralytic, "*Take heart* [Courage], son; your sins are forgiven" (Matthew 9:2). To the woman with the twelve-year hemorrhage he said, "*Take heart* [Courage], daughter, your faith has healed you" (Matthew 9:22). To his frightened disciples as he came to them across the storm-tossed Sea of Galilee he said, "*Take courage*! It is I. Don't be afraid" (Matthew 14:27). In the Upper Room, on the night of his crucifixion, he said, "*Take heart* [Courage]! I have overcome the world" (John 16:33). This is Christ's unique word for all who are trying to serve him, however feebly!

Paul had this courage throughout the rest of his ministry. In fact, when he finally got to Rome and his confinement there, he sang out, "Now I want you to know, brothers, that what has happened to me has really served to advance the gospel. . . . Because of my chains, most of the brothers in the Lord have been encouraged to speak the word of God more courageously and fearlessly" (Philippians 1:12, 14). Paul's courageous obedience to Christ encouraged the beleaguered Christian minority in mighty Rome! We too must look upward and keep serving our Lord!

Ancient historians record that horse traders brought a beautiful black horse to the court of Philip, Alexander the Great's father. The horse was at first so vicious, plunging and kicking at everyone who came near, that the king's horseman was about to reject him. But Alexander was greatly taken with the animal and asked permission to ride him. Noting that the horse was frightened by his shadow, Alexander turned the animal's head toward the sun, then leaped upon his back and galloped back and forth before the king.[2]

As we look up to the Son of righteousness, we can exercise courage.

> *"Fear not, for I have redeemed you; I have called you by name; you are mine. When you pass through the waters, I will be with you; and when you pass through the rivers, they will not sweep over you. When you walk through the fire, you will not be burned; the flames will not set you ablaze." (Isaiah 43:1b-2)*

Christ also promised Paul further ministry in Rome: "Take courage! As you have testified about me in Jerusalem, so you must also testify in Rome."

In June 1926 a young missionary in his mid-twenties, Raymond Edman, fell ill from typhus fever in a mountain village in Ecuador. So grave was his illness that he was carried by train and stretcher from Riobamba to Guayaquil, the port city of Ecuador. Soon his wife followed. When she arrived at the hospital, the attending North American physician told Mrs. Edman that her husband's feet were already cold — he would soon die. A fellow missionary ordered a black, cloth-covered coffin for the missionary's burial. Because Mrs. Edman had no black dress, she had her wedding dress dyed black. They even set the time and date for the funeral — 3 P.M., July 4.[3]

Many years later, in 1967, Dr. V. Raymond Edman, the fourth president of Wheaton College, was addressing the student body when he suddenly collapsed after a slow half-turn and moments later passed into the presence of the King of kings.[4] Dr. Edman had known forty-one years of fruitful service since those dark days in Guayaquil. *God's servants are immortal until their work is done. No servant of God dies a premature death.*

God had a job for Paul to do, and no one or no thing could thwart God's plans. Christ's words greatly encouraged Paul, and he never never wavered again, despite all the immense perils that later came upon him. Christ's presence beside him, Christ's galvanizing call to courage, and Christ's promise of further ministry helped Paul to firmly believe and to keep serving his Lord.

PROVIDENTIAL CARE (23:12-24)

According to verses 12-15, some forty radicals (Zealots or dagger-carrying assassins) literally "anathematized themselves with an anathema" (compare the Greek in verse 14), vowing not to eat or drink until they killed Paul. They even asked the chief priests and elders to urge the Sanhedrin to ask the tribune to bring Paul back for more questioning, thus giving them an opportunity to murder the apostle. This could have easily brought about the end of Paul's life, except for one thing, as verses 16 and 17 relate:

> *But when the son of Paul's sister heard of this plot, he went into the barracks and told Paul. Then Paul called one of the centurions and said, "Take this young man to the commander; he has something to tell him."*

Prior to this passage we did not know Paul had a sister, let alone a nephew! In fact, this is the only record in all of Scripture of their existence. What was Paul's nephew doing in Jerusalem? How old was he? How did he find out about the dangerous conspiracy? How did he get in to see Paul? (Possibly the latter occurred because he was a harmless youth.) Apart from what we read here, about the only thing we know regarding Paul's family is that they had apparently disowned him (see Philippians 3:8).

God intervened on his servant's behalf by taking an unidentified nephew and placing him in just the right place at just the right time to learn about the murderous plot. Paul surely praised God for this.

Paul's stay in Jerusalem ended in style, for after the tribune heard the nephew's story:

> *The commander dismissed the young man and cautioned him, "Don't tell anyone that you have reported this to me." Then he called two of*

> *his centurions and ordered them, "Get ready a detachment of two hundred soldiers, seventy horsemen and two hundred spearmen to go to Caesarea at nine tonight. Provide mounts for Paul so that he may be taken safely to Governor Felix." (vv. 22-24)*

Paul left town on horseback surrounded by 470 soldiers. He left town more like a king than a criminal! Meanwhile, his assassins were left in town fighting insistent hunger pains.

Christ had told Paul, "Take courage! As you have testified about me in Jerusalem, so you must also testify in Rome." And Paul told Christ, "Lord, I believe you with all my heart." May we tell our Savior the same!

A FINAL WORD

Paderewski, the famous composer-pianist, was scheduled to perform at a great concert hall in America. It was an evening to remember — a black-tux-long-evening-dress, high-society extravaganza. In the audience that evening sat a mother with her fidgety nine-year-old son. Weary of waiting for the concert to begin, the lad squirmed constantly in his seat. His mother hoped her boy would be encouraged to practice the piano once he heard the immortal Padereweski. That is why, against his wishes, he was there.

When his mother turned to talk with some friends, the impatient boy could stay seated no longer. He slipped away from her side, strangely drawn to the ebony concert grand Steinway and its leather-tufted stool on the huge stage flooded with brilliant lights. Largely ignored by the sophisticated audience, the boy sat down at the stool, staring wide-eyed at the black and white keys. He placed his small, trembling fingers in the right location and began to play "Chopsticks." The roar of the crowd quickly ceased as hundreds of frowning faces turned in his direction. Irritated and embarrassed, they began to shout at the bold youngster.

Backstage the master, overhearing the sounds, hurriedly grabbed his coat and rushed toward the stage, where he stood behind the boy and began to improvise a countermelody to harmonize with and enhance "Chopsticks." As the two of them played together, Paderewski kept whispering in the boy's ears, "Keep going. Do not quit, son. Keep on playing. Do not stop. Do not quit." What a gracious genius!

We have been called to play a spiritual tune for Christ. Though we have generally wanted to do our best, we have occasionally said the wrong thing to the wrong person at the wrong time. Perhaps we have not lived up to our own expectations, not to mention *his* standards of service. Perhaps our best service is sometimes more like "Chopsticks" than *Swan Lake*. Maybe some in the galleries are trying to yell us off the stage. We know we have a heavenly calling, and we want to keep playing for God, but we desperately need encouragement.

At such times Christ stands beside us, his presence vivid and sustaining. He tells us, "Have courage, my dear servant. I have more work for you to do. Keep playing . . . Keep going . . . Do not stop . . . Do not quit." He adds his amazing and superior countermelody to ours, making the result something that honors him and is beautiful.

PRAYER

O God, as we examine our opportunities for service, the challenges that threaten to turn us back, the dangers posed by the world, the flesh, and the devil, may we find our courage in you. Remind us often of your presence that comforts and your promises that encourage and your power that equips. In Jesus' name, Amen.

37

On Giving and Receiving God's Word

ACTS 24:1-27

After leaving Jerusalem under armed guard and being escorted to Caesarea, Paul was arraigned before Antonius Felix, the provincial governor. He then withstood the clever attacks of Tertullus, a lawyer hired by the Sanhedrin (vv. 1-21).

In verses 22-26 Governor Felix, having heard enough, dismissed Paul's accusers while still keeping Paul under a kind of house arrest, a situation that made possible a fateful interview between Paul and Felix and his wife Drusilla. Paul's example shows us how to share the Word, and the example of Felix and Drusilla shows us how *not* to receive the Word.

Background information about Felix and Drusilla helps us catch the full import of this celebrated interview. Antonius Felix was the first slave in the history of the Roman Empire to become the governor of a Roman province. That would have been quite a distinction if he had earned it, but that was not the case. As a child, Felix, along with his brother Pallas, had been freed by Antonia, the mother of Prince Claudius, a future Caesar. As they grew up, Pallas became a close friend of Claudius, so much so that when Claudius became emperor, Pallas persuaded him to make Felix a government official in Palestine under Cumanus. When Cumanus was deposed, Felix obtained Cumanus' office through shameful intrigue.

During Felix's governorship, insurrections and anarchy dramatically increased throughout Palestine because of his brutality. Josephus tells us that he repeatedly crucified the leaders of various uprisings.[1] The Roman historian Tacitus described him as "a master of cruelty and lust who exercised the powers of a king with the spirit of a slave."[2] Antonius Felix was an unscrupulous, avaricious, brutal, scheming politician.

Drusilla was his third wife, and Felix was her second husband. Drusilla was the youngest daughter of Agrippa I and had originally married Azizus, king of Emesa, a small kingdom in Syria. She did not find Azizus very exciting and won Felix's affection with the help of a magician named Atomas, eventually becoming Felix's illicit lover and "wife." She was barely twenty at the time. Unusually beautiful, her ambition and lust equalled that of her new husband. Unlike Felix, a pagan, Drusilla had been raised as a Jew (v. 24), though she no longer had an active faith in the one God.

Evidently after Paul's hearing, during his continuing house arrest, Felix and Drusilla left town. However, when they returned, they sought Paul out (v. 24). The opening exchange gives us insight in how to proclaim the Word of God.

WISDOM IN DELIVERING GOD'S WORD

Paul delivered God's Word with *boldness*, as verse 24 and the beginning of verse 25 make very clear:

> *Several days later Felix came with his wife Drusilla, who was a Jewess. He sent for Paul and listened to him as he spoke about faith in Christ Jesus. As Paul discoursed on righteousness, self-control and the judgment to come . . .*

This was not the message this illicit couple wanted to hear! They probably thought they would hear some learned dissertation on the future resurrection or some arcane point of rabbinic theology. But Paul quickly left off preaching and went to meddling.

Hugh Latimer, the English Reformer, often preached before Henry VIII and on one occasion offended the king with his boldness. So he was commanded to preach the following weekend and make an apology. On the next Sunday, after reading the text, he addressed himself as he began to preach:

> Hugh Latimer, dost thou know before whom thou art this day to speak? To the high and mighty monarch, the king's most excellent majesty, who can take away thy life if thou offendest; therefore, take heed that thou speakest not a word that may displease; but then consider well, Hugh, dost thou not know from whence thou comest; upon whose message thou art sent? Even by the great and mighty God! who is all-present, and who beholdeth all thy ways, and is able to cast thy soul in hell! Therefore, take care that thou deliverest thy message faithfully.

He then gave Henry the *same* sermon he had preached the week before — with even more energy![3] Paul had that kind of boldness.

One of the high-school boys in my youth ministry some years back was like that. We had gone out to share Christ at a summer resort area, and Jeff approached a group of older college-aged people and asked if they could give him a few minutes to share his faith. The biggest guy responded that if he did, he would throw him in the lake. Jeff walked away, thought about it, then returned and told them the good news of Jesus Christ. When he finished, he was indeed tossed into the lake — gently and in good fun. A loving boldness like Paul's delights the heart of God.

Paul was also *straightforward in his witness.* Felix and Drusilla "listened to him as he spoke about faith in Christ Jesus" (v. 24), though basically they had come to be entertained. Paul got their attention with a clear presentation of the gospel, emphasizing that if they would truly put their faith in Christ their lives would change. He understood their vain pursuits, their looking for love in all the wrong places, their sleepless nights, and he was convinced that Christ could make the difference.

The apostle not only presented the theology of personal salvation but discussed personal morality — "righteousness," no doubt emphasizing God's holiness and his requirements for the inhabitants of Planet Earth. The conversation probably included thoughts like those expressed in the epistle to the Romans: "There is no one righteous, not even one" (3:10); "the wrath of God is being revealed from heaven against all the godlessness and wickedness of men who suppress the truth by their wickedness" (1:18).

Paul also told these two who had always followed their passions about "self-control." Perhaps he taught, as he did in Galatians 5, that such self-discipline can only be accomplished by the indwelling Holy Spirit.

Finally, he emphasized "the judgment to come," warning them that they would not escape divine accountability. Undoubtedly he pointed out that God would not only judge their outward actions but also their hearts. Wanting to win their souls to the Savior who alone could save them, Paul did not soft-pedal the truth. Preaching the gospel (the good news) must include the lostness of man and God's universal moral demands. If we leave this out, we are not preaching the authentic gospel of Christ.

How did all this affect Felix and his bejeweled lover? Did they respond with contempt — mockery — confusion? In Drusilla's case, we cannot say. But the text is clear regarding Felix: "Felix was afraid" (literally, "terrified"). Paul saw fear in the ruler's eyes.

Actually, this was the continental divide of Felix's life. He was being weighed on the scale of God's holiness. It was time to make a choice — believing repentance or continuing rejection. The scale trembled and hesitated for a moment, and then Felix said, "That's enough for now! You may leave. When I find it convenient, I will send for you" (v. 25b). In a very real sense, his soul died at that moment — a tragedy of infinite proportions.

Two tragedies are possible for every human soul. The first is the tragedy of never trembling — of never coming to face one's sin before a holy God. "Blessed are those who mourn, for they will be comforted" (Matthew 5:4). The second is the tragedy of disregarding such Spirit-produced trembling. The one whom God has brought to fear for his soul must not turn away.

WISDOM IN RECEIVING GOD'S WORD

Felix did not say he never wanted to hear Paul and his saving message again. He just made the potentially fatal error of procrastination. When God's Word comes to us with convicting power, we must never put off our response, for several reasons.

Though we might hear the same truth again, it might not bring conviction again. That was pathetically true of Felix who sent Paul away, saying he would summon him another time. But "at the same time he was hoping that Paul would offer him a bribe, so he sent for him frequently and talked with him" (v. 26). He frequently talked with Paul for greed's sake, but he only trembled once. Repetition dulls truth's potency. Some who have heard the good news for years and years greet extraordinary truth with a yawn.

Moreover, *truths not acted upon can harden us so that we cannot understand them.* Jesus said, "This is why I speak to them in parables: Though seeing, they do not see; though hearing, they do not hear or understand" (Matthew 13:13). That is precisely what happened to the Pharisees and those like them. They even lost some of the truth they once possessed: "Whoever has will be given more, and he will have an abundance. Whoever does not have, even what he has will be taken from him" (v. 12). Whenever we come under conviction while hearing the truth, we must take immediate action or suffer spiritual loss. If the Spirit is prompting us to teach, we must quickly take first steps to do so. If he is moving us to give, we must do it. If he is prompting some ethical or social involvement, we must respond. One of the reasons some evangelical churches have such a weak social and ethical witness is that they have ignored God's voice so long that they can no longer hear it! If God is speaking, we must answer!

If Felix is the classic example of what not to do, the Philippian jailer is a good example of what to do. The phrase that describes his fear, in the original, is almost identical with that describing Felix (compare 16:20-30, esp. v. 29). However, instead of delay, the jailer allowed his fear to catapult him into eternal life: "Men, what must I do to be saved?" Responding to God's appeal brings new life. Delay may result in eternal death.

He was going to be all that a mortal should be
Tomorrow
No one would be better than he
Tomorrow
Each morning he stacked up the letters he would write
Tomorrow
It was too bad indeed he was too busy to see his friend,
but he promised to do it
Tomorrow
The greatest of workers this man would have been
Tomorrow
The world would have known him had he ever seen
Tomorrow
But the fact is he died and faded from view, and all that
was left when living was through
Was a mountain of things he intended to do
Tomorrow.

If God is speaking to us, we must not put off our obedience. It is always the right time to do the right thing! Paul's words in 2 Corinthians 6:2 say it perfectly: "We urge you not to receive God's grace in vain. For he says, 'In the time of my favor I heard you, and in the day of salvation I helped you.' I tell you, now is the time of God's favor, now is the day of salvation."

We must each respond to God's Word as it comes to us individually. There is to be no procrastination, no equivocation, but rather a full receiving and a full giving.

PRAYER

O God of Heaven, help us each to be sure that we have personally received your Son, the Lord Jesus Christ, as our Savior from sin and judgment. May we not be in awe of the Judge and yet turn away, but rather bow before you for forgiveness and eternal life. And if we have indeed come into your kingdom and possess your salvation, may we now boldly, wisely, and lovingly proclaim the gospel to those who do not know you. Grant us success, O Lord, as we seek to yield to you more and more and to win others to you. In Jesus' name, Amen.

38

The Accused

ACTS 25:1-12

In the early morning hours of October 4, 1980, a young nursing student was brutally murdered in the Chicago suburb of Oak Park. Following the advice of well-meaning friends, Steve Linscott, a student at Emmaus Bible College, told police about a dream he'd had the night of the crime. Oak Park police later arrested him, interpreting his dream account as the roundabout confession of a psychopathic killer. Later a jury found Linscott guilty, and he was sentenced to forty years in prison. There was just one problem — Linscott was innocent! Only after time in prison and numerous legal appeals — a process that lasted twelve years — was Linscott free and vindicated![1]

Those years undoubtedly brought the most difficult challenges Linscott will ever face — separated from his wife and children for three and a half years except for brief visits, wondering if he had somehow brought all this on himself and why God had allowed it to happen, surviving prison violence. Those were tough years, and yet years of growth and a growing awareness of the goodness of God. In Linscott's words:

> I have come to realize that we cannot judge God's purposes, nor where He places us, nor why He chooses one path for our lives as opposed to another.
>
> The Bible itself is replete with accounts of divine action (or inaction) that does not seem fair, that does not make sense except when viewed in light of God's perfect plan. Thousands of Egyptian children were massacred while a baby named Moses was spared. Jacob was a liar and a thief, and yet it was he, not his faithful brother Esau, who received the blessing of their father Isaac and of God. On one level it

> makes no sense that God would allow His Son to die for the sins of humankind. But God has a plan — a perfect plan.[2]

Though our life circumstances may not be as extreme as Linscott's, none of us likes to be falsely accused. To do what is right and be charged with doing wrong, to work hard to maintain a good job record or reputation and have someone smear it — such injustice can easily crush the human spirit, even in a follower of Jesus Christ. We know the truth, we know who we are in Christ, but slander hurts.

The Apostle Paul, one of the most devoted servants of Jesus Christ in the history of the Church, was at times hated, persecuted, and falsely charged. Acts 25:1-12 recounts such a time.

Consider what Paul had already endured. He had been arrested in Jerusalem though he had done nothing wrong, had spoken to an angry mob, had addressed the Sanhedrin, had been transferred to Caesarea to avoid assassination, had been tried before Felix, and now was about to appear before Festus, the new governor. He had not committed any crime, and yet he was a prisoner of the Roman Empire and on the receiving end of spurious accusations of hateful Jews.

To fully appreciate this passage, we need to catch a whiff of the cell that had been the apostle's home for two years, to feel the burden of his iron manacles, to share his heart's burden for the spiritual bankruptcy of Rome. How the apostle's soul must have longed for personal vindication but also, much more, to be unleashed to minister the gospel freely wherever and to whomever he wished.

Festus was a welcomed successor to the miserably debauched Felix, governor of Judea (24:27). When he took over, tension with the Jews was near the breaking point. Only days after his arrival in Caesarea, he traveled to meet with Jewish leaders in Jerusalem (25:1). The Jews attempted to persuade him to deliver Paul to Jerusalem for another trial before the Sanhedrin. Their plan was to either murder the apostle (in their eyes, the apostate) en route or to sentence him to death for profaning the temple (v. 3).

FALSELY ACCUSED (vv. 1-6)

Festus, like most new rulers or government leaders, was probably anxious to curry the favor of his subjects. He knew they had brought charges against Paul, though obviously they did not have much of a case since the apostle had been sitting in a cell for two years. He may also have known that his predecessor, Felix, had kept Paul under arrest because he was hoping for a bribe (24:26).

Festus refused to bring Paul up to Jerusalem but kept the legal situation intact, inviting the Jews to send selected spokesmen to Caesarea to testify against the apostle. Did Festus know about the Jews' plot to murder Paul along the road, or did the governor have some other reason for his decision? We do not know. We can be sure, however, that God was in control and was continuing to protect his servant.

On the face of it, the Jews' request was fair — to have the hearing in their holy city, not in a foreign locale. But beneath the surface lay evil motives and violent plans against the Lord's evangelist. No matter how devious men may be, the Lord of Heaven is not fooled. Of course, years later the Roman Empire did manage to end the earthly life of the apostle — but only because it was God's will. The sovereign God is always in control.

The Apostle Paul was not the first of God's workers to be falsely accused. Joseph, one of very few Bible characters about whom the Bible has nothing negative to say, knew what it is to be betrayed, hated, and slandered. Sold into slavery by jealous brothers, accused of a crime he did not commit (in fact, no one did), imprisoned and even forgotten by a fellow prisoner he had helped, Joseph could have become bitter toward man and God. Instead, he kept a heavenly focus ("You intended to harm me, but God intended it for good," Genesis 50:20).

> Do you ever wonder if Joseph counted the passing days with slash marks on the wall of his prison cell? Or do you think he gave up worrying about how long he had been there? Do you think he gave up hoping the cupbearer would keep his promise? Joseph knew his interpretation had been correct, and he knew that every day the cupbearer stood in a position of power and influence. Maybe one day that man would remember his promise. But then again, maybe not. How long can a person cling to a dusty promise?[3]

As long as he hangs on to Jesus Christ for dear life, that's how long. As Paul put it, "Since, then, you have been raised with Christ, set your hearts on things above, where Christ is seated at the right hand of God. Set your minds on things above, not on earthly things. For you died, and your life is now hidden with Christ in God" (Colossians 3:1-3).

Turn your eyes upon Jesus,
Look full in His wonderful face
And the things of earth will grow strangely dim
In the light of His glory and grace.

Or consider Daniel, deemed a criminal and thrown into a pit of hungry lions. His crime? Praying to the only true God (Daniel 6). How dare he! Why, Daniel must have been as villainous as William Tyndale, who actually dared to translate the Bible into English, or the ten Boom family, who dared to hide Jews rather than let the Nazis take them away to concentration camps! To defy the authority of man in order to obey God is, in the eyes of human government, improper. But God is honored and pleased with such obedience to him. In the words of the great reformer John Calvin:

> Christ's servants . . . must be all the more courageous to carry on through good and evil reports; they should not think it anything remarkable that evil is spoken of them when they have done good. At the same time, they must easily defend themselves before men when the opportunity arises.[4]

How do God's servants not only survive but thrive in such straits? "When Daniel was lifted from the den, no wound was found on him, because *he had trusted in his God*" (Daniel 6:23). "Everyone born of God has overcome the world. This is the victory that has overcome the world, even our *faith*" (1 John 5:4).

The false accusations of men and women, though they may hurt us and alienate us from those we love, can do us no ultimate harm. We require only God's approval and acceptance, and if Jesus Christ is our Savior, we have it.

> *He hath made us accepted in the beloved. (Ephesians 1:6, KJV)*

> *"May they be brought to complete unity to let the world know that you sent me and have loved them even as you have loved me." (John 17:23)*

> *Who will bring any charge against those whom God has chosen? It is is God who justifies. Who is he that condemns? Christ Jesus, who died — more than that, who was raised to life — is at the right hand of God and is also interceding for us. . . . For I am convinced that neither death nor life, neither angels nor demons, neither the present nor the future, nor any powers, neither height nor depth, nor anything else in all creation will be able to separate us from the love of God that is in Christ Jesus our Lord. (Romans 8:33-34, 38-39)*

Slandered by his own people, Paul knew the security of the love of his precious Savior. The same assurance can fuel our lives.

AN INNOCENT MAN (vv. 7-8)

When the chosen Jewish spokesmen came to Caesarea to testify against the Apostle Paul, they apparently did not have much to say. About all they could do was throw their charges at Paul, with no evidence to support them —"which they could not prove" (v. 7). Christ's apostle had been confined in a jail cell for two years and his accusers still had no case on him!

It is sad to see how evil is so entrenched in our world. Why do pro-abortion politicians get reelected more easily than pro-life candidates? Why does a drunk driver walk away from a wreck while a darling two-year-old is killed? Why do the media so effectively portray Christian activists as meddlesome, Constitution-stomping kooks but God-denying radicals as heroes — and why do people believe them? Why did innocent Steve Linscott go to prison but some serial murderers are never caught?

Like us, the psalmist Asaph lamented the apparent immunity of the wicked. "Pride is their necklace; they clothe themselves with violence . . . the evil conceits of their minds know no limits . . . their tongues take possession of the earth . . . people turn to them and drink up waters in abundance" (Psalm 73:6-7, 9-10). It is easy to mourn this seeming injustice, to forget that God is still Judge and that he will make all things right in their time: "till I entered the sanctuary of God; then I understood their final destiny" (v. 17).

When we are wrongly accused, slandered, or treated harshly, we must remember that God, the Judge of Heaven, will hold men accountable. We must also keep on loving our enemies, as Jesus commanded (Matthew 5:43-44). Rather than becoming bitter or giving up hope, we must recognize the futility and temporality of our opponents' efforts against us. In the words of the great preacher C. H. Spurgeon, "We ought never to fear those who are defending the wrong side, for since God is not with them their wisdom is folly, their strength is weakness, and their glory is their shame."

Furthermore, times of malicious accusation and mistreatment are opportunities for prayer and trust in God. Again quoting Spurgeon, "Often the less we say to our foes, and the more we say to our best Friend, the better it will fare with us." When faced with groundless accusations, Paul did not go on a rampage but clearly and calmly stated the facts of his innocence. Perhaps he remembered the opening verses of Psalm 109:

> *O God, whom I praise, do not remain silent, for wicked and deceitful men have opened their mouths against me; they have spoken against me with lying tongues. With words of hatred they surround me; they attack me without cause. In return for my friendship they accuse me, but I am a man of prayer. (vv. 1-4)*

We must also maintain an honest view of ourselves. Even when the charges leveled against us — whether in a legal proceeding or in a passing conversation with a friend or in misguided media panning Christian believers — are unfounded, there is an element of truth. None of us is perfect. We all have areas in which we need to grow spiritually. First John 1:8-10 makes this painfully clear.

At the same time, recognizing our shortcomings and limitations, we can serve our Lord with a clear conscience, confess our sins to him, and allow him to help us become the persons he wants us to be. Balance is crucial if we are to serve our Savior effectively.

Why do wicked people — those who reject Christ and shut him out of their hearts and lives — love to slander good people — those who believe in Christ and seek to serve him? And how should Christian believers respond to their accusers? The ungodly would like to do away with any convincing argument for the truth of Christ's gospel, the existence of a God who holds men accountable to him, the reality of moral absolutes in our world, so they can live as they wish, without fear of divine penalty. Sadly, they are walking blindly toward judgment and eternal darkness.

The supreme example of godly behavior toward one's evil accusers is Jesus Christ himself.

> *Christ suffered for you, leaving you an example, that you should follow in his steps. "He committed no sin, and no deceit was found in his mouth." When they hurled their insults at him, he did not retaliate; when he suffered, he made no threats. Instead, he entrusted himself to him who judges justly. (1 Peter 2:21-23)*

AN APPEAL TO CAESAR (vv. 9-12)

Apparently at this point Festus wanted to try one more time to use the situation for his own advantage — "to do the Jews a favor" (v. 9) and help himself in the process. Why was Festus suddenly willing to do what he had refused to do earlier (namely, to transfer his famous prisoner to Jerusalem for trial there)? We are not sure, but we do know that the self-seeking governor was being unfair to Paul — there was clearly not enough evidence to warrant Paul's continuing imprisonment or to justify another trial. And yet to Festus' credit, he gave Paul a choice and did not force the situation to go his way. This was probably due to his high respect for Paul's Roman citizenship, though certainly the sovereignty of God was the overriding factor.

Paul's response at this juncture is most admirable:

> *"I am now standing before Caesar's court, where I ought to be tried. I have not done any wrong to the Jews, as you yourself know very well. If, however, I am guilty of doing anything deserving death, I do not refuse to die. But if the charges brought against me by these Jews*

are not true, no one has the right to hand me over to them. I appeal to Caesar!"

As Paul again declared his innocence, he was not being egotistical or boastful. He was simply, and truthfully, saying that he had not committed any crime — that his arrest and imprisonment were unjustified. He also stated publicly that Festus *knew* the apostle was innocent, and thus for that ruler to go along with the situation was to participate in a charade — always a tragic state of affairs for a man God has chosen for political authority. Paul added that if in fact he was guilty of any violation against the law, he was willing to suffer the appropriate penalty, even death. Only a man with spiritual conviction and a clean conscience could say that.

Christ's brave ambassador then took a bold step, for his own safety and for the further proclamation of Christ — "I appeal to Caesar!" Realizing he would not receive justice from Festus or from the Jews, he submitted his case to the authority of the emperor himself. This was a right possessed by every Roman citizen. Paul did not do this because Caesar was a Christian or a just leader — he was neither, but because it was the apostle's final hope. Perhaps he also felt Spirit-led to make this appeal because God had told him he would minister in Rome.

Some believers might criticize Paul here, saying he should have simply waited on God and allowed him to direct the apostle's circumstances however he willed. But certainly there is no fault with using the provisions God gives us for our lives and ministries. As John Calvin stated, "God, who has appointed courts of law, also gives his people liberty to use them lawfully."[5] Romans 13:1-7 clearly teaches that God ordained human governments to punish wrongdoers and to reward those who do right. Paul did well to use his rights as a Roman citizen to protect himself and to extend his ministry.

Just think of what God has done through his servants who used that which God made available to them. For example, William Wilberforce, a strong Christian and a member of the British Parliament in the late eighteenth and early nineteenth centuries, championed the abolition of slavery. Exercising spiritual determination, using all the legitimate political resources at his disposal, he persevered in his calling for more than twenty years and was used by God to bring an end to slavery in the British Empire.

Festus then conferred with a council of leading citizens, as the Roman governors did in those days. Perhaps he tried to convince them to send Paul to Jerusalem, perhaps not. But they had no choice. Paul, a Roman citizen, had appealed to Caesar, and that is where he had to go. Thus Festus was now obligated to send Paul to Caesar even though there were no solid charges against him.

A FINAL WORD

This must have been an exhilarating time for the Apostle Paul. Granted, he was again faced with serious charges of which he was totally innocent ("I have done nothing wrong against the law of the Jews or against the temple or against Caesar . . . I have not done any wrong to the Jews," vv. 8, 10). Certainly these accusations hurt. Not even the great apostle was immune to emotional wounds when injustice was heaped on his shoulders.

But Paul also had the satisfaction of knowing that though men maligned him, his Lord loved him and continued to be with him. What matters the spite of mere humans when the God of Heaven says, "You are my child and will be forever — I am with you — I love you"? Combined with this was the excitement Paul felt because he was going to Rome and was sure God would use him mightily in that great city, just as he had promised!

PRAYER

> *O Lord, when we are unfairly criticized or misjudged or wrongly charged with misbehavior, please help us respond with love, not hate; forgiveness, not bitterness; hope, not despair. When circumstances threaten to thwart our ministry or our spiritual growth, help us to look up to you — our life, our salvation, our God. Remind us again and again, O Lord, that as we cooperate with you, we will be fruitful ambassadors, through your strength and for your glory! In Jesus' name, Amen.*

39

Blessed Madness

ACTS 26:1-32

In the late 1800s a clergyman by the name of Bishop Wright thought it was impossible for man to fly. "Flight," he said, "is reserved for the angels." On December 17, 1903 his oldest son, Wilbur, took his seat in the first power-driven plane ever built and was airborne at Kitty Hawk, North Carolina, for twelve seconds and 120 feet. There were some who thought the Wright brothers were a little touched before that fateful day, but today they are everyone's heroes.

It was the same for Christopher Columbus. People were so sure this crazy explorer would sail off the end of the earth that many of their coins carried the Latin inscription, "Ne Plus Ultra" — "no more beyond." After 1492 when he sailed the ocean blue, the new coins read "Plus Ultra" — "more beyond."

When Robert Fulton gave his first public demonstration of his steamboat, some bystanders chanted, "It will never start, never start, never start . . ." When it started, the astonished crowd began to repeat, "It will never stop, never stop, never stop . . ."

Similarly, many of the Apostle Paul's contemporaries considered him out of touch with reality. Even today some maintain that Paul had a hallucination on the Damascus Road and that his subsequent teachings perverted Judaism. But the fact of the matter is, Paul was the sanest of theologians, and his teachings were anointed by God.

Acts 26 records Paul's sanity being questioned. Besides the great apostle, the cast of characters in this divinely orchestrated drama includes Festus, whom we met in Acts 25, and Agrippa and Bernice, a couple who were even more unsavory than Felix and Drusilla.

A LOST COUPLE

King Agrippa II was the latest of the Herod Dynasty, the last of the Herods to meddle with Christ or his followers. His great-grandfather was the King Herod who had feared the birth of the Christ-child and murdered the male children in the vicinity of Bethlehem. The grand-uncle of Agrippa II had murdered John the Baptist, and his father, Agrippa I, had executed James and imprisoned Peter and was eaten with worms as punishment for allowing people to worship him as a god right there in Caesarea (12:20-23).[1]

With Agrippa was Bernice, his sister, who was one year younger. She had once been engaged to Marcus, a nephew of the philosopher Philo. Then she married her uncle — Herod, King of Chalcis. But now she was living incestuously with her full blood brother Agrippa. So notorious was her conduct that when she later became the Emperor Titus' mistress, he had to send her away because of the moral outcry of pagan Rome.[2] Agrippa and Bernice were a sick, sin-infested couple.

To make matters even more outrageous, Rome considered Agrippa an authority on the Jewish religion. Because he was a Herod, he was appointed curator of the temple and thus had the power to appoint the high priest and to administer the temple treasury.[3]

Festus was elated at the appearance of Agrippa and his willingness to interview Paul, because Festus could now receive expert advice on what to write to Rome about his prisoner.

> *Agrippa and Bernice came with great pomp and entered the audience room with the high ranking officers and the leading men of the city. At the command of Festus, Paul was brought in. (23:25)*

The phrase "with great pomp" comes from the Greek word *phantasia*, from which we derive our English word *fantasy*. Certainly the event was something of a fantasy: Agrippa and Bernice arrayed in purple, Festus in red, chiliarchs (commanders of thousands), rigid legionnaires, manipulative politicians, and Paul appearing even smaller and more insignificant in his manacles and humble dress. The scene was carefully constructed to intimidate.

But the Apostle Paul, mighty in the Lord, towered above the king and governor and their petty dignitaries. This is just what Paul had longed for during his bleak two years in prison — a knowledgeable judge and a non-antagonistic audience before whom he could make his case. Speaking with remarkable optimism and fervor, Paul's speech was not so much a personal defense as a positive presentation of the gospel and an evangelistic appeal.

However, not all went as he'd hoped. Since coming to Jerusalem Paul hadn't been allowed to finish a public speech, and this occasion was no exception. Just when he was making his strongest plea, Festus excitedly interrupted him.

> *"You are out of your mind, Paul!" he shouted."Your great learning is driving you insane." (26:24)*

This is a pastor's nightmare — preaching with enthusiasm, hoping for great results, when suddenly someone stands up and shouts, "Pastor, you're crazy!" and those around nod their assent.

What prompted Festus to assert that Paul was mad? Despite conventional references to Roman gods, the typical Roman, as Charles Cochrane points out in *Christianity and Classical Culture*, worshiped imperial fortune — the prominence and success of the Empire.[4] Festus, being first and last a politician, worshiped power and was a practical materialist. A sensible Roman, he could not believe in the resurrection of a dead man. And even if he did privately accept such a bizarre view, he would not allow it to interfere with practical living or to challenge accepted views and values. Being politically and spiritually correct was everything to him.

Paul's testimony of his encounter with and commission by Christ on the road to Damascus (26:13-18) stretched Festus' rationality to the limit. Further, Paul's dogged obedience to Christ's commission despite persecution (vv. 19-21) offended Festus' instinctive hedonism. It made no sense to him for Paul to choose a path that not only brought the apostle less pleasure but more suffering! When the apostle asserted that the resurrection of a man named Jesus was the nexus of his argument and appeal (vv. 22-23), it was simply too much, and the Roman Festus shouted, "Paul, you are insane! Your long studying has broken your mind!" (TLB). In other words, "Paul, you are a real nutcase!"

CHRIST'S CRAZY APOSTLES

The world has always thought that Christ's ambassadors were crazy. To those outside the faith, Paul's utter devotion to Jesus Christ could only appear as a mad obsession. For the sake of the Savior, he tossed aside everything that others value. That which others treasured, he called waste.

> *. . . circumcised on my eighth day, Israelite by race, of the tribe of Benjamin, a Hebrew born and bred; in my attitude to the law, a Pharisee; in pious zeal, a persecutor of the church; in legal rectitude, faultless. But all such assets I have written off because of Christ. I would say more: I count everything sheer loss, because all is far outweighed by the gain of knowing Christ Jesus my Lord, for whose sake I did in*

fact lose everything. I count it so much garbage, for the sake of gaining Christ. (Philippians 3:5-7, New English Bible)

Paul also wrote, "For to me, to live is Christ and to die is gain" (Philippians 1:21). Those on the outside said, "That's crazy!" Subsequent Pauls have suffered the same stigma. In 1913 when William Borden, age twenty-six, a graduate of Yale and Princeton, left his palatial home near Chicago's Lake Shore Drive, giving away over $500,000 to become a missionary to the Muslim world, many of his contemporaries thought he was crazy. And when he died six months later from cerebral meningitis amidst the flies and heat of a Cairo hospital, some were sure he was mentally unbalanced. God did not share their opinion.

In 1885 when the Cambridge Seven, including C. T. Studd, England's most famous athlete, left for China, they were ridiculed for their "enthusiasm," a polite British way of saying "mad fanaticism."

The prophetic words of the later martyred Chet Bitterman, "I would not be a bit surprised if the Lord required martyrdom of somebody in Wycliffe, maybe someone in Colombia, I am willing,"[5] seem insane if you are a Festus or an Agrippa.

The world system has always thought Pauls were crazy! But actually it is the world that is insane. The July-September 1982 issue of *Sparks* magazine, in an article entitled "Faith as Madness," documented the then official Soviet position of religion: "Belief in God . . . is considered a delusion." At that time the treatment for dissenters frequently included drugs for psychosis and torture. The patients were not the ones who were mad.

Such insanity is not confined to Marxist materialists. It also flourishes in the West, even today. Millions of people starve, while on the other side of the world people pay hundreds of dollars for a pair of Calvin Klein jeans just because they were worn by some celebrity bombshell. Or consider the insanity seen when society mourns the terrible epidemic of AIDS and other diseases due to sexual license but mocks those who suggest that the solution is chastity. To be earnest about wealth or power or science or pleasure or athletic championships is not crazy from the world's viewpoint. But to be fervent about spiritual things is called madness.

True sanity lies with the Pauls of this world — those who build their lives on the gospel of the Lord Jesus Christ. It is mad to live, as the majority does, as though ultimate reality resides in what we can see, taste, and touch. As Paul stated so aptly in 2 Corinthians 4:18:

So we fix our eyes not on what is seen, but on what is unseen. For what is seen is temporary, but what is unseen is eternal.

It is mad to suppose, as some do, that we can find fulfillment in our possessions. John Paul Getty, asked "How much is enough?" answered, "Just a little bit more." Jesus' words, "A man's life does not consist in the abundance of his possessions" (Luke 12:15), must be taken into account.

It is also crazy to think that life will come together when we achieve position or status or prominence. Agrippa and Bernice had prestige — the political good life. But their life was little more than a fantasy and, ultimately, a desert. The Pauls of this world are the sane ones, not the Agrippas, because they have Jesus.

To be honest, even the church sometimes holds God's Pauls suspect. Some of the believers in Corinth criticized Paul for being too enthusiastic. Paul answered them by saying, "If we are out of our mind, it is for the sake of God" (2 Corinthians 5:13). That is, "If I seem a little touched, it is because the love of Jesus takes over my heart. There are times when I simply cannot contain myself!"

Charles Finney, the great though sometimes controversial evangelist who founded Oberlin College, wrote:

> If you have much of the Spirit of God, it is not unlikely you will be thought deranged by many. We judge men to be deranged when they act differently from what we think to be according to prudence and common sense, and when they come to conclusions for which we can see no good reasons. Paul was accused of being deranged by those who did not understand the views of things under which he acted. This is by no means uncommon. Multitudes have appeared, to those who had no spirituality, as if they were deranged. Yet they saw good reasons for doing as they did. God was leading their minds to act in such a way that those who were not spiritual could not see the reasons.[6]

How would modern-day Christians regard Paul? Too excitable? Too one-sided? Many believers would be uncomfortable in his presence. The crowd outside the church would say he was not playing with all his marbles. But without doubt God would say, "I would like to see more of this blessed madness." Most of us believe everything Paul believed, but we have not carried our faith to its logical end like Paul did. Our world would be a saner, happier place if more of us bore a spiritual resemblance to the Apostle Paul.

Festus had rudely interrupted Paul, saying he was out of his mind. "'I am not insane, most excellent Festus,' Paul replied. 'What I am saying is true and reasonable'" (v. 25). Paul remained cool and unruffled by the governor's outburst. Refusing to accept the charge against him, he courteously deflected Festus' putdown, then used it to pursue Agrippa's dark heart on behalf of Jesus Christ.

"The king is familiar with these things, and I can speak freely to him. I am convinced that none of this has escaped his notice, because it was not done in a corner. King Agrippa, do you believe the prophets? I know you do." (v. 26)

The psychology of Paul's plea is beautiful. He told Festus he was sure that official knew and understood a great deal about the story of Christ, then asked Agrippa if he believed the prophets (v. 27), a belief that Paul hoped would take him directly to Christ.

Agrippa was caught off-guard and was embarrassed. His public image would require him to say he believed in the prophets, but he saw where Paul was trying to lead him and did not want to go there. So he parried Paul's question with a clever, though rather inane, counterquestion: "Do you think that in such a short time you can persuade me to be a Christian?" (v. 28). Agrippa was the crazy man! Sadly, if he never came to Christ, he will have all eternity to consider the madness of his response.

How did Paul respond to Agrippa's red herring?

"Short time or long — I pray God that not only you but all who are listening to me today may become what I am, except for these chains." (v. 29)

Though a mere speck of a man before the majestic red and purple of Rome, the surging tide of Christ's life in the Apostle Paul flowed out to Agrippa and Bernice and Festus. His was a blessed madness!

What would Paul say to people today? To unbelievers, he would say, "I wish you knew Christ like I do." To those who know Christ, he would say, "Even if others think you are crazy, keep on serving Christ!"

Like Paul, Christ has sent us "to open their eyes and turn them from darkness to light, and from the power of Satan to God, so that they may receive forgiveness of sins and a place among those who are sanctified by faith in me" (v. 18). That is our high calling and special privilege.

PRAYER

O God, help us to not worry about what people think of us — whether they respect us or think we are crazy. Rather, remind us daily of who you are and who we are in Christ. Give us the courage to speak the truth of the gospel to those who need to hear it so desperately. And may many of those to whom we witness truly turn to you and receive him in whom is life eternal. In Jesus' name, Amen.

40

Anchors in the Storm

ACTS 27:1-44

On April 15, 1912, at approximately 2:20 A.M. the stern of the White Star liner *Titanic* swung slowly upward toward the stars. Her lights went out, flashed on again, then went out for good. Only a single kerosene lantern flickered high in the aftermast. As her stern reached higher, a steady roar thundered across the water as every movable thing aboard her broke loose. There has never been a mixture like it: 15,000 bottles of ale and stout, huge anchor chains (each link weighed 175 pounds), thirty cases of golf clubs, 30,000 fresh eggs, potted palms, five grand pianos, a cask of china for Tiffany's, a case of gloves for Marshall Field's, and, most valuable of all, 1,500 passengers who had not been able to get off the great ship.

The great and the unknown tumbled together in a writhing heap as the bow eased deeper and the stern rose higher. The *Titanic* was now absolutely vertical, with her three dripping propellers glistening in the darkness. For nearly two minutes she stood poised as the noise finally stopped. Then she began sliding slowly under, until the sea closed over the flagstaff on her stern with an audible gulp.[1]

A wreck of any kind is a terrifying experience, whether it be a train derailment, an automobile collision, or the crash of an airplane. But probably the most terrifying of all is a shipwreck, because of the prolonged agony that the passengers and crew endure. Acts 27 is the tale of one of the most famous shipwrecks in history — that of the Apostle Paul on his way to Rome. It is also one of the best-told, most-detailed shipwreck accounts in ancient history — and certainly the most profitable to the hearer.

Having appealed to Caesar, Paul was put in the custody of a kindly Roman centurion named Julius and placed on an Adramyttian ship destined for Italy — the focus of his ministry dreams. Being a Roman citizen and an obvious gentleman, Paul was allowed to take along his companions Dr. Luke and Aristarchus, a devoted Christian brother from Thessalonica. Paul was treated so well that the next day, when they put in at Sidon, he was allowed to disembark and visit his friends there. So far, so good. But from this point on the voyage rapidly deteriorated.

After leaving Sidon they had to sail up and around Cyprus, rather than straight toward Italy in the west, because the winds were contrary. Finally landing in Asia Minor, the centurion transferred Paul and the other prisoners onto a large Egyptian grain ship. The typical grain freighter was 140 feet long and thirty-six feet wide and bore a thirty-three-foot draught. It was a sturdy ship, but in high seas it had definite disadvantages. It had no rudder like a modern ship but was steered by two great paddles extending from the stern. It had only one mast on which was a great square sail. Chief among its drawbacks was that it could not sail into the wind.

Departing Myra in the freighter, they reached nearby Cnidus only with great difficulty. Then they were forced to sail south under the shelter of Crete so that with further difficulty they reached Crete's small southern port of Fair Havens.

Here, according to verses 9 and 10, Paul, an experienced traveler, warned the centurion that they should stay in Fair Havens because it was after Passover (mid-October) and everyone knew it was dangerous to make that voyage at that time of year. However, because Fair Havens was a rather boring port and the harbor was not ideal for wintering and an enticing south wind began to blow, the captain decided to take a chance and set sail for the much nicer port of Phoenix, about forty miles away.

Once they were underway, it seemed as if all the forces of evil broke loose upon them! According to verse 14 (NASB), the sailors had a name for this gale — "Euraquilo." From their point of view, Euroclydon, the terror of seamen, had been watching and waiting from the top of Mount Ida (the fabled abode of Zeus) to drive them to destruction. Now the battle was on! They were in the grips of a deadly "northeaster" (NIV) that was driving them due west the length of the Mediterranean. Verses 14 through 20 describe the terror:

> *Before very long, a wind of hurricane force, called the "northeaster," swept down from the island. The ship was caught by the storm and could not head into the wind; so we gave way to it and were driven along. As we passed to the lee of a small island called Cauda, we were hardly able to make the lifeboat secure. When the men had hoisted it aboard, they passed ropes under the ship itself to hold it together. Fearing that they would run aground on the sandbars of Syrtis, they lowered the sea anchor and let the ship be driven along. We took such*

a violent battering from the storm that the next day they began to throw the cargo overboard. On the third day, they threw the ship's tackle overboard with their own hands. When neither sun nor stars appeared for many days and the storm continued raging, we finally gave up all hope of being saved.

Those of us who have been made ill by a storm while on water can relate to this picture of abysmal misery. I once heard of a woman who became seasick while on a day-long sport fishing boat and staggered to the captain holding out the keys to her new car, saying he could have it if he would just turn around. The plight of Paul and his friends was a thousand times worse.

The dangers faced by the 276 crewmen and passengers worsened rapidly. So with great difficulty they secured the dinghy, then proceeded to pass great ropes around the hull and winch them tight in an effort to tie the ship together. Next they jettisoned the cargo and cut away the tangled gear that littered the deck. Day after day for fourteen days, with no light of sun by day and no stars by night, they wallowed in the deep until finally they gave up all hope of being saved. They occupied a ghost ship that again and again climbed toward the unseen heavens, then dove back to the deadly, dark depths.

Two years earlier (23:11) Christ had appeared in Paul's cell in Caesarea and told him to take courage, for he would bear witness for the Savior in Rome. This was an unconditional promise. Paul would go to Rome — no doubt about it. However, God did not promise smooth sailing along the way. As we serve Christ, there will be storms, hardships, high seas, breakdowns — but also peace, assurance, fruitfulness, the sustaining presence of God.

We read in the fourteenth chapter of Matthew that Christ came walking to his disciples on the stormy Sea of Galilee when their ship was about to sink. They were in danger precisely because they had followed the orders of Jesus — he had told them to go out onto the lake, and they obeyed. Those who claim that all who follow Christ will always have smooth sailing are misunderstanding and misrepresenting the Word of God. F. B. Meyer wrote: "If I am told that I am to take a journey that is a dangerous trip, every jolt along the way will remind me that I am on the right road." Christ warned his disciples they would face trials, but he also assured them he would be with them. The record of Paul's shipwreck in Acts 27 is intriguing history, but it is also a metaphor of what all Christians experience in their voyage through life.

Paul's courage in the midst of a hopeless storm would have made a perfect part for Charlton Heston under Cecil B. DeMille's direction. Paul must have had to shout above the spray of the howling storm: "Men, you should have taken my advice not to sail from Crete; then you would have spared yourselves this damage and loss. But now I urge you to keep up your courage, because not one of you will be lost; only the ship will be destroyed" (vv. 21-22). Huge waves were assaulting the ship, but Paul's soul was as calm as a windless pond. Why? He was anchored in a way the rest knew nothing about. Every Christian can have courage amidst life's storms if he or she uses the proper anchors.

COURAGE IN LIFE'S STORMS THROUGH THE ANCHOR OF GOD'S PRESENCE

In the opening sentence of verse 23 Paul continued, "Last night an angel of the God whose I am and whom I serve stood beside me." On the deck of a sinking ship in a raging storm, Paul was anchored in God's presence, an ongoing reality for him. This was not the first time the apostle experienced this assurance. In Corinth Christ came to him in a vision, as Acts 18:9-10 records: "Do not be afraid; keep on speaking, do not be silent. For I am with you, and no one is going to attack and harm you, because I have many people in this city." In Caesarea Christ actually stood with the apostle in the flesh (23:11): "The following night the Lord stood near Paul and said, 'Take courage! As you have testified about me in Jerusalem, so you must also testify in Rome.'" Later in Rome, according to 2 Timothy 4:16-17, Christ again stood with him. As the writer of Hebrews (and this may have been Paul himself) put it, "God has said, 'Never will I leave you; never will I forsake you'" (13:5).

There, west of Crete, with mountains of ocean on all sides, if God had opened their eyes they would have seen supernatural beings gliding on the deck. "So to faith's enlightened sight . . . All the mountains flamed with light!"

How do we become aware of God's presence? Rarely through an audible voice, but rather through the still, gentle assurance of the Holy Spirit and through God's holy Word. Remaining alert to his presence with us in the midst of the storms is a key to spiritual health and courage. C. S. Lewis put it like this: "He walks everywhere incognito. And the incognito is not always hard to penetrate. The real labour is to remember, to attend. In fact, to come awake. Still more, to remain awake."[2]

When we are anchored to God's presence, we will display amazing courage in the worst storms. And just as important, when we are thus anchored, we can sustain others, just as Paul did. There was a time when I was going through some dark days, some of the darkest I have ever known in the ministry. I felt alone. I could not sense the presence or help of God. As I was sharing this late one night with my wife, her life-giving words to me were, "Hold on to my faith. I have enough faith for both of us." God's presence through her was an anchor to my soul.

COURAGE IN LIFE'S STORMS THROUGH THE ANCHOR OF GOD'S OWNERSHIP

Paul mastered the storm because he knew he belonged to God: "Last night an angel of the God *whose I am* and whom I serve stood beside me" (v. 23). He saw himself as God's property!

How do we belong to God? *Like a bride belongs to the bridegroom.* The Song of Songs says, "My lover is mine and I am his" (2:16). In fact, the Bible often uses the intimacies between husband and wife to illustrate our union with the Lord. In Ephesians 5, Paul's description of the marriage relationship, he concludes by saying, "This is a profound mystery — but I am talking about Christ and the church."

We belong to him in the most exalted and personal way — *like sheep to a shepherd.* Jesus said, "I am the good shepherd; I know my sheep and my sheep know me — just as the Father knows me and I know the Father" (John 10:14-15a).

We also belong to him *like a child belongs to his father.* When Alan Redpath's two daughters were younger, he heard his wife say, "Girls, go get your father for breakfast." The oldest bounded up the steps, and by the time the youngest (who was considerably younger) made it to the room puffing from the race, her big sister said, "I have already told Daddy breakfast is ready, and besides I have all of Daddy." The little one took that pronouncement hard, and a tear began to run down her cheek, so her father sat her on his knee. She put her head on his shoulder, then smiled big and said to her sister, "You might have all of Daddy, but Daddy has all of me." Paul was his Father's possession, and that truth so permeated his inner being that he described God as "the God whose I am."

We belong to God *because he bought us.* First Corinthians 6:19-20 says, "Do you not know that your body is a temple of the Holy Spirit, who is in you, whom you have received from God? You are not your own; you were bought at a price." Paul traced God's possession of him not to the fact that God is Creator, but to the one transcendent act of divine love in which Christ gave his life to purchase us for himself.

God's ownership enabled Paul to stand tall in the deadly storm.

COURAGE IN LIFE'S STORMS THROUGH THE ANCHOR OF SERVICE FOR GOD

Paul had courage because he was anchored in the fact that he was on business for God — "the God whose I am and *whom I serve*" (v. 23). He knew nothing could harm him unless God allowed it.

In another storm on the same sea centuries earlier, Jonah had no such anchor. He refused to serve God. In contrast to Paul's witness to his Gentile associates, Jonah was reproved by the ship's crew. All those who are Christ's, who consciously serve him as best they can, experience sustaining assurance. This is one of God's gracious gifts to the committed, and Paul knew it to the fullest.

COURAGE IN LIFE'S STORMS THROUGH THE ANCHOR OF TRUST IN GOD

The apostle told the others on the endangered ship, "[God's angel] said, 'Do not be afraid, Paul. You must stand trial before Caesar; and God has graciously given you the lives of all who sail with you.' So keep up your courage, men, for I have faith in God that it will happen just as he told me" (vv. 24-25). The reason Paul displayed such courage was that *he believed God!* If our hearts bear the anchors of the Lord's presence, ownership, and service, we will be able to stand tall in any storm.

Truly trusting and resting in God's omnipresence, omniscience, and omnipotence will enable us to be men of courage and to shout words of encouragement above the storm. Dr. Barnhouse and his wife used to have the perfect squelch for each other when one or the other displayed a lack of faith over some problem. One would say to the other, "Well, we *think* that all things work together for good." At that, the other would be brought up short and would say, "For we *know* that all things work together for good."

In an impossible situation Paul said, "So keep up your courage, men, for I have faith in God that it will happen just as he told me." He was anchored to Christ by faith, and that made all the difference in the world. The remaining story of the shipwreck reveals how Paul's example brought courage to the others.

After Paul's encouragement, before God saved them all from the sinking ship, things got even worse. As the darkness continued, their sounding lines revealed that the ship was nearing shore and certain death! In a final effort the sailors cast off four anchors from the stern, and they held! The men desperately prayed for daybreak. Some of the sailors tried to escape in the ship's dinghy under the pretense of laying more anchors, but Paul warned the centurion that unless all the men remained on the ship to help navigate a landing, all would be lost. The boat was cast away in obedience to the apostle and the God he served. Paul then encouraged them all to eat. They did, and their spirits picked up. Verses 37 through 44 record their salvation by shipwreck:

> *Altogether there were 276 of us on board. When they had eaten as much as they wanted, they lightened the ship by throwing the grain*

into the sea. When daylight came, they did not recognize the land, but they saw a bay with a sandy beach, where they decided to run the ship aground if they could. Cutting loose the anchors, they left them in the sea and at the same time untied the ropes that held the rudders. Then they hoisted the foresail to the wind and made for the beach. But the ship struck a sandbar and ran aground. The bow stuck fast and would not move, and the stern was broken to pieces by the pounding of the surf. The soldiers planned to kill the prisoners to prevent any of them from swimming away and escaping. But the centurion wanted to spare Paul's life and kept them from carrying out their plan. He ordered those who could swim to jump overboard first and get to land. The rest were to get there on planks or on pieces of the ship. In this way everyone reached land in safety.

Another ho-hum day in the life of the Apostle Paul! What a man! And what a God! Not one soul was lost, and God's name was wonderfully glorified!

Why are there storms and shipwrecks? God, who controls the winds and waves, could certainly have spared Paul this dire strait. We know that whatever God allows to come our way, he loves us and will give us sufficient grace to endure and remain faithful to him. Of course, sometimes a trial is the work of Satan. Paul wrote the Thessalonians, "For we wanted to come to you — certainly I, Paul, did again and again — but Satan stopped us" (1 Thessalonians 2:18). At the same time, the story of Job teaches us that Satan must obtain God's permission before he can touch one of God's children.

Furthermore, storms and shipwrecks can actually be for our benefit. Oswald Sanders put it this way:

When God wants to drill a man
And thrill a man,
And skill a man,
When God wants to mold a man
To play the noblest part;
When he yearns with all his heart
To create so great and bold a man
That all the world shall be amazed,
Watch his methods, watch his ways!
How he ruthlessly perfects
Whom he royally elects!
How he hammers him and hurts him
And with mighty blows converts him
Into trial shapes of clay which
Only God understands;

While his tortured heart is crying
And he lifts beseeching hands!
How he bends but never breaks
While his good he undertakes;
How he uses whom he chooses
And with every purpose fuses him;
By every act induces him
To try his splendor out —
God knows what He's about![3]

Paul was mature in Christ but was still being shaped through trials. We are often *objective*-oriented, but God is *process*-oriented. We just want to get to Rome, but God is even more interested in *how* we get there.

Storms can also be for others' good. Aboard ship people learn about each other very quickly. The imminent threat of death on that floundering Egyptian freighter revealed the secrets of each man's character, and Paul was head and shoulders above them all. Perhaps many found Christ in those following months on Malta. Sometimes storms come so that others will look beyond us to Christ.

Are you in a storm? Does it look like your ship is about to go under? If so, you need some anchors:

The anchor of God's presence. He is with you — "an angel of the God whose I am and whom I serve stood beside me."

The anchor of God's ownership. You are his possession — "the God whose I am."

The anchor that comes through serving God. ". . . the God . . . whom I serve."

The anchor of faith. "So keep up your courage, men, for I have faith in God that it will happen just as he told me."

With anchors like these, God's servants will stand strong and true.

PRAYER

O Lord, as we sail through life's storms, may your presence and rule in our lives preserve our trust in you. May we not allow the winds and waves to draw us aside from serving you faithfully, wholeheartedly, courageously. When we must decide whether to believe circumstances or the Sovereign Lord, may we again and again choose to trust in you. And may others see you in us and come to know you too. In Jesus' name, Amen.

41

Building an Indomitable Spirit

ACTS 28:1-30

On a hot summer day in 1967 Joni Eareckson Tada dove into the Chesapeake Bay and lost touch with her body forever — in this life anyway. The story of her battle for life and an even greater battle for her soul is well-known today, as is her indomitable, buoyant spirit. Seeing her speak, sing, and charm a live audience only serves to confirm what her first book, *Joni*, so beautifully affirms — she possesses one of the unconquerable spirits of our time, because of her strong faith in Jesus Christ. Her positive example has both shamed and lured us toward a more courageous, faith-filled outlook on life.

The secret of such an unchained spirit is taught in many passages of Scripture, including Acts 28, where we see another unconquerable spirit, the great Apostle Paul. From the time he met Christ on the Damascus Road, he lived a life of bravery through Christ. His missionary journeys reveal a man of God who refused to be repressed by anyone or anything. He withstood Elymas the sorcerer face to face. When he was stoned in Lystra and his disciples were mourning over his apparent corpse, he revived and went right back into Lystra!

After a miserable beating in Philippi, he and Silas gave the first gospel concert in Europe. He withstood the heady intellectualism of Athens, the corruption of Corinth, and the violence of Ephesus. In Jerusalem and Caesarea he was magnificent amidst the abuse of his kinsmen and the Roman governors. And he was absolutely amazing as he inspired courage in others during the storm and shipwreck described so vividly in Acts 27.

In chapter 28 we see Paul standing on the shore of what is today called St. Paul's Bay on the tiny island of Malta. His indomitable spirit prevailed first through his casual dealing with a serpent's bite and then through the healing of the governor's father and subsequent ministry. Three months later when Paul finally left Malta, he left more like an honored dignitary than a prisoner of Rome — and in God's eyes he was.

In verses 11-16 Luke describes the subsequent journey on to Rome. They sailed from Malta in another Alexandrian grain ship, which carried on its bow the carved effigy of the "the twin gods Castor and Pollux." They stopped at Syracuse in Sicily, then Rhegium on the toe of Italy, then Puteoli on the bay of modern Naples. From there they walked the 140 miles to Rome. About forty-three miles outside Rome the most wonderful thing happened — Christian brothers and sisters came out to greet him at the Market of Appius. Another ten miles closer, at "the Three Taverns," yet others greeted him. A joyous throng marched the remaining distance along the Appian Way to the so-called Eternal City.

Luke helps us catch the excitement and optimism of that time, concluding in verse 16, "When we got to Rome, Paul was allowed to live by himself, with a soldier to guard him." *Even in chains, Paul was an unconquered, indomitable victor.*

What are the secrets to having such an unconquerable spirit? We see two in the general history of Paul's life and a third in Acts 28:16-24.

THE FIRST SECRET OF AN UNCONQUERABLE SPIRIT: VISION

Paul was a man of massive spiritual vision — namely, the conversion of his own people and the evangelization of the entire known world! Concerning his own people, he said, "For I could wish that I myself were cursed and cut off from Christ for the sake of my brothers, those of my own race" (Romans 9:3). Concerning the Gentiles, he said, "It has always been my ambition to preach the gospel where Christ was not known" (Romans 15:20). He longed to see Jews and Gentiles reconciled as one body through the cross (Ephesians 2:16).

A man of great vision, Paul also knew how to set intermediate objectives. Our broad vision should be for the world, but within that there needs to be a more focused vision — perhaps to work with youth or to minister to homosexuals or to be a medical missionary in the Third Word. The infinite tragedy of the church is that many believers never see this, often because they do not ask God to show it to them.

Paul clearly saw his call because he had one of the clearest visions of Christ of any man who has ever lived.

> *Since, then, you have been raised with Christ, set your hearts on things above, where Christ is seated at the right hand of God. Set your mind on things above, not on earthly things. (Colossians 3:1-2)*

Because he himself did this, God gave him an expanded vision for life on this earth — and an unconquerable inner spirit! Without such vision we will never come anywhere near Paul's spiritual vitality and perseverance.

This was painfully seen in 1968 when the University Christian movement voted itself out of existence, posting this sign on their doors: "Gone out of business . . . did not know what our business was." Do we have a vision for a friend? A Sunday school class? The publishing of truth? A people group? Persevering prayer? If so, we have a basic ingredient of what can become an unconquerable spirit.

THE SECOND SECRET OF AN UNCONQUERABLE SPIRIT: FAITH

A certain American prisoner held in North Viet Nam, led to believe that if he cooperated with his captors he would be set free, had done quite well despite two years in captivity. With this vision before him, he even became the leader of a prison thought-reform group. However, the day his vision dissolved and he realized he was being deceived, he curled up on his bunk, refused nourishment, and was dead in a couple of weeks. When faith in his vision was removed, he could no longer cope.

Unlike man, God never reneges on his word, and Paul drew strength from that. Part of Paul's vision was God's promise of a ministry in Rome, a promise of which Paul was sure! Thus amidst the storm-tossed sea he confidently told his shipmates:

> *"I urge you to keep up your courage, because not one of you will be lost; only the ship will be destroyed. Last night an angel of the God whose I am and whom I serve stood beside me and said, 'Do not be afraid, Paul. You must stand trial before Caesar.'"* (27:22-24)

Because Paul believed, he acquired an unconquerable spirit!

Moreover, Paul's faith was not derailed when his ministry in Rome did turn out not as he had envisioned. Initially he probably saw himself preaching to vast crowds in the forum and reasoning freely with intellectuals in their gardens. But when the time came, he was confined to a single dwelling and chained to a soldier. Yet he remained undaunted!

We must realize that when we get to our Rome, the reality may not be what we had pictured. J. B. Phillips said of his own experience, "There is an apparent capriciousness and arbitrariness about the working of the Spirit of God which is singularly exasperating to the tidy-minded." God does not always conform to our neat preconceptions. God gives us the essence of our dreams, but not in the way we expect. But *God's way is always better. God knows what he is doing.* As Paul said, "The one who calls you is faithful and he will do it" (1 Thessalonians 5:24).

THE THIRD SECRET OF AN UNCONQUERABLE SPIRIT: A WILLINGNESS TO FIGHT

Incredibly, when Paul arrived in Rome, though he was confined to an apartment under house-arrest and was chained to a soldier, he came out swinging! After all he had been through, he only gave himself three days to get situated before calling the leading Jews of all the synagogues together and making a forthright defense.

> *When they had assembled, Paul said to them: "My brothers, although I have done nothing against our people or against the customs of our ancestors, I was arrested in Jerusalem and handed over to the Romans. They examined me and wanted to release me, because I was not guilty of any crime deserving death. But when the Jews objected, I was compelled to appeal to Caesar — not that I had any charge to bring against my own people. For this reason I have asked to see you and talk with you. It is because of the hope of Israel that I am bound with this chain." (vv. 17-20)*

Surprisingly, the leaders responded mildly:

> *"We have not received any letters from Judea concerning you, and none of the brothers who have come from there has reported or said anything bad about you. But we want to hear what your views are, for we know that people everywhere are talking against this sect." (vv. 21-22)*

Their claim to know nothing about Paul was undoubtedly untrue. Christianity had been known among the Jewish community for many years, and there had been such division over it that Emperor Claudius banished all Jews from the city of Rome. The truth is, the Jews wanted as little to do with Paul and Christianity as possible — they wanted Caesar to take care of it. Their true feelings came through, however, in calling Christianity a "sect," a translation of the same Greek word from which our English word *heresy* is derived.

However, Paul got what he wanted because they agreed to meet again, and with the next meeting Paul was really in the thick of it.

They arranged to meet Paul on a certain day, and came in even larger numbers to the place where he was staying. From morning till evening he explained and declared to them the kingdom of God and tried to convince them about Jesus from the Law of Moses and from the Prophets. Some were convinced by what he said, but others would not believe. (vv. 23-24)

Large numbers came to the apostle's lodging — the most exciting home Bible study in history! We can be sure Paul aimed high in this unique opportunity to share the gospel. The word translated "explained" means "to set out or place before." Paul gave his argument with detailed logic and care. This culminated in his trying "to convince them about Jesus." All his persuasive powers were brought to bear upon his hearers "from morning till evening." This was not an hour of study and then cookies and punch. It was ten to twelve hours of serious discussion daily. *The Apostle Paul was a fighter.* As always, some were persuaded, and some simply would not believe regardless of Paul's logic and passion or the Spirit's urging. The same fire that melts wax hardens clay.

During the gymnastics portion of the 1976 Olympics a Japanese athlete broke his leg during one of his routines, and everyone thought he was finished. As the competition turned out, the last day's performances would determine whether the championship went to the Japanese or the Russians. Despite the fact that his leg was broken, the injured athlete mounted the rings for a final performance, and it was sparkling. The look of pride on his face as he ran through the exercise was magnificent. But there was also obvious anguish as from ten feet in the air he came hurtling to the floor for his dismount, landing on his broken leg. His fighting spirit made him indomitable. With his goal firmly in mind, he refused to quit, no matter how severe the pain.

Paul used his limitations to do exploits for his God. Who would ever have thought that a chained prisoner could reach Rome and more? As James Stalker so beautifully pointed out, *Paul's room became a fulcrum from which he moved the world.* How did that come to be? As Paul explains in Philippians 1:12-13:

Now I want you to know, brothers, that what has happened to me has really served to advance the gospel. As a result, it has become clear throughout the whole palace guard and to everyone else that I am in chains for Christ.

As each shift brought a new guard to share a manacle with the apostle, Paul had a captive audience. At first these elite Praetorian guards were probably aloof, but eventually the reality of his life and of his Savior living within him penetrated their hearts. Soon some of the guards were trading palace duty to get more time with Paul!

Today in Rome you can see a square of plaster cut from the wall of the barracks in the Palace of the Caesars. On it is scratched a human figure with a donkey's head. The figure is nailed to a cross, and a man is pictured kneeling before it. This artwork is an obvious insult to a Roman soldier who converted to Christianity, for the picture bears the inscription, "Anexamenos worships his God."[1] Some of Rome's imperial elite came to know Christ! And that is not all — they led some of their privileged friends to Christ. In Philippians 4:22 Paul writes, "All the saints send you greetings, especially those who belong to Caesar's household."

According to the last verse of Acts, Paul witnessed to all visitors "boldly and without hindrance." Furthermore, while a prisoner Paul, through the Holy Spirit, wrote the New Testament books of Philippians, Philemon, Ephesians, Colossians, and 2 Timothy, the first four of which, as John Stott has pointed out, are the most Christological of all his writings. God did great things during Paul's difficult years and despite his personal and circumstantial limitations. As Paul wrote shortly before being martyred for Christ, "I am suffering even to the point of being chained like a criminal. But God's word is not chained" (2 Timothy 2:9).

Joni Eareckson Tada understands completely.

> Few of us have the luxury — it took me forever to think of it as that — to come to ground zero with God. Before the accident, my questions had always been, "How will God fit into this situation? How will He affect my dating life? My career plans? The things I enjoy?" All those options were gone. It was me, just a helpless body, and God.
>
> I had no other identity but God, and gradually He became enough. I became overwhelmed with the phenomenon of the personal God, who created the universe, living in my life. He would make me attractive and worthwhile. . . .
>
> Maybe God's gift to me is my dependence on Him. I will never reach the place where I am self-sufficient, where God is crowded out of my life. I am aware of His grace to me every moment. My need for help is obvious every day when I wake up, flat on my back, waiting for someone to come dress me. I cannot even comb my hair or blow my nose alone!
>
> And there's one more thing. I have hope for the future. The Bible speaks of our bodies being "glorified" in Heaven. In high school that was always a hazy, foreign concept. But now I realize that I will be healed. I have not been cheated out of being a complete person — I

am just going through a forty-year delay, and God is with me even through that.

Being "glorified" — I know the meaning of that now. It's the time, after my death here, when I will be on my feet dancing.[2]

What have we done with our limitations? Have we taken them into a pit of self-pity so we can wallow in hopelessness and impotency? Or have we given them to God so he can do his greatest works through us, not the least of which is building a gloriously indomitable spirit?

Am I a soldier of the cross,
a foll'wer of the Lamb,
And shall I fear to own His cause,
or blush to speak His name?
Must I be carried to the skies
on flowery beds of ease,
While others fought to win the prize,
and sailed thro' bloody seas?
Are there no foes for me to face?
Must I not stem the flood?
Is this vile world a friend to grace,
to help me on to God?
Sure I must fight if I would reign;
increase my courage, Lord;
I will bear the toil, endure the pain,
supported by Thy Word.[3]

Vision, faith, a willingness to fight — these are the secrets of an unconquerable life.

PRAYER

O Lord, may we each share your vision for our lives, our families, our churches, our nation. May your heart's desires be ours — your compassion, your hope, your love for all. May we dare to believe that what you say you can accomplish in and through us, you can and will do. May we not evade the battle but fight it — in your strength, covered with your armor, depending only on you for triumph. In Jesus' name, Amen.

42

The Twenty-ninth Chapter of Acts

Lloyd Ogilvie, now chaplain of the U.S. Senate, tells a story from his student days about the memorable experience of sailing on the *Queen Mary* from New York to Southampton. He recalls that she was a magnificent ship. Though his student's budget put him on deck Double D, he spent most of his time walking the top deck so he could enjoy the cold salt wind and watch the historic craft cut her way through the high waves. As he explored the ship, he tried to imagine what it must have been like to be aboard the *Queen Mary* in her prime — as a lovely pleasure vessel and then as a troop ship carefully evading enemy submarines.

It was years before he saw the *Queen Mary* again — as a museum piece, docked in Long Beach Harbor, California. Her gigantic engine was gone, as was most of her sailing equipment. Souvenir shops now lined her decks. The dining and lounge areas had been adapted for special groups and conventions. Her cabins were refurbished hotel rooms. Actors had been hired to play the parts of officers and crew, complete with professional British accents.

Ogilvie was understandably disappointed. His own words best describe what happened:

> While on board the motionless *Queen* I reviewed a documentary movie about how she was built and the way she had served through wars and changing history. The movie ended with a triumphant but somehow tragic statement, supported by an upsweep of dramatic music: "The greatest ship that ever went to sea is now the greatest ship to come and see."
>
> The words were still on my mind the next day when I greeted the

> congregation of my Hollywood Presbyterian Church after worship. A woman visitor from Iowa made a comment she meant to be a compliment. The similarity to the closing lines of the movie made it just the opposite. She had heard about Hollywood Church for years and had been inspired by the influence of its preaching and program upon America. With excitement she said, "I have waited for years to visit Hollywood Presbyterian Church to see all the great things that used to happen here!"[1]

Not exactly what a pastor wants to hear! Of course, that woman's well-meaning statement was not true of Hollywood Presbyterian Church. But every church faces the danger of becoming merely a historical monument. No church is more than a generation away from such a possibility.

The church that is not a monument but is steaming ahead is a living extension of the book of Acts — an Acts Twenty-nine Church. Such a church has three distinctives that are not only found in Acts but are clearly stated in the rest of Scripture.

THE UPWARD CHARACTERISTIC: WORSHIP

Luke's portrait of the infant church in Acts 2:42 shows that it was a worshiping church: "They devoted themselves to the apostles' teaching and to the fellowship, to the breaking of bread and to prayer." An upward focus pervaded their lives. They daily worshiped in the temple, and as they took their meals together, they used the bread and wine to remember the Lord's death (cf. 2:46). Moreover, Paul, the primary earthly figure in Acts, was dominated by a profound focus on heaven, as his epistles repeatedly testify. Paul lived in the heavenlies.

Love and worship have always been the highest priority for God's people. The *shema*, the fundamental summary statement of Israel's law, commanded it.

> *Hear, O Israel: The LORD our God, the LORD is one. Love the LORD your God with all your heart and with all your soul and with all your strength. (Deuteronomy 6:4-5)*

In the Old Testament this call to love and worship was codified in an effort to ensure that God's people would be fit worshipers. But when the Spirit came at Pentecost, no legal strictures were needed. Worship became as natural as breathing.

Worship is the primary characteristic of the church that refuses to become a monument. The immense tragedy of the contemporary church is that most people worship their work, work at their play, and play at their worship. A. W. Tozer, a man who was a prophet to the modern church, put it this way:

> We have lost our spirit of worship and our ability to withdraw inwardly to meet God in adoring silence. Modern Christianity is simply not producing the kind of Christian who can appreciate or experience the life in the Spirit. The words, "Be still, and know that I am God," mean next to nothing to the self-confident, bustling worshiper in this middle period of the twentieth century.[2]

A vast host of hurrying, scurrying believers seldom slow down enough to even glance upward when they are in church. The opening prayer is a time to shut one's eyes and reflect on what has to be done that day or week. The hymns are opportunities to slip into neutral. The preaching of God's Word is something to endure. One "Dear Abby" column described a poll the writer took, asking churchgoers why they went to church. Not one of them mentioned worship. That is not always the fault of the attenders because church leaders address God like a busy grocery store clerk, pick hymns at random, and deliver the sermon with little regard for what God's Word actually says or means for us today. Such conditions will ultimately produce a relic of a church.

If we desire to be an extension of the book of Acts, we must first give careful attention to worship, including our own private adoration and thanksgiving. William Temple's definition of worship is helpful: "To quicken the conscience by the holiness of God, to feed the mind with the truth of God, to purge the imagination by the beauty of God, to open up the heart to the love of God, to devote the will to the purpose of God." The conscience, the mind, the imagination, the heart, the will — our entire being — are to be devoted to God and given to him as sacred gifts. Weekly corporate worship, no matter how authentic it appears, is a charade if through the week we are not reaching up to God. All of us should give ourselves to making the prayers our own as we pray, to sing the *Gloria* to God only, to sing the great hymns with both heart and mind so that we ourselves do not become dead monuments.

THE INWARD CHARACTERISTIC: CARE FOR CHRIST'S BODY, THE CHURCH

Acts 2:42 tells us, "They devoted themselves to . . . the fellowship." The root idea of "fellowship" in the Greek is "commonness" — not in the sense of ordinariness, but of joint participation. Every time this word is used in the New Testament, it denotes some kind of sharing, either sharing something with someone else (for instance, in 2 Corinthians 8:4 and 9:13 it means offering a contribution), or sharing in what someone else is experiencing. Here in Acts the emphasis is on giving — caring for one another. Verses 44 and 45 make this beautifully clear:

> *All the believers were together and had everything in common. Selling their possessions and goods, they gave to anyone as he had need.*

They cared for one another. They were socially and materially part of one another's lives.

Translated into our own situation, care for those within a local body of Christ is to be second only to worship. Paul expressed this to the Corinthian church when he said, "So I will very gladly spend for you everything I have and expend myself as well" (2 Corinthians 12:15). Care — a concern for one another's material welfare — is to be the inward characteristic of the church. Those who are prospering are to aid those who are in difficulty. Christian generosity must prevail.

Members of the body are also to encourage one another, look after each other's spiritual well-being, and pray for one another While we cannot legislate such mutually beneficial ministry, each local church should have within its fellowship numerous cross-generational groups that build up one another and reach out to those around them. Spiritual care is an indispensable part of being the people of God.

Ultimately, care for the body means grace for the world! When Jesus said, "All men will know that you are my disciples if you love one another" (John 13:35), he was saying that when others truly see loving care within the Body of Christ, they will conclude that we are disciples of the living God. It was precisely this caring ambience that allowed the early church to storm the world. It was irresistible!

THE OUTWARD CHARACTERISTIC: TAKING THE MESSAGE OF CHRIST TO THE WORLD

Sharing the good news of Jesus Christ with the world is the theme of the book of Acts. Chapters 1 — 7 tell of its spread "in Jerusalem," chapters 8 — 11 of the witness "in all Judea and Samaria," and chapters 12 — 28 "to the ends of the earth." So incendiary was the flame of the gospel that soon Christians could be found in all parts of the Empire.

The comprehensiveness of the early church's outreach — from their homeland and on out to the ends of the world — forbids the evangelistic schizophrenia to which we so easily fall prey — lavishing our attention on foreign missions while neglecting our neighbors, or attending to the immediate needs around us while millions overseas have never heard about Jesus. We need balance. We must reach our neighbors *and* the world with our gospel witness, our social witness, our money, our time, ourselves, our offspring. We must put all we have and are in the hands of Christ and allow him to use it all in his way, in his time, for others' salvation, for his glory.

An Acts Twenty-nine Church is an *upward* church, a worshiping church. Lewis said in *The Four Loves*, "Every Christian would agree that a man's spiritual health is exactly proportional to his love for God." Add to this a divine *inwardness* — a caring church — so that the world begins to believe. Such a church is also an *outward* church — evangelistic, mission-minded — that triumphantly extends the book of Acts in its own day.

In the final verses of Acts 28, we see the Apostle Paul and the leaders of the Jewish synagogues in Rome having an ongoing morning-to-evening debate. As a result, some were persuaded, while others refused to believe. As the unbelieving were departing, the apostle gave them a parting exhortation, a quotation given originally to the newly commissioned prophet Isaiah by God as an explanation of why his people would ignore him (Isaiah 6:9-10).

> *They disagreed among themselves and began to leave after Paul had made this final statement: "The Holy Spirit spoke the truth to your forefathers when he said through Isaiah the prophet: 'Go to this people and say, "You will be ever hearing but never understanding; you will be ever seeing but never perceiving." For this people's heart has become calloused; they hardly hear with their ears, and they have closed their eyes. Otherwise they might see with their eyes, hear with their ears, understand with their hearts and turn, and I would heal them.'"* (vv. 25-27)

This was also quoted by Jesus as an explanation as to why the Pharisees would not hear him (Matthew 13:14-15).

Paul says that the unbelieving departed because while seeing they were blind and while hearing they were deaf. Their hearts had become dull, or as the Greek literally says, "fat." To the Jew who daily dressed his own meat, the image was perfectly clear — a heart surrounded so closely with fatty tissue that it was constricted and thus prevented from functioning properly. The application to us is all too obvious, for the things that can constrict our hearts are too numerous to mention.

How are our hearts? Sluggish? Constricted? Thick with fat? On that fateful day some very learned, religious men walked out the door and, spiritually speaking, precluded the writing of any new spiritual chapters in their lives. Others remained and listened and heeded because their hearts were lean and vital. Their lives were not monuments but a movement. They were the twenty-ninth chapter of Acts.

Soli Deo gloria!

Notes

Chapter One: "You Shall Be My Witnesses"

1. Lloyd John Ogilvie, *The Drumbeat of Love* (Waco, TX: Word, 1976), p. 12.
2. William Barclay, *The Acts of the Apostles* (Philadelphia: Westminster, 1955), p. 5.
3. Clarence Edward Macartney, *Preaching Without Notes* (Grand Rapids, MI: Baker, 1946), p. 183.
4. Alexander Maclaren, *Exposition of Holy Scripture*, Volume 10 (Grand Rapids, MI: Baker, 1974), p. 228.
5. Charles Swindoll, "Insight for Living," taped sermon on the book of Acts.

Chapter Two: Expectant Prayer

1. L. J. Ogilvie, *The Cup of Wonder* (Wheaton, IL: Tyndale House, 1976), p. 123.
2. Herbert Danby, trans., *The Mishnah*, Sotah 5:3 (London: Oxford University Press, 1933), p. 298.
3. A. T. Robertson, *Word Pictures in the New Testament*, Volume III, *The Acts of the Apostles* (Nashville: Broadman, 1930), p. 14.
4. Donald Grey Barnhouse, *Acts* (Grand Rapids, MI: Zondervan, 1979), p. 25.

Chapter Three: Pentecost

1. Richard N. Longenecker, *The Expositor's Bible Commentary*, Volume 9, *John-Acts* (Grand Rapids, MI: Zondervan, 1981), p. 269.
2. A. T. Robertson, *Word Pictures in the New Testament*, Volume III, *The Acts of the Apostles* (Nashville: Broadman, 1930), p. 20.
3. Thomas Walker, *The Acts of the Apostles* (Chicago: Moody, 1965), p. 33.
4. NASB margin.
5. James Gilchrist Lawson, *Deeper Life Experiences of Famous People* (Anderson, IN: Warner Press, 1911), p. 267.
6. *Ibid.*, pp. 262, 263.

Chapter Four: Peter's Greatest Sermon

1. Bob L. Ross, *A Pictorial Biography of C. H. Spurgeon* (Pasadena, TX: Pilgrim Publications, 1974), p. 88.
2. William Barclay, *A Spiritual Biography* (Grand Rapids, MI: Eerdmans, 1975), p. 84.
3. Warren Wiersbe, *Listening to the Giants* (Grand Rapids, MI: Baker, 1980), p. 198.
4. T. H. L. Parker, *Karl Barth* (Grand Rapids, MI: Eerdmans, 1970), p. 42.

Chapter Five: The Church Where the Spirit Reigned

1. Richard N. Longenecker, *The Expositor's Bible Commentary*, Volume 9, *John-Acts* (Grand Rapids, MI: Zondervan, 1981), p. 286.
2. Thomas Walker, *The Acts of the Apostles* (Chicago: Moody, 1965), p. 61.

Chapter Six: When Life Is Jumping

1. *War I*, 201, Volume 3.
2. H. L. Strack and Billerbeck, *P Kommentar zum Neuen Testament aus Talmud und Midrash*, Volume I (Munich: Beck, 1961), pp. 387, 388.
3. G. Campbell Morgan, *The Acts of the Apostles* (Westwood, NJ: Revell, 1924), p. 47.

Chapter Seven: The Bliss of Persecution

1. Dietrich Bonhoeffer, *The Cost of Discipleship* (New York: Macmillan, 1977), pp. 100, 101.
2. Alexander Maclaren, *Expositions of Holy Scripture*, Volume 10 (Grand Rapids, MI: Baker, 1974), p. 140.

Chapter Eight: When the Church Is Great

1. Earle Cairns, *Christianity Through the Centuries* (Grand Rapids, MI: Zondervan, 1981), pp. 93, 94.
2. Alan Richardson, *A Theological Word Book of the New Testament* (New York: Macmillan, 1950), p. 145.
3. W. H. Griffith Thomas, *Outline Studies in Acts* (Grand Rapids, MI: Eerdmans, 1956), p. 104.
4. *Ibid.*, p. 112.
5. A. W. Tozer, *The Pursuit of God* (Harrisburg, PA: Christian Publications, 1948), p. 97.
6. F. F. Bruce, *The Spreading Flame* (Grand Rapids, MI: Eerdmans, 1954), quoting from Ignatius, Letter to the Romans, preface.

Chapter Nine: Keeping Things on the Up and Up

1. Donald Grey Barnhouse, *Acts* (Grand Rapids, MI: Zondervan, 1979), p. 52.
2. Thomas Walker, *The Acts of the Apostles* (Chicago: Moody, 1965), p. 114.
3. Richard N. Longenecker, *The Expositor's Bible Commentary*, Volume 9, *John-Acts* (Grand Rapids, MI: Zondervan, 1981), p. 314.
4. *Ibid.*
5. *Canto*, XXIII, line 67.
6. William James, *Principles of Psychology* (Chicago: William Benton, 1952), p. 83.
7. William Barclay, *The Letters to the Galatians and Ephesians* (Philadelphia: Westminster, 1958), p. 183.

Chapter Ten: The Liberty of God's Children

1. Xenia Howard-Johnson and Michael Bourdeaux, *The Evidence That Convicted Aida Skripnikova* (Elgin, IL: David C. Cook, 1973).
2. Herbert Danby, trans., *The Mishnah*, Sotah 9:15 (London: Oxford University Press, 1933), p. 306.

Chapter Eleven: Maintaining the Ministry

1. J. Dwight Pentecost, *The Joy of Living* (Grand Rapids, MI: Zondervan, 1973), p. 55.
2. G. Campbell Morgan, *The Acts of the Apostles* (Westwood, NJ: Revell, 1924), p. 174.
3. *Ibid.*
4. J. H. Jowett, *The Preacher and His Life Work* (New York: Hodder and Stoughton, n.d.), pp. 66-68.
5. Phillips Brooks, *Lectures on Preaching* (Manchester, England: James Robinson, 1899), pp. 93, 94.
6. Donald Grey Barnhouse, *Acts* (Grand Rapids, MI: Zondervan, 1979), p. 59.
7. Kenneth N. Taylor, *Romans for the Family Hour* (Chicago: Moody Press, 1959), pp. 170, 171.

Chapter Twelve: Standing Tall

1. Herbert Lockyer, *Last Words of Saints and Sinners* (Grand Rapids, MI: Kregel, 1969), p. 133.
2. *Ibid.*, p. 64.

3. *Ibid.*, p. 70.
4. *Ibid.*, p. 55.
5. Paul S. Rees, *Man of Action in the Book of Acts* (Westwood, NJ: Revell, 1966), p. 32.
6. Frederick Buechner, *Peculiar Treasures* (San Francisco: Harper & Row, 1979), p. 162.

CHAPTER THIRTEEN: GOD'S WAY

1. Gustaf Dalman, *The Words of Jesus* (Edinburgh: T & T Clark, 1909), p. 200.
2. W. A. Criswell, *Acts, an Exposition*, Volume I (Grand Rapids, MI: Zondervan, 1978), p. 271.
3. *Ibid.*, p. 270.

CHAPTER FOURTEEN: PHILIP: THE TOUCH OF GOD

1. Myra Brooks Welch, "The Touch of the Master's Hand," in Hazel Sellmen, ed., *The Best Loved Poems of the American People* (New York: Doubleday, 1936), p. 222.
2. Lloyd John Ogilvie, *The Drumbeat of Love* (Waco, TX: Word, 1976), p. 119.
3. Richard N. Longenecker, *The Expositor's Bible Commentary*, Volume 9, *John-Acts* (Grand Rapids, MI: Zondervan, 1981), p. 365.

CHAPTER FIFTEEN: SAUL: THE HUNTER HUNTED

1. Richard Connell, *The Most Dangerous Game* (New York: Berkley, 1957), p. 15.
2. A. T. Robertson, *Word Pictures in the New Testament*, Volume III, *The Acts of the Apostles* (Nashville: Broadman, 1930), p. 113.
3. C. S. Lewis, *Surprised by Joy* (New York: Harcourt, Brace & World, 1955), p. 229.

CHAPTER SIXTEEN: SAUL'S PREPARATION FOR MINISTRY

1. G. Campbell Morgan, *The Acts of the Apostles* (Westwood, NJ: Revell, 1924), p. 237.
2. Lloyd John Ogilvie, *Drumbeat of Love* (Waco, TX: Word, 1976), pp. 134, 135.

CHAPTER SEVENTEEN: PETER'S PREPARATION FOR GREATER MINISTRY

1. H. A. Ironside, *Lectures on the Book of Acts* (Neptune, NJ: Loizeaux, 1943), p. 250.
2. Alexander Whyte, *Bible Characters* (Grand Rapids, MI: Zondervan, 1967), p. 164.
3. *Ibid.*, pp. 164, 165.

CHAPTER EIGHTEEN: OPENING THE CHURCH'S ARMS

1. William Barclay, *The Acts of the Apostles* (Philadelphia: Westminster, 1955), p. 91.
2. Allan Emery, *Turtle on a Fencepost* (Waco, TX: Word, 1979), p. 96.

CHAPTER NINETEEN: THE FIRST CHRISTIANS

1. J. Rawson Lumby, *The Acts of the Apostles* (Cambridge: At the University Press, 1904), p. 226.
2. H. A. Ironside, *Lectures on the Book of Acts* (Neptune, NJ: Loizeaux, 1943), p. 284.
3. D. Elton Trueblood, *The People Called Quakers* (New York: Harper & Row, 1966), p. 6.
4. Alexander Maclaren, *Expositions of Holy Scripture, Acts 1 — 12* (Grand Rapids, MI: Baker, 1974), p. 337.
5. Richard Longenecker, *The Expositor's Bible Commentary*, Volume 9, *John-Acts* (Grand Rapids, MI: Zondervan, 1981), p. 402.
6. Maclaren, *Acts 1— 12*, p. 346.
7. W. A. Criswell, *Acts*, Volume II (Grand Rapids, MI: Zondervan, 1979), p. 99.

CHAPTER TWENTY: GETTING ACQUAINTED WITH OUR POWER

1. Herbert Danby, trans., *The Mishnah*, M Bikkurim 3:4 (London: Oxford University Press, 1933), p. 97.
2. A. T. Robertson, *Word Pictures in the New Testament*, Volume III, *The Acts of the Apostles* (Nashville: Broadman, 1930), p. 165.
3. Ray Stedman, *Acts 1 — 12, Birth of the Body* (Santa Ana, CA: Vision House, 1974), p. 199.
4. Geoffrey Gregson, ed., *Faber Book of Epigrams and Epigraphs*, "Upon My Thirty-third Birthday" (Winchester, MA: Faber & Faber, 1977).
5. Dr. Howard Hendricks related this anecdote on March 4, 1982 in his message to the International Congress on Biblical Inerrancy in San Diego, California.

CHAPTER TWENTY-ONE: REALITIES OF THE CHURCH MILITANT

1. William Barclay, *The Acts of the Apostles* (Philadelphia: Westminster, 1955), p. 106.
2. G. Campbell Morgan, *The Acts of the Apostles* (Westwood, NJ: Revell, 1924), p. 317.
3. Ray C. Stedman, *Growth of the Body* (Santa Ana, CA: Vision House, 1976), pp. 14, 15.
4. H. A. Ironside, *Lectures on the Book of Acts* (Neptune, NJ: Loizeaux, 1943), p. 307.

CHAPTER TWENTY-TWO: STICKING TO THE TASK, REGARDLESS

1. *Reader's Digest*, July 1965.
2. William Barclay, *The Acts of the Apostles* (Philadelphia: Westminster, 1955), p. 115.
3. Donald Grey Barnhouse, *Acts* (Grand Rapids, MI: Zondervan, 1979), p. 129.
4. Richard N. Longenecker, *The Expositor's Bible Commentary*, Volume 9, *John-Acts* (Grand Rapids, MI: Zondervan, 1981), p. 435.
5. Lloyd John Ogilvie, *Drumbeat of Love* (Waco, TX: Word, 1976), pp. 185, 186.
6. David Howard, *The Power of the Holy Spirit* (Downers Grove, IL: InterVarsity Press, 1979), pp. 43, 44.
7. John Claypool, *The Preaching Event* (Waco, TX: Word, 1980), pp. 61, 62.

CHAPTER TWENTY-THREE: GRACE ALONE

1. Lloyd John Ogilvie, *Drumbeat of Love* (Waco, TX: Word, 1976), pp. 190, 191.
2. *Ibid*, p. 192.
3. Richard N. Longenecker, *The Expositor's Bible Commentary*, Volume 9, *John-Acts* (Grand Rapids, MI: Zondervan, 1981), p. 435.
4. John Claypool, *The Preaching Event* (Waco, TX: Word, 1980), pp. 61, 62.
5. International Council on Biblical Inerrancy, San Diego, California, March 4, 1982.

CHAPTER TWENTY-FOUR: GOD'S GUIDANCE

1. Richard N. Longenecker, *The Expositor's Bible Commentary*, Volume 9, *John-Acts* (Grand Rapids, MI: Zondervan, 1981), p. 458.
2. G. Campbell Morgan, *The Acts of the Apostles* (Westwood, NJ: Revell, 1924), p. 369.
3. James McGraw, *Great Evangelical Preachers of Yesterday* (Nashville: Abingdon, 1961), p. 37.
4. Clyde E. Fant and William M. Pinson, Jr., *Twenty Centuries of Great Preaching*, Volume 6 (Waco, TX: Word, 1971), p. 114.
5. Longenecker, *The Expositor's Bible Commentary*, Volume 9, *John-Acts*, p. 248.
6 Morgan, *The Acts of the Apostles*, p. 337.

CHAPTER TWENTY-FIVE: BEACHHEAD IN EUROPE

1. G. Campbell Morgan, *The Acts of the Apostles* (Westwood, NJ: Revell, 1924), p. 249.
2. Richard N. Longenecker, *The Expositor's Bible Commentary*, Volume 9, *John-Acts* (Grand Rapids, MI: Zondervan, 1981), p. 460.

3. Richard Collier, *The General Next to God* (London: Collins, 1965), p. 175.
4. A. T. Robertson, *Word Pictures in the New Testament*, Volume III, *The Acts of the Apostles* (Nashville: Broadman, 1930), p. 260.
5. H. A. Ironside, *Lectures on the Book of Acts* (Neptune, NJ: Loizeaux, 1943), p. 384.

CHAPTER TWENTY-SIX: GOD'S NOBLES

1. John Powell, *Fully Human, Fully Alive* (Niles, IL: Argus Communications, 1976), pp. 19, 20.
2. Em Griffin, *The Mind Changers* (Wheaton, IL: Tyndale, 1976), p. 28.
3. A. T. Robertson, *Word Pictures in the New Testament*, Volume III, *The Acts of the Apostles* (Nashville: Broadman, 1930), p. 270.
4. J. C. Rolfe, trans., Seutonius, *Vita Claudius* 25:4 (Cambridge, MA: The Loeb Classical Library, 1914).
5. G. Campbell Morgan, *The Acts of the Apostles* (Westwood, NJ: Revell, 1924), p. 404.
6. Robertson, *Word Pictures in the New Testament*, p. 274.
7. J. I. Packer, *Knowing God* (Downers Grove, IL: InterVarsity Press, 1973), p. 34.
8. James Hastings, ed., *Speaker's Bible*, Volume 12 (Grand Rapids, MI: Baker, 1971), p. 36.

CHAPTER TWENTY-SEVEN: PAUL VERSUS ATHENS

1. W. M. Ramsay as quoted by W. M. Smith, *Therefore Stand* (Grand Rapids, MI: Baker, 1945), p. 260.
2. F. F. Bruce, *Commentary on the Book of Acts* (Grand Rapids, MI: Eerdmans, 1955), p. 360.
3. Miguel de Unamuno, *The Tragic Sense of Life* (New York: Dover, 1954), pp. 49, 50.

CHAPTER TWENTY-EIGHT: REJUVENATING GOD'S SERVANTS

1. Clarence Macartney, *Macartney's Illustrations* (Nashville: Abingdon, 1945), p. 415.
2. *Ibid.*
3. Lloyd John Ogilvie, *Drumbeat of Love* (Waco, TX: Word, 1976), p. 224.
4. A. W. Tozer, *The Knowledge of the Holy* (New York: Harper & Row, 1961), p. 80.

CHAPTER TWENTY-NINE: THE MISSING INGREDIENT

1. G. Campbell Morgan, *Westminster Pulpit I* (Old Tappan, NJ: Revell, n.d.), p. 234.
2. A. T. Robertson, *Types of Preachers in the New Testament* (New York: George H. Doran, 1922), p. 15.
3. A. J. Gossip, *In Christ's Stead* (London: Hodder and Stoughton, 1925), p. 65.
4. Lloyd John Ogilvie, *Drumbeat of Love* (Waco, TX: Word, 1976), p. 231.
5. Earle Cairns, *Christianity Through the Centuries* (Grand Rapids, MI: Zondervan, 1954), p. 382.
6. Donald Grey Barnhouse, *Let Me Illustrate* (Old Tappan, NJ: Revell, 1967), pp. 159, 160.

CHAPTER THIRTY: ASSAULTING THE CASTLE DARK

1. Richard N. Longenecker, *The Expositor's Bible Commentary*, Volume 9, *John-Acts* (Grand Rapids, MI: Zondervan, 1981), p. 495.
2. A. T. Robertson, *Word Pictures in the New Testament*, Volume III, *The Acts of the Apostles* (Nashville: Broadman, 1930), p. 316.
3. Ray Stedman, *The Growth of the Body*, Volume 2, *Acts 13 — 20* (Santa Ana, CA: Vision House, 1976), pp. 160, 161.
4. F. F. Bruce, *New Testament History* (Garden City, NY: Doubleday, 1980), p. 328.

Chapter Thirty-one: When the Leaves Fall Away

1. Donald Grey Barnhouse, *Let Me Illustrate* (Old Tappan, NJ: Revell, 1967), p. 97.
2. W. A. Criswell, *Acts, III* (Grand Rapids, MI: Zondervan, 1980), p. 27.
3. Quoted by G. T. Stokes, *Acts, Expositor's Bible* (New York: A. C. Armstrong and Son, 1903), p. 367.
4. Richard Collier, *The General Next to God* (London: Collins, 1965), pp. 104, 109.

Chapter Thirty-two: Falling Asleep in Church

1. Thomas Walker, *The Acts of the Apostles* (Chicago: Moody, 1965), p. 438.
2. C. S. Lewis, *Screwtape Letters* (New York: Macmillan, 1961), p. 56.
3. Sheldon Vanauken, *A Severe Mercy* (San Francisco: Harper & Row, 1977), pp. 105, 106.
4. Phillips Brooks, *Lectures on Preaching* (Manchester, England: James Robinson, 1899), pp. 25, 26.
5. Clarence E. Macartney, *Chariots of Fire* (Nashville: Abingdon, 1951), pp. 50, 51.

Chapter Thirty-three: Paul's Approach to Ministry

1. General Douglas MacArthur, *Reminiscences* (New York: McGraw-Hill, 1964), pp. 142, 143.
2. Ethel May Baldwin and David V. Benson, *Henrietta Mears and How She Did It* (Glendale, CA: Regal, 1967), p. 148.
3. C. S. Lewis, *Letters to Malcolm* (New York: Harcourt, Brace & World, 1964), p. 98.

Chapter Thirty-four: Man's Word or God's Word?

1. Philip Schaff, *History of the Christian Church*, Volume 7 (Grand Rapids, MI: Eerdmans, 1974), p. 298.
2. Roland H. Bainton, *Here I Stand* (Nashville: Pierce and Smith, 1950), p. 141.
3. Ewald M. Plass, *What Luther Says*, Volume 3 (St. Louis: Concordia, 1959), pp. 1107, 1108.
4. Bainton, *Here I Stand*, p. 144.
5. Herbert Hendin, *The Age of Sensation* (New York: Norton, 1975), p. 13.
6. Oswald Chambers, *My Utmost for His Highest* (Grand Rapids, MI: Discovery House, 1992), p. 223.
7. Richard N. Longenecker, *The Expositor's Bible Commentary*, Volume 9, *John-Acts* (Grand Rapids, MI: Zondervan, 1981), p. 515.
8. Chambers, *My Utmost for His Highest*, p. 223.
9. For valuable and helpful reading on this topic, see Ray Pritchard, *The Road Best Traveled* (Wheaton, IL: Crossway Books, 1995).
10. Clarence Macartney, *Macartney's Illustrations* (Nashville: Abingdon, 1945), p. 409.

Chapter Thirty-five: A Dangerous Heart

1. Herbert Danby, trans., *The Mishnah*, Nazir 6:6ff. (London: Oxford University Press, 1933), p. 288 and Numbers 6:14.
2. F. F. Bruce, *Commentary on the Book of Acts* (Grand Rapids, MI: Eerdmans, 1955), p. 432.
3. Donald Grey Barnhouse, *Acts* (Grand Rapids, MI: Zondervan, 1979), pp. 192, 193.

Chapter Thirty-six: Encouraged in the Night

1. John Farrow, *The Story of Thomas More* (Garden City, NY: Doubleday, 1968), p. 152.
2. C. E. Macartney, *You Can Conquer* (Nashville: Abingdon, 1954), p. 9.

3. Earle E. Cairns, *V. Raymond Edman, In the Presence of the King* (Chicago: Moody, 1972), p. 51.
4. *Ibid.*, p. 192.

CHAPTER THIRTY-SEVEN: ON GIVING AND RECEIVING GOD'S WORD

1. *Wars II*, 253, 263, xii 205.
2. *Historiae* 5.9.
3. C. H. Spurgeon, *Metropolitan Tabernacle Pulpit*, Volume 10 (Pasadena, TX: Pilgrim Publications, 1973), p. 407.

CHAPTER THIRTY-EIGHT: THE ACCUSED

1. Steven Linscott with Randall L. Frame, *Maximum Security* (Wheaton, IL: Crossway Books, 1994).
2. *Ibid.*, p. 189.
3. Gary R. Mayes, *Now What!* (Wheaton, IL: Crossway Books, 1995), p. 152.
4. John Calvin, *Acts* (Wheaton, IL: Crossway Books, 1995), p. 384.
5. *Ibid.*, p. 385.

CHAPTER THIRTY-NINE: BLESSED MADNESS

1. Lloyd John Ogilvie, *Drumbeat of Love* (Waco, TX: Word, 1976), p. 269.
2. Earnest Cary, trans., *Dio's Roman History* (Cambridge, MA: Harvard University Press, 1961), 56:18.
3. Richard N. Longenecker, *The Expositor's Bible Commentary*, Volume 9, *John-Acts* (Grand Rapids, MI: Zondervan, 1981), p. 548.
4. Charles Cochrane, *Christianity and Classical Culture* (London: Oxford University Press, 1944), p. 113.
5. *Chicago Tribune*, February 6, 1982.
6. Charles Finney, *Revival Lectures* (Grand Rapids, MI: Charles Finney, n.d.), p. 125.

CHAPTER FORTY: ANCHORS IN THE STORM

1. Walter Lord, *A Night to Remember* (New York: Holt, 1955), pp. 13-175.
2. C. S. Lewis, *Letters to Malcolm: Chiefly on Prayer* (New York: Harcourt, Brace & World, 1964), p. 75.
3. J. Oswald Sanders, *Spiritual Leadership* (Chicago: Moody, 1980), p. 141.

CHAPTER FORTY-ONE: BUILDING AN INDOMITABLE SPIRIT

1. Albert Basil Orme Wilberforce, *The Purpose of God* (London: E. Stock, 1917), p. 23.
2. Philip Yancey, *Where Is God When it Hurts?* (Grand Rapids, MI: Zondervan, 1977), pp. 119, 120.
3. "Am I a Soldier of the Cross?," *Hymns for the Living Church*, #510.

CHAPTER FORTY-TWO: THE TWENTY-NINTH CHAPTER OF ACTS

1. Lloyd John Ogilvie, *Drumbeat of Love* (Waco, TX: Word, 1976), pp. 281, 282.
2. A. W. Tozer, *Knowledge of the Holy* (New York: Harper & Row, 1961), p. 6.

Scripture Index

General Index

Index of Sermon Illustrations

About the Book Jacket

The design of the book jacket brings together the talents of several Christian artists. The design centers around the beautiful banner created by artist Marge Gieser. It is photographed here on the jacket at about one-twentieth of its original size.

Concerning the symbolism used in the banner for *Acts* Marge Gieser writes:

> The imagery of the flames engulfing the globe is a visual symbol of what happened in Luke's account of the Acts of the Apostles. It began with a flaming Pentecost, which then set the world on fire for the gospel. Historically, fire has come to symbolize what God does through the Holy Spirit. It is also used as a symbol of religious fervor.

Other artists contributing their talents to the creation of the jacket include: Bill Koechling, photography, and Cindy Kiple, art direction.